# THE NAVAL WAR OF 1812

# Theodore Roosevelt

# The Naval War of 1812

*Series Introduction by Caleb Carr*

*Introduction by John Allen Gable*

THE MODERN LIBRARY

NEW YORK

1999 Modern Library Paperback Edition

Biographical note copyright © 1996 by Random House, Inc.
Series Introduction copyright © 1999 by Caleb Carr
Introduction copyright © 1999 by John Allen Gable

LIBRARY OF CONGRESS CATALOGING-IN-PUBLICATION DATA
Roosevelt, Theodore, 1858–1919.
[Naval War of 1812, or, The history of the United States Navy
during the last war with Great Britain]
The naval War of 1812/Theodore Roosevelt.
p.  cm.
Previously published: The naval War of 1812, or, The history of
the United States Navy during the last war with Great Britain.
Annapolis, Md.: Naval Institute Press, c1987.
Includes bibliographical references and index.
ISBN 0-375-75419-9
1. United States—History—War of 1812—Naval operations.
2. United States.  Navy—History—War of 1812.  3. New Orleans
(La.), Battle of, 1815.  I. Title.
E360.R86  1999
973.5'25—dc21       98-48973

Modern Library website address: www.modernlibrary.com

Printed in the United States of America

2  4  6  8  9  7  5  3  1

# THEODORE ROOSEVELT

Theodore Roosevelt—the naturalist, writer, historian, soldier, and politician who became twenty-sixth president of the United States—was born in New York City on October 27, 1858, into a distinguished family. He was the second of four children of Theodore Roosevelt, Sr., a wealthy philanthropist of Dutch descent, and the former Martha ("Mittie") Bulloch, an aristocratic Southern belle. An endlessly inquisitive young man, he was especially interested in natural history, which became the focus of his first published works, *Summer Birds of the Adirondacks* (1877) and *Notes on Some of the Birds of Oyster Bay* (1879). Upon graduating Phi Beta Kappa from Harvard in 1880 Roosevelt briefly studied law. The next year he was elected to the New York State Assembly on the Republican ticket and soon made a name for himself as a historian with *The Naval War of 1812* (1882).

Following the death of his wife, Alice, in childbirth in 1884, Roosevelt sought change and headed west to ranch lands he had acquired in the Dakota Territory. The young outdoorsman chronicled his years in the Bad Lands in *Hunting Trips of a Ranchman* (1885), the first volume in the nature trilogy that eventually included *Ranch Life and the Hunting-Trail* (1888) and *The Wilderness Hunter* (1893). After failing to win the New York City mayoral election in 1886 as a self-styled "Cowboy Candidate," Roosevelt married childhood sweetheart Edith Kermit Carow and retired for a time to Sagamore Hill, his estate at Oyster Bay, Long Island. He wrote *Gouveneur Morris* (1888), a biography of the revolutionary-era statesman intended as a companion to the political memoir *Life of Thomas Hart Benton* (1887) and conceived the masterly four-volume history *The Winning of the West* (1889–1896).

Roosevelt returned to public life in 1889. Appointed Civil Service Commissioner he spent the next six years in Washington energetically pushing for reform of the government system, all the while propelling himself into the national spotlight. In 1895 he accepted a position as member, and later president, of the Board of Police Commissioners of New York City. Known as "a man you can't cajole, can't frighten, can't buy," Roosevelt continued to enjoy growing prestige nationwide, and within two years he was named assistant secretary of the navy under President William McKinley. Resigning this office in May 1898 at the outbreak of the Spanish-American War, Roosevelt helped organize and train the "Rough Riders," a regiment of the First U.S. Volunteer Cavalry whose legendary exploits he recorded in *The Rough Riders* (1899). A popular hero upon returning from Cuba, Roosevelt was elected governor of New York in November 1898, and two years later he became vice president of the United States in the second administration of William McKinley.

The assassination of President McKinley in September 1901 placed Roosevelt in the White House, and he was elected president in 1904. For the remainder of the decade he embodied the boundless confidence of the nation as it entered the American Century. He promised a square deal for the workingman, brought about trust-busting reforms aimed at regulating big business, and instituted modern-day environmental measures. The first American leader to play an important role in world affairs, Roosevelt guided construction of the Panama Canal, advocated a "big stick" policy to enforce the Monroe Doctrine, and sought to keep the Open Door course in China. In 1906 he was awarded the Nobel Peace Prize for resolving the Russo-Japanese War.

After leaving office in 1909 he took an almost yearlong hunting trip to Africa and described his adventures in *African Game Trails* (1910). In 1912 he made a bid for reelection on the progressive Bull Moose ticket but lost to Woodrow Wilson, who became a bitter enemy. Afterward he completed *Theodore Roosevelt: An Autobiography* (1913) and *Through the Brazilian Wilderness* (1914), an account of his explorations in South America. With the outbreak of World War I, Roosevelt became an outspoken advocate of United States military preparedness in books such as *America and the World War* (1915). His last work, *The Great Adventure*, appeared in 1918. Still entertaining the idea of running again for office, Theodore Roosevelt died in his sleep at Sagamore Hill on January 6, 1919.

# Introduction to the Modern Library War Series

*Caleb Carr*

The term "military history" has always been a bit of a problem for me, as it has, I suspect, for many other students of the discipline. The uninitiated seem to have a prejudicial belief that those who study war are an exceedingly odd lot: men (few women enter the field) who at best have never outgrown boyhood and at worst are somewhat alienated, perhaps even dangerous, characters. Of course, much of this general attitude was formed during the sixties and early seventies (my own high school and college years), when an interest in the details of human conflict was one of the most socially ostracizing qualities a person could have. That tarnish has never quite disappeared: In our own day the popular belief that military historians are somehow, well, *off,* endures in many circles.

By way of counterargument let me claim that enthusiasts of military history are often among the most committed and well-read people one might hope to encounter. Rarely does an important work of military history go out of print; and those who know war well can usually hold their own in discussions of political and social history, as well. The reason for this is simple: The history of war represents fully half the tale of mankind's social interactions, and one cannot understand war without understanding its political and social underpinnings. (Conversely, one cannot understand political history or cultural development without understanding war.) Add to this the fact that military history very often involves tales of high adventure—peopled by extreme and fascinating characters and told by some of the best writers ever to take up a pen—and you have the actual secret of why the subject has remained so popular over the ages.

The new Modern Library War Series has been designed to both introduce the uninitiated to this, the real nature of military history, and to reacquaint the initiated with important works that they may have either forgotten or overlooked. For the sake of coherence, we have chosen to focus our four initial offerings on American military history specifically, in order to show how the study of war illuminates so many other aspects of a particular people's experience and character. Francis Parkman's *Montcalm and Wolfe,* for example, not only shows how very much about the psychology of pre-Revolutionary leaders one must understand in order to grasp the conflict known in North America as the French and Indian War, but is also the work of one of the great American prose stylists of the nineteenth century. Ulysses S. Grant's *Personal Memoirs* (which owe more than a little to the editorial efforts of one of Grant's champions, Mark Twain) contrast the remarkable humility of their author with the overwhelmingly dramatic circumstances into which Fate flung him, and that he struggled so hard—in the end, successfully—to master. Theodore Roosevelt's *The Naval War of 1812,* too long neglected, was the first work to reveal the prodigious intellect, irrepressible character, and remarkably entertaining style of this future president, who (his father having spent most of the family fortune on charities) consistently made a good part of his income through writing. And finally we have *A Soldier's Story,* the memoirs of Omar Bradley, "the G.I. General," who, surrounded by a sea of prima donnas during World War II, never stopped quietly learning his trade, until he became, during the conquest of Germany in 1945, arguably the most progressive and important senior American commander in the European theater.

To read any or all of these books is to see that military history is neither an obscure nor a peculiar subject, but one critical to any understanding of the development of human civilization. That warfare itself is violent is true and unfortunate; that it has been a central method through which every nation in the world has established and maintained its independence, however, makes it a critical field of study. The fact that the personalities and stories involved in war are often so compelling is simply a bonus—but it is the kind of bonus that few academic disciplines can boast.

# INTRODUCTION

*by John Allen Gable*

On December 3, 1881, twenty-three-year-old Theodore Roosevelt, elected the month before to the New York State Assembly (he was the youngest member of the legislature), turned in to G. P. Putnam's Sons the manuscript of his first book, a five hundred-page study, *The Naval War of 1812*. *The Naval War of 1812*, published in 1882, immediately established the author as a notable historian, and the book has endured, generation after generation, as a classic in the canon of American naval history.

Theodore began writing *The Naval War of 1812* during his senior year at Harvard, 1879–1880. He graduated from Harvard, Phi Beta Kappa and magna cum laude, on June 30, 1880; then he went hunting in the Midwest; entered law school at Columbia University in the fall; and on his twenty-second birthday, October 27, 1880, married Alice Hathaway Lee. After his first year of law school, the young couple toured Europe and Roosevelt climbed the Matterhorn. In the fall of 1881, he was back in law school. He was nominated for the New York State Assembly in October and campaigned for office, was elected on November 9, 1881, and finished *The Naval War of 1812* by December 3.

It seems amazing that Roosevelt was able to accomplish so much, both in his personal life and for his career, in such a short, crowded period of time. But Theodore Roosevelt, it is generally conceded, was one of the most amazing Americans of all time. "Roosevelt was a many-sided man and every side was like an electric battery. Such versatility, such vitality, such thoroughness, such copiousness, have rarely been united in one man," said his friend the nature-writer John Burroughs.

TR was the author of over thirty-five books and hundreds of essays on a dazzling variety of subjects; hunter, naturalist, explorer, and conservationist; Dakota rancher and police commissioner of New York City; colonel of the Rough Riders and winner of the Nobel Peace Prize; founder of the NCAA and president of the American Historical Association; man in the arena of count-less political battles who for a time had his own political party; trustbuster and builder of the Panama Canal; advocate of the strenuous life and the Square Deal; creator of the U.S. Forest Service and the Fish and Wildlife Service; gov-ernor of New York State and vice president; president of the United States at the age of forty-two. TR was, in short, an American Renaissance man.

It was natural that the many-sided TR would have an interest in naval affairs and history, because the sea was very much a part of his heritage. The Roosevelts had lived on the island of Manhattan since the 1640s, when they had immigrated from the Netherlands, and many of the Roosevelts had been importers. Theodore Roosevelt, Senior, father of the future president, was an importer of plate glass, and had been appointed, though not confirmed, as collector of the Port of New York shortly before his death. The younger Theodore had sailed and rowed in the waters of Long Island since boyhood, and many of the Roo-sevelts over the years were well known in yachting circles.

TR's mother, Martha Bulloch Roosevelt, who came from Georgia, had two brothers who made their mark in naval history. James Dunwody Bulloch was in the U.S. Navy and became an admiral in the Confederate navy during the Civil War. He built ships, including the *Alabama,* in Great Britain for the Con-federacy. His younger brother Irvine Bulloch served on the *Alabama* and, TR related, "fired the last gun discharged from her batteries in the fight with the *Kearsarge.*" After the war, the Bulloch brothers lived in exile in England, be-coming cotton merchants. TR and his family, in spite of the distance, main-tained close ties with the Bullochs in England, and visited them on trips to Europe. TR told his friend the Reverend Ferdinand Cowle Inglehart, a Methodist minister, in the 1890s:

> From my earliest recollection I have been fed on tales of the sea and of ships. My mother's brother was an admiral in the Confederate navy, and her deep interest in the Southern cause and her brother's calling led her to talk to me as a little shaver about ships, ships, ships, and fighting of ships, till they sank into the depths of my soul. And when I first began to think, in any independent and consecutive order, ... I began to write a his-tory of the Naval War of 1812.

Theodore had borrowed from the library of the Porcellian Club a noted work by an English historian, William James's *The Naval History of Great Britain from the Declaration of War by France in 1793 to the Accession of George IV,* six vol-umes (1837). Roosevelt was infuriated by James's denigration of the perfor-mance of the American navy in the War of 1812. James's history was biased and inaccurate, as Roosevelt demonstrated again and again in *The Naval War of 1812*. James had produced "an invaluable work, written with fulness and care; on the other hand it is also a piece of special pleading by a bitter and not over-scrupulous partisan," Roosevelt concluded.

Yet it was obvious to TR that American accounts of the war, such as the novelist James Fenimore Cooper's history of the American navy, were equally biased as well as sadly lacking in historical scholarship. "It is to be regretted that most of the histories written on the subject, on either side of the Atlantic, should be of the 'hurrah' order of literature, with no attempt whatever to get at the truth, but merely to explain away the defeats or immensely exaggerate the victories suffered or gained by their own side," Roosevelt wrote. He set for himself the goal of producing an accurate and fair account of naval operations. "Without abating a jot from one's devotion to his country and flag, I think a history can be made just enough to warrant its being received as an authority equally among Americans and Englishmen," he told his readers.

Roosevelt began mastering the tactics, technology, and terminology of naval warfare. He prepared elaborate diagrams of major battles. He read every source he could get his hands on. He made his own translations of French historians for use in the text of his book. It was his habit in 1880 and 1881 to attend classes at Columbia law school in the morning, and then go to the Astor Library to work on his book in the afternoon. Evenings were often devoted to the active social life he led with his wife, Alice.

When he and Alice were in Germany on their much belated honeymoon trip in 1881, Roosevelt met Simeon E. Baldwin, Connecticut jurist and law professor, who helped TR obtain original documents from the Navy Department. It is interesting to note that in 1910, during a heated political campaign, when Baldwin was the Democratic candidate for governor of Connecticut, he sued TR for libel after TR attacked his conservative legal views. Baldwin won the election and dropped the suit.

From The Hague, on August 21, 1881, in a letter to his sister Anna, TR discussed "that favorite chateau-en-espagne of mine, the Naval History." He noted: "You would be amused to see me writing it here. I have plenty of information now, but I can't get it into words; I am afraid it is too big a task for me. I wonder if I won't find everything in life too big for my abilities. Well, time will tell."

In Liverpool some weeks later, Theodore's visit with his "Uncle Jimmie" Bulloch proved to be an important event in the annals of American naval history as the creative sparks were struck and fanned into flame for two important historical works. James Bulloch read his nephew's manuscript and gave Theodore first-hand information and advice about naval strategy and warfare. In the Preface to *The Naval War of 1812*, TR expressed his "sincerest thanks" to "Captain James D. Bulloch, formerly of the United States Navy, ... without whose advice and sympathy this work would probably never have been written or even begun."

For his part, TR encouraged his uncle to write his memoirs of the Civil War. In a letter from Liverpool, on September 14, 1881, Theodore told his mother, Martha Bulloch Roosevelt, that he was "with the blessed old sea-captain, talking over naval history, and helping him arrange his papers of which he has literally thousands." "I enjoy talking to the dear old fellow more than I can tell," TR wrote his mother, "he is such a modest high souled old fellow that I just love and respect him. And I think he enjoys having some one to talk to who really enjoys listening." *The Secret Service of the Confederate States in Europe,* two volumes by James D. Bulloch, was published in London in 1883.

Back in New York in the fall of 1881, TR wrote in his diary: "Am working fairly hard at my law, hard at politics, and hardest of all at my book." Roosevelt's self-discipline, energy, productivity, sense of direction, and ability to lead a multifaceted style of life were much in evidence in the fall of 1881. We have a glimpse of TR at this time from his friend Owen Wister, who dedicated his novel *The Virginian* to TR:

> . . . He finished his *Naval History of the War of 1812* mostly standing on one leg at the bookcases in his New York house, the other leg crossed behind, toe touching the floor, heedless of dinner engagements and the flight of time. A slide drew out from the bookcase. On this he had open the leading authorities on navigation, of which he knew nothing. He knew that when a ship's course was one way, with the wind another, the ship had to sail at angles, and this was called tacking or beating. By exhaustive study and drawing of models, he pertinaciously got it all right, whatever of it came into the naval engagements he was writing about.
>
> His wife used to look in at his oblivious back, and exclaim in a plaintive drawl:
>
> "We're dining out in twenty minutes, and Teedy's drawing little ships!"

Published in 1882, *The Naval War of 1812* received laudatory reviews on both sides of the Atlantic. "The volume is an excellent one in every respect," said *The New York Times,* and the *New York Evening Post* declared that the book was "remarkable and worthy of praise," judgments echoed by historians down through the years. The military historian Edward K. Eckert writes: "*The Naval War of 1812* marked an important turning point in American naval historiography. For the first time an operational history based upon careful research in original sources had been written."

*The Naval War of 1812* went through two editions, or printings, in 1882; and then in 1883 for the third edition Roosevelt added both a long preface, in which he summarized the land operations during the war, and a new concluding chapter on the Battle of New Orleans. While the naval war had showed Americans at their best, military operations on land had gone badly for the United States, except for the victory at New Orleans, which of course took place after peace had been concluded in far-off Europe. By regulations adopted in 1886, at least one copy of *The Naval War of 1812* was to be placed on board every vessel in the U.S. Navy. The book was reprinted in the U.S. Naval Institute's "Classics of Naval Literature" series in 1987.

What about Roosevelt's goal of producing with *The Naval War of 1812* a fair and balanced history of the naval conflict that would be accepted in both Great Britain and the United States? That question was definitively answered when Roosevelt was asked to write the section on the War of 1812 in the official history of the Royal Navy, edited by William Laird Clowes. TR's new account, "The War with the United States, 1812–1815 was published in 1901 in volume VI of *The Royal Navy: A History*, which was reprinted in the United States by Little, Brown and Company as a 290-page book entitled *The Naval Operations of the War Between Great Britain and the United States, 1812–1815* (1901).

Back in 1882 the book sold well, and *The New York Times* said that TR had "a brisk and interesting way of telling events." Times and tastes differ. Edward K. Eckert pays high tribute to TR's writing: "Roosevelt's descriptions of battles display a low-key but intense drama unsurpassed until the British novelist C. S. Forester wrote *The Age of Fighting Sail* in 1956." Some modern readers may be more in agreement with biographer Edmund Morris, who says the book's "merits are as simple as those of any serious piece of academic writing: clarity, accuracy, and completeness, backed by massive documentation." Those with an interest in military history or naval tactics and strategy will discover a rich and rewarding experience in reading this classic volume. *The Naval War of 1812*, of course, cannot be ignored by any serious student of Theodore Roosevelt's life and work.

Roosevelt's moderate "social Darwinism" periodically intrudes on his analysis of the war, with assertions about the cultural superiority of the British and Americans; and his ethnic remarks about the relative nautical merits of the Portuguese, Italians, and others reveal the limitations of his intellect as well as the prejudices of period and place. While TR shows that he is quite familiar with the composition of the crews of the American ships, he does not mention the large number of free blacks in the U.S. Navy. During the War of 1812, approximately one sailor in six serving on the American frigates was a free black. However, in his account of the Battle of New Orleans, which was added to the book in the third edition of 1883, Roosevelt takes note of the African Americans in the American army:

> …One band had in its formation something that was curiously pathetic. It was composed of free men of color, who had gathered to defend the land which kept the men of their race in slavery; who were to shed their blood for the Flag that symbolized to their kind not freedom but bondage; who were to die bravely as freemen, only that their brethren might live on ignobly as slaves. Surely there was never a stranger instance than this of the irony of fate.

As much as TR admired and loved his Southern mother and his Confederate uncles, intellectually and spiritually, just like his Knickerbocker father, he was a Northerner who believed in the Union cause. TR's pointed remarks about the fighting free African Americans at New Orleans, and his bitter attacks on Thomas Jefferson and his followers throughout *The Naval War of 1812*, show that Roosevelt was part of the patrician nationalist school of historians from the northeastern regions of the United States.

This school included writers like Francis Parkman, Henry Adams, James Ford Rhodes, Henry Cabot Lodge, and William Roscoe Thayer—many of them TR's friends—nonacademic gentlemen scholars (few had professional training, most had inherited money) who upheld the traditions of the Federalist, Whig, and Republican parties. *The Naval War of 1812* clearly reflected the views of the patrician nationalists, as did TR's later biography of the Federalist statesman Gouverneur Morris (1888). The Jeffersonians had won most of the elections, and the hearts of the people, but the battle of the books clearly went to the neo-Federalists during the nineteenth century. The tide would turn after 1900.

When change came, Theodore Roosevelt was part of the progressive movement, which influenced every field of thought as well as the course of American politics and government. But Roosevelt retained, defended, and adapted some of the core beliefs of the old patrician school of historians, particularly nationalism, and the concept that history is not just a social science but also a branch of literature. TR's progressive platform was called the "New Nationalism," and his inaugural address as president of the American Historical Association in 1912 was entitled "History as Literature."

Roosevelt in *The Naval War of 1812* was attempting to make military preparedness, particularly naval power, an integral part of American nationalism, as it had been for the leaders of the Federalist Party in the 1790s. In 1888, TR was invited by Admiral Stephen B. Luce to speak at the new Naval War College in Newport, Rhode Island, on the topic, the "True Conditions of the War of 1812." This was the first of many visits to the Naval War College, and the beginning of TR's friendship with Captain Alfred Thayer Mahan, president of the Naval War College. With the publication in 1890 of Mahan's book *The Influence of Sea Power Upon History*, which was enthusiastically praised by Roosevelt in his review in the *Atlantic Monthly*, the subject of naval affairs became an important focus of the patrician nationalist school of history, following the trail blazed by TR with *The Naval War of 1812*. TR and Mahan were soon associated in the public mind as the great apostles of naval power.

What Roosevelt found in his study of the War of 1812 was that the small but first-rate navy built by the Federalists in the 1790s, in spite of the neglect by Presidents Thomas Jefferson and James Madison, remained sufficiently strong to defeat the "mightiest naval power the world has ever seen." It wasn't courage or wishful thinking that won out. "As a whole, it must be said that both sides showed equal courage and resolution." The difference was most of all in the quality of the American ships. Comparing the past with his present, Roosevelt wrote:

> The reason of these striking and unexpected successes was that our navy in 1812 was the exact reverse of what our navy is now, in 1882.... Whereas we now have a large number of worthless vessels, standing very low down in their respective classes, we then possessed a few vessels, each unsurpassed by any foreign ship of her class.... If in 1812 our ships had borne the same relation to the British ships that they do now, not all the courage and skill of our sailors would have won us a single success.

In contrast to American successes on the sea, the operations on land show the results of Jefferson's frugal budgets and antimilitarism. The American Army was weak, and therefore was "thrashed" by the seasoned British troops, except at New Orleans. Of the American defeats, including the capture and destruction of the nation's capital, TR said: "They teach us nothing new; it is the old, old lesson, that a miserly economy in preparation may in the end involve a lavish outlay of men and money, which after all, comes too late to offset the evils produced by the original short-sighted parsimony." In other words, military preparedness is less expensive than losing a war or rebuilding Washington, D.C. Moreover, TR claimed that a strong defense posture usually preserves peace.

When *The Naval War of 1812* was published, the U.S. Navy was at perhaps its lowest point in history, ranking below the top ten navies of the world. "At the time I wrote the book, in the early eighties, the navy had reached its nadir," TR recalled in his *Autobiography,* "and we were then utterly incompetent to fight Spain or any other power that had a navy at all. Shortly afterwards we began timidly and hesitatingly to build up a fleet."

In 1897, in part because of his authorship of *The Naval War of 1812* and his identification with naval studies, TR was appointed assistant secretary of the Navy, the first of five members of his family to hold this position. (The others are Franklin D. Roosevelt; Theodore Roosevelt, Jr.; TR's nephew Theodore Douglas Robinson; and Henry Latrobe Roosevelt.) TR helped prepare the Navy for the war he saw coming with Spain, and his biographers have assigned him some of the credit for the spectacular naval victories of the war of 1898.

The rest of the story is fairly familiar. TR became a war hero with the Rough Riders in the Spanish-American War, was elected governor of New York and vice president, and became the twenty-sixth president of the United States in 1901 when William McKinley was assassinated. When he left the White House in 1909, TR had raised the United States Navy to the top ranks of the world's naval powers, and had sent the Great White Fleet on a spectacular voyage around the world. The American Navy was TR's "big stick," and he could speak softly and be heard clearly anywhere in the world. It is not surprising that Theodore Roosevelt is known as the "father of the modern navy."

## BIBLIOGRAPHICAL NOTE

Theodore Roosevelt, *The Naval War of 1812, or the History of the United States Navy During the Last War With Great Britain* (New York: G. P. Putnam's Sons, 1882, 498 pp., illustrated, 8vo, royal blue or olive green; the third edition was brown or green).

The book was printed twice in 1882, and in 1883 a "third edition" had a lengthy additional Preface with an account of the war on land and a new concluding chapter (Chapter X), "The Battle of New Orleans." There were ten numbered editions. The fourth edition (1889) added Appendix E, in which Roosevelt responded to an English critic H. T. Powell.

The book has been frequently reprinted in many editions. *The Naval War of 1812* is volume VII in Hermann Hagedorn, editor, *The Works of Theodore Roosevelt: Memorial Edition* (24 vols., New York: Charles Scribner's Sons, 1923–1926), and volume VI in the *National Edition* (1926).

———

JOHN ALLEN GABLE, Ph.D., is the executive director of the Theodore Roosevelt Association.

# CONTENTS

I. INTRODUCTORY    3

Causes of the War of 1812 · Conflicting views of America and Britain as regards neutral rights · Those of the former power right · Impossibility of avoiding hostilities · Declaration of war · General features of the contest · Racial identity of contestants · The treaty of peace nominally leaves the situation unchanged · But practically settles the dispute in our favor in respect to maritime rights · The British navy and its reputation prior to 1812 · Comparison with other European navies · British and American authorities consulted in the present work

II.    14

Overwhelming naval supremacy of England when America declared war against her · Race identity of the combatants · American navy at the beginning of the war · Officers well trained · Causes tending to make our seamen especially efficient · Close similarity between British and American sailors · Our ships manned chiefly by native Americans, many of whom had formerly been impressed into the British navy · Quotas of seamen contributed by the different States · Navy-yards · Lists of officers and men · List of vessels · Tonnage · Different ways of estimating it in Britain and America · Ratings · American ships properly rated · Armaments of the frigates and corvettes · Three styles of guns used · Difference between long guns and carronades · Short weight of American shot · Comparison of British frigates rating 38, and American frigates rating 44 guns · Compared with a 74

III. 1812. ON THE OCEAN    42

Commodore Rodgers' cruise and unsuccessful chase of the *Belvidera* · Cruise of the *Essex* · Captain Hull's cruise, and escape from the squadron of Commodore Broke · *Constitution* captures *Guerrière* · *Wasp* captures *Frolic* · Second unsuccessful cruise of Commodore Rodgers · *United States* captures *Macedonian* · *Constitution* captures *Java* · *Essex* starts on a cruise · Summary

tillery duels · Great battle of January 8th, 1815 · Slaughtering repulse of the main attack · Rout of the Americans on the right bank of the river · Final retreat of the British · Observations on the character of the troops and commanders engaged

# PREFACE

The history of the naval events of the War of 1812 has been repeatedly presented both to the American and the English reader. Historical writers have treated it either in connection with a general account of the contest on land and sea, or as forming a part of the complete record of the navies of the two nations. A few monographs, which confine themselves strictly to the naval occurrences, have also appeared. But none of these works can be regarded as giving a satisfactorily full or impartial account of the war—some of them being of the "popular" and loosely-constructed order, while others treat it from a purely partisan standpoint. No single book can be quoted which would be accepted by the modern reader as doing justice to both sides, or, indeed, as telling the whole story. Any one specially interested in the subject must read all; and then it will seem almost a hopeless task to reconcile the many and widely contradictory statements he will meet with.

There appear to be three works which, taken in combination, give the best satisfaction on the subject. First, in James' "Naval History of Great Britain" (which supplies both the material and the opinions of almost every subsequent English or Canadian historian) can be found the British view of the case. It is an invaluable work, written with fulness and care; on the other hand it is also a piece of special pleading by a bitter and not over-scrupulous partisan. This, in the second place, can be partially supplemented by Fenimore Cooper's "Naval History of the United States." The latter gives the American view of the cruises and battles; but it is much less of an authority than James', both because it is written without great regard for exactness, and because all figures for the

American side need to be supplied from Lieutenant (now Admiral) George E. Emmons' statistical "History of the United States Navy," which is the third of the works in question.

But even after comparing these three authors, many contradictions remain unexplained, and the truth can only be reached in such cases by a careful examination of the navy "Records," the London "Naval Chronicle," "Niles' Register," and other similar documentary publications. Almost the only good criticisms on the actions are those incidentally given in standard works on other subjects, such as Lord Howard Douglass' "Naval Gunnery," and Admiral Jurien de la Graviére's "Guerres Maritimes." Much of the material in our Navy Department has never been touched at all. In short, no full, accurate, and unprejudiced history of the war has ever been written.

The subject merits a closer scrutiny than it has received. At present people are beginning to realize that it is folly for the great English-speaking Republic to rely for defence upon a navy composed partly of antiquated hulks, and partly of new vessels rather more worthless than the old. It is worth while to study with some care that period of our history during which our navy stood at the highest pitch of its fame; and to learn any thing from the past it is necessary to know, as near as may be, the exact truth. Accordingly the work should be written impartially, if only from the narrowest motives. Without abating a jot from one's devotion to his country and flag, I think a history can be made just enough to warrant its being received as an authority equally among Americans and Englishmen. I have endeavored to supply such a work. It is impossible that errors, both of fact and opinion, should not have crept into it; and although I have sought to make it in character as non-partisan as possible, these errors will probably be in favor of the American side.

As my only object is to give an accurate narrative of events, I shall esteem it a particular favor if any one will furnish me with the means of rectifying such mistakes; and if I have done injustice to any commander, or officer of any grade, whether American or British, I shall consider myself under great obligations to those who will set me right.

I have been unable to get access to the original reports of the British commanders, the logs of the British ships, or their muster-rolls, and so have been obliged to take them at second hand from the "Gazette," or "Naval Chronicle," or some standard history. The American official letters, log-books, original contracts, muster-rolls, etc., however, being preserved in the Archives at Washington, I have been able, thanks to the courtesy of the Hon. Wm. H. Hunt, Secretary of the Navy, to look them over. The set of letters from the officers is very complete, in three series,—"Captains' Letters," "Masters' Commandant Letters," and "Officers' Letters," there being several volumes for each year. The books of contracts contain valuable information as to the size and build of some of the vessels. The log-books are rather exasperating, often being very incomplete. Thus when I turned from Decatur's extremely vague official letter describing the capture of the *Macedonian* to the log-book of the Frigate *United*

*States,* not a fact about the fight could be gleaned. The last entry in the log on the day of the fight is "strange sail discovered to be a frigate under English colors," and the next entry (on the following day) relates to the removal of the prisoners. The log of the *Enterprise* is very full indeed, for most of the time, but is a perfect blank for the period during which she was commanded by Lieutenant Burrows, and in which she fought the *Boxer.* I have not been able to find the *Peacock's* log at all, though there is a very full set of letters from her commander. Probably the fire of 1837 destroyed a great deal of valuable material. When ever it was possible I have referred to printed matter in preference to manuscript, and my authorities can thus, in most cases, be easily consulted.

In conclusion I desire to express my sincerest thanks to Captain James D. Bulloch, formerly of the United States Navy, and Commander Adolf Mensing, formerly of the German Navy, without whose advice and sympathy this work would probably never have been written or even begun.

*New York City, 1882*

# PREFACE TO
# THIRD EDITION

I originally intended to write a companion volume to this, which should deal with the operations on land. But a short examination showed that these operations were hardly worth serious study. They teach nothing new; it is the old, old lesson, that a miserly economy in preparation may in the end involve a lavish outlay of men and money, which, after all, comes too late to more than partially offset the evils produced by the original short-sighted parsimony. This might be a lesson worth dwelling on did it have any practical bearing on the issues of the present day; but it has none, as far as the army is concerned. It was criminal folly for Jefferson, and his follower Madison, to neglect to give us a force either of regulars or of well-trained volunteers during the twelve years they had in which to prepare for the struggle that any one might see was inevitable; but there is now far less need of an army than there was then. Circumstances have altered widely since 1812. Instead of the decaying might of Spain on our southern frontier, we have the still weaker power of Mexico. Instead of the great Indian nations of the interior, able to keep civilization at bay, to hold in check strong armies, to ravage large stretches of territory, and needing formidable military expeditions to overcome them, there are now only left broken and scattered bands, which are sources of annoyance merely. To the north we are still hemmed in by the Canadian possessions of Great Britain; but since 1812 our strength has increased so prodigiously, both absolutely and relatively, while England's military power has remained almost stationary, that we need now be under no apprehensions from her land-forces; for, even if checked in the beginning, we could not help conquering in the end by sheer weight of numbers, if by nothing else. So that there is now no cause for our keeping up a large army; while, on the contrary, the necessity for an efficient navy is so evident that only our almost incredible short-sightedness prevents our at once preparing one.

Not only do the events of the war on land teach very little to the statesman who studies history in order to avoid in the present the mistakes of the past, but besides this, the battles and campaigns are of very little interest to the student of military matters. The British regulars, trained in many wars, thrashed the raw troops opposed to them whenever they had any thing like a fair chance; but this is not to be wondered at, for the same thing has always happened the world over under similar conditions. Our defeats were exactly such as any man might have foreseen, and there is nothing to be learned from the follies committed by incompetent commanders and untrained troops when in the presence of skilled officers having under them disciplined soldiers. The humiliating surrenders, abortive attacks, and panic routs of our armies can all be paralleled in the campaigns waged by Napoleon's marshals against the Spaniards and Portuguese in the years immediately preceding the outbreak of our own war. The Peninsular troops were as little able to withstand the French veterans as were our militia to hold their own against the British regulars. But it must always be remembered, to our credit, that while seven years of fighting failed to make the Spaniards able to face the French,[1] two years of warfare gave us soldiers who could stand against the best men of Britain. On the northern frontier we never developed a great general,—Brown's claim to the title rests only on his not having committed the phenomenal follies of his predecessors,—but by 1814 our soldiers had become seasoned, and we had acquired some good brigade commanders, notably Scott, so that in that year we played on even terms with the British. But the battles, though marked by as bloody and obstinate fighting as ever took place, were waged between small bodies of men, and were not distinguished by any feats of generalship, so that they are not of any special interest to the historian. In fact, the only really noteworthy feat of arms of the war took place at New Orleans, and the only military genius that the struggle developed was Andrew Jackson. His deeds are worthy of all praise, and the battle he won was in many ways so peculiar as to make it well worth a much closer study than it has yet received. It was by far the most prominent event of the war; it was a victory which reflected high honor on the general and soldiers who won it, and it was in its way as remarkable as any of the great battles that took place about the same time in Europe. Such being the case, I have devoted a chapter to its consideration at the conclusion of the chapters devoted to the naval operations.

---

[1] At the closing battle of Toulouse, fought between the allies and the French, the flight of the Spaniards was so rapid and universal as to draw from the Duke of Wellington the bitter observation, that "though he had seen a good many remarkable things in the course of his life, yet this was the first time he had ever seen ten thousand men running a race."

As before said, the other campaigns on land do not deserve very minute attention; but, for the sake of rendering the account of the battle of New Orleans more intelligible, I will give a hasty sketch of the principal engagements that took place elsewhere.

The war opened in mid-summer of 1812, by the campaign of General Hull on the Michigan frontier. With two or three thousand raw troops he invaded Canada. About the same time Fort Mackinaw was surrendered by its garrison of 60 Americans to a British and Indian force of 600. Hull's campaign was unfortunate from the beginning. Near Brownstown the American Colonel Van Horne, with some 200 men, was ambushed and routed by Tecumseh and his Indians. In revenge Col. Miller, with 600 Americans, at Maguaga attacked 150 British and Canadians under Capt. Muir, and 250 Indians under Tecumseh, and whipped them,—Tecumseh's Indians standing their ground longest. The Americans lost 75, their foes 180 men. At Chicago the small force of 66 Americans was surprised and massacred by the Indians. Meanwhile, General Brock, the British commander, advanced against Hull with a rapidity and decision that seemed to paralyze his senile and irresolute opponent. The latter retreated to Detroit, where, without striking a blow, he surrendered 1,400 men to Brock's nearly equal force, which consisted nearly one half of Indians under Tecumseh. On the Niagara frontier, an estimable and honest old gentleman and worthy citizen, who knew nothing of military matters, Gen. Van Rensselaer, tried to cross over and attack the British at Queenstown; 1,100 Americans got across and were almost all killed or captured by a nearly equal number of British, Canadians, and Indians, while on the opposite side a larger number of their countrymen looked on, and with abject cowardice refused to cross to their assistance. The command of the army was then handed over to a ridiculous personage named Smythe, who issued proclamations so bombastic that they really must have come from an unsound mind, and then made a ludicrously abortive effort at invasion, which failed almost of its own accord. A British and Canadian force of less than 400 men was foiled in an assault on Ogdensburg, after a slight skirmish, by about 1,000 Americans under Brown; and with this trifling success the military operations of the year came to an end.

Early in 1813, Ogdensburg was again attacked, this time by between 500 and 600 British, who took it after a brisk resistance from some 300 militia; the British lost 60 and the Americans 20, in killed and wounded. General Harrison, meanwhile, had begun the campaign in the Northwest. At Frenchtown, on the River Raisin, Winchester's command of about 900 Western troops was surprised by a force of 1,100 men, half of them Indians, under the British Colonel Proctor. The right division, taken by surprise, gave up at once; the left division, mainly Kentucky riflemen, and strongly posted in houses and stockaded enclosures, made a stout resistance, and only surrendered after a bloody fight, in which 180 British and about half as many Indians were killed or wounded. Over 300 Americans were slain, some in the battle, but most in the bloody massacre that followed. After this, General Harrison went into camp at Fort Meigs, where, with about 1,100 men, he was besieged by 1,000 British and Canadians under Proctor and 1,200 Indians under Tecumseh. A force of 1,200 Kentucky militia advanced to his relief and tried to cut its way into the fort while the garrison made a sortie. The sortie was fairly successful, but the Kentuckians were scattered like chaff by the British regulars in the open, and when broken were cut to pieces by the Indians in the woods. Nearly two thirds of the relieving troops were killed or captured; about 400 got into the fort. Soon afterward Proctor abandoned the siege. Fort Stephenson, garrisoned by Major Croghan and 160 men, was attacked by a force of 391 British regulars, who tried to carry it by assault, and were repulsed with the loss of a fourth of their number. Some four thousand Indians joined Proctor, but most of them left him after Perry's victory on Lake Erie. Then Harrison, having received large reinforcements, invaded Canada. At the River Thames his army of 3,500 men encountered and routed between 600 and 700 British under Proctor, and about 1,000 Indians under Tecumseh. The battle was decided at once by a charge of the Kentucky mounted riflemen, who broke through the regulars, took them in rear, and captured them, and then dismounting attacked the flank of the Indians, who were also assailed by the infantry. Proctor escaped by the skin of his teeth and Tecumseh died fighting, like the hero that he was. This battle ended the campaign in the Northwest. In this quarter it must be remembered that the war was, on the part of the Americans, mainly one against Indians; the latter always forming over half of the British forces. Many of the remainder were French Canadians, and the others were regulars. The American armies, on the contrary, were composed of the armed settlers of Kentucky and Ohio, native Americans, of English speech and blood, who were battling for lands that were to form the heritage of their children. In the West the war was only the closing act of the struggle that for many years had been waged by the hardy and restless pioneers of our race, as with rifle and axe they carved out the mighty empire that we their children inherit; it was but the final effort with which they wrested from the Indian lords of the soil the wide and fair domain that now forms the heart of our great Republic. It was the breaking down of the last barrier that stayed the flood of our civilization; it settled, once and for ever, that henceforth the law, the tongue, and the blood of the land should be neither Indian, nor yet French, but English. The few French of the West were fighting against a race that was to leave as little trace of them as of the doomed Indian peoples with whom they made common cause. The presence of the British mercenaries did not alter the character of the contest; it merely served to show the bitter and narrow hatred with which the Mother-Island regarded her greater daughter, predestined as the latter was to be queen of the lands that lay beyond the Atlantic.

Meanwhile, on Lake Ontario, the Americans made successful descents on York and Fort George, scattering or capturing their comparatively small garrisons; while a counter descent by the British on Sackett's Harbor failed, the attacking force being too small. After the capture of Fort George, the Americans invaded Canada; but their advance guard, 1,400 strong, under Generals Chandler and Winder, was surprised in the night by 800 British, who, advancing with the bayonet, broke up the camp, capturing both the generals and half the artillery. Though the assailants, who lost 220 of their small number, suffered much more than the Americans, yet the latter were completely demoralized, and at once retreated to Fort George. Soon afterward, Col. Boerstler with about 600 men surrendered with shamefully brief resistance to a somewhat smaller force of British and Indians. Then about 300 British crossed the Niagara to attack Black Rock, which they took, but were afterward driven off by a large body of militia with the loss of 40 men. Later in the season the American General McClure wantonly burned the village of Newark, and then retreated in panic flight across the Niagara. In retaliation the British in turn crossed the river; 600 regulars surprised and captured in the night Fort Niagara, with its garrison of 400 men; two thousand troops attacked Black Rock, and, after losing over a hundred men in a smart engagement with somewhat over 1,500 militia whom they easily dispersed, captured and burned both it and Buffalo. Before these last events took place another invasion of Canada had been attempted, this time under General Wilkinson, "an unprincipled imbecile," as Scott very properly styled him. It was mismanaged in every possible way, and was a total failure; it was attended with but one battle, that of Chrystler's Farm, in which 1,000 British, with the loss of less than 200 men, beat back double their number of Americans, who lost nearly 500 men and also one piece of artillery. The American army near Lake Champlain had done nothing, its commander, General Wade Hampton, being, if possible, even more incompetent than Wilkinson. He remained stationary while a small force of British plundered Plattsburg and Burlington; then, with 5,000 men he crossed into Canada, but returned almost immediately, after a small skirmish at Chauteaugay between his advance guard and some 500 Canadians, in which the former lost 41 and the latter 22 men. This affair, in which hardly a tenth of the American force was engaged, has been, absurdly enough, designated a "battle" by most British and Canadian historians. In reality it was the incompetency of their general and not the valor of their foes that caused the retreat of the Americans. The same comment, by the way, applies to the so-called "Battle" of Plattsburg, in the following year, which may have been lost by Sir George Prevost, but was certainly not won by the Americans. And, again, a similar criticism should be passed on General Wilkinson's attack on La Colle Mill, near the head of the same lake. Neither one of the three affairs was a stand-up fight; in each a greatly superior force, led by an utterly incapable general, retreated after a slight skirmish with an enemy whose rout would have been a matter of certainty had the engagement been permitted to grow serious.

In the early spring of 1814 a small force of 160 American regulars, under Captain Holmes, fighting from behind felled logs, routed 200 British with a loss of 65 men, they themselves losing but 8. On Lake Ontario the British made a descent on Oswego and took it by fair assault; and afterward lost 180 men who tried to cut out some American transports, and were killed or captured to a man. All through the spring and early summer the army on the Niagara frontier was carefully drilled by Brown, and more especially by Scott, and the results of this drilling were seen in the immensely improved effectiveness of the soldiers in the campaign that opened in July. Fort Erie was captured with little resistance, and on the 4th of July, at the river Chippeway, Brown, with two brigades of regulars, each about 1,200 strong, under Scott and Ripley, and a brigade of 800 militia and Indians under Porter, making a total of about 3,200 men, won a stand-up fight against the British General Riall, who had nearly 2,500 men, 1,800 of them regulars. Porter's brigade opened by driving in the Canadian militia and the Indians; but was itself checked by the British light-troops. Ripley's brigade took very little part in the battle, three of the regiments not being engaged at all, and the fourth so slightly as to lose but five men. The entire brunt of the action was born by Scott's brigade, which was fiercely attacked by the bulk of the British regulars under Riall. The latter advanced with great bravery, but were terribly cut up by the fire of Scott's regulars; and when they had come nearly up to him, Scott charged with the bayonet and drove them clean off the field. The American loss was 322, including 23 Indians; the British loss was 515, excluding that of the Indians. The number of Americans actually engaged did not exceed that of the British; and Scott's brigade, in fair fight, closed by a bayonet charge, defeated an equal force of British regulars.

On July 25th occurred the Battle of Niagara, or Lundy's Lane, fought between General Brown with 3,100[1] Americans and General Drummond with 3,500[2] British. It was brought on by accident in the evening, and was waged with obstinate courage and savage slaughter till midnight. On both sides the forces straggled into action by detachments. The Americans formed the attacking party. As before, Scott's brigade bore the brunt of the fight, and over half of his men were killed or wounded; he himself was disabled and borne from the field. The struggle was of the most desperate character, the combatants showing a stubborn courage that could not be surpassed.[3] Charge after charge was made with the bayonet, and the artillery was taken and retaken once and again. The loss was nearly equal: on the side of the Americans, 854 men (including Generals Brown and Scott, wounded) and two guns; on that of the British, 878 men (including General Riall captured) and one gun. Each side claimed it as a vic-

---

[1] As near as can be found out; most American authorities make it much less; Lossing, for example, says only 2,400.

[2] General Drummond in his official letter makes it but 2,800; James, who gives the details, makes it 3,000 rank and file; adding 13 per cent. for the officers, sergeants, and drummers, brings it up to 3,400; and we still have to count in the artillery drivers, etc.

[3] General Drummond writes: "In so determined a manner were their attacks directed against our guns that our artillerymen were bayoneted while in the act of loading, and the muzzle of the enemy's guns were advanced within a few yards of ours." Even James says: "Upon the whole, however, the American troops fought bravely; and the conduct of many of the officers, of the artillery corps especially, would have done honor to any service."

tory over superior numbers. The truth is beyond question that the British had the advantage in numbers, and a still greater advantage in position; while it is equally beyond question that it was a defeat and not a victory for the Americans. They left the field and retired in perfect order to Fort Erie, while the British held the field and the next day pursued their foes.

Having received some reinforcements General Drummond, now with about 3,600 men, pushed forward to besiege Fort Erie, in which was the American army, some 2,400 strong, under General Gaines. Col. Tucker with 500 British regulars was sent across the Niagara to destroy the batteries at Black Rock, but was defeated by 300 American regulars under Major Morgan, fighting from behind a strong breastwork of felled trees, with a creek in front. On the night of the 15th of August, the British in three columns advanced to storm the American works, but after making a most determined assault were beaten off. The assailants lost 900 men, the assailed about 80. After this nothing was done till Sept. 17th, when General Brown, who had resumed command of the American forces, determined upon and executed a sortie. Each side had received reinforcements; the Americans numbered over 3,000, the British nearly 4,000. The fighting was severe, the Americans losing 500 men; but their opponents lost 600 men, and most of their batteries were destroyed. Each side, as usual, claimed the victory; but, exactly as Lundy's Lane must be accounted an American defeat, as our forces retreated from the ground, so this must be considered an American victory, for after it the British broke up camp and drew off to Chippeway. Nothing more was done, and on November 5th the American army recrossed the Niagara. Though marked by some brilliant feats of arms this four months' invasion of Canada, like those that had preceded it, thus came to nothing. But at the same time a British invasion of the United States was repulsed far more disgracefully. Sir George Prevost, with an army of 13,000 veteran troops, marched south along the shores of Lake Champlain to Plattsburg, which was held by General Macomb with 2,000 regulars, and perhaps double that number of nearly worthless militia;—a force that the British could have scattered to the winds, though, as they were strongly posted, not without severe loss. But the British fleet was captured by Commodore MacDonough in the fight on the lake; and then Sir George, after some heavy skirmishing between the outposts of the armies, in which the Americans had the advantage, fled precipitately back to Canada.

All through the war the sea-coasts of the United States had been harried by small predatory excursions; a part of what is now the State of Maine was conquered with little resistance, and kept until the close of hostilities; and some of the towns on the shores of Chesapeake Bay had been plundered or burnt. In August, 1814, a more serious invasion was planned, and some 5,000 troops—regulars, sailors, and marines—were landed, under the command of General Ross. So utterly helpless was the Democratic Administration at Washington, that during the two years of warfare hardly any steps had been taken to protect the Capitol, or the country round about; what little was done, was done entirely too late, and bungled badly in addition. History has not yet done justice to the ludicrous and painful folly and stupidity of which the government founded by Jefferson, and carried on by Madison, was guilty, both in its preparations for, and in its way of carrying on, this war; nor is it yet realized that the men just mentioned, and their associates, are primarily responsible for the loss we suffered in it, and the bitter humiliation some of its incidents caused us. The small British army marched at will through Virginia and Maryland, burned Washington, and finally retreated from before Baltimore and re-embarked to take part in the expedition against New Orleans. Twice, at Bladensburg and North Point, it came in contact with superior numbers of militia in fairly good position. In each case the result was the same. After some preliminary skirmishing, manœuvring, and volley firing, the British charged with the bayonet. The rawest regiments among the American militia then broke at once; the others kept pretty steady, pouring in quite a destructive fire, until the regulars had come up close to them, when they also fled. The British regulars were too heavily loaded to pursue, and, owing to their mode of attack, and the rapidity with which their opponents ran away, the loss of the latter was in each case very slight. At North Point, however, the militia, being more experienced, behaved better than at Bladensburg. In neither case were the British put to any trouble to win their victory.

The above is a brief sketch of the campaigns of the war. It is not cheerful reading for an American, nor yet of interest to a military student; and its lessons have been taught so often by similar occurrences in other lands under like circumstances, and, moreover, teach such self-evident truths, that they scarcely need to be brought to the notice of an historian. But the crowning event of the war was the Battle of New Orleans; remarkable in its military aspect, and a source of pride to every American. It is well worth a more careful study, and to it I have devoted the last chapter of this work.

*New York City, 1883*

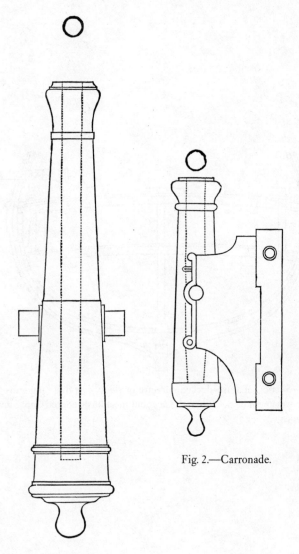

Fig. 1.—Long gun.

Fig. 2.—Carronade.

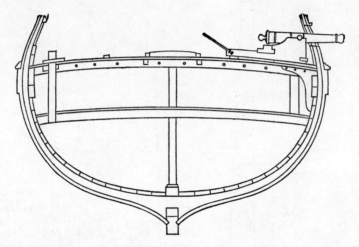

Fig. 3.—Section of flush-decked corvette or sloop, carrying long guns. Such was the armament of the *Pike* and *Adams,* but most flush-decked ships mounted carronades.

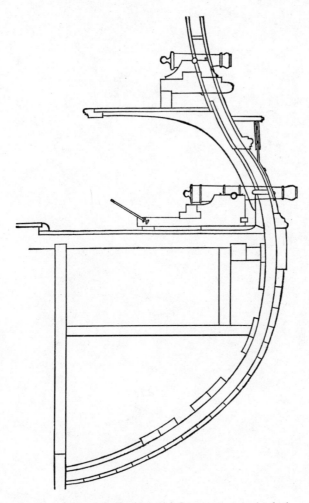

Fig. 4.—Section of frigate-built ship, with long gun on main-deck and car-ronade on spar-deck. Taken from the "American Artillerist's Companion," by Louis de Toussard (Philadelphia, 1811).

# Principal Authorities
## Referred To

(SEE ALSO IN ALPHABETICAL PLACE IN INDEX.)

American State Papers.

Brenton, E. P. Naval History of Great Britain, 1783 to 1836. 2 vols., octavo. London, 1837.

Broke, Adm., Memoir of, by Rev. J. G. Brighton. Octavo. London, 1866.

"Captains' Letters" in Archives at Washington.

Codrington, Adm. Sir E. Memoirs, edited by his daughter. 2 vols., octavo. London, 1873.

Coggeshall, George. History of American Privateers. New York, 1876.

Cooper, J. F. Naval History of the United States. New York, 1856.

Dundonald, Earl. Autobiography of a Seaman. London, 1860.

Douglass, Lord Howard. Naval Gunnery. Octavo. London, 1860.

Emmons, Lieut. G. E. Statistical History of United States Navy, 1853.

Farragut, Adm. D. G., Life of, by his son, Loyall Farragut. Octavo. New York, 1878.

Gravière, Adm., J. de la. Guerres Maritimes. 2 vols., octavo. Paris, 1881.

James, William. Naval History of Great Britain. 6 vols., octavo. London, 1837.

James, William. Naval Occurrences with the Americans. Octavo. London, 1817.

Lossing, Benson J. Field-book of the War of 1812. Octavo. New York, 1869.

Low, C. R. History of the Indian Navy, 1613 to 1863. 2 vols., octavo. London, 1877.

*London Naval Chronicle.*

Marshall. Royal Naval Biography. 12 vols., octavo. London, 1825.

"Masters-Commandant Letters" in the Archives at Washington.

Morris, Com. Charles. Autobiography. Annapolis, 1880.

Naval Archives at Washington.

Niles. *Weekly Register.*

Pielat, B. La Vie et les Actions Mémorables du St. Michel du Ruyter. Amsterdam, 1677.

Rivière, Lieut H. La Marine Française sous le Régime de Louis XV. Paris, 1859.

Tatnall, Commod., Life, by C. C. Jones, Jr. Savannah, 1878.

Toussard, L. de. American Artillerists' Companion. Phila., 1811.

Troude, O. Batailles Navales de la France. Paris, 1868.

Ward, Com. J. H. Manual of Naval Tactics. 1859.

Yonge, Charles Duke. History of the British Navy. 3 vols., octavo. London, 1866.

# AUTHORITIES REFERRED TO
# IN CHAPTER X

Alison, Sir A. History of Europe. Ninth edition. 20 vols. London, 1852. Pages 260, 263, 267, 268.

Butler, Adjutant-General Robert. Official Report for the Morning of Jan. 8, 1815. Page 263.

Codrington, Admiral Sir Edward. Memoir of, by lady Bourchier. London, 1873. Pages 260, 262, 267.

Cole, John William. Memoirs of British Generals Distinguished during the Peninsular War. London, 1856. Pages 262, 270.

Court of Inquiry on Conduct of General Morgan. Official Report. Page 267.

Gleig, Ensign H. R. Narrative of the Campaigns of the British Army at Washington, Baltimore, and New Orleans. Philadelphia, 1821. Pages 257, 258, 259, 260, 261, 263, 269.

Jackson, Andrew. As a Public Man. A sketch by W. G. Sumner. Boston, 1882. Page 270.

Jackson, General Andrew. Official Letters. Pages 256, 269.

James, William. Military Occurrences of the Late War. 2 vols. London, 1818. Pages 256, 260, 262, 267, 271.

Keane, Major-General John. Letter, December 26, 1814. Pages 254, 257, 258.

Lambert, General. Letters, January 10 and 28, 1815. Pages 268, 269.

Latour, Major A. Lacarriex. Historical Memoir of the War in West Florida and Louisiana. Translated from the French by H. P. Nugent. Philadelphia, 1816. Pages 254, 255, 258, 259, 260, 263, 264, 267.

Lossing, Benson J. Field-Book of the War of 1812. New York, 1859. Page 259.

Patterson, Com. Daniel G. Letters, Dec. 20, 1814, and Jan. 13, 1815. Pages 255, 267.

Monroe, James. Sketch of His Life, by Daniel C. Gilman. 16mo. Boston, 1883. Page 252.

Napier, Maj.-Gen. Sir W. F. P. History of the War in the Peninsula. 5 vols. New York, 1882. Pages 253, 256, 261, 262, 265, 270.

Scott, Lieut.-Gen. W. Memoirs, by himself. 2 vols. New York, 1864. Page 252.

Thornton, Col. W. Letter, Jan. 8, 1815. Page 267.

# THE NAVAL
# WAR OF
# 1812

# I

# INTRODUCTORY

Causes of the War of 1812 · Conflicting views of America and Britain as regards neutral rights · Those of the former power right · Impossibility of avoiding hostilities · Declaration of war · General features of the contest · Racial
identity of the contestants · The treaty of peace nominally leaves the situation
unchanged · But practically settles the dispute in our favor in respect to maritime rights · The British navy and its reputation prior to 1812 · Comparison
with other European navies · British and American authorities consulted in the
present work

The view professed by Great Britain in 1812 respecting the rights of belliger-
ents and neutrals was diametrically opposite to that held by the United States.
"Between England and the United States of America," writes a British author,
"a spirit of animosity, caused chiefly by the impressment of British seamen, or
of seamen asserted to be such, from on board of American merchant vessels,
had unhappily subsisted for a long time" prior to the war. "It is, we believe," he
continues, "an acknowledged maxim of public law, as well that no nation but
the one he belongs to can release a subject from his natural allegiance, as that,
provided the jurisdiction of another independent state be not infringed, every
nation has a right to enforce the services of her subjects wherever they may be
found. Nor has any neutral nation such a jurisdiction over her merchant vessels
upon the high seas as to exclude a belligerent nation from the right of searching them for contraband of war or for the property or persons of her enemies.
And if, in the exercise of that right, the belligerent should discover on board of
the neutral vessel a subject who has withdrawn himself from his lawful allegiance, the neutral can have no fair ground for refusing to deliver him up; more
especially if that subject is proved to be a deserter from the sea or land service
of the former."[1]

Great Britain's doctrine was "once a subject always a subject." On the other
hand, the United States maintained that any foreigner, after five years' resi-

---

[1] "The Naval History of Great Britain," by William James, vol. iv, p. 324. (New edition by Captain
Chamier, R. N., London, 1837.)

dence within her territory, and after having complied with certain forms, became one of her citizens as completely as if he was native born. Great Britain contended that her war ships possessed the right of searching all neutral vessels for the property and persons of her foes. The United States, resisting this claim, asserted that "free bottoms made free goods," and that consequently her ships when on the high seas should not be molested on any pretext whatever. Finally, Great Britain's system of impressment,[1] by which men could be forcibly seized and made to serve in her navy, no matter at what cost to themselves, was repugnant to every American idea.

Such wide differences in the views of the two nations produced endless difficulties. To escape the press-gang, or for other reasons, many British seamen took service under the American flag; and if they were demanded back, it is not likely that they or their American shipmates had much hesitation in swearing either that they were not British at all, or else that they had been naturalized as Americans. Equally probable is it that the American blockade-runners were guilty of a great deal of fraud and more or less thinly veiled perjury. But the wrongs done by the Americans were insignificant compared with those they received. Any innocent merchant vessel was liable to seizure at any moment; and when overhauled by a British cruiser short of men was sure to be stripped of most of her crew. The British officers were themselves the judges as to whether a seaman should be pronounced a native of America or of Britain, and there was no appeal from their judgment. If a captain lacked his full complement there was little doubt as to the view he would take of any man's nationality. The wrongs inflicted on our seafaring countrymen by their impressment into foreign ships formed the main cause of the war.

There were still other grievances which are thus presented by the British Admiral Cochrane.[2] "Our treatment of its (America's) citizens was scarcely in accordance with the national privileges to which the young Republic had become entitled. There were no doubt many individuals among the American people who, caring little for the Federal Government, considered it more profitable to break than to keep the laws of nations by aiding and supporting our enemy (France), and it was against such that the efforts of the squadron had chiefly been directed; but the way the object was carried out was scarcely less an infraction of those national laws which we were professedly enforcing. The practice of taking English (and American) seamen out of American ships without regard to the safety of navigating them when thus deprived of their hands has been already mentioned. To this may be added the detention of vessels against which nothing contrary to international neutrality could be established, whereby their cargoes became damaged compelling them, on suspicion only, to proceed to ports other than those to which they were destined; and gen-

[1] The best idea of which can be gained by reading Marryatt's novels.
[2] "Autobiography of a Seaman," by Thomas, tenth Earl of Dundonald, Admiral of the Red; Rear-Admiral of the Fleet, London, 1860, vol. i, p. 24.

erally treating them as though they were engaged in contraband trade. \* \* \*
American ships were not permitted to quit English ports without giving secu-
rity for the discharge of their cargoes in some other British or neutral port." On
the same subject James[1] writes: "When, by the maritime supremacy of England,
France could no longer trade for herself, America proffered her services, as a
neutral, to trade for her; and American merchants and their agents, in the gains
that flowed in, soon found a compensation for all the perjury and fraud necessary to cheat the former out of her belligerent rights. The high commercial importance of the United States thus obtained, coupled with a similarity of
language and, to a superficial observer, a resemblance in person between the
natives of America and Great Britain, has caused the former to be the chief, if
not the only sufferers by the exercise of the right of search. Chiefly indebted
for their growth and prosperity to emigration from Europe, the United States
hold out every allurement to foreigners, particularly to British seamen, whom,
by a process peculiarly their own, they can naturalize as quickly as a dollar can
exchange masters and a blank form, ready signed and sworn to, can be filled up.[2]
It is the knowledge of this fact that makes British naval officers when searching
for deserters from their service, so harsh in their scrutiny, and so sceptical of
American oaths and asseverations."

The last sentence of the foregoing from James is an euphemistic way of saying that whenever a British commander short of men came across an American
vessel he impressed all of her crew that he wanted, whether they were citizens
of the United States or not. It must be remembered, however, that the only reason why Great Britain did us more injury than any other power was because she
was better able to do so. None of her acts were more offensive than Napoleon's
Milan decree, by which it was declared that any neutral vessel which permitted
itself to be searched by a British cruiser should be considered as British, and as
the lawful prize of any French vessel. French frigates and privateers were very
apt to snap up any American vessel they came across, and were only withheld
at all by the memory of the sharp dressing they had received in the West Indies
during the quasi-war of 1799–1800. What we undoubtedly ought to have done
was to have adopted the measure actually proposed in Congress, and declared
war on both France and England. As it was, we chose as a foe the one that had
done, and could still do, us the greatest injury.

The principles for which the United States contended in 1812 are now universally accepted, and those so tenaciously maintained by Great Britain find no
advocates in the civilized world. That England herself was afterward completely reconciled to our views was amply shown by her intense indignation
when Commodore Wilkes, in the exercise of the right of search for the persons
of the foes of his country, stopped the neutral British ship *Trent;* while the ap-
plause with which the act was greeted in America proves pretty clearly another

---

[1] *L. c.,* iv, 325.
[2] This is an exaggeration.

fact, that we had warred for the right, not because it *was* the right, but because it agreed with our self-interest to do so. We were contending for "Free Trade and Sailors' Rights": meaning by the former expression, freedom to trade wherever we chose without hindrance save from the power with whom we were trading; and by the latter, that a man who happened to be on the sea should have the same protection accorded to a man who remained on land. Nominally, neither of these questions was settled by, or even alluded to, in the treaty of peace; but the immense increase of reputation that the navy acquired during the war practically decided both points in our favor. Our sailors had gained too great a name for any one to molest them with impunity again.

Holding views on these maritime subjects so radically different from each other, the two nations could not but be continually dealing with causes of quarrel. Not only did British cruisers molest our merchant-men, but at length one of them, the 50-gun ship *Leopard*, attacked an American frigate, the *Chesapeake*, when the latter was so lumbered up that she could not return a shot, killed or disabled some twenty of her men and took away four others, one Briton and three Americans, who were claimed as deserters. For this act an apology was offered, but it failed to restore harmony between the two nations. Soon afterward another action was fought. The American frigate *President*, Commodore Rodgers, attacked the British sloop *Little Belt*, Captain Bingham, and exchanged one or two broadsides with her,—the frigate escaping scot-free while the sloop was nearly knocked to pieces. Mutual recriminations followed, each side insisting that the other was the assailant.

When Great Britain issued her Orders in Council forbidding our trading with France, we retaliated by passing an embargo act, which prevented us from trading at all. There could be but one result to such a succession of incidents, and that was war. Accordingly, in June, 1812, war was declared; and as a contest for the rights of seamen, it was largely waged on the ocean. We also had not a little fighting to do on land, in which, as a rule, we came out second-best. Few or no preparations for the war had been made, and the result was such as might have been anticipated. After dragging on through three dreary and uneventful years it came to an end in 1815, by a peace which left matters in almost precisely the state in which the war had found them. On land and water the contest took the form of a succession of petty actions, in which the glory acquired by the victor seldom eclipsed the disgrace incurred by the vanquished. Neither side succeeded in doing what it intended. Americans declared that Canada must and should be conquered, but the conquering came quite as near being the other way. British writers insisted that the American navy should be swept from the seas; and, during the sweeping process it increased fourfold.

When the United States declared war, Great Britain was straining every nerve and muscle in a death struggle with the most formidable military despotism of modern times, and was obliged to entrust the defence of her Canadian colonies to a mere handful of regulars, aided by the local fencibles. But Congress had provided even fewer trained soldiers, and relied on militia. The latter chiefly exercised their fighting abilities upon one another in duelling, and, as a rule, were afflicted with conscientious scruples whenever it was necessary to cross the frontier and attack the enemy. Accordingly, the campaign opened with the bloodless surrender of an American general to a much inferior British force, and the war continued much as it had begun; we suffered disgrace after disgrace, while the losses we inflicted, in turn, on Great Britain were so slight as hardly to attract her attention. At last, having crushed her greater foe, she turned to crush the lesser, and, in her turn, suffered ignominious defeat. By this time events had gradually developed a small number of soldiers on our northern frontier, who, commanded by Scott and Brown, were able to contend on equal terms with the veteran troops to whom they were opposed, though these formed part of what was then undoubtedly the most formidable fighting infantry any European nation possessed. The battles at this period of the struggle were remarkable for the skill and stubborn courage with which they were waged, as well as for the heavy loss involved; but the number of combatants was so small that in Europe they would have been regarded as mere outpost skirmishes, and they wholly failed to attract any attention abroad in that period of colossal armies.

When Great Britain seriously turned her attention to her transatlantic foe, and assembled in Canada an army of 14,000 men at the head of Lake Champlain, Congressional forethought enabled it to be opposed by soldiers who, it is true, were as well disciplined, as hardy, and as well commanded as any in the world, but who were only a few hundred strong, backed by more or less incompetent militia. Only McDonough's skill and Sir George Prevost's incapacity saved us from a serious disaster; the sea-fight reflected high honor on our seamen, but the retreat of the British land-forces was due to their commander and not to their antagonists. Meanwhile a large British fleet in the Chesapeake had not achieved much glory by the destruction of local oyster-boats and the burning of a few farmers' houses, so an army was landed to strike a decisive blow. At Bladensburg[1] the five thousand British regulars, utterly worn out by heat and fatigue, by their mere appearance, frightened into a panic double their number of American militia well posted. But the only success attained was burning the public buildings of Washington, and that result was of dubious value. Baltimore was attacked next, and the attack repulsed, after the forts and ships had shelled one another with the slight results that usually attend that spectacular and harmless species of warfare.

The close of the contest was marked by the extraordinary battle of New Orleans. It was a perfectly useless shedding of blood, since peace had already been declared. There is hardly another contest of modern times where the defeated side suffered such frightful carnage, while the victors came off almost scatheless. It is quite in accordance with the rest of the war that the militia, hitherto worse than useless, should on this occasion win against great odds in

---

[1] See the "Capture of Washington," by Edward D. Ingraham (Philadelphia, 1849).

point of numbers; and, moreover, that their splendid victory should have been of little consequence in its effects upon the result. On the whole, the contest by land, where we certainly ought to have been successful, reflected greater credit on our antagonists than upon us, in spite of the services of Scott, Brown, and Jackson. Our small force of regulars and volunteers did excellently; as for the militia, New Orleans proved that they *could* fight superbly, and the other battles that they generally *would not* fight at all.

At sea, as will appear, the circumstances were widely different. Here we possessed a small but highly effective force, the ships well built, manned by thoroughly trained men, and commanded by able and experienced officers. The deeds of our navy form a part of history over which any American can be pardoned for lingering.

———

Such was the origin, issue, and general character of the war. It may now be well to proceed to a comparison of the authorities on the subject. Allusion has already been made to them in the preface, but a fuller reference seems to be necessary in this connection.

At the close of the contest, the large majority of historians who wrote of it were so bitterly rancorous that their statements must be received with caution. For the main facts, I have relied, wherever it was practicable, upon the official letters of the commanding officers, taking each as authority for his own force and loss.[1] For all the British victories we have British official letters, which tally almost exactly, as regards matters of *fact* and not of *opinion*, with the corresponding American accounts. For the first year the British also published official accounts of their defeats, which in the cases of the *Guerrière, Macedonian* and *Frolic,* I have followed as closely as the accounts of the American victors. The last British official letter published announcing a defeat was that in the case of the *Java,* and it is the only letter that I have not strictly accepted. The fact that no more were published thereafter is of itself unfortunate; and from the various contradictions it contains it would appear to have been tampered with. The surgeon's report accompanying it is certainly false. Subsequent to 1812 no letter of a defeated British commander was published,[2] and I have to depend upon the various British historians, especially James, of whom more anon.

The American and British historians from whom we are thus at times forced to draw our material regard the war from very different stand-points, and their accounts generally differ. Each writer naturally so colored the affair as to have it appear favorable to his own side. Sometimes this was done intentionally and

[1] As where Broke states his own force at 330, his antagonists at 440, and the American court of inquiry makes the numbers 396 and 379, I have taken them as being 330 and 379 respectively. This is the only just method; I take it for granted that each commander meant to tell the truth, and of course knew his own force, while he might very naturally and in perfect good faith exaggerate his antagonist's.

[2] Except about the battles on the Lakes, where I have accordingly given the same credit to the accounts both of the British and of the Americans.

sometimes not. Not infrequently errors are made against the historian's own side; as when the British author, Brenton, says that the British brig *Peacock* mounted 32's instead of 24's, while Lossing in his "Field-Book of the War of 1812" makes the same mistake about the arming of the American brig *Argus*. Errors of this description are, of course, as carefully to be guarded against as any others. Mere hearsay reports, such as "it has been said," "a prisoner on board the opposing fleet has observed," "an American (or British) newspaper of such and such a date has remarked," are of course to be rejected. There is a curious parallelism in the errors on both sides. For example, the American, Mr. Low, writing in 1813, tells how the *Constitution,* 44, captured the *Guerrière* of 49 guns, while the British Lieutenant Low, writing in 1880, tells how the *Pelican,* 18, captured the *Argus* of 20 guns. Each records the truth but not the whole truth, for although rating 44 and 18 the victors carried respectively 54 and 21 guns, of heavier metal than those of their antagonists. Such errors are generally intentional. Similarly, most American writers mention the actions in which the privateers were victorious, but do not mention those in which they were defeated; while the British, in turn, record every successful "cutting-out" expedition, but ignore entirely those which terminated unfavorably. Other errors arise from honest ignorance. Thus, James in speaking of the repulse of the *Endymion*'s boats by the *Neufchatel* gives the latter a crew of 120 men; she had more than this number originally, but only 40 were in her at the time of the attack. So also when the captain of the *Pelican* writes that the officers of the *Argus* report her loss at 40, when they really reported it at 24 or when Captain Dacres thought the *Constitution* had lost about 20 men instead of 14. The American gun-boat captains in recounting their engagements with the British frigates invariably greatly overestimated the loss of the latter. So that on both sides there were some intentional misstatements or garblings, and a much more numerous class of simple blunders, arising largely from an incapacity for seeing more than one side of the question.

Among the early British writers upon this war, the ablest was James. He devoted one work, his "Naval Occurrences," entirely to it; and it occupies the largest part of the sixth volume of his more extensive "History of the British Navy."[1] Two other British writers, Lieutenant Marshall[2] and Captain Brenton,[3] wrote histories of the same events, about the same time; but neither of these naval officers produced half as valuable a work as did the civilian James. Marshall wrote a dozen volumes, each filled with several scores of dreary panegyrics, or memoirs of as many different officers. There is no attempt at order, hardly any thing about the ships, guns, or composition of the crews; and not even the pretence of giving both sides, the object being to make every Englishman appear in his best light. The work is analogous to the numerous lives of Decatur, Bain-

---

[1] A new edition, London, 1826.
[2] "Royal Navy Biography," by John Marshall (London, 1823–1835).
[3] "Naval History of Great Britain," by Edward Pelham Brenton (new edition, London, 1837).

bridge, Porter, etc., that appeared in the United States about the same time, and is quite as untrustworthy. Brenton made a far better and very interesting book, written on a good and well-connected plan, and apparently with a sincere desire to tell the truth. He accepts the British official accounts as needing nothing whatever to supplement them, precisely as Cooper accepts the American officials'. A more serious fault is his inability to be accurate. That this inaccuracy is not intentional is proved by the fact that it tells as often against his own side as against his opponents. He says, for example, that the guns of Perry's and Barclay's squadrons "were about equal in number and weight," that the *Peacock* (British) was armed with 32's instead of 24's, and underestimates the force of the second *Wasp.* But the blunders are quite as bad when distributed as when confined to one side; in addition, Brenton's disregard of all details makes him of but little use.

James, as already said, is by far the most valuable authority on the war, as regards *purely British* affairs. He enters minutely into details, and has evidently laboriously hunted up his authorities. He has examined the ships' logs, the Admiralty reports, various treatises, all the *Gazette* reports, gives very well-chosen extracts, has arranged his work in chronological order, discriminates between the officers that deserve praise and those that deserve blame, and in fact writes a work which ought to be consulted by every student of naval affairs. But he is unfortunately afflicted with a hatred toward the Americans that amounts to a monomania. He wishes to make out as strong a case as possible against them. The *animus* of his work may be gathered from the not over complimentary account of the education of the youthful seafaring American, which can be found in vol. vi, p. 113, of his "History." On page 153 he asserts that he is an "impartial historian"; and about three lines before mentions that "it may suit the Americans to invent any falsehood, no matter how barefaced, to foist a valiant character on themselves." On page 419 he says that Captain Porter is to be believed, "so far as is borne out by proof (the only safe way where an American is concerned),"—which somewhat sweeping denunciation of the veracity of all of Captain Porter's compatriots would seem to indicate that James was not, perhaps, in that dispassionate frame of mind best suited for writing history. That he should be biassed against individual captains can be understood, but when he makes rabid onslaughts upon the American people as a whole, he renders it difficult for an American, at any rate, to put implicit credence in him. His statements are all the harder to confute when they are erroneous, because they are intentionally so. It is not, as with Brenton and Marshall, because he really thinks a British captain *cannot* be beaten, except by some kind of distorted special providence, for no man says worse things than he does about certain officers and crews. A writer of James' undoubted ability must have known perfectly well that his statements were untrue in many instances, as where he garbles Hilyar's account of Porter's loss, or misstates the comparative force of the fleets on Lake Champlain.

When he says (p. 194) that Captain Bainbridge wished to run away from the *Java,* and would have done so if he had not been withheld by the advice of his first lieutenant, who was a renegade Englishman,[1] it is not of much consequence whether his making the statement was due to excessive credulity or petty meanness, for, in either case, whether the defect was in his mind or his morals, it is enough to greatly impair the value of his other "facts." Again, when James (p. 165) states that Decatur ran away from the *Macedonian* until, by some marvellous optical delusion, he mistook her for a 32, he merely detracts a good deal from the worth of his own account. When the Americans adopt boarding helmets, he considers it as proving conclusively that they are suffering from an acute attack of cowardice. On p. 122 he says that "had the *President,* when she fell in with the *Belvidera,* been cruising alone * * * Commodore Rodgers would have magnified the British frigate into a line-of-battle ship, and have done his utmost to avoid her," which gives an excellent idea of the weight to be attached to the various other anecdotes he relates of the much-abused Commodore Rodgers.

But it must always be remembered that untrustworthy as James is in any thing referring purely to the Americans, he is no worse than his compeers of both nationalities. The misstatements of Niles in his "Weekly Register" about the British are quite as flagrant, and his information about his own side even more valuable.[2] Every little American author crowed over Perry's "Nelsonic victory over a greatly superior force." The *Constitution* was declared to have been at a disadvantage when she fought the *Guerrière,* and so on *ad infinitum.* But these writers have all faded into oblivion, and their writings are not even referred to, much less believed. James, on the contrary, has passed through edition after edition, is considered as unquestionable authority in his own country, and largely throughout Europe, and has furnished the basis for every subsequent account by British authors. From Alison to Lieutenant Low, almost every English work, whether of a popular character or not, is, in so far as it touches on the war, simply a "rehash" of the works written by James. The consequence is that the British and American accounts have astonishingly little resemblance. One ascribes the capture of the British frigates simply to the fact that their opponents were "cut down line-of-battle ships"; the other gives all the glory to the "undaunted heroism," etc., of the Yankee sailors.

One not very creditable trait of the early American naval historians gave their rivals a great advantage. The object of the former was to make out that the *Constitution,* for example, won her victories against an equal foe, and an exact statement of the forces showed the contrary; so they always avoided figures,

---

[1] Who, by the way, was Mr. Parker, born in Virginia, and never in England in his life.

[2] In Niles, by the way, can be found excellent examples of the traditional American "spread-eagle" style. In one place I remember his describing "The Immortal Rodgers," baulked of his natural prey, the British, as "soaring about like the bold bald eagle of his native land," seeking whom he might devour. The accounts he gives of British line-of-battle ships fleeing from American 44's quite match James' anecdotes of the latter's avoidance of British 38's and 36's for fear they might mount twenty-four-pounders. The two works taken together give a very good idea of the war; separately, either is utterly unreliable, especially in matters of opinion.

and thus left the ground clear for James' careful misstatements. Even when they criticised him they never went into details, confining themselves to some remark about "hurling" his figures in his face with "loathing." Even Cooper, interesting though his work is, has gone far less into figures than he should, and seems to have paid little if any attention to the British official statements, which of course should be received as of equal weight with the American. His comments on the actions are generally very fair, the book never being disfigured by bitterness toward the British; but he is certainly wrong, for example, in ascribing the loss of the *Chesapeake* solely to accident, that of the *Argus* solely to her inferiority in force, and so on. His disposition to praise *all* the American commanders may be generous, but is nevertheless unjust. If Decatur's surrender of the *President* is at least impliedly praised, then Porter's defence of the *Essex* can hardly receive its just award. There is no weight in the commendation bestowed upon Hull, if commendation, the same in kind though less in degree, is bestowed upon Rodgers. It is a great pity that Cooper did not write a criticism on James, for no one could have done it more thoroughly. But he never mentions him, except once in speaking of Barclay's fleet. In all probability this silence arose from sheer contempt, and the certainty that most of James' remarks were false; but the effect was that very many foreigners believe him to have shirked the subject. He rarely gives any data by which the statements of James can be disproved, and it is for this reason that I have been obliged to criticise the latter's work very fully. Many of James' remarks, however, defy criticism from their random nature, as when he states that American midshipmen were chiefly masters and mates of merchantmen, and does not give a single proof to support the assertion. It would be nearly as true to assert that the British midshipmen were for the most part ex-members of the prize-ring, and as much labor would be needed to disprove it. In other instances it is quite enough to let his words speak for themselves, as where he says (p. 155) that of the American sailors one third in number and one half in point of effectiveness were in reality British. That is, of the 450 men the *Constitution* had when she fought the *Java* 150 were British, and the remaining 300 could have been as effectively replaced by 150 more British. So a very little logic works out a result that James certainly did not intend to arrive at; namely, that 300 British led by American officers could beat, with ease and comparative impunity, 400 British led by their own officers. He also forgets that the whole consists of the sum of the parts. He accounts for the victories of the Americans by stating (p. 280) that they were lucky enough to meet with frigates and brigs who had unskilful gunners or worthless crews; he also carefully shows that the *Macedonian* was incompetently handled, the *Peacock* commanded by a mere martinet, the *Avon's* crew unpractised at the guns, the *Epervier's* mutinous and cowardly, the *Penguin's* weak and unskilful, the *Java's* exceedingly poor, and more to the same effect. Now the Americans took in single fight three frigates and seven sloops, and when as many as ten vessels are met it is exceedingly probable that they represent the fair average; so that James' strictures, so far as true, simply show that the average British ship was very apt to possess, comparatively speaking, an incompetent captain or unskilful crew. These disadvantages were not felt when opposed to navies in which they existed to an even greater extent, but became very apparent when brought into contact with a power whose few officers knew how to play their own parts very nearly to perfection, and, something equally important, knew how to make first-rate crews out of what was already good raw material. Finally, a large proportion of James' abuse of the Americans sufficiently refutes itself, and perhaps Cooper's method of contemptuously disregarding him was the best; but no harm can follow from devoting a little space to commenting upon him.

Much the best American work is Lieutenant George E. Emmons' statistical "History of the United States Navy." Unfortunately it is merely a mass of excellently arranged and classified statistics, and while of invaluable importance to the student, is not interesting to the average reader. Almost all the statements I have made of the force, tonnage, and armament of the American vessels, though I have whenever practicable taken them from the Navy Records, etc., yet could be just as well quoted from Emmons. Copies of most of the American official letters which I have quoted can be found in "Niles' Register," volumes 1 to 10, and all of the British ones in the "London Naval Chronicle" for the same years. It is to these two authorities that I am most indebted, and nearly as much so to the "American State Papers," vol. xiv. Next in order come Emmons, Cooper, and the invaluable, albeit somewhat scurrilous, James; and a great many others whose names I have quoted in their proper places. In commenting upon the actions, I have, whenever possible, drawn from some standard work, such as Jurien de la Gravière's "Guerres Maritimes," Lord Howard Douglass' "Naval Gunnery," or, better still, from the lives and memoirs of Admirals Farragut, Codrington, Broke, or Durham. The titles of the various works will be found given in full as they are referred to.[1] In a few cases, where extreme accuracy was necessary, or where, as in the case of the *President*'s capture, it was desirable that there should be no room for dispute as to the facts, I have given the authority for each sentence; but in general this would be too cumbersome, and so I have confined myself to referring, at or near the beginning of the account of each action, to the authorities from whom I have taken it. For the less important facts on which every one is agreed I have often given no references.

---

[1] To get an idea of the American seamen of that time Cooper's novels, "Miles Wallingford," "Home as Found," and the "Pilot," are far better than any history; in the "Two Admirals" the description of the fleet manœuvring is unrivalled. His view of Jack's life is rather rose-colored however. "Tom Cringle's log" ought to be read for the information it gives. Marryatt's novels will show some of the darker aspects of sailor life.

# II

During the early years of this century England's naval power stood at a height never reached before or since by that of any other nation. On every sea her navies rode, not only triumphant, but with none to dispute their sway. The island folk had long claimed the mastery of the ocean, and they had certainly succeeded in making their claim completely good during the time of bloody warfare that followed the breaking out of the French Revolution. Since the year 1792 each European nation, in turn, had learned to feel bitter dread of the weight of England's hand. In the Baltic, Sir Samuel Hood had taught the Russians that they must needs keep in port when the English cruisers were in the offing. The descendants of the Vikings had seen their whole navy destroyed at Copenhagen. No Dutch fleet ever put out after the day when, off Camperdown, Lord Duncan took possession of De Winter's shattered ships. But a few years before 1812, the greatest sea-fighter of all time had died in Trafalgar Bay, and in dying had crumbled to pieces the navies of France and of Spain.

From that day England's task was but to keep in port such of her foes' vessels as she had not destroyed. France alone still possessed fleets that could be rendered formidable, and so, from the Scheldt to Toulon, her harbors were watched and her coasts harried by the blockading squadrons of the English. Elsewhere the latter had no fear of their power being seriously assailed; but their vast commerce and numerous colonies needed ceaseless protection. Accordingly in every sea their cruisers could be found, of all sizes, from the stately ship-of-the-line, with her tiers of heavy cannon and her many hundreds of men, down to the little cutter carrying but a score of souls and a couple of light guns. All these cruisers, but especially those of the lesser rates, were continually brought into contact with such of the hostile vessels as had run through the blockade, or were too small to be affected by it. French and Italian frigates were often fought and captured when they were skirting their own coasts, or had started off on a plundering cruise through the Atlantic, or to the Indian Ocean; and though the Danes had lost their larger ships they kept up a spirited warfare with brigs and gun-boats. So the English marine was in constant exercise, attended with almost invariable success.

Such was Great Britain's naval power when the Congress of the United States declared war upon her. While she could number her thousand sail, the American navy included but half a dozen frigates, and six or eight sloops and brigs; and it is small matter for surprise that the British officers should have regarded their new foe with contemptuous indifference. Hitherto the American seamen had never been heard of except in connection with two or three engagements with French frigates, and some obscure skirmishes against the Moors of Tripoli; none of which could possibly attract attention in the years that saw Aboukir, Copenhagen, and Trafalgar. And yet these same petty wars were the school which raised our marine to the highest standard of excellence. A continuous course of victory, won mainly by seamanship, had made the English sailor overweeningly self-confident, and caused him to pay but little regard to manœuvring or even to gunnery. Meanwhile the American learned, by receiving hard knocks, how to give them, and belonged to a service too young to feel an over-confidence in itself. One side had let its training relax, while the other had carried it to the highest possible point. Hence our ships proved, on the whole, victorious in the apparently unequal struggle, and the men who had conquered the best seamen of Europe were now in turn obliged to succumb. Compared with the great naval battles of the preceding few years, our bloodiest conflicts were mere skirmishes, but they were skirmishes between the hitherto acknowledged kings of the ocean, and new men who yet proved to be more than their equals. For over a hundred years, or since the time when they had contended on equal terms with the great Dutch admirals, the British had shown a decided superiority to their various foes, and during the latter quarter of the time this superiority, as already said, was very marked, indeed; in consequence, the victories of the new enemy atttacted an amount of attention altogether disproportionate to their material effects. And it is a curious fact that our little navy, in which the art of handling and fighting the old broadside, sailing frigate in single conflict was brought to the highest point of perfection ever reached, that this same navy should have contained the first representative of the modern war steamer, and also the torpedo—the two terrible engines which were to drive from the ocean the very white-winged craft that had first won honor for the starry flag. The tactical skill of Hull or Decatur is now of merely archaic interest, and has but little more bearing on the manœuvring of a modern fleet than have the tactics of the Athenian gallies. But the war still conveys some most practical lessons as to the value of efficient ships and, above all, of efficient men in them. Had we only possessed the miserable gun-boats, our men could have done nothing; had we not possessed good men, the heavy frigates would have availed as little. Poor ships and impotent artillery had lost the Dutch almost their entire navy; fine ships and heavy cannon had not saved the French and Spanish from the like fate. We owed our success to putting sailors even better than the Dutch on ships even finer than those built by the two Latin seaboard powers.

The first point to be remembered in order to write a fair account of this war is that the difference in fighting skill, which certainly existed between the two parties, was due mainly to training, and not to the nature of the men. It seems certain that the American had in the beginning somewhat the advantage, because his surroundings, partly physical and partly social and political, had forced him into habits of greater self-reliance. Therefore, on the average, he offered rather the best material to start with; but the difference was very slight, and totally disappeared under good training. The combatants were men of the same race, differing but little from one another. On the New England coast the English blood was as pure as in any part of Britain; in New York and New Jersey it was mixed with that of the Dutch settlers—and the Dutch are by race nearer to the true old English of Alfred and Harold than are, for example, the thoroughly anglicized Welsh of Cornwall. Otherwise, the infusion of new blood into the English race on this side of the Atlantic has been chiefly from three sources—German, Irish, and Norse; and these three sources represent the elemental parts of the composite English stock in about the same proportions in which they were originally combined,—mainly Teutonic, largely Celtic, and with a Scandinavian admixture. The descendant of the German becomes as much an Anglo-American as the descendant of the Strathclyde Celt has already become an Anglo-Briton. Looking through names of the combatants it would be difficult to find any of one navy that could not be matched in the other—Hull or Lawrence, Allen, Perry, or Stewart. And among all the English names on both sides will be found many Scotch, Irish, or Welsh—McDonough, O'Brien, or Jones. Still stranger ones appear: the Huguenot Tattnall is one among the American defenders of the *Constellation,* and another Huguenot Tattnall is among the British assailants at Lake Borgne. It must always be kept in mind that the Americans and the British are two substantially similar branches of the great English race, which both before and after their separation have assimilated, and made Englishmen of many other peoples.[1] The lessons taught by the war can hardly be learned unless this identity is kept in mind.[2]

---

[1] The inhabitants of Great Britain are best designated as "British"—English being either too narrow or too broad a term, in one case meaning the inhabitants of but a part of Britain, and in the other the whole Anglo-Saxon people.

[2] It was practically a civil war, and was waged with much harshness and bitterness on both sides. I have already spoken of the numerous grievances of the Americans; the British, in turn, looked upon our blockade-runners which entered the French ports exactly as we regarded, at a later date, the British

To understand aright the efficiency of our navy, it is necessary to take a brief look at the character and antecedents of the officers and men who served in it.

When war broke out the United States Navy was but a few years old, yet it already had a far from dishonorable history. The captains and lieutenants of 1812 had been taught their duties in a very practical school, and the flag under which they fought was endeared to them already by not a few glorious traditions—though these, perhaps, like others of their kind, had lost none of their glory in the telling. A few of the older men had served in the war of the Revolution, and all still kept fresh in mind the doughty deeds of the old-time privateering war craft. Men still talked of Biddle's daring cruises and Barney's stubborn fights, or told of Scotch Paul and the grim work they had who followed his fortunes. Besides these memories of an older generation, most of the officers had themselves taken part, when younger in years and rank, in deeds not a whit less glorious. Almost every man had had a share in some gallant feat, to which he, in part at least, owed his present position. The captain had perhaps been a midshipman under Truxton when he took the *Vengeauce,* and had been sent aboard the captured French frigate with the prize-master; the lieutenant had borne a part in the various attacks on Tripoli, and had led his men in the desperate hand-to-hand fights in which the Yankee cutlass proved an overmatch for the Turkish and Moorish scimitars. Nearly every senior officer had extricated himself by his own prowess or skill from the dangers of battle or storm; he owed his rank to the fact that he had proved worthy of it. Thrown upon his own resources, he had learned self-reliance; he was a first-rate practical seaman, and prided himself on the way his vessel was handled. Having reached his rank by hard work, and knowing what real fighting meant, he was careful to see that his men were trained in the *essentials* of discipline, and that they knew how to handle the guns in battle as well as polish them in peace. Beyond almost any of his countrymen, he worshipped the "Gridiron Flag," and, having been brought up in the Navy, regarded its honor as his own. It was, perhaps, the Navy alone that thought itself a match, ship against ship, for Great Britain. The remainder of the nation pinned its faith to the army, or rather to that weakest of weak reeds, the militia. The officers of the navy, with their strong *esprit de corps,* their jealousy of their own name and record, and the knowledge, by actual experience, that the British ships sailed no faster and were no better handled than their own, had no desire to shirk a conflict with any foe, and having tried their bravery in actual service, they made it doubly formidable by cool, wary skill. Even the younger men, who had never been in action, had been so well trained by the tried veterans over them that the lack of experience was not sensibly felt.

---

steamers that ran into Wilmington and Charleston. It is curious to see how illogical writers are. The careers of the *Argus* and *Alabama* for example, were strikingly similar in many ways, yet the same writer who speaks of one as an "heroic little brig," will call the other a "black pirate." Of course there can be no possible comparison as to the *causes* for which the two vessels were fighting; but the cruises themselves were very much alike, both in character and history.

The sailors comprising the crews of our ships were well worthy of their leaders. There was no better seaman in the world than American Jack; he had been bred to his work from infancy, and had been off in a fishing dory almost as soon as he could walk. When he grew older, he shipped on a merchant-man or whaler, and in those warlike times, when our large merchant-marine was compelled to rely pretty much on itself for protection, each craft *had* to be well handled; all who were not were soon weeded out by a process of natural selection, of which the agents were French picaroons, Spanish buccaneers, and Malay pirates. It was a rough school, but it taught Jack to be both skilful and self-reliant; and he was all the better fitted to become a man-of-war's man, because he knew more about fire-arms than most of his kind in foreign lands. At home he had used his ponderous ducking gun with good effect on the flocks of canvasbacks in the reedy flats of the Chesapeake, or among the sea-coots in the rough water off the New England cliffs; and when he went on a sailing voyage the chances were even that there would be some use for the long guns before he returned, for the American merchant sailor could trust to no armed escort.

The wonderful effectiveness of our seamen at the date of which I am writing as well as long subsequently to it was largely due to the curious condition of things in Europe. For thirty years all the European nations had been in a state of continuous and very complicated warfare, during the course of which each nation in turn fought almost every other, England being usually at loggerheads with all. One effect of this was to force an enormous proportion of the carrying trade of the world into American bottoms. The old Massachusetts town of Salem was then one of the main depots of the East India trade; the Baltimore clippers carried goods into the French and German ports with small regard to the blockade; New Bedford and Sag Harbor fitted out whalers for the Arctic seas as well as for the South Pacific; the rich merchants of Philadelphia and New York sent their ships to all parts of the world; and every small port had some craft in the coasting trade. On the New England seaboard but few of the boys would reach manhood without having made at least one voyage to the Newfoundland Banks after codfish; and in the whaling towns of Long Island it used to be an old saying that no man could marry till he struck his whale. The wealthy merchants of the large cities would often send their sons on a voyage or two before they let them enter their counting-houses. Thus it came about that a large portion of our population was engaged in seafaring pursuits of a nature strongly tending to develop a resolute and hardy character in the men that followed them. The British merchant-men sailed in huge convoys, guarded by men-of-war, while, as said before, our vessels went alone, and relied for protection on themselves. If a fishing smack went to the Banks it knew that it ran a chance of falling in with some not over-scrupulous Nova Scotian privateer. The barques that sailed from Salem to the Spice Islands kept their men well trained both at great guns and musketry, so as to be able to beat off either Malay proas, or Chinese junks. The New York ships, loaded for the West Indies, were prepared to do battle with the picaroons that swarmed in the Spanish main; while the fast craft from Baltimore could fight as well as they could run. Wherever an American seaman went, he not only had to contend with all the legitimate perils of the sea, but he had also to regard almost every stranger as a foe. Whether this foe called himself pirate or privateer mattered but little. French, Spaniards, Algerines, Malays, from all alike our commerce suffered, and against all, our merchants were forced to defend themselves. The effect of such a state of things, which made commerce so remunerative that the bolder spirits could hardly keep out of it, and so hazardous that only the most skilful and daring could succeed in it, was to raise up as fine a set of seamen as ever manned a navy. The stern school in which the American was brought up, forced him into habits of independent thought and action which it was impossible that the more protected Briton could possess. He worked more intelligently and less from routine, and while perfectly obedient and amenable to discipline, was yet able to judge for himself in an emergency. He was more easily managed than most of his kind—being shrewd, quiet, and, in fact, comparatively speaking, rather moral than otherwise; if he was a New Englander, when he retired from a sea life he was not unapt to end his days as a deacon. Altogether there could not have been better material for a fighting crew than cool, gritty American Jack. Moreover, there was a good nucleus of veterans to begin with, who were well fitted to fill the more responsible positions, such as captains of guns, etc. These were men who had cruised in the little *Enterprise* after French privateers, who had been in the *Constellation* in her two victorious fights, or who, perhaps, had followed Decatur when with only eighty men he cut out the *Philadelphia,* manned by fivefold his force and surrounded by hostile batteries and war vessels,—one of the boldest expeditions of the kind on record.

It is to be noted, furthermore, in this connection, that by a singular turn of fortune, Great Britain, whose system of impressing American sailors had been one of the chief causes of the war, herself became, in consequence of that very system, in some sort, a nursery for the seamen of the young Republican navy. The American sailor feared nothing more than being impressed on a British ship—dreading beyond measure the hard life and cruel discipline aboard of her; but once there, he usually did well enough, and in course of time often rose to be of some little consequence. For years before 1812, the number of these impressed sailors was in reality greater than the entire number serving in the American navy, from which it will readily be seen that they formed a good stock to draw upon. Very much to their credit, they never lost their devotion to the home of their birth, more than two thousand of them being imprisoned at the beginning of the war because they refused to serve against their country. When Commodore Decatur captured the

*Macedonian,* that officer, as we learn from Marshall's "Naval Biography" (ii, 1019), stated that most of the seamen of his own frigate, the *United States,* had served in British war vessels, and that some had been with Lord Nelson in the *Victory,* and had even been bargemen to the great Admiral,—a pretty sure proof that the American sailors did not show at a disadvantage when compared with others.[1]

Good seamen as the impressed American proved to be, yet he seldom missed an opportunity to escape from the British service, by desertion or otherwise. In the first place, the life was very hard, and, in the second, the American seaman was very patriotic. He had an honest and deep affection for his own flag; while, on the contrary, he felt a curiously strong hatred for England, as distinguished from Englishmen. This hatred was partly an abstract feeling, cherished through a vague traditional respect for Bunker Hill, and partly something very real and vivid, owing to the injuries he, and others like him, had received. Whether he lived in Maryland or Massachusetts, he certainly knew men whose ships had been seized by British cruisers, their goods confiscated, and the vessels condemned. Some of his friends had fallen victims to the odious right of search, and had never been heard of afterward. He had suffered many an injury to friend, fortune, or person, and some day he hoped to repay them all; and when the war did come, he fought all the better because he knew it was in his own quarrel. But, as I have said, this hatred was against England, not against Englishmen. Then, as now, sailors were scattered about over the world without any great regard for nationality; and the resulting intermingling of natives and foreigners in every mercantile marine was especially great in those of Britain and America, whose people spoke the same tongue and wore the same aspect. When chance drifted the American into Liverpool or London, he was ready enough to ship in an Indiaman or whaler, caring little for the fact that he served under the British flag; and the Briton, in turn, who found himself in New York or Philadelphia, willingly sailed in one of the clipper-built barques, whether it floated the stars and stripes or not. When Captain Porter wrought such havoc among the British whalers in the South Seas, he found that no inconsiderable portion of their crews consisted of Americans, some of whom enlisted on board his own vessel; and among the crews of the American whalers were many British. In fact, though the skipper of each ship might brag loudly of his nationality, yet in practical life he knew well enough that there was very little to choose between a

---

[1] With perfect gravity, James and his followers assume Decatur's statement to be equivalent to saying that he had chiefly British seamen on board; whereas, even as quoted by Marshall, Decatur merely said that "his seamen had served on board a British man-of-war," and that some "had served under Lord Nelson." Like the *Constitution,* the *United States* had rid herself of most of the British subjects on board, before sailing. Decatur's remark simply referred to the number of his American seamen who had been impressed on board British ships. Whenever James says that an American ship had a large proportion of British sailors aboard, the explanation is that a large number of the crew were Americans who had been impressed on British ships. It would be no more absurd to claim Trafalgar as an American victory because there was a certain number of Americans in Nelson's fleet, than it is to assert that the Americans were victorious in 1812, because there were a few renegade British on board their ships.

Yankee and a Briton.[1] Both were bold and hardy, cool and intelligent, quick with their hands, and showing at their best in an emergency. They looked alike and spoke alike; when they took the trouble to think, they thought alike; and when they got drunk, which was not an infrequent occurrence, they quarrelled alike.

Mingled with them were a few seamen of other nationalities. The Irishman, if he came from the old Dano-Irish towns of Waterford, Dublin, and Wexford, or from the Ulster coast, was very much like the two chief combatants; the Celto-Turanian kern of the west did not often appear on shipboard. The French, Danes, and Dutch were hemmed in at home; they had enough to do on their own seaboard, and could not send men into foreign fleets. A few Norse, however, did come in, and excellent sailors and fighters they made. With the Portuguese and Italians, of whom some were to be found serving under the union-jack, and others under the stars and stripes, it was different; although there were many excellent exceptions they did not, as a rule, make the best kind of seamen. They were treacherous, fond of the knife, less ready with their hands, and likely to lose either their wits or their courage when in a tight place.

In the American navy, unlike the British, there was no impressment; the sailor was a volunteer, and he shipped in whatever craft his fancy selected. Throughout the war there were no "picked crews" on the American side,[2] excepting on the last two cruises of the *Constitution.* In fact (as seen by the letter of Captains Stewart and Bainbridge to Secretary Hamilton), there was often much difficulty in getting enough men.[3] Many sailors preferred to serve in the

---

[1] What choice there was, was in favor of the American. In point of courage there was no difference whatever. The *Essex* and the *Lawrence,* as well as the *Frolic* and the *Reindeer,* were defended with the same stubborn, desperate, cool bravery that marks the English race on both sides of the Atlantic. But the American was a free citizen, any one's equal, a voter with a personal interest in his country's welfare, and, above all, without having perpetually before his eyes the degrading fear of the press-gang. In consequence, he was more tractable than the Englishman, more self-reliant, and possessed greater judgment. In the fight between the *Wasp* and the *Frolic,* the latter's crew had apparently been well trained at the guns, for they aimed well; but they fired at the wrong time, and never corrected the error; while their antagonists, delivering their broadsides far more slowly, by intelligently waiting until the proper moment, worked frightful havoc. But though there was a certain slight difference between the seamen of the two nations, it must never be forgotten that it was very much less than that between the various individuals of the same nation; and when the British had been trained for a few years by such commanders as Broke and Manners, it was impossible to surpass them, and it needed our best men to equal them.

[2] James' statements to the contrary being in every case utterly without foundation. He is also wrong in his assertion that the American ships had no boys; they had nearly as many in proportion as the British. The *Constitution* had 31, the *Adams* 15, etc. So, when he states that our midshipmen were generally masters and mates of merchantmen; they were generally from eleven to seventeen years old at the beginning of the war, and, besides, had rarely or never been in the merchant marine.

[3] Reading through the volumes of official letters about this war, which are preserved in the office of the Secretary of the Navy, one of the most noticeable things is the continual complaints about the difficulty of getting men. The *Adams* at one time had a crew of but nineteen men—"fourteen of whom are marines," adds the aggrieved commander. A log-book of one of the gun-boats records the fact that after much difficulty *two* men were enlisted—from the jail, with a parenthetical memorandum to the effect that they were both very drunk. British ships were much more easily manned, as they could always have recourse to impressment.

innumerable privateers, and, the two above-mentioned officers, in urging the necessity of building line-of-battle ships, state that it was hard work to recruit men for vessels of an inferior grade, so long as the enemy had ships of the line.

One of the standard statements made by the British historians about this war is that our ships were mainly or largely manned by British sailors. This, if true, would not interfere with the lessons which it teaches; and, besides that, it is *not* true.

In this, as in every thing else, all the modern writers have merely followed James or Brenton, and I shall accordingly confine myself to examining their assertions. The former begins (vol. iv, p. 470) by diffidently stating that there is a "similarity" of language between the inhabitants of the two countries—an interesting philological discovery that but few will attempt to controvert. In vol. vi, p. 154, he mentions that a number of blanks occur in the American Navy List in the column "Where Born"; and in proof of the fact that these blanks are there because the men were not Americans, he says that their names "are all English and Irish."[1] They certainly are; and so are all the other names in the list. It could not well be otherwise, as the United States Navy was not officered by Indians. In looking over this same Navy List (of 1816) it will be seen that but a little over 5 per cent. of the officers were born abroad—a smaller proportion by far than would exist in the population of the country at large—and most of these had come to America when under ten years of age. On p. 155 James adds that the British sailors composed "one third in number and one half in point of effectiveness" of the American crews. Brenton in his "Naval History" writes: "It was said, and I have no rea-son to doubt the fact, that there were 200 British seamen aboard the *Constitution*."[2] These statements are mere assertions, unsupported by proof, and of such a loose character as to be difficult to refute. As our navy was small, it may be best to take each ship in turn. The only ones of which the British could write authoritatively were, of course, those which they captured. The first one taken was the *Wasp*. James says many British were discovered among her crew, instancing especially one sailor named Jack Lang; now Jack Lang was born in the town of Brunswick, New Jersey, *but had been impressed and*

---

The *Constitution* on starting out on her last cruises had an extraordinary number of able seamen aboard, viz., 218, with but 92 ordinary seamen, 12 boys, and 44 marines, making, with the officers a total of 440 men. (See letter of Captain Bainbridge, Oct. 16, 1814; it is letter No. 51, in the fortieth volume of "Captains' Letters," in the clerk's office of the Secretary of the Navy.)

[1] For example, James writes: "Out of the 32 captains one only, Thomas Tingey, has England marked as his birthplace.... Three blanks occur, and we consider it rather creditable to Captains John Shaw, Daniel S. Patterson, and John Ord Creighton, that they were ashamed to tell where they were born." I have not been able to find out the latter's birth-place, but Captain Shaw was born in New York, and I have seen Captain Patterson incidentally alluded to as "born and bred in America." Generally, whenever I have been able to fill up the vacancies in the column "Where Born," I have found that it was in Amer-ica. From these facts it would appear that James was somewhat hasty in concluding that the omission of the birth-place proved the owner of the name to be a native of Great Britain.

[2] New edition, London, 1837, vol. ii, p. 456.

*forced to serve in the British Navy.* The same was doubtless true of the rest of the "many British" seamen of her crew; at any rate, as the only instance James mentions (Jack Lang) was an American, he can hardly be trusted for those whom he does not name.

Of the 95 men composing the crew of the *Nautilus* when she was captured, "6 were detained and sent to England to await examination as being suspected of being British subjects."[1] Of the other small brigs, the *Viper, Vixen, Rattlesnake,* and *Syren,* James does not mention the composition of the crew, and I do not know that any were claimed as British. Of the crew of the *Argus* "about 10 or 12 were believed to be British subjects; the American officers swore the crew contained none" (James, "Naval Occurrences," p. 278). From 0 to 10 per cent. can be allowed. When the *Frolic* was captured "her crew consisted of native Americans" (*do.* p. 340). James speaks ("History," p. 418) of "a portion of the British subjects on board the *Essex,*" but without giving a word of proof or stating his grounds of belief. One man was claimed as a deserter by the British, but he turned out to be a New Yorker. There were certainly a certain number of British aboard, but the number probably did not exceed thirty. Of the *President's* crew he says ("Naval Occurrences," p. 448): "In the opinion of several British officers there were among them many British seamen"; but Commodore Decatur, Lieutenant Gallagher, and the other officers swore that there were none. Of the crew of the *Chesapeake,* he says, "about 32" were British subjects, or about 10 per cent. One or two of these were afterward shot, and some 25, together with a Portuguese boatswain's mate, entered into the British service. So that of the vessels captured by the British, the *Chesapeake* had the largest number of British (about 10 per cent. of her crew) on board, the others ranging from that number down to none at all, as in the case of the *Wasp.*

As these eleven ships would probably represent a fair average, this proportion, of from 0 to 10 per cent., should be taken as the proper one. James, however, is of the opinion that those ships manned by Americans were more apt to be captured than those manned by the braver British; which calls for an examination of the crews of the remaining vessels. Of the American sloop *Peacock,* James says ("Naval Occurrences," p. 348) that "several of her men were recognized as British seamen"; even if this were true, "several" could not probably mean more than sixteen, or 10 per cent. Of the second *Wasp* he says, "Captain Blakely was a native of Dublin, and, along with some English and Scotch, did not, it may be certain, neglect to have in his crew a great many Irish." Now Captain Blakely left Ireland when he was but 16 months old, and

---

[1] Quoted from letter of Commodore Rodgers of September 12, 1812 (in Naval Archives, "Captains' Letters," vol. xxv, No. 43), enclosing a "List of American prisoners of war discharged out of custody of Lieutenant William Miller, agent at the port of Halifax," in exchange for some of the British captured by Porter. This list, by the way, shows the crew of the *Nautilus* (counting the six men detained as British) to have been 95 in number, instead of 106, as stated by James. Commodore Rodgers adds that he has detained 12 men of the *Guerrière's* crew as an offset to the 6 men belonging to the *Nautilus.*

the rest of James' statement is avowedly mere conjecture. It was asserted positively in the American newspapers that the *Wasp*, which sailed from Portsmouth, was manned exclusively by New Englanders, except a small draft of men from a Baltimore privateer, and that there was not a foreigner in her crew. Of the *Hornet* James states that "some of her men were natives of the United Kingdom"; but he gives no authority, and the men he refers to were in all probability those spoken of in the journal of one of the *Hornet*'s officers, which says that "many of our men (Americans) had been impressed in the British service." As regards the gun-boats, James asserts that they were commanded by "Commodore Joshua Barney, a native of Ireland." This officer, however, was born at Baltimore on July 6, 1759. As to the *Constitution*, Brenton, as already mentioned, supposes the number of British sailors in her crew to have been 200; James makes it less, or about 150. Respecting this, the only definite statements I can find in British works are the following: In the "Naval Chronicle," vol. xxix, p. 452, an officer of the *Java* states that most of the *Constitution*'s men were British, many being from the *Guerrière;* which should be read in connection with James' statement (vol. vi, p. 156) that but eight of the *Guerrière*'s crew deserted, and but two shipped on board the *Constitution.* Moreover, as a matter of fact, these eight men were all impressed Americans. In the "Naval Chronicle" it is also said that the *Chesapeake*'s surgeon was an Irishman, formerly of the British navy; he was born in Baltimore, and was never in the British navy in his life. The third lieutenant "was supposed to be an Irishman" (Brenton, ii, 456). The first lieutenant "was a native of Great Britain, we have been informed" (James, vi, 194); he was Mr. George Parker, born and bred in Virginia. The remaining three citations, if true, prove nothing. "One man had served under Mr. Kent" of the *Guerrière* (James, vi, p. 153). "One had been in the *Achille*" and "one in the *Eurydice*" (Brenton, ii, 456). These three men were most probably American seamen who had been impressed on British ships. From Cooper (in "Putnam's Magazine," vol. I, p. 593) as well as from several places in the *Constitution*'s log,[1] we learn that those of the crew who were British deserters were discharged from the *Constitution* before she left port, as they were afraid to serve in a war against Great Britain. That this fear was justifiable may be seen by reading James, vol. iv, p. 483. Of the four men taken by the *Leopard* from the *Chesapeake,* as deserters, one was hung and three scourged. In reality the crew of the *Constitution* probably did not contain a dozen British sailors; in her last cruises she was manned almost exclusively by New Englanders. The only remaining vessel is the *United States,* respecting whose crew

---

[1] See her log-book (vol. ii, Feb. 1, 1812 to Dec. 13, 1813); especially on July 12th, when twelve men were discharged. In some of Hull's letters he alludes to the desire of the British part of the crew to serve on the gun-boats or in the ports; and then writes that "in accordance with the instructions sent him by the Secretary of the Navy" he had allowed the British-born portion to leave the ship. The log-books are in the Bureau of Navigation.

some remarkable statements have been made. Marshall (vol. ii, p. 1019) writes that Commodore Decatur "declared there was not a seaman in his ship who had not served from 5 to 12 years in a British man-of-war," from which he concludes that they were British themselves. It may be questioned whether Decatur ever made such an assertion; or if he did, it is safe to assume again that his men were long-impressed Americans.[1]

Of the *Carolina*'s crew of 70 men, five were British. This fact was not found out till three deserted, when an investigation was made and the two other British discharged. Captain Henly, in reporting these facts, made no concealment of his surprise that there should be any British at all in his crew.[2]

From these facts and citations we may accordingly conclude that the proportion of British seamen serving on American ships *after the war broke out,* varied between none, as on the *Wasp* and *Constitution,* to ten per cent., as on the *Chesapeake* and *Essex.* On the average, nine tenths of each of our crews were American seamen, and about one twentieth British, the remainder being a mixture of various nationalities.

On the other hand, it is to be said that the British frigate *Guerrière* had ten Americans among her crew, who were permitted to go below during action, and the *Macedonian* eight, who were not allowed that privilege, three of them being killed. Three of the British sloop *Peacock*'s men were Americans, who were forced to fight against the *Hornet;* one of them was killed. Two of the *Epervier*'s men were Americans, who were also forced to fight. When the crew of the *Nautilus* was exchanged, a number of other American prisoners were sent with them; among these were a number of American seamen who had been serving in the *Shannon, Acasta, Africa,* and various other vessels. So there was also a certain proportion of Americans among the British crews, although forming a smaller percentage of them than the British did on board

---

[1] At the beginning of the war there were on record in the American State Department 6,257 cases of impressed American seamen. These could represent but a small part of the whole, which must have amounted to 20,000 men, or more than sufficient to man our entire navy five times over. According to the British Admiralty Report to the House of Commons, February 1, 1815, 2,548 impressed American seamen, who refused to serve against their country, were imprisoned in 1812. According to Lord Castlereagh's speech in the House, February 18, 1813, 3,300 men claiming to be American subjects were serving in the British navy in January, 1811, and he certainly did not give any thing like the whole number. In the American service the term of enlistment extended for two years, and the frigate, *United States,* referred to, had not had her crew for any very great length of time as yet. If such a crew were selected at random from American sailors, among them there would be, owing to the small number serving in our own navy and the enormous number impressed into the British navy, probably but one of the former to two of the latter. As already mentioned the American always left a British man-of-war as soon as he could, by desertion or discharge; but he had no unwillingness to serve in the home navy, where the pay was larger, and the discipline far more humane, not to speak of motives of patriotism. Even if the ex-British man-of-war's man kept out of service for some time, he would be very apt to enlist when a war broke out, which his country undertook largely to avenge his own wrongs.

[2] See his letter in "Letters of Masters' Commandant," 1814, I, No. 116.

the American ships. In neither case was the number sufficient to at all affect the result.

The crews of our ships being thus mainly native Americans, it may be interesting to try to find out the proportions that were furnished by the different sections of the country. There is not much difficulty about the officers. The captains, masters commandant, lieutenants, marine officers, whose birthplaces are given in the Navy List of 1816,—240 in all,—came from the various States as follows:

| New England | N. H., | 5 | |
| | Mass., | 20 | 42 |
| | R. I., | 11 | |
| | Conn., | 6 | |
| Middle States | N. Y., | 17 | |
| | N. J., | 22 | 78 |
| | Penn., | 35 | |
| | Del., | 4 | |
| District of Columbia | D. C., | 4 | 4 |
| Southern States | Md., | 46 | |
| | Va., | 42 | |
| | N. C., | 4 | |
| | S. C., | 16 | 116 |
| | Ga., | 2 | |
| | La., | 4 | |
| | Ky., | 2 | |
| Total of given birthplaces | | | 240 |

Thus, Maryland furnished, both absolutely and proportionately, the greatest number of officers, Virginia, then the most populous of all the States, coming next; four fifths of the remainder came from the Northern States.

It is more difficult to get at the birthplaces of the sailors. Something can be inferred from the number of privateers and letters of marque fitted out. Here Baltimore again headed the list; following closely came New York, Philadelphia, and the New England coast towns, with, alone among the Southern ports, Charleston, S. C. A more accurate idea of the quotas of sailors furnished by the different sections can be arrived at by comparing the total amount of tonnage the country possessed at the outbreak of the war. Speaking roughly, 44 per cent. of it belonged to New England, 32 per cent. to the Middle States, and 11 per cent. to Maryland. This makes it *probable* (but of course not certain) that three fourths of the common sailors hailed from the Northern States, half the remainder from Maryland, and the rest chiefly from Virginia and South Carolina.

———

Having thus discussed somewhat at length the character of our officers and crews, it will now be necessary to present some statistical tables to give a more accurate idea of the composition of the navy; the tonnage, complements, and armaments of the ships, etc.

At the beginning of the war the Government possessed six navy yards (all but the last established in 1801) as follows:[1]

| | PLACE. | ORIGINAL COST. | MINIMUM NUMBER OF MEN EMPLOYED. |
|---|---|---|---|
| 1. | Portsmouth, N. H., | $ 5,500 | 10 |
| 2. | Charleston, Mass., | 39,214 | 20 |
| 3. | New York, | 40,000 | 102 |
| 4. | Philadelphia, | 37,000 | 13 |
| 5. | Washington, | 4,000 | 36 |
| 6. | Gosport, | 12,000 | 16 |

In 1812 the following was the number of officers in the navy:[2]

| | |
|---|---|
| 12 | captains |
| 10 | masters commandant |
| 73 | lieutenants |
| 53 | masters |
| 310 | midshipmen |
| 42 | marine officers |
| 500 | |

At the opening of the year, the number of seamen, ordinary seamen, and boys in service was 4,010, and enough more were recruited to increase it to 5,230, of whom only 2,346 were destined for the cruising war vessels, the remainder being detailed for forts, gun-boats, navy yards, the lakes, etc.[3] The marine corps was already ample, consisting of 1,523 men.[4]

No regular navy lists were published till 1816, and I have been able to get very little information respecting the increase in officers and men during 1813 and 1814; but we have full returns for 1815, which may be summarized as follows:[5]

[1] Report of Naval Secretary Jones, Nov. 30, 1814.
[2] "List of Vessels," etc., by Geo. H. Preble, U.S.N. (1874).
[3] Report of Secretary Paul Hamilton, Feb. 21, 1812.
[4] *Ibid.*
[5] Seybert's "Statistical Annals," p. 676 (Philadelphia, 1818).

30  captains,
25  masters commandant,
141  lieutenants,
24  commanders,
510  midshipmen,
230  sailing-masters,
50  surgeons,
12  chaplains,
50  pursers,
10  coast pilots,
45  captain's clerks,
80  surgeon's mates,
530  boatswains, gunners, carpenters, and sail-makers,
268  boatswain's mates, gunner's mates, etc.,
1,106  quarter gunners, etc.,
5,000  able seamen,
6,849  ordinary seamen and boys.
Making a total of 14,960, with 2,715 marines.[1]

Comparing this list with the figures given before, it can be seen that during the course of the war our navy grew enormously, increasing to between three and four times its original size.

At the beginning of the year 1812, the navy of the United States on the ocean consisted of the following vessels, which either were, or could have been, made available during the war.[2]

| RATE (GUNS). | NAME. | WHERE BUILT. | WHEN BUILT. | TON-NAGE. | COST. |
|---|---|---|---|---|---|
| 44 | *United States,* | Philadelphia, | 1797 | 1576 | $299,336 |
| 44 | *Constitution,* | Boston, | 1797 | 1576 | 302,718 |
| 44 | *President,* | New York, | 1800 | 1576 | 220,910 |
| 38 | *Constellation,* | Baltimore, | 1797 | 1265 | 314,212 |
| 38 | *Congress,* | Portsmouth, | 1799 | 1268 | 197,246 |
| 38 | *Chesapeake,* | Norfolk, | 1799 | 1244 | 220,677 |
| 32 | *Essex,* | Salem, | 1799 | 860 | 139,362 |
| 28 | *Adams,* | New York, | 1799 | 560 | 76,622 |
| 18 | *Hornet,* | Baltimore, | 1805 | 480 | 52,603 |
| 18 | *Wasp,* | Washington, | 1806 | 450 | 40,000 |
| 16 | *Argus,* | Boston, | 1803 | 298 | 37,428 |
| 16 | *Syren,* | Philadelphia, | 1803 | 250 | 32,521 |
| 14 | *Nautilus,* | Baltimore, | 1803 | 185 | 18,763 |
| 14 | *Vixen,* | Baltimore, | 1803 | 185 | 20,872 |
| 12 | *Enterprise,* | Baltimore, | 1799 | 165 | 16,240 |
| 12 | *Viper,* | Purchased, | 1810 | 148 | |

[1] Report of Secretary B. W. Crowninshield, April 18, 1816.
[2] Letter of Secretary Benjamin Stoddart to Fifth Congress, Dec. 24, 1798; Letter of Secretary Paul Hamilton, Feb. 21, 1812; "American State Papers," vol. xix, p. 149. See also the "History of the Navy of

There also appeared on the lists the *New York*, 36, *Boston*, 28, and *John Adams*, 28. The two former were condemned hulks; the latter was entirely re-built after the war. The *Hornet* was originally a brig of 440 tons, and 18 guns; having been transformed into a ship, she was pierced for 20 guns, and in size was of an intermediate grade between the *Wasp* and the heavy sloops, built somewhat later, of 509 tons. Her armament consisted of 32-pound car-ronades, with the exception of the two bow-guns, which were long 12's. The whole broadside was in nominal weight just 300 pounds; in actual weight about 277 pounds. Her complement of men was 140, but during the war she generally left port with 150.[1] The *Wasp* had been a ship from the beginning, mounted the number of guns she rated (of the same calibres as the *Hornet*'s) and carried some ten men less. She was about the same length as the British 18-gun brig-sloop, but, being narrower, measured nearly 30 tons less. The *Argus* and *Syren* were similar and very fine brigs, the former being the longer. Each carried two more guns than she rated; and the *Argus*, in addition, had a couple thrust through the bridle-ports. The guns were 24-pound carronades, with two long 12's for bow-chasers. The proper complement of men was 100, but each sailed usually with about 125. The four smaller craft were originally schooners, armed with the same number of light long guns as they rated, and carrying some 70 men apiece; but they had been very effectually ruined by being changed into brigs, with crews increased to a hundred men. Each was armed with 18-pound carronades, carrying two more than she rated. The *En-terprise*, in fact, mounted 16 guns, having two long nines thrust through the bridle-ports. These little brigs were slow, not very seaworthy, and over-crowded with men and guns; they all fell into the enemy's hands without doing any good whatever, with the single exception of the *Enterprise*, which escaped capture by sheer good luck, and in her only battle happened to be pitted against one of the corresponding and equally bad class of British gun-brigs. The *Adams* after several changes of form finally became a flush-decked corvette. The *Essex* had originally mounted twenty-six long 12's on her main-deck, and sixteen 24-pound carronades on her spar-deck; but official wisdom changed this, giving her 46 guns, twenty-four 32-pound carronades, and two long 12's on the main-deck, and sixteen 32-pound carronades with four long 12's on the spar-deck. When Captain Porter had command of her he was deeply sensible of the disadvantages of an armament which put him at the mercy of any ordinary antagonist who could choose his distance; accordingly he petitioned several times, but always without success, to have his long 12's returned to him.

---

the United States," by Lieut. G. E. Emmons, U.S.N. (published in Washington, MDCCCLIII, under the au-thority of the Navy Department.)

[1] In the *Hornet*'s log of Oct. 25, 1812, while in port, it is mentioned that she had 158 men; four men who were sick were left behind before she started. (See, in the Navy Archives, the Log-book, *Hornet*, *Wasp*, and *Argus*, July 20, 1809, to Oct. 6, 1813.)

The American 38's were about the size of the British frigates of the same rate, and armed almost exactly in the same way, each having 28 long 18's on the main-deck and 20 32-pound carronades on the spar-deck. The proper complement was 300 men, but each carried from 40 to 80 more.[1]

Our three 44-gun ships were the finest frigates then afloat (although the British possessed some as heavy, such as the *Egyptienne,* 44). They were beautifully modelled, with very thick scantling, extremely stout masts, and heavy cannon. Each carried on her main-deck thirty long 24's, and on her spar-deck two long bow-chasers, and twenty or twenty-two carronades—42-pounders on the *President* and *United States,* 32-pounders on the *Constitution.* Each sailed with a crew of about 450 men—50 in excess of the regular complement.[2]

It may be as well to mention here the only other class of vessels that we employed during the war. This was composed of the ship-sloops built in 1813, which got to sea in 1814. They were very fine vessels, measuring 509 tons apiece,[3] with very thick scantling and stout masts and spars. Each carried twenty 32-pound carronades and two long 12's with a crew nominally of 160 men, but with usually a few supernumeraries.[4]

The British vessels encountered were similar, but generally inferior, to our own. The only 24-pounder frigate we encountered was the *Endymion* of about a fifth less force than the *President.* Their 38-gun frigates were almost exactly like ours, but with fewer men in crew as a rule. They were three times matched against our 44-gun frigates, to which they were inferior about as

---

[1] The *Chesapeake,* by some curious mistake, was frequently rated as a 44, and this drew in its train a number of attendant errors. When she was captured, James says that in one of her lockers was found a letter, dated in February, 1811, from Robert Smith, the Secretary of War, to Captain Evans, at Boston, directing him to open houses of rendezvous for manning the *Chesapeake,* and enumerating her crew at a total of 443. Naturally this gave British historians the idea that such was the ordinary complement of our 38-gun frigates. But the ordering so large a crew was merely a mistake, as may be seen by a letter from Captain Bainbridge to the Secretary of the Navy, which is given in full in the "Captains' Letters," vol. xxv, No. 19 (Navy Archives). In it he mentions the extraordinary number of men ordered for the *Chesapeake,* saying, "There is a mistake in the crew ordered for the *Chesapeake,* as it equals in number the crews of our 44-gun frigates, whereas the *Chesapeake* is of the class of the *Congress* and *Constellation."*

[2] The *President* when in action with the *Endymion* had 450 men aboard, as sworn by Decatur; the muster-roll of the *Constitution,* a few days before her action with the *Guerrière* contains 464 names (including 51 marines); 8 men were absent in a prize, so she had aboard in the action 456. Her muster-roll just before the action with the *Cyane* and *Levant* shows 461 names.

[3] The dimensions were 117 feet 11 inches upon the gun-deck, 97 feet 6 inches keel for tonnage, measuring from one foot before the forward perpendicular and along the base line to the front of the rabbet of the port, deducting ⅗ of the moulded breadth of the beam, which is 31 feet 6 inches; making 509²¹/₉₅ tons. (See in Navy Archives, "Contracts," vol. ii, p. 137.)

[4] The *Peacock* had 166 men, as we learn from her commander Warrington's letter of June 1st (Letter No. 140 in "Masters' Commandant Letters," 1814, vol. i). The *Frolic* took aboard "10 or 12 men beyond her regular complement" (see letter of Joseph Bainbridge, No. 51, in same vol.). Accordingly when she was captured by the *Orpheus,* the commander of the latter, Captain Hugh Pigot, reported the number of men aboard to be 171. The *Wasp* left port with 173 men, with which she fought her first action; she had a much smaller number aboard in her second.

three is to four. Their 36-gun frigates were larger than the *Essex*, with a more numerous crew, but the same number of guns; carrying on the lower deck, however, long 18's instead of 32-pound carronades,—a much more effective armament. The 32-gun frigates were smaller, with long 12's on the main-deck. The largest sloops were also frigate-built, carrying twenty-two 32-pound carronades on the main-deck, and twelve lighter guns on the quarter-deck and forecastle, with a crew of 180. The large flush-decked ship-sloops carried 21 or 23 guns, with a crew of 140 men. But our vessels most often came in contact with the British 18-gun brig-sloop; this was a tubby craft, heavier than any of our brigs, being about the size of the *Hornet*. The crew consisted of from 110 to 135 men; ordinarily each was armed with six-teen 32-pound carronades, two long 6's, and a shifting 12-pound carronade; often with a light long gun as a stern-chaser, making 20 in all. The *Reindeer* and *Peacock* had only 24-pound carronades; the *Epervier* had but eighteen guns, all carronades.[1]

Among the stock accusations against our navy of 1812, were, and are, statements that our vessels were rated at less than their real force, and in par-ticular that our large frigates were "disguised line-of-battle ships." As regards the ratings, most vessels of that time carried more guns than they rated; the disparity was less in the French than in either the British or American navies. Our 38-gun frigates carried 48 guns, the exact number the British 38's pos-sessed. The worst case of underrating in our navy was the *Essex*, which rated 32, and carried 46 guns, so that her real was 44 per cent. in excess of her nom-inal force; but this was not as bad as the British sloop *Cyane*, which was rated a 20 or 22, and carried 34 guns, so that she had either 55 or 70 per cent. greater real than nominal force. At the beginning of the war we owned two 18-gun ship-sloops, one mounting 18 and the other 20 guns; the 18-gun brig-sloops they captured mounted each 19 guns, so the average was the same. Later we built sloops that rated 18 and mounted 22 guns, but when one was captured it was also put down in the British navy list as an 18-gun ship-sloop. During all the combats of the war there were but four vessels that carried as few guns as they rated. Two were British, the *Epervier* and *Levant*, and two American, the *Wasp* and *Adams*. One navy was certainly as deceptive as an-other, as far as underrating went.

The force of the statement that our large frigates were disguised line-of-battle ships, of course depends entirely upon what the words "frigate" and "line-of-battle ship" mean. When on the 10th of August, 1653, De Ruyter saved a great convoy by beating off Sir George Ayscough's fleet of 38 sail, the largest of the Dutch admiral's "33 sail of the line" carried but 30 guns

---

[1] The *Epervier* was taken into our service under the same name and rate. Both Preble and Emmons describe her as of 477 tons. Warrington, her captor, however, says: "The surveyor of the port has just measured the *Epervier* and reports her 467 tons." (In the Navy Archives, "Masters' Commandant Let-ters," 1814, i, No. 125.)

For a full discussion of tonnage, see Appendix A.

and 150 men, and his own flag-ship but 28 guns and 134 men.[1] The Dutch book from which this statement is taken speaks indifferently of frigates of 18, 40, and 58 guns. Toward the end of the eighteenth century the terms had crystallized. Frigate then meant a so-called single-decked ship; it in reality possessed two decks, the main- or gun-deck, and the upper one, which had no name at all, until our sailors christened it spar-deck. The gun-deck possessed a complete battery, and the spar-deck an interrupted one, mounting guns on the forecastle and quarter-deck. At that time all "two-decked" or "three-decked" (in reality three- and four-decked) ships were liners. But in 1812 this had changed somewhat; as the various nations built more and more powerful vessels, the lower rates of the different divisions were dropped. Thus the British ship *Cyane,* captured by the *Constitution,* was in reality a small frigate, with a main-deck battery of 22 guns, and 12 guns on the spar-deck; a few years before she would have been called a 24-gun frigate, but she then ranked merely as a 22-gun sloop. Similarly the 50- and 64-gun ships that had fought in the line at the Doggerbank, Camperdown, and even at Aboukir, were now no longer deemed fit for that purpose, and the 74 was the lowest line-of-battle ship.

The *Constitution, President,* and *States* must then be compared with the existing European vessels that were classed as frigates. The French in 1812 had no 24-pounder frigates, for the very good reason that they had all fallen victims to the English 18-pounder's; but in July of that year a Danish frigate, the *Nayaden,* which carried long 24's, was destroyed by the English ship *Dictator,* 64.

The British frigates were of several rates. The lowest rated 32, carrying in all 40 guns, 26 long 12's on the main-deck and 14 24-pound carronades on the spar-deck—a broadside of 324 pounds.[2] The 36-gun frigates, like the *Phœbe,* carried 46 guns, 26 long 18's on the gun-deck and 32-pound carronades above. The 38-gun frigates, like the *Macedonian,* carried 48 or 49 guns, long 18's below and 32-pound carronades above. The 32-gun frigates, then, presented in broadside 13 long 12's below and 7 24-pound carronades above; the 38-gun frigates, 14 long 18's below and 10 32-pound carronades above; so that a 44-gun frigate would naturally present 15 long 24's below and 12 42-pound carronades above, as the *United States* did at first. The rate was perfectly proper, for French, British, and Danes already possessed 24-pounder frigates; and there was really less disparity between the force and rate of a 44 that carried 54 guns, than there was in a 38 that carried 49, or, like the *Shannon,* 52. Nor was this all. Two of our three victories were won by the *Constitution,* which only carried 32-pound carronades, and once 54 and once 52 guns; and as two thirds

---

[1] "La Vie et les Actions Memorables du Sr. Michel de Ruyter, à Amsterdam, Chez Henry et Theodore Boom, MDCLXXVII. The work is by Barthelemy Pielat, a surgeon in de Ruyter's fleet, and personally present during many of his battles. It is written in French, but is in tone more strongly anti-French than anti-English.

[2] In all these vessels there were generally two long 6's or 9's substituted for the bow-chase carronades.

of the work was thus done by this vessel, I shall now compare her with the largest British frigates. Her broadside force consisted of 15 long 24's on the main-deck, and on the spar-deck one long 24, and in one case 10, in the other 11 32-pound carronades—a broadside of 704 or 736 pounds.[1] There was then in the British navy the *Acasta,* 40, carrying in broadside 15 long 18's and 11 32-pound carronades; when the spar-deck batteries are equal, the addition of 90 pounds to the main-deck broadside (which is all the superiority of the *Constitution* over the *Acasta*) is certainly not enough to make the distinction between a frigate and a disguised 74. But not considering the *Acasta,* there were in the British navy three 24-pounder frigates, the *Cornwallis, Indefatigable,* and *Endymion.* We only came in contact with the latter in 1815, when the *Constitution* had but 52 guns. The *Endymion* then had an armament of 28 long 24's, 2 long 18's, and 20 32-pound carronades, making a broadside of 674 pounds,[2] or including a shifting 24-pound carronade, of 698 pounds—just *six pounds,* or 1 per cent., less than the force of that "disguised line-of-battle ship" the *Constitution!* As the *Endymion* only rated as a 40, and the *Constitution* as a 44, it was in reality the former and not the latter which was underrated. I have taken the *Constitution,* because the British had more to do with her than they did with our other two 44's taken together. The latter were both of heavier metal than the *Constitution,* carrying 42-pound carronades. In 1812 the *United States* carried her full 54 guns, throwing a broadside of 846 pounds; when captured, the *President* carried 53, having substituted a 24-pound carronade for two of her 42's, and her broadside amounted to 828 pounds, or 16 per cent. *nominal,* and, on account of the short weight of her shot, 9 per cent. *real* excess over the *Endymion.* If this difference made her a line-of-battle ship, then the *Endymion* was doubly a line-of-battle ship compared to the *Congress* or *Constellation.* Moreover, the American commanders found their 42-pound carronades too heavy; as I have said the *Constitution* only mounted 32's, and the *United States* landed 6 of her guns. When, in 1813, she attempted to break the blockade, she carried but 48 guns, throwing a broadside of 720 pounds—just 3 per cent. more than the *Endymion.*[3] If our frigates were line-of-battle ships the disguise was certainly marvellously complete, and they had a number of companions equally disguised in the British ranks.

The 44's were thus *true frigates,* with one complete battery of long guns and one interrupted one of carronades. That they were better than any other

[1] Nominally; in reality about 7 per cent. less on account of the short weight in the metal.

[2] According to James 664 pounds; he omits the chase guns for no reason.

[3] It was on account of this difference of 3 per cent. that Captain Hardy refused to allow the *Endymion* to meet the *States* (James, vi, p. 470). This was during the course of some challenges and counter-challenges which ended in nothing, Decatur in his turn being unwilling to have the *Macedonian* meet the *Statira,* unless the latter should agree not to take on a picked crew. He was perfectly right in this; but he ought never to have sent the challenge at all, as two ships but an hour or two out of port would be at a frightful disadvantage in a fight.

frigates was highly creditable to our ingenuity and national skill. We cannot, perhaps, lay claim to the invention and first use of the heavy frigate, for 24-pounder frigates were already in the service of at least three nations, and the French 36-pound carronade, in use on their spar-decks, threw a heavier ball than our 42-pounder. But we had enlarged and perfected the heavy frigate, and were the first nation that ever used it effectively. The French *Forte* and the Danish *Nayaden* shared the fate of ships carrying guns of lighter calibre; and the British 24-pounders, like the *Endymion*, had never accomplished anything. Hitherto there had been a strong feeling, especially in England, that an 18-pound gun was as effective as a 24- in arming a frigate; we made a complete revolution in this respect. England had been building only 18-pounder vessels when she ought to have been building 24-pounders. It was greatly to our credit that our average frigate was superior to the average British frigate; exactly as it was to our discredit that the *Essex* was so ineffectively armed. Captain Porter owed his defeat chiefly to his ineffective guns, but also to having lost his topmast, to the weather being unfavorable, and, still more, to the admirable skill with which Hilyar used his superior armament. The *Java*, *Macedonian*, and *Guerrière* owed their defeat partly to their lighter guns, but much more to the fact that their captains and seamen did not display either as good seamanship or as good gunnery as their foes. Inferiority in armament was a factor to be taken into account in all the four cases, but it was more marked in that of the *Essex* than in the other three; it would have been fairer for Porter to say that he had been captured by a line-of-battle ship, than for the captain of the *Java* to make that assertion. In this last case the forces of the two ships compared almost exactly as their rates. A 44 was matched against a 38; it was not surprising that she should win, but it *was* surprising that she should win with ease and impunity. The long 24's on the *Constitution*'s gun-deck no more made her a line-of-battle ship than the 32-pound carronades mounted on an English frigate's quarter-deck and forecastle made *her* a line-of-battle ship when opposed to a Frenchman with only 8's and 6's on his spar-deck. When, a few years before, the English *Phœbe* had captured the French *Nereide*, their broadsides were respectively 407 and 258 pounds, a greater disparity than in any of our successful fights; yet no author thought of claiming that the *Phœbe* was any thing but a frigate. So with the *Clyde*, throwing 425 lbs., which took the *Vestale*, throwing but 246. The facts were that 18-pounder frigates had captured 12-pounders, exactly as our 24-pounders in turn captured the 18-pounders.

Shortly before Great Britain declared war on us, one of her 18-pounder frigates, the *San Florenzo*, throwing 476 lbs. in a broadside, captured the 12-pounder French frigate *Psyché*, whose broadside was only 246 lbs. The force of the former was thus almost double that of the latter, yet the battle was long and desperate, the English losing 48 and the French 124 men. This conflict, then, reflected as much credit on the skill and seamanship of the defeated as of the victorious side; the difference in loss could fairly be ascribed to the difference in weight of metal. But where, as in the famous ship-duels of 1812, the difference in force is only a fifth, instead of a half and yet the slaughter, instead of being as five is to two, is as six to one, then the victory is certainly to be ascribed as much to superiority in skill as to superiority in force. But, on the other hand, it should always be remembered that there was a very decided superiority in force. It is a very discreditable feature of many of our naval histories that they utterly ignore this superiority, seeming ashamed to confess that it existed. In reality it was something to be proud of. It was highly to the credit of the United States that her frigates were of better make and armament than any others; it always speaks well for a nation's energy and capacity that any of her implements of warfare are of superior kind. This is a perfectly legitimate reason for pride.

It spoke well for the Prussians in 1866 that they opposed breech-loaders to the muzzle-loaders of the Austrians; but it would be folly to give all the credit of the victory to the breech-loaders and none to Moltke and his lieutenants. Thus, it must be remembered that two things contributed to our victories. One was the excellent make and armament of our ships; the other was the skilful seamanship, excellent discipline, and superb gunnery of the men who were in them. British writers are apt only to speak of the first, and Americans only of the last, whereas both should be taken into consideration.

To sum up: the American 44-gun frigate was a true frigate, in build and armament, properly rated, stronger than a 38-gun frigate just about in the proportion of 44 to 38, and not exceeding in strength an 18-pounder frigate as much as the latter exceeded one carrying 12-pounders. They were in no way whatever line-of-battle ships; but they were superior to any other frigates afloat, and, what is still more important, they were better manned and commanded than the *average* frigate of any other navy. Lord Codrington says ("Memoirs," i, p. 310): "But I well know the system of favoritism and borough corruption prevails so very much that many people are promoted and kept in command that should be dismissed the service, and while such is the case the few Americans chosen for their merit may be expected to follow up their successes except where they meet with our best officers on even terms."[1] The small size of our navy was probably to a certain extent effective in keeping it up to a high standard; but this is not the only explanation, as can be seen by Portugal's small and poor navy. On the other hand, the cham-

[1] To show that I am not quoting an authority biassed in our favor I will give Sir Edward Codrington's opinion of our rural better class (i, 318). "It is curious to observe the animosity which prevails here among what is called the better order of people, which I think is more a misnomer here than in any other country I have ever been. Their *whig* and *tory* are democrat and federalist, and it would seem for the sake of giving vent to that bitterness of hatred which marks the Yankee character, every gentleman (God save the term) who takes possession of a property adopts the opposite political creed to that of his nearest neighbor."

pions or pick of a large navy *ought* to be better than the champions of a small one.[1]

Again, the armaments of the American as well as of the British ships were composed of three very different styles of guns. The first, or long gun, was enormously long and thick-barrelled in comparison to its bore, and in consequence very heavy; it possessed a very long range, and varied in calibre from two to forty-two pounds. The ordinary calibres in our navy were 6, 9, 12, 18, and 24. The second style was the carronade, a short, light gun of large bore; compared to a long gun of the same weight it carried a much heavier ball for a much shorter distance. The chief calibres were 9, 12, 18, 24, 32, 42, and 68-pounders, the first and the last being hardly in use in our navy. The third style was the columbiad, of an intermediate grade between the first two. Thus it is seen that a gun of one style by no means corresponds to a gun of another style of the same calibre. As a rough example, a long 12, a columbiad 18, and a 32-pound carronade would be about equivalent to one another. These guns were mounted on two different types of vessel. The first was flush-decked; that is, it had a single straight open deck on which all the guns were mounted. This class included one heavy corvette (the *Adams*), the ship-sloops, and the brig-sloops. Through the bow-chase port, on each side, each of these mounted a long gun; the rest of their guns were carronades, except in the case of the *Adams*, which had all long guns. Above these came the frigates, whose gun-deck was covered

---

[1] In speaking of tonnage I wish I could have got better authority than James for the British side of the question. He is so bitter that it involuntarily gives one a distrust of his judgment. Thus, in speaking of the *Penguin*'s capture, he, in endeavoring to show that the *Hornet*'s loss was greater than she acknowledged, says, "several of the dangerously wounded were thrown overboard because the surgeon was afraid to amputate, owing to his want of experience" ("Naval Occurrences," 492). Now what could persuade a writer to make such a foolish accusation? No matter how utterly depraved and brutal Captain Biddle might be, he would certainly not throw his wounded over alive because he feared they might die. Again, in vol. vi, p. 546, he says: "Captain Stewart had caused the *Cyane* to be painted to resemble a 36-gun frigate. The object of this was to aggrandize his exploit in the eyes of the gaping citizens of Boston." No matter how skilful an artist Captain Stewart was, and no matter how great the gaping capacities of the Bostonians, the *Cyane* (which by the way went to New York and not Boston) could no more be painted to look like a 36-gun frigate than a schooner could be painted to look like a brig. Instances of rancor like these two occur constantly in his work, and make it very difficult to separate what is matter of fact from what is matter of opinion. I always rely on the British official accounts when they can be reached, except in the case of the *Java*, which seem garbled. That such was sometimes the case with British officials is testified to by both James (vol. iv, p. 17) and Brenton (vol. ii, p. 454, note). From the "Memoir of Admiral Broke" we learn that his public letter was wrong in a number of particulars. See also any one of the numerous biographies of Lord Dundonald, the hero of the little *Speedy*'s fight. It is very unfortunate that the British stopped publishing official accounts of their defeats; it could not well help giving rise to unpleasant suspicions.

It may be as well to mention here, again, that James' accusations do not really detract from the interest attaching to the war, and its value for purposes of study. If, as he says, the American commanders were cowards, and their crews renegades, it is well worth while to learn the lesson that good training will make such men able to beat brave officers with loyal crews. And why did the British have such bad average crews as he makes out? He says, for instance, that the *Java*'s was unusually bad; yet Brenton says (vol. ii, p. 461) it was like "the generality of our crews." It is worth while explaining the reason that such a crew was generally better than a French and worse than an American one.

above by another deck; on the fore and aft parts (forecastle and quarter-deck) of this upper, open deck were also mounted guns. The main-deck guns were all long, except on the *Essex*, which had carronades; on the quarter-deck were mounted carronades, and on the forecastle also carronades, with two long bow-chasers.

Where two ships of similar armament fought one another, it is easy to get the comparative force by simply comparing the weight in broadsides, each side presenting very nearly the same proportion of long guns to carronades. For such a broadside we take half the guns mounted in the ordinary way; and all guns mounted on pivots or shifting. Thus Perry's force in guns was 54 to Barclay's 63; yet each presented 34 in broadside. Again, each of the British brig-sloops mounted 19 guns, presenting 10 in broadside. Besides these, some ships mounted bow-chasers run through the bridle-ports, or stern-chasers, neither of which could be used in broadsides. Nevertheless, I include them, both because it works in about an equal number of cases against each navy, and because they were sometimes terribly effective. James excludes the *Guerrière's* bow-chaser; in reality he ought to have included both it and its fellow, as they worked more damage than all the broadside guns put together. Again, he excludes the *Endymion's* bow-chasers, though in her action they proved invaluable. Yet he includes those of the *Enterprise* and *Argus,* though the former's were probably not fired. So I shall take the half of the fixed, plus all the movable guns aboard, in comparing broadside force.

But the chief difficulty appears when guns of one style are matched against those of another. If a ship armed with long 12's, meets one armed with 32-pound carronades, which is superior in force? At long range the first, and at short range the second; and of course each captain is pretty sure to insist that "circumstances" forced him to fight at a disadvantage. The result would depend largely on the skill or luck of each commander in choosing position.

One thing is certain; long guns are more formidable than carronades of the same calibre. There are exemplifications of this rule on both sides; of course, American writers, as a rule, only pay attention to one set of cases, and British to the others. The *Cyane* and *Levant* threw a heavier broadside than the *Constitution* but were certainly less formidably armed; and the *Essex* threw a heavier broadside than the *Phœbe,* yet was also less formidable. On Lake Ontario the American ship *General Pike* threw less metal at a broadside than either of her two chief antagonists, but neither could be called her equal; while on Lake Champlain a parallel case is afforded by the British ship *Confiance.* Supposing that two ships throw the same broadside weight of metal, one from long guns, the other from carronades, at short range they are equal; at long, one has it all her own way. Her captain thus certainly has a great superiority of force, and if he does not take advantage of it it is owing to his adversary's skill or his own mismanagement. As a mere approximation, it may be assumed, in comparing the broadsides of two vessels or squadrons, that long guns count for at least twice as much as carronades of the same calibre. Thus on Lake Champlain

Captain Downie possessed an immense advantage in his long guns, which Commodore Macdonough's exceedingly good arrangements nullified. Sometimes part of the advantage may be willingly foregone, so as to acquire some other. Had the *Constitution* kept at long bowls with the *Cyane* and *Levant* she could have probably captured one without any loss to herself, while the other would have escaped; she preferred to run down close so as to insure the capture of both, knowing that even at close quarters long guns are somewhat better than short ones (not to mention her other advantages in thick scantling, speed, etc.). The British carronades often upset in action; this was either owing to their having been insufficiently secured, and to this remaining undiscovered because the men were not exercised at the guns, or else it was because the unpractised sailors would greatly overcharge them. Our better-trained sailors on the ocean rarely committed these blunders, but the less-skilled crews on the lakes did so as often as their antagonists.

But while the Americans thus, as a rule, had heavier and better-fitted guns, they labored under one or two disadvantages. Our foundries were generally not as good as those of the British, and our guns, in consequence, more likely to burst; it was an accident of this nature which saved the British *Belvidera;* and the *General Pike*, under Commodore Chauncy, and the new American frigate *Guerrière* suffered in the same way; while often the muzzles of the guns would crack. A more universal disadvantage was in the short weight of our shot. When Captain Blakely sunk the *Avon* he officially reported that her four shot which came aboard weighed just 32 pounds apiece, a pound and three quarters more than his *heaviest;* this would make his average shot about 2½ pounds less, or rather over 7 per cent. Exactly similar statements were made by the officers of the *Constitution* in her three engagements. Thus when she fought the *Java*, she threw at a broadside, as already stated, 704 pounds; the *Java* mounted 28 long 18's, 18 32-pound carronades, 2 long 12's, and one shifting 24-pound carronade, a broadside of 576 pounds. Yet by the actual weighing of all the different shot on both sides it was found that the difference in broadside force was only about 77 pounds, or the *Constitution's* shot were about 7 per cent. short weight. The long 24's of the *United States* each threw a shot but 4¼ pounds heavier than the long 18's of the *Macedonian;* here again the difference was about 7 per cent. The same difference existed in favor of the *Penguin* and *Epervier* compared with the *Wasp* and *Hornet.* Mr. Fenimore Cooper[1] weighed a great number of shot some time after the war. The later castings, even, weighed nearly 5 per cent. less than the British shot, and some of the older ones, about 9 per cent. The average is safe to take at 7 per cent. less, and I shall throughout make this allowance for ocean cruisers. The deficit was sometimes owing to windage, but more often the shot was of full size but defective in density. The effect of this can be gathered from the following quotation from the work of a British artillerist: "The greater the density of shot of like cali-

[1] See "Naval History," i, p. 380.

bres, projected with equal velocity and elevation, the greater the range, accuracy, and penetration."[1] This defectiveness in density might be a serious injury in a contest at a long distance, but would make but little difference at close quarters (although it may have been partly owing to their short weight that so many of the *Chesapeake*'s shot failed to penetrate the *Shannon*'s hull). Thus in the actions with the *Macedonian* and *Java* the American frigates showed excellent practice when the contest was carried on within fair distance, while their first broadsides at long range went very wild; but in the case of the *Guerrière*, the *Constitution* reserved her fire for close quarters, and was probably not at all affected by the short weight of her shot.

As to the officers and crew of a 44-gun frigate, the following was the regular complement established by law:[2]

| | | | |
|---|---|---|---|
| 1 | captain, | 1 | purser, |
| 4 | lieutenants, | 1 | surgeon, |
| 2 | lieutenants of marines, | 2 | surgeon's mates, |
| 2 | sailing-masters, | 1 | clerk, |
| 2 | master's mates, | 1 | carpenter, |
| 7 | midshipmen, | 2 | carpenter's mates, |
| 1 | boatswain, | 1 | cook, |
| 2 | boatswain's mates, | 1 | chaplain. |
| 1 | yeoman of gun-room, | | —— |
| 1 | gunner, | 50 | |

| | | | |
|---|---|---|---|
| 11 | quarter gunners, | 120 | able seamen, |
| 1 | coxswain, | 150 | ordinary seamen, |
| 1 | sailmaker, | 30 | boys, |
| 1 | cooper, | 50 | marines. |
| 1 | steward, | | —— |
| 1 | armorer, | 400 | in all. |
| 1 | master of arms, | | |

An 18-gun ship had 32 officers and petty officers, 30 able seamen, 46 ordinary seamen, 12 boys, and 20 marines—140 in all. Sometimes ships put to sea without their full complements (as in the case of the first *Wasp*), but more often with supernumeraries aboard. The weapons for close quarters were pikes, cutlasses, and a few axes; while the marines and some of the topmen had muskets, and occasionally rifles.

[1] "Heavy Ordnance," Captain T. F. Simmons, R. A., London, 1837. James supposes that the "Yankee captains" have in each case hunted round till they could get particularly small American shot to weigh; and also denies that short weight is a disadvantage. The last proposition carried out logically would lead to some rather astonishing results.

[2] See State Papers, vol. xiv, 159 (Washington, 1834).

In comparing the forces of the contestants I have always given the number of men in crew; but this in most cases was unnecessary. When there were plenty of men to handle the guns, trim the sails, make repairs, act as marines, etc., any additional number simply served to increase the slaughter on board. The *Guerrière* undoubtedly suffered from being short-handed, but neither the *Macedonian* nor *Java* would have been benefited by the presence of a hundred additional men. Barclay possessed about as many men as Perry, but this did not give him an equality of force. The *Penguin* and *Frolic* would have been taken just as surely had the *Hornet* and *Wasp* had a dozen men less apiece than they did.

The principal case where numbers would help would be in a hand-to-hand fight. Thus the *Chesapeake* having fifty more men than the *Shannon* ought to have been successful; but she was not, because the superiority of her crew in numbers was more than counterbalanced by the superiority of the *Shannon's* crew in other respects. The result of the battle of Lake Champlain, which was fought at anchor, with the fleets too far apart for musketry to reach, was not in the slightest degree affected by the number of men on either side, as both combatants had amply enough to manage the guns and perform every other service.

In all these conflicts the courage of both parties is taken for granted; it was not so much a factor in gaining the victory, as one which if lacking was fatal to all chances of success. In the engagements between regular cruisers, not a single one was gained by superiority in courage. The crews of both the *Argus* and *Epervier* certainly flinched; but had they fought never so bravely they were too unskilful to win. The *Chesapeake's* crew could hardly be said to lack courage; it was more that they were inferior to their opponents in discipline as well as in skill.

There was but one conflict during the war where the victory could be said to be owing to superiority in pluck. This was when the *Neufchatel* privateer beat off the boats of the *Endymion.* The privateersmen suffered a heavier proportional loss than their assailants, and they gained the victory by sheer ability to stand punishment.

For convenience in comparing them I give in tabulated form the force of the three British 38's taken by American 44's (allowing for short weight of metal of latter).

| CONSTITUTION. | GUERRIÈRE. |
|---|---|
| 30 long 24's, | 30 long 18's, |
| 2 long 24's, | 2 long 12's, |
| 22 short 32's. | 16 short 32's, |
|  | 1 short 18. |
| Broadside, nominal, 736 lbs. | |
| real, 684 lbs. | Broadside, 556 lbs. |

|  UNITED STATES. |  MACEDONIAN. |
| --- | --- |
| 30  long 24's, | 28  long 18's, |
| 2  long 24's, | 2  long 12's, |
| 22  short 42's. | 2  long  9's, |
|  | 16  short 32's, |
|  | 1  short 18. |

Broadside, nominal, 846 lbs.
real, 786 lbs.

Broadside, 547 lbs.

|  CONSTITUTION. |  JAVA. |
| --- | --- |
| 30  long 24's, | 28  long 18's, |
| 2  long 24's, | 2  long 12's, |
| 20  short 32's. | 18  short 32's, |
|  | 1  short 24. |

Broadside, nominal, 704 lbs.
real, 654 lbs.　　Broadside, 576 lbs.

The smallest line-of-battle ship, the 74, with only long 18's on the second deck, was armed as follows:

|  |  |  |
| --- | --- | --- |
| 28 | long | 32's, |
| 28 | " | 18's, |
| 6 | " | 12's, |
| 14 | short | 32's, |
| 7 | " | 18's, |

or a broadside of 1,032 lbs., 736 from long guns, 296 from carronades; while the *Constitution* threw (in reality) 684 lbs., 356 from long guns, and 328 from her carronades, and the *United States* 102 lbs. more from her carronades. Remembering the difference between long guns and carronades, and considering sixteen of the 74's long 18's as being replaced by 42-pound carronades[1] (so as to get the metal on the ships distributed in similar proportions between the two styles of cannon), we get as the 74's broadside 592 lbs. from long guns, and 632 from carronades. The *United States* threw nominally 360 and 486, and the *Constitution* nominally 360 and 352; so the 74 was superior even to the former nominally about as three is to two; while the *Constitution,* if "a line-of-battle ship," was disguised to such a degree that she was in reality of but little more than *one half* the force of one of the smallest *true* liners England possessed!

[1] That this change would leave the force about as it was, can be gathered from the fact that the *Adams* and *John Adams* both of which had been armed with 42-pound carronades (which were sent to Sackett's Harbor), had them replaced by long and medium 18-pounders, these being considered to be more formidable; so that the substitution of 42-pound carronades would, if any thing, reduce the force of the 74.

# III

# 1812

# ON THE OCEAN

Commodore Rodgers' cruise and unsuccessful chase of the *Belvidera* · Cruise of the *Essex* · Captain Hull's cruise, and escape from the squadron of Commodore Broke · *Constitution* captures *Guerrière* · *Wasp* captures *Frolic* · Second unsuccessful cruise of Commodore Rodgers · *United States* captures *Macedonian* · *Constitution* captures *Java* · *Essex* starts on a cruise · Summary

At the time of the declaration of war, June 18, 1812, the American navy was but partially prepared for effective service. The *Wasp*, 18, was still at sea, on her return voyage from France; the *Constellation*, 38, was lying in the Chesapeake river, unable to receive a crew for several months to come; the *Chesapeake*, 38, was lying in a similar condition in Boston harbor; the *Adams*, 28, was at Washington, being cut down and lengthened from a frigate into a corvette. These three cruisers were none of them fit to go to sea till after the end of the year. The *Essex*, 32, was in New York harbor, but, having some repairs to make, was not yet ready to put out. The *Constitution*, 44, was at Annapolis, without all of her stores, and engaged in shipping a new crew, the time of the old one being up. The *Nautilus*, 14, was cruising off New Jersey, and the other small brigs were also off the coast. The only vessels immediately available were those under the command of Commodore Rodgers, at New York, consisting of his own ship, the *President*, 44, and of the *United States*, 44, Commodore Decatur, *Congress*, 38, Captain Smith, *Hornet*, 18, Captain Lawrence, and *Argus*, 16, Lieut. Sinclair. It seems marvellous that any nation should have permitted its ships to be so scattered, and many of them in such an unfit condition, at the beginning of hostilities. The British vessels cruising off the coast were not at that time very numerous or formidable, consisting of the *Africa*, 64, *Acasta*, 40, *Shannon*, 38, *Guerrière*, 38, *Belvidera*, 36, *Æolus*, 32, *Southampton*, 32, and *Minerva*, 32, with a number of corvettes and sloops; their force was, however, strong enough to render it impossible for Commodore Rodgers to make any attempt on the coast towns of Canada or the West Indies. But the homeward bound plate fleet had sailed from Jamaica on May 20th, and was only protected by the *Thalia,* 36, Capt. Vashon, and *Reindeer,* 18, Capt. Manners. Its capture or destruction would have been a serious blow, and one which there seemed a good chance of striking, as the fleet would have to pass along the American coast, running with the Gulf Stream. Commodore Rodgers had made every preparation, in expectation of war being declared, and an hour after official intelligence of it, together with his instructions, had been received, his squadron put to sea, on June 21st, and ran off toward the south-east[1] to get at the Jamaica ships. Having learned from an American brig that she had passed the plate fleet four days before in lat. 36° N., long. 67° W., the Commodore made all sail in that direction. At 6 A.M. on June 23d a sail was made out in the N.E., which proved to be the British frigate *Belvidera,* 36, Capt. Richard Byron.[2] The latter had sighted some of Commodore Rodgers' squadron some time before, and stood toward them, till at 6.30 she made out the three largest ships to be frigates. Having been informed of the likelihood of war by a New York pilot boat, the *Belvidera* now stood away, going N.E. by E., the wind being fresh from the west. The Americans made all sail in chase, the *President,* a very fast ship off the wind, leading, and the *Congress* coming next. At noon the *President* bore S.W., distant 2¾ miles from the *Belvidera,* Nantucket shoals bearing 100 miles N. and 48 miles E.[3] The wind grew lighter, shifting more toward the south-west, while the ships continued steadily in their course, going N.E. by E. As the *President* kept gaining, Captain Byron cleared his ship for action, and shifted to the stern ports two long eighteen pounders on the main-deck and two thirty-two pound carronades on the quarter-deck.

At 4.30[4] the *President'*s starboard forecastle bow-gun was fired by Commodore Rodgers himself; the corresponding main-deck gun was next discharged, and then Commodore Rodgers fired again. These three shots all struck the stern of the *Belvidera,* killing and wounding nine men,—one of them went through the rudder coat, into the after gun-room, the other two into the captain's cabin. A few more such shots would have rendered the *Belvidera'*s capture certain, but when the *President'*s main-deck gun was discharged for the second time it burst, blowing up the forecastle deck and killing and wounding 16 men, among them the Commodore himself, whose leg was broken. This saved the British frigate. Such an explosion always causes a half panic, every gun being at once suspected. In the midst of the confusion Captain Byron's stern-chasers opened with spirit and effect, killing or wounding six men more. Had the *President* still pushed steadily on, only using her bow-chasers until she closed abreast, which she could probably have done, the *Belvidera* could still have been taken; but, instead, the former now bore up and fired her port broadside, cutting her antagonist's rigging slightly, but doing no other damage, while the *Belvidera* kept up a brisk and

---

[1] Letter of Commodore John Rodgers to the Secretary of the Navy, Sept. 1, 1812.

[2] Brenton, v. 46.

[3] Log of *Belvidera,* June 23, 1812.

[4] Cooper, ii, 151. According to James, vi, 117, the *President* was then 600 yards distant from the *Belvidera,* half a point on her weather or port quarter.

galling fire, although the long bolts, breeching-hooks, and breechings of the guns now broke continually, wounding several of the men, including Captain Byron. The *President* had lost ground by yawing, but she soon regained it, and, coming up closer than before, again opened from her bow-chasers a well-directed fire, which severely wounded her opponent's main-top mast, cross-jack yard, and one or two other spars;[1] but shortly afterward she repeated her former tactics and again lost ground by yawing to discharge another broadside, even more ineffectual than the first. Once more she came up closer than ever, and once more yawed; the single shots from her bow-chasers doing considerable damage, but her raking broadsides none.[2] Meanwhile the active crew of the *Belvidera* repaired every thing as fast as it was damaged, while under the superintendence of Lieutenants Sykes, Bruce, and Campbell, no less than 300 shot were fired from her stern guns.[3] Finding that if the *President* ceased yawing she could easily run alongside, Captain Byron cut away one bower, one stream, and two sheet anchors, the barge, yawl, gig, and jolly boat, and started 14 tons of water. The effect of this was at once apparent, and she began to gain; meanwhile the damage the sails of the combatants had received had enabled the *Congress* to close, and when abreast of his consort Captain Smith opened with his bow-chasers, but the shot fell short. The *Belvidera* soon altered her course to east by south, set her starboard studding-sails, and by midnight was out of danger; and three days afterward reached Halifax harbor.

Lord Howard Douglass' criticisms on this encounter seem very just. He says that the *President* opened very well with her bow-chasers (in fact the Americans seem to have aimed better and to have done more execution with these guns than the British with their stern-chasers); but that she lost so much ground by yawing and delivering harmless broadsides as to enable her antagonist to escape. Certainly if it had not been for the time thus lost to no purpose, the Commodore would have run alongside his opponent, and the fate of the little 36 would have been sealed. On the other hand it must be remembered that it was only the bursting of the gun on board the *President*, causing such direful confusion and loss, and especially harmful in disabling her commander, that gave the *Belvidera* any chance of escape at all. At any rate, whether the American frigate does, or does not, deserve blame, Captain Byron and his crew do most emphatically deserve praise for the skill with which their guns were served and repairs made, the coolness with which measures to escape were adopted, and the courage with which they resisted so superior a force. On this occasion Captain Byron showed himself as good a seaman and as brave a man as he subsequently proved a humane and generous enemy when engaged in the blockade of the Chesapeake.[4]

[1] James, vi, 119. He says the *President* was within 400 yards.

[2] Lord Howard Douglass, "Naval Gunnery," p. 419 (third edition).

[3] James, vi, 118.

[4] Even Niles, unscrupulously bitter as he is toward the British, does justice to the humanity of Captains Byron and Hardy—which certainly shone in comparison to some of the rather buccaneering exploits of Cockburn's followers in Chesapeake Bay.

This was not a very auspicious opening of hostilities for America. The loss of the *Belvidera* was not the only thing to be regretted, for the distance the chase took the pursuers out of their course probably saved the plate fleet. When the *Belvidera* was first made out, Commodore Rodgers was in latitude 39° 26′ N., and longitude 71° 10′ W.; at noon the same day the *Thalia* and her convoy were in latitude 39° N., longitude 62° W. Had they not chased the *Belvidera* the Americans would probably have run across the plate fleet.

The American squadron reached the western edge of the Newfoundland Banks on June 29th,[1] and on July 1st, a little to the east of the Banks, fell in with large quantities of cocoa-nut shells, orange peels, etc., which filled every one with great hopes of overtaking the quarry. On July 9th, the *Hornet* captured a British privateer, in latitude 45° 30′ N., and longitude 23° W., and her master reported that he had seen the Jamaica-men the previous evening; but nothing further was heard or seen of them, and on July 13th, being within twenty hours' sail of the English Channel, Commodore Rodgers reluctantly turned southward, reaching Madeira July 21st. Thence he cruised toward the Azores and by the Grand Banks home, there being considerable sickness on the ships. On August 31st he reached Boston after a very unfortunate cruise, in which he had made but seven prizes, all merchant-men, and had recaptured one American vessel.

On July 3d the *Essex*, 32, Captain David Porter, put out of New York. As has been already explained she was most inefficiently armed, almost entirely with carronades. This placed her at the mercy of any frigate with long guns which could keep at a distance of a few hundred yards; but in spite of Captain Porter's petitions and remonstrances he was not allowed to change his armament. On the 11th of July at 2 A.M., latitude 33° N., longitude 66° W., the *Essex* fell in with the *Minerva*, 32, Captain Richard Hawkins, convoying seven transports, each containing about 200 troops, bound from Barbadoes to Quebec. The convoy was sailing in open order, and, there being a dull moon, the *Essex* ran in and cut out transport No. 299, with 197 soldiers aboard. Having taken out the soldiers, Captain Porter stood back to the convoy, expecting Captain Hawkins to come out and fight him; but this the latter would not do, keeping the convoy in close order around him. The transports were all armed and still contained in the aggregate 1,200 soldiers. As the *Essex* could only fight at close quarters these heavy odds rendered it hopeless for her to try to cut out the *Minerva*. Her carronades would have to be used at short range to be effective, and it would of course have been folly to run in right among the convoy, and expose herself to the certainty of being boarded by five times as many men as she possessed. The *Minerva* had three less guns a side, and on her spar-deck carried 24-pound carronades instead of 32's, and, moreover, had fifty men less than the *Essex*, which had about 270 men this cruise; on the other hand, her main-deck was armed with long 12's, so that it is hard to say whether she did right or not in refusing

---

[1] Letter of Commodore Rodgers, Sept. 1st.

to fight. She was of the same force as the *Southampton* whose captain, Sir James Lucas Yeo, subsequently challenged Porter, but never appointed a meeting-place. In the event of a meeting, the advantage, in ships of such radically different armaments, would have been with that captain who succeeded in outmanœuvring the other and in making the fight come off at the distance best suited to himself. At long range either the *Minerva* or *Southampton* would possess an immense superiority; but if Porter could have contrived to run up within a couple of hundred yards, or still better, to board, his superiority in weight of metal and number of men would have enabled him to carry either of them. Porter's crew was better trained for boarding than almost any other American commander's; and probably none of the British frigates on the American station, except the *Shannon* and *Tenedos,* would have stood a chance with the *Essex* in a hand-to-hand struggle. Among her youngest midshipmen was one, by name David Glasgow Farragut, then but thirteen years old, who afterward became the first and greatest admiral of the United States. His own words on this point will be read with interest. "Every day," he says,[1] "the crew were exercised at the great guns, small arms, and single stick. And I may here mention the fact that I have never been on a ship where the crew of the old *Essex* was represented but that I found them to be the best swordsmen on board. They had been so thoroughly trained as boarders that every man was prepared for such an emergency, with his cutlass as sharp as a razor, a dirk made by the ship's armorer out of a file, and a pistol."[2]

On August 13th a sail was made out to windward, which proved to be the British ship-sloop *Alert,* 16, Captain T. L. O. Laugharne, carrying 20 eighteen-pound carronades and 100 men.[3] As soon as the *Essex* discovered the *Alert* she put out drags astern, and led the enemy to believe she was trying to escape by sending a few men aloft to shake out the reefs and make sail. Concluding the frigate to be a merchant-man, the *Alert* bore down on her; while the Americans went to quarters and cleared for action, although the tompions were left in the

---

[1] "Life of Farragut" (embodying his journal and letters), p. 31. By his son, Loyall Farragut, New York, 1879.

[2] James says: "Had Captain Porter really endeavored to bring the *Minerva* to action we do not see what could have prevented the *Essex* with her superiority of sailing, from coming alongside of her. But no such thought, we are sure, entered into Captain Porter's head." What "prevented the *Essex*" was the *Minerva's* not venturing out of the convoy. Farragut, in his journal writes: "The captured British officers were very anxious for us to have a fight with the *Minerva,* as they considered her a good match for the *Essex,* and Captain Porter replied that he should gratify them with pleasure if his majesty's commander was of their taste. So we stood toward the convoy and when within gunshot hove to, and awaited the *Minerva,* but she tacked and stood in among the convoy, to the utter amazement of our prisoners, who denounced the commander as a base coward, and expressed their determination to report him to the Admiralty." An incident of reported "flinching" like this is not worth mentioning; I allude to it only to show the value of James' sneers.

[3] James (History, vi, p. 128) says "86 men." In the Naval Archives at Washington in the "Captains' Letters" for 1812 (vol. ii, No. 182) can be found enclosed in Porter's letter the parole of the officers and crew of the *Alert* signed by Captain Laugharne; it contains either 100 or 101 names of the crew of the *Alert* besides those of a number of other prisoners sent back in the same cartel.

guns, and the ports kept closed.[1] The *Alert* fired a gun and the *Essex* hove to, when the former passed under her stern, and when on her lee quarter poured in a broadside of grape and canister; but the sloop was so far abaft the frigate's beam that her shot did not enter the ports and caused no damage. Thereupon Porter put up his helm and opened as soon as his guns would bear, tompions and all. The *Alert* now discovered her error and made off, but too late, for in eight minutes the *Essex* was along side, and the *Alert* fired a musket and struck, three men being wounded and several feet of water in the hold. She was disarmed and sent as a cartel into St. Johns. It has been the fashion among American writers to speak of her as if she were "unworthily" given up, but such an accusation is entirely groundless. The *Essex* was four times her force, and all that could possibly be expected of her was to do as she did—exchange broadsides and strike, having suffered some loss and damage. The *Essex* returned to New York on September 7th, having made 10 prizes, containing 423 men.[2]

The *Belvidera*, as has been stated, carried the news of the war to Halifax. On July 5th Vice-Admiral Sawyer despatched a squadron to cruise against the United States, commanded by Philip Vere Broke, of the *Shannon*, 38, having under him the *Belvidera*, 36, Captain Richard Byron, *Africa*, 64, Captain John Bastard, and *Æolus*, 32, Captain Lord James Townsend. On the 9th, while off Nantucket, they were joined by the *Guerrière*, 38, Captain James Richard Dacres. On the 16th the squadron fell in with and captured the United States brig *Nautilus*, 14, Lieutenant Crane, which, like all the little brigs, was overloaded with guns and men. She threw her lee guns overboard and made use of every expedient to escape, but to no purpose. At 3 P.M. of the following day, when the British ships were abreast of Barnegat, about four leagues off shore, a strange sail was seen and immediately chased, in the south by east, or windward quarter, standing to the north-east. This was the United States frigate *Constitution*, 44, Captain Isaac Hull.[3] When the war broke out he was in the Chesapeake River getting a new crew aboard. Having shipped over 450 men (counting officers), he put out of harbor on the 12th of July. His crew was entirely new, drafts of men coming on board up to the last moment.[4] On the 17th,

---

[1] "Life of Farragut," p. 16.

[2] Before entering New York the *Essex* fell in with a British force which, in both Porter's and Farragut's works, is said to have been composed of the *Acasta* and *Shannon*, each of fifty guns, and *Ringdove*, of twenty. James says it was the *Shannon*, accompanied by a merchant vessel. It is not a point of much importance, as nothing came of the meeting, and the *Shannon*, alone, with her immensely superior armament, ought to have been a match twice over for the *Essex*; although, if James is right, as seems probable, it gives rather a comical turn to Porter's account of his "extraordinary escape."

[3] For the ensuing chase I have relied mainly on Cooper; see also "Memoir of Admiral Broke," p. 240; James, vi, 133; and Marshall's "Naval Biography" (London, 1825), ii, 625.

[4] In a letter to the Secretary of the Navy ("Captains' Letters," 1812, ii, No. 85), Hull, after speaking of the way his men were arriving, says: "The crew are as yet unacquainted with a ship of war, as many have but lately joined and have never been on an armed ship before. * * * We are doing all that we can to make them acquainted with their duty, and in a few days we shall have nothing to fear from any single-decked ship."

at 2 P.M., Hull discovered four sail, in the northern board, heading to the westward. At 3, the wind being very light, the *Constitution* made sail and tacked, in 18½ fathoms. At 4, in the N.E., a fifth sail appeared, which afterward proved to be the *Guerrière.* The first four ships bore N.N.W., and were all on the starboard tack; while by 6 o'clock the fifth bore E.N.E. At 6.15 the wind shifted and blew lightly from the south, bringing the American ship to windward. She then wore round with her head to the eastward, set her light studding-sails and stay-sails, and at 7.30 beat to action, intending to speak the nearest vessel, the *Guerrière.* The two frigates neared one another gradually and at 10 the *Constitution* began making signals, which she continued for over an hour. At 3.30 A.M. on the 18th the *Guerrière,* going gradually toward the *Constitution* on the port tack, and but one half mile distant, discovered on her lee beam the *Belvidera* and the other British vessels, and signalled to them. They did not answer the signals, thinking she must know who they were—a circumstance which afterward gave rise to sharp recriminations among the captains—and Dacres, concluding them to be Commodore Rodgers' squadron, tacked, and then wore round and stood away from the *Constitution* for some time before discovering his mistake.

At 5 A.M. Hull had just enough steerage way on to keep his head to the east, on the starboard tack; on his lee quarter, bearing N.E. by N., were the *Belvidera* and *Guerrière* and astern the *Shannon, Æolus,* and *Africa.* At 5.30 it fell entirely calm, and Hull put out his boats to tow the ship, always going southward. At the same time he whipped up a 24 from the main-deck, and got the forecastle-chaser aft, cutting away the taffrail to give the two guns more freedom to work in and also running out, through the cabin windows, two of the long main-deck 24's. The British boats were towing also. At 6 A.M. a light breeze sprang up, and the *Constitution* set studding-sails and stay-sails; the *Shannon* opened at her with her bow guns, but ceased when she found she could not reach her. At 6.30, the wind having died away, the *Shannon* began to gain, almost all the boats of the squadron towing her. Having sounded in 26 fathoms, Lieutenant Charles Morris suggested to Hull to try kedging. All the spare rope was bent on to the cables, payed out into the cutters, and a kedge run out half a mile ahead and let go; then the crew clapped on and walked away with the ship, overrunning and tripping the kedge as she came up with the end of the line. Meanwhile, fresh lines and another kedge were carried ahead, and the frigate glided away from her pursuers. At 7.30 A.M. a little breeze sprang up, when the *Constitution* set her ensign and fired a shot at the *Shannon.* It soon fell calm again and the *Shannon* neared. At 9.10 a light air from the southward struck the ship, bringing her to windward. As the breeze was seen coming, her sails were trimmed, and as soon as she obeyed her helm she was brought close up on the port tack. The boats dropped in alongside; those that belonged to the davits were run up, while the others were just lifted clear of the water, by purchases on the spare spars, stowed outboard, where they could be used again at a minute's notice. Meanwhile, on her lee beam, the *Guerrière* opened fire; but her shot fell short, and the Americans paid not the slightest heed to it. Soon it again fell calm, when Hull had 2,000 gallons of water started, and again put out his boats to tow. The *Shannon* with some of the other boats of the squadron helping her, gained on the *Constitution* but by severe exertion was again left behind. Shortly afterward, a slight wind springing up, the *Belvidera* gained on the other British ships, and when it fell calm she was nearer to the *Constitution* than any of her consorts, their boats being put on to her.[1] At 10.30, observing the benefit that the *Constitution* had derived from warping, Captain Byron did the same, bending all his hawsers to one another, and working two kedge anchors at the same time by paying the warp out through one hawse-hole as it was run in through the other opposite. Having men from the other frigates aboard, and a lighter ship to work, Captain Byron, at 2 P.M. was near enough to exchange bow- and stern-chasers with the *Constitution,* out of range however. Hull expected to be overtaken, and made every arrangement to try in such case to disable the first frigate before her consorts could close. But neither the *Belvidera* nor the *Shannon* dared to tow very near for fear of having their boats sunk by the American's stern-chasers.

The *Constitution*'s crew showed the most excellent spirit. Officers and men relieved each other regularly, the former snatching their rest any where on deck, the latter sleeping at the guns. Gradually the *Constitution* drew ahead, but the situation continued most critical. All through the afternoon the British frigates kept towing and kedging, being barely out of gunshot. At 3 P.M. a light breeze sprung up, and blew fitfully at intervals; every puff was watched closely and taken advantage of to the utmost. At 7 in the evening the wind almost died out, and for four more weary hours the worn-out sailors towed and kedged. At 10.45 a little breeze struck the frigate, when the boats dropped alongside and were hoisted up, excepting the first cutter. Throughout the night the wind continued very light, the *Belvidera* forging ahead till she was off the *Constitution*'s lee beam; and at 4 A.M. on the morning of the 19th, she tacked to the eastward, the breeze being light from the south by east. At 4.20 the *Constitution* tacked also; and at 5.15 the *Æolus,* which had drawn ahead, passed on the contrary tack. Soon afterward the wind freshened so that Captain Hull took in his cutter. The *Africa* was now so far to leeward as to be almost out of the race; while the five frigates were all running on the starboard tack with every stitch of canvas set. At 9 A.M. an American merchant-man hove in sight and bore down toward the squadron. The *Belvidera,* by way of decoy, hoisted American colors, when the *Constitution* hoisted the British flag, and the merchant vessel hauled off. The breeze continued light till noon, when Hull found he had dropped the British frigates well behind; the nearest was the *Belvidera,* exactly in his wake, bearing W.N.W. 2½ miles distant. The *Shannon* was on his lee, bearing N. by W. ½ W. distant 3½ miles. The other two frigates were five miles off on the lee quarter. Soon afterward the breeze freshened, and "old Ironsides" drew slowly ahead

---

[1] Cooper speaks as if this was the *Shannon;* but from Marshall's "Naval Biography" we learn that it was the *Belvidera.* At other times he confuses the *Belvidera* with the *Guerrière.* Captain Hull, of course, could not accurately distinguish the names of his pursuers. My account is drawn from a careful comparison of Marshall, Cooper, and James.

from her foes, her sails being watched and tended with the most consummate skill. At 4 P.M. the breeze again lightened, but even the *Belvidera* was now four miles astern and to leeward. At 6.45 there were indications of a heavy rain squall, which once more permitted Hull to show that in seamanship he excelled even the able captains against whom he was pitted. The crew were stationed and every thing kept fast till the last minute, when all was clewed up just before the squall struck the ship. The light canvas was furled, a second reef taken in the mizzen top-sail, and the ship almost instantly brought under short sail. The British vessels seeing this began to let go and haul down without waiting for the wind, and were steering on different tacks when the first gust struck them. But Hull as soon as he got the weight of the wind sheeted home, hoisted his fore and main-top gallant sails, and went off on an easy bowline at the rate of 11 knots. At 7.40 sight was again obtained of the enemy, the squall having passed to leeward; the *Belvidera,* the nearest vessel, had altered her bearings two points to leeward, and was a long way astern. Next came the *Shannon;* the *Guerrière* and *Æolus* were hull down, and the *Africa* barely visible. The wind now kept light, shifting occasionally in a very baffling manner, but the *Constitution* gained steadily, wetting her sails from the sky-sails to the courses. At 6 A.M, on the morning of the 20th the pursuers were almost out of sight; and at 8.15 A.M. they abandoned the chase. Hull at once stopped to investigate the character of two strange vessels, but found them to be only Americans; then, at midday, he stood toward the east, and went into Boston on July 26th.

In this chase Captain Isaac Hull was matched against five British captains, two of whom, Broke and Byron, were fully equal to any in their navy; and while the latter showed great perseverance, good seamanship, and ready imitation, there can be no doubt that the palm in every way belongs to the cool old Yankee. Every daring expedient known to the most perfect seamanship was tried, and tried with success; and no victorious fight could reflect more credit on the conqueror than this three days' chase did on Hull. Later, on two occasions, the *Constitution* proved herself far superior in gunnery to the average British frigate; this time her officers and men showed that they could handle the sails as well as they could the guns. Hull out-manœuvred Broke and Byron as cleverly as a month later he out-fought Dacres. His successful escape and victorious fight were both performed in a way that place him above any single ship captain of the war.

On Aug. 2d the *Constitution* made sail from Boston[1] and stood to the eastward, in hopes of falling in with some of the British cruisers. She was unsuccessful, however, and met nothing. Then she ran down to the Bay of Fundy, steered along the coast of Nova Scotia, and thence toward Newfoundland, and finally took her station off Cape Race in the Gulf of St. Lawrence, where she took and burned two brigs of little value. On the 15th she recaptured an American brig from the British ship-sloop *Avenger,* though the latter escaped; Capt. Hull

---

[1] Letter of Capt. Isaac Hull, Aug. 28, 1812.

manned his prize and sent her in. He then sailed southward, and on the night of the 18th spoke a Salem privateer which gave him news of a British frigate to the south; thither he stood, and at 2 P.M. on the 19th, in lat. 41° 30′ N. and 55° W., made out a large sail bearing E.S.E. and to leeward,[1] which proved to be his old acquaintance, the frigate *Guerrière,* Captain Dacres. It was a cloudy day and the wind was blowing fresh from the northwest. The *Guerrière* was standing by the wind on the starboard tack, under easy canvas[2]; she hauled up her courses, took in her top-gallant sails, and at 4.30 backed her main-top sail. Hull then very deliberately began to shorten sail, taking in top-gallant sails, stay-sails, and flying jib, sending down the royal yards and putting another reef in the top-sails. Soon the Englishman hoisted three ensigns, when the American also set his colors, one at each mast-head, and one at the mizzen peak.

The *Constitution* now ran down with the wind nearly aft. The *Guerrière* was on the starboard tack, and at five o'clock opened with her weather-guns,[3] the shot falling short, then wore round and fired her port broadside, of which two shot struck her opponent, the rest passing over and through her rigging.[4] As the British frigate again wore to open with her starboard battery, the *Constitution* yawed a little and fired two or three of her port bow-guns. Three or four times the *Guerrière* repeated this manœuvre, wearing and firing alternate broadsides, but with little or no effect, while the *Constitution* yawed as often to avoid being raked, and occasionally fired one of her bow guns. This continued nearly an hour, as the vessels were very far apart when the action began, hardly any loss or damage being inflicted by either party. At 6.00 the *Guerrière* bore up and ran off under her top-sails and jib, with the wind almost astern, a little on her port quarter; when the *Constitution* set her main-top gallant sail and foresail, and at 6.05 closed within half pistol-shot distance on her adversary's port beam.[5] Immediately a furious cannonade opened, each ship firing as the guns bore. By the time the ships were fairly abreast, at 6.20, the *Constitution* shot away the *Guerrière*'s mizzen-mast, which fell over the starboard quarter, knocking a large hole in the counter, and bringing the ship round against her helm. Hitherto she had suffered very greatly and the *Constitution* hardly at all. The latter, finding that she was ranging ahead, put her helm aport and then luffed short round her enemy's bows,[6] delivering a heavy raking fire with the starboard guns and shooting away the *Guerrière*'s main-yard. Then she wore and again passed her adversary's bows, raking with her port guns. The mizzen-

---

[1] *Do.,* Aug. 30th.

[2] Letter of Capt. James R. Dacres, Sept. 7, 1812.

[3] Log of *Guerrière.*

[4] See in the Naval Archives (Bureau of Navigation) the *Constitution*'s Log-Book (vol. ii, from Feb. 1, 1812, to Dec. 13, 1813). The point is of some little importance because Hull, in his letter, speaks as if *both* the first broadsides fell short, whereas the log distinctly says that the second went over the ship, except two shot, which came home. The hypothesis of the *Guerrière* having damaged powder was founded purely on this supposed falling short of the first two broadsides.

[5] "Autobiography of Commodore Morris" (Annapolis, 1880), p. 164.

[6] Log of *Constitution.*

mast of the *Guerrière,* dragging in the water, had by this time pulled her bow round till the wind came on her starboard quarter; and so near were the two ships that the Englishman's bowsprit passed diagonally over the *Constitution's* quarter-deck, and as the latter ship fell off it got foul of her mizzen-rigging, and the vessels then lay with the *Guerrière's* starboard bow against the *Constitution's* port, or lee quarter-gallery.[1] The Englishman's bow guns played havoc with Captain Hull's cabin, setting fire to it; but the flames were soon extinguished by Lieutenant Hoffmann. On both sides the boarders were called away; the British ran forward, but Captain Dacres relinquished the idea of attacking[2] when he saw the crowds of men on the American's decks. Meanwhile, on the *Constitution,* the boarders and marines gathered aft, but such a heavy sea was running that they could not get on the *Guerrière.* Both sides suffered heavily from the closeness of the musketry fire; indeed, almost the entire loss on the *Constitution* occurred at this juncture. As Lieutenant Bush, of the marines, sprang upon the taffrail to leap on the enemy's decks, a British marine shot him dead; Mr. Morris, the first Lieutenant, and Mr. Alwyn, the master, had also both leaped on the taffrail, and both were at the same moment wounded by the musketry fire. On the *Guerrière* the loss was far heavier, almost all the men on the forecastle being picked off. Captain Dacres himself was shot in the back and severely wounded by one of the American mizzen topmen, while he was standing on the starboard forecastle hammocks cheering on his crew[3]; two of the lieutenants and the master were also shot down. The ships gradually worked round till the wind was again on the port quarter, when they separated, and the *Guerrière's* foremast and main-mast at once went by the board, and fell over on the starboard side, leaving her a defenseless hulk, rolling her maindeck guns into the water.[4] At 6.30 the *Constitution* hauled aboard her tacks, ran off a little distance to the eastward, and lay to. Her braces and standing and running rigging were much cut up and some of the spars wounded, but a few minutes sufficed to repair damages, when Captain Hull stood under his adversary's lee, and the latter at once struck, at 7.00 P.M.,[5] just two hours after she had fired the first shot. On the part of the *Constitution,* however, the actual fighting, exclusive of six or eight guns fired during the first hour, while closing, occupied less than 30 minutes.

The tonnage and metal of the combatants have already been referred to. The *Constitution* had, as already said, about 456 men aboard, while of the *Guerrière's* crew, 267 prisoners were received aboard the *Constitution;* deducting 10 who were Americans and would not fight, and adding the 15 killed outright, we get 272; 28 men were absent in prizes.

[1] Cooper, in "Putnam's Magazine," i, 475.
[2] Address of Captain Dacres to the court-martial at Halifax.
[3] James, vi, 144.
[4] Brenton, v, 51.
[5] Log of the *Constitution.*

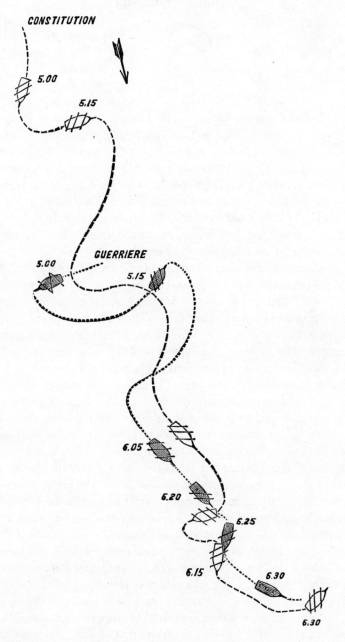

CONSTITUTION

5.00

5.15

GUERRIERE

5.00
5.15

6.05

6.20

6.25

6.15
6.30

6.30

This diagram is taken from Commodore Morris' autobiography and the log of the *Guerrière*; the official accounts apparently consider "larboard" and "starboard" as interchangeable terms.

COMPARATIVE FORCE

| | TONS. | GUNS. | BROAD-SIDE. | MEN. | LOSS. | COMPARATIVE FORCE. | COMPARATIVE LOSS INFLICTED. |
|---|---|---|---|---|---|---|---|
| *Constitution* | 1576 | 27 | 684 | 456 | 14 | 1.00 | 1.00 |
| *Guerrière* | 1338 | 25 | 556 | 272 | 79 | .70 | .18 |

The loss of the *Constitution* included Lieutenant William S. Bush, of the marines, and six seamen killed, and her first lieutenant, Charles Morris, Master, John C. Alwyn, four seamen, and one marine, wounded. Total, seven killed and seven wounded. Almost all this loss occurred when the ships came foul, and was due to the *Guerrière's* musketry and the two guns in her bridle-ports.

The *Guerrière* lost 23 killed and mortally wounded, including her second lieutenant, Henry Ready, and 56 wounded severely and slightly, including Captain Dacres himself, the first lieutenant, Bartholomew Kent, Master, Robert Scott, two master's mates, and one midshipman.

The third lieutenant of the *Constitution,* Mr. George Campbell Read, was sent on board the prize, and the *Constitution* remained by her during the night; but at daylight it was found that she was in danger of sinking. Captain Hull at once began removing the prisoners, and at three o'clock in the afternoon set the *Guerrière* on fire, and in a quarter of an hour she blew up. He then set sail for Boston, where he arrived on August 30th. "Captain Hull and his officers," writes Captain Dacres in his official letter, "have treated us like brave and generous enemies; the greatest care has been taken that we should not lose the smallest trifle."

The British laid very great stress on the rotten and decayed condition of the *Guerrière;* mentioning in particular that the main-mast fell solely because of the weight of the falling foremast. But it must be remembered that until the action occurred she was considered a very fine ship. Thus, in Brighton's "Memoir of Admiral Broke," it is declared that Dacres freely expressed the opinion that she could take a ship in half the time the *Shannon* could. The fall of the main-mast occurred when the fight was practically over; it had no influence whatever on the conflict. It was also asserted that her powder was bad, but on no authority; her first broadside fell short, but so, under similar circumstances, did the first broadside of the *United States.* None of these causes account for the fact that her shot did not hit. Her opponent was of such superior force—nearly in the proportion of 3 to 2—that success would have been very difficult in any event, and no one can doubt the gallantry and pluck with which the British ship was fought; but the execution was very greatly disproportioned to the force. The gunnery of the *Guerrière* was very poor, and that of the *Constitution* excellent; during the few minutes the ships were yard-arm and yard-arm, the latter was not hulled once, while no less than 30 shot took effect on the former's engaged side,[1] five sheets of copper beneath the bends. The *Guerrière,* moreover, was

---

[1] Captain Dacres' address to the court-martial.

out-manœuvred; "in wearing several times and exchanging broadsides in such rapid and continual changes of position, her fire was much more harmless than it would have been if she had kept more steady."[1] The *Constitution* was handled faultlessly; Captain Hull displayed the coolness and skill of a veteran in the way in which he managed, first to avoid being raked, and then to improve the advantage which the precision and rapidity of his fire had gained. "After making every allowance claimed by the enemy, the character of this victory is not essentially altered. Its peculiarities were a fine display of seamanship in the approach, extraordinary efficiency in the attack, and great readiness in repairing damages; all of which denote cool and capable officers, with an expert and trained crew; in a word, a disciplined man-of-war."[2] The disparity of force, 10 to 7, is not enough to account for the disparity of execution, 10 to 2. Of course, something must be allowed for the decayed state of the Englishman's masts, although I really do not think it had any influence on the battle, for he was beaten when the main-mast fell; and it must be remembered, on the other hand, that the American crew was absolutely new, while the *Guerrière* was manned by old hands. So that, while admitting and admiring the gallantry, and, on the whole, the seamanship of Captain Dacres and his crew, and acknowledging that he fought at a great disadvantage, especially in being short-handed, yet all must acknowledge that the combat showed a marked superiority, particularly in gunnery, on the part of the Americans. Had the ships not come foul, Captain Hull would probably not have lost more than three or four men; as it was, he suffered but slightly. That the *Guerrière* was not so weak as she was represented to be can be gathered from the fact that she mounted two more main-deck guns than the rest of her class; thus carrying on her main-deck 30 long 18-pounders in battery, to oppose to the 30 long 24's, or rather (allowing for the short weight of shot) long 22's, of the *Constitution*. Characteristically enough, James, though he carefully reckons in the long bow-chasers in the bridle-ports of the *Argus* and *Enterprise*, yet refuses to count the two long eighteens mounted through the bridle-ports on the *Guerrière's* main-deck. Now, as it turned out, these two bow guns were used very effectively, when the ships got foul, and caused more damage and loss than all of the other main-deck guns put together.

Captain Dacres, very much to his credit, allowed the ten Americans on board to go below, so as not to fight against their flag; and in his address to the court-martial mentions, among the reasons for his defeat, "that he was very much weakened by permitting the Americans on board to quit their quarters." Coupling this with the assertion made by James and most other British writers that the *Constitution* was largely manned by Englishmen, we reach the somewhat remarkable conclusion, that the British ship was defeated because the Americans on board would *not* fight against their country, and that the American was victorious because the British on board *would*. However, as I

---

[1] Lord Howard Douglass, "Treatise on Naval Gunnery" (London, 1851), p. 454.
[2] Cooper, ii, 173.

have shown, in reality there were probably not a score of British on board the *Constitution*.

In this, as well as the two succeeding frigate actions, every one must admit that there was a great superiority in force on the side of the victors, and British historians have insisted that this superiority was so great as to preclude any hopes of a successful resistance. That this was not true, and that the disparity between the combatants was not as great as had been the case in a number of encounters in which English frigates had taken French ones, can be best shown by a few accounts taken from the French historian Troude, who would certainly not exaggerate the difference. Thus on March 1, 1799, the English 38-gun 18-pounder frigate *Sybil,* captured the French 44-gun 24-pounder frigate *Forte,* after an action of two hours and ten minutes.[1] In *actual* weight the shot thrown by one of the main-deck guns of the defeated *Forte* was over six pounds heavier than the shot thrown by one of the main-deck guns of the victorious *Constitution* or *United States.*[2]

There are later examples than this. But a very few years before the declaration of war by the United States, and in the same struggle that was then still raging, there had been at least two victories gained by English frigates over French foes as superior to themselves as the American 44's were to the British ships they captured. On Aug 10, 1805, the *Phœnix,* 36, captured the *Didon,* 40, after 3½ hours' fighting, the comparative broadside force being:[3]

| PHŒNIX. | DIDON. |
|---|---|
| $13 \times 18$ | $14 \times 18$ |
| $2 \times 9$ | $2 \times 8$ |
| $6 \times 32$ | $7 \times 36$ |
| 21 guns, 444 lbs. | 23 guns, 522 lbs. (nominal; about 600, real). |

On March 8, 1808, the *San Florenzo,* 36, captured the *Piédmontaise,* 40, the force being exactly what it was in the case of the *Phœnix* and *Didon.*[4] Comparing the real, not the nominal weight of metal, we find that the *Didon* and *Piédmontaise* were proportionately of greater force compared to the *Phœnix* and *San Florenzo,* than the *Constitution* was compared to the *Guerrière* or *Java.* The French 18's threw each a shot weighing but about two pounds less than that thrown by an American 24 of 1812, while their 36-pound carronades each threw a shot over 10 pounds heavier than that thrown by one of the *Constitution's* spar-deck 32's.

That a 24-pounder can not always whip an 18-pounder frigate is shown by the action of the British frigate *Eurotas* with the French frigate *Chlorinde,* on Feb.

[1] "Batailles Navales de la France," O. Troude (Paris, 1868), iv, 171.
[2] See Appendix B, for actual weight of French shot.
[3] *Ibid.,* iii, 425.
[4] *Ibid.,* iii, 499.

25, 1814.[1] The first with a crew of 329 men threw 625 pounds of shot at a broadside, the latter carrying 344 men and throwing 463 pounds; yet the result was indecisive. The French lost 90 and the British 60 men. The action showed that heavy metal was not of much use unless used well.

To appreciate rightly the exultation Hull's victory caused in the United States, and the intense annoyance it created in England, it must be remembered that during the past twenty years the Island Power had been at war with almost every state in Europe, at one time or another, and in the course of about two hundred single conflicts between ships of approximately equal force (that is, where the difference was less than one half), waged against French, Spanish, Italian, Turkish, Algerine, Russian, Danish, and Dutch antagonists, her ships had been beaten and captured in but five instances. Then war broke out with America, and in eight months five single-ship actions occurred, in every one of which the British vessel was captured. Even had the victories been due solely to superior force this would have been no mean triumph for the United States.

On October 13, 1812, the American 18-gun ship-sloop *Wasp*, Captain Jacob Jones, with 137 men aboard, sailed from the Delaware and ran off south-east to get into the track of the West India vessels; on the 16th a heavy gale began to blow, causing the loss of the jib-boom and two men who were on it. The next day the weather moderated somewhat, and at 11.30 P.M., in latitude 37° N., longitude 65° W., several sail were descried.[2] These were part of a convoy of 14 merchant-men which had quitted the bay of Honduras on September 12th, bound for England,[3] under the convoy of the British 18-gun brig-sloop *Frolic*, of 19 guns and 110 men, Captain Thomas Whinyates. They had been dispersed by the gale of the 16th, during which the *Frolic*'s main-yard was carried away and both her top-sails torn to pieces[4]; next day she spent in repairing damages, and by dark six of the missing ships had joined her. The day broke almost cloudless on the 18th (Sunday), showing the convoy, ahead and to leeward of the American ship, still some distance off, as Captain Jones had not thought it prudent to close during the night, while he was ignorant of the force of his antagonists. The *Wasp* now sent down her top-gallant yards, close reefed her top-sails, and bore down under short fighting canvas; while the *Frolic* removed her main-yard from the casks, lashed it on deck, and then hauled to the wind under her boom main-sail and close-reefed foretop-sail, hoisting Spanish colors to decoy the stranger under her guns, and permit the convoy to escape. At 11.32 the action began—the two ships running parallel on the starboard tack, not 60 yards apart, the *Wasp* firing her port, and the *Frolic* her starboard, guns. The latter fired very rapidly, delivering three broadsides to the *Wasp*'s two,[5] both crews cheering loudly as the ships wallowed through the water. There was a very heavy sea

---

[1] James, vi, 391.
[2] Capt. Jones' official letter, Nov. 24, 1812.
[3] James' History, vi, 158.
[4] Capt. Whinyates' official letter, Oct. 18, 1812.
[5] Cooper, 182.

running, which caused the vessels to pitch and roll heavily. The Americans fired as the engaged side of their ship was going down, aiming at their opponent's hull[1]; while the British delivered their broadsides while on the crests of the seas, the shot going high. The water dashed in clouds of spray over both crews, and the vessels rolled so that the muzzles of the guns went under.[2] But in spite of the rough weather, the firing was not only spirited but well directed. At 11.36 the *Wasp*'s maintop-mast was shot away and fell, with its yard, across the port fore and foretop-sail braces, rendering the head yards unmanageable; at 11.46 the gaff and mizzentop-gallant mast came down, and by 11.52 every brace and most of the rigging was shot away.[3] It would now have been very difficult to brace any of the yards. But meanwhile the *Frolic* suffered dreadfully in her hull and lower masts, and had her gaff and head braces shot away.[4] The slaughter among her crew was very great, but the survivors kept at their work with the dogged courage of their race. At first the two vessels ran side by side, but the American gradually forged ahead, throwing in her fire from a position in which she herself received little injury; by degrees the vessels got so close that the Americans struck the *Frolic*'s side with their rammers in loading,[5] and the British brig was raked with dreadful effect. The *Frolic* then fell aboard her antagonist, her jib-boom coming in between the main- and mizzen-rigging of the *Wasp* and passing over the heads of Captain Jones and Lieutenant Biddle, who were standing near the capstan. This forced the *Wasp* up in the wind, and she again raked her antagonist, Captain Jones trying to restrain his men from boarding till he could put in another broadside. But they could no longer be held back, and Jack Lang, a New Jersey seaman, leaped on the *Frolic*'s bowsprit. Lieutenant Biddle then mounted on the hammock cloth to board, but his feet got entangled in the rigging, and one of the midshipmen seizing his coat-tails to help himself up, the lieutenant tumbled back on the deck. At the next swell he succeeded in getting on the bowsprit, on which there were already two seamen whom he passed on the forecastle. But there was no one to oppose him; not twenty Englishmen were left unhurt.[6] The man at the wheel was still at his post, grim and undaunted, and two or three more were on deck, including Captain Whinyates and Lieutenant Wintle, both so severely wounded that they could not stand without support.[7] There could be no more resistance, and Lieutenant Biddle lowered the flag at 12.15—just 43 minutes after the beginning of the fight.[8] A minute or two afterward both the *Frolic*'s masts went by the

---

[1] Niles' Register, iii, p. 324.
[2] *Do.*
[3] Capt. Jones' letter.
[4] Capt. Whinyates' letter.
[5] Capt. Jones' letter.
[6] Capt. Whinyates' letter.
[7] James, vi, 161.
[8] Capt. Jones' letter.

board—the foremast about fifteen feet above the deck, the other short off. Of her crew, as already said, not twenty men had escaped unhurt. Every officer was wounded; two of them, the first lieutenant, Charles McKay, and master, John Stephens, soon died. Her total loss was thus over 90[1]; about 30 of whom were killed outright or died later. The *Wasp* suffered very severely in her rigging and aloft generally, but only two or three shots struck her hull; five of her men were killed—two in her mizzen-top and one in her maintop-mast rigging—and five wounded,[2] chiefly while aloft.

The two vessels were practically of equal force. The loss of the *Frolic's* main-yard had merely converted her into a brigantine, and, as the roughness of the sea made it necessary to fight under very short canvas, her inferiority in men was fully compensated for by her superiority in metal. She had been desperately defended; no men could have fought more bravely than Captain Whinyates and his crew. On the other hand, the Americans had done their work with a coolness and skill that could not be surpassed; the contest had been mainly one of gunnery, and had been decided by the greatly superior judgment and accuracy with which they fired. Both officers and crew had behaved well; Captain Jones particularly mentions Lieutenant Claxton, who, though too ill to be of any service, persisted in remaining on deck throughout the engagement.

DIAGRAM[3]

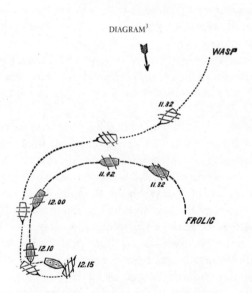

---

[1] Capt. Whinyates' official letter thus states it, and is, of course, to be taken as authority; the Bermuda account makes it 69, and James only 62.

[2] Capt. Jones' letter.

[3] It is difficult to reconcile the accounts of the manœuvres in this action. James says "larboard" where Cooper says "starboard"; one says the *Wasp* wore, the other says that she could not do so, etc.

The *Wasp* was armed with 2 long 12's and 16 32-pound carronades; the *Frolic* with 2 long 6's, 16 32-pound carronades, and 1 shifting 12-pound carronade.

### COMPARATIVE FORCE

|  | TONS. | NO. GUNS. | WEIGHT METAL. | CREWS. | LOSS. |
|---|---|---|---|---|---|
| *Wasp* | 450 | 9 | 250 | 135 | 10 |
| *Frolic* | 467 | 10 | 274 | 110 | 90 |

Vice-Admiral Jurien de la Gravière comments on this action as follows[1]:

"The American fire showed itself to be as accurate as it was rapid. On occasions when the roughness of the sea would seem to render all aim excessively uncertain, the effects of their artillery were not less murderous than under more advantageous conditions. The corvette *Wasp* fought the brig *Frolic* in an enormous sea, under very short canvas, and yet, forty minutes after the beginning of the action, when the two vessels came together, the Americans who leaped aboard the brig found on the deck, covered with dead and dying, but one brave man, who had not left the wheel, and three officers, all wounded, who threw down their swords at the feet of the victors." Admiral de la Gravière's criticisms are especially valuable, because they are those of an expert, who only refers to the war of 1812 in order to apply to the French navy the lessons which it teaches, and who is perfectly unprejudiced. He cares for the lesson taught, not the teacher, and is quite as willing to learn from the defeat of the *Chesapeake* as from the victories of the *Constitution*—while most American critics only pay heed to the latter.

The characteristics of the action are the practical equality of the contestants in point of force and the enormous disparity in the damage each suffered; numerically, the *Wasp* was superior by 5 per cent., and inflicted a ninefold greater loss.

Captain Jones was not destined to bring his prize into port, for a few hours afterward the *Poictiers*, a British 74, Captain John Poer Beresford, hove in sight. Now appeared the value of the *Frolic*'s desperate defence; if she could not prevent herself from being captured, she had at least ensured her own recapture, and also the capture of the foe. When the *Wasp* shook out her sails they were found to be cut into ribbons aloft, and she could not make off with sufficient speed. As the *Poictiers* passed the *Frolic*, rolling like a log in the water, she threw a shot over her, and soon overtook the *Wasp*. Both vessels were carried into Bermuda. Captain Whinyates was again put in command of the *Frolic*. Captain Jones and his men were soon exchanged; 25,000 dollars prize-money was voted them by Congress, and the Captain and Lieutenant Biddle were both promoted, the former receiving the captured ship *Macedonian*. Unluckily the blockade was too close for him to succeed in getting out during the remainder of the war.

---

[1] "Guerres Maritimes," ii, 287 (Septième Édition, Paris, 1881).

On Oct. 8th Commodore Rodgers left Boston on his second cruise, with the *President, United States, Congress,* and *Argus,*[1] leaving the *Hornet* in port. Four days out, the *United States* and *Argus* separated, while the remaining two frigates continued their cruise together. The *Argus,*[2] Captain Sinclair, cruised to the eastward, making prizes of 6 valuable merchant-men, and returned to port on January 3d. During the cruise she was chased for three days and three nights (the latter being moonlight) by a British squadron, and was obliged to cut away her boats and anchors and start some of her water. But she saved her guns, and was so cleverly handled that during the chase she actually succeeding in taking and manning a prize, though the enemy got near enough to open fire as the vessels separated. Before relating what befell the *United States,* we shall bring Commodore Rodgers' cruise to an end.

On Oct. 10th the Commodore chased, but failed to overtake, the British frigate *Nymphe,* 38, Captain Epworth. On the 18th, off the great Bank of Newfoundland, he captured the Jamaica packet *Swallow,* homeward bound, with 200,000 dollars in specie aboard. On the 31st, at 9 A.M., lat. 33° N., long. 32° W., his two frigates fell in with the British frigate *Galatea,* 36, Captain Woodley Losack, convoying two South Sea ships, to windward. The *Galatea* ran down to reconnoitre, and at 10 A.M., recognizing her foes, hauled up on the starboard tack to escape. The American frigates made all sail in chase, and continued beating to windward, tacking several times, for about three hours. Seeing that she was being overhauled, the *Galatea* now edged away to get on her best point of sailing; at the same moment one of her convoy, the *Argo,* bore up to cross the hawse of her foes, but was intercepted by the *Congress,* who lay to to secure her. Meanwhile the *President* kept after the *Galatea;* she set her top-mast, top-gallant mast and lower studding-sails, and when it was dusk had gained greatly upon her. But the night was very dark, the *President* lost sight of the chase, and, toward midnight, hauled to the wind to rejoin her consort. The two frigates cruised to the east as far as 22° W., and then ran down to 17° N.; but during the month of November they did not see a sail. They had but slightly better luck on their return toward home. Passing 120 miles north of Bermuda, and cruising a little while toward the Virginia capes, they reëntered Boston on Dec. 31st, having made 9 prizes, most of them of little value.

When four days out, on Oct. 12th, Commodore Decatur had separated from the rest of Rodgers' squadron and cruised east; on the 25th, in lat. 29° N., and long. 29° 30′ W., while going close-hauled on the port tack, with the wind fresh from the S.S.E., a sail was descried on the weather beam, about 12 miles distant.[3] This was the British 38-gun frigate *Macedonian,* Captain John Surnam Carden. She was not, like the *Guerrière,* an old ship captured from the French, but newly built of oak, and larger than any American 18-pounder frigate; she was reputed (very wrongfully) to be a "crack ship." According to Lieut. David Hope, "the

---

[1] Letter of Commodore Rodgers, Jan. 1, 1813.
[2] Letter of Capt. Arthur Sinclair, Jan. 4, 1813.
[3] Official letter of Commodore Decatur, Oct. 30, 1812.

state of discipline on board was excellent; in no British ship was more attention paid to gunnery. Before this cruise the ship had been engaged almost every day with the enemy; and in time of peace the crew were constantly exercised at the great guns."[1] How they could have practised so much and learned so little is certainly marvellous.

The *Macedonian* set her foretop-mast and top-gallant studding sails and bore away in chase,[2] edging down with the wind a little aft the starboard beam. Her first lieutenant wished to continue on this course and pass down ahead of the *United States*,[3] but Captain Carden's over-anxiety to keep the weather-gage lost him this opportunity of closing.[4] Accordingly he hauled by the wind and passed way to windward of the American. As Commodore Decatur got within range, he eased off and fired a broadside, most of which fell short[5]; he then kept his luff, and, the next time he fired, his long 24's told heavily, while he received very little injury himself.[6] The fire from his main-deck (for he did not use his carronades at all for the first half hour)[7] was so very rapid that it seemed as if the ship was on fire; his broadsides were delivered with almost twice the rapidity of those of the Englishman.[8] The latter soon found he could not play at long bowls with any chance of success; and, having already erred either from timidity or bad judgment, Captain Carden decided to add rashness to the catalogue of his virtues. Accordingly he bore up, and came down end on toward his adversary, with the wind on his port quarter. The *States* now (10.15) laid her main-topsail aback and made heavy play with her long guns, and, as her adversary came nearer, with her carronades also. The British ship would reply with her starboard guns, hauling up to do so; as she came down, the American would ease off, run a little way and again come to, keeping up a terrific fire. As the *Macedonian* bore down to close, the chocks of all her forecastle guns (which were mounted on the outside) were cut away[9]; her fire caused some damage to the American's rigging, but hardly touched her hull, while she herself suffered so heavily both alow and aloft that she gradually dropped to leeward, while the American fore-reached on her. Finding herself ahead and to windward, the *States* tacked and ranged up under her adversary's lee, when the latter struck her colors at 11.15, just an hour and a half after the beginning of the action.[10]

The *United States* had suffered surprisingly little; what damage had been done was aloft. Her mizzen top-gallant mast was cut away, some of the spars were wounded, and the rigging a good deal cut; the hull was only struck two or

[1] Marshall's "Naval Biography," vol. iv, p. 1018.
[2] Capt. Carden to Mr. Croker, Oct. 28, 1812.
[3] James, vi, 166.
[4] Sentence of Court-martial held on the *San Domingo*, 74, at the Bermudas, May 27, 1812.
[5] Marshall, iv, 1080.
[6] Cooper, ii, 178.
[7] Letter of Commodore Decatur.
[8] James, vi, 169.
[9] Letter of Captain Carden.
[10] Letter of Commodore Decatur.

three times. The ships were never close enough to be within fair range of grape and musketry,[1] and the wounds were mostly inflicted by round shot and were thus apt to be fatal. Hence the loss of the Americans amounted to Lieutenant John Messer Funk (5th of the ship) and six seamen killed or mortally wounded, and only five severely and slightly wounded.

The *Macedonian,* on the other hand, had received over a hundred shot in her hull, several between wind and water; her mizzen-mast had gone by the board; her fore- and maintop-masts had been shot away by the caps, and her main-yard in the slings; almost all her rigging was cut away (only the fore-sail being left); on the engaged side all of her carronades but two, and two of her main-deck guns, were dismounted. Of her crew 43 were killed and mortally wounded, and 61 (including her first and third lieutenants) severely and slightly wounded.[2] Among her crew were eight Americans (as shown by her muster-roll); these asked permission to go below before the battle, but it was refused by Captain Carden, and three were killed during the action. James says that they *were* allowed to go below, but this is untrue; for if they had, the three would not have been slain. The others testified that they had been forced to fight, and they afterward entered the American service—the only ones of the *Macedonian's* crew who did, or who were asked to.

The *Macedonian* had her full complement of 301 men; the *States* had, by her muster-roll of October 20th, 428 officers, petty officers, seamen, and boys, and 50 officers and privates of marines, a total of 478 (instead of 509 as Marshall in his "Naval Biography" makes it).

COMPARATIVE FORCE

|  | SIZE. | BROADSIDE GUNS. | WEIGHT METAL. | MEN. | LOSS. |
|---|---|---|---|---|---|
| *United States* | 1576 | 27 | 786 | 478 | 12 |
| *Macedonian* | 1325 | 25 | 547 | 301 | 104 |

|  | COMPARATIVE FORCE. | COMPARATIVE LOSS INFLICTED. |
|---|---|---|
| *States* | 100 | 100 |
| *Macedonian* | 66 | 11 |

That is, the relative force being about as three is to two,[3] the damage done was as nine to one!

---

[1] Letter of Commodore Decatur.

[2] Letter of Captain Carden.

[3] I have considered the *United States* as mounting her full allowance of 54 guns; but it is possible that she had no more than 49. In Decatur's letter of challenge of Jan. 17, 1814 (which challenge, by the way, was a most blustering affair, reflecting credit neither on Decatur, nor his opponent, Captain Hope, nor on any one else, excepting Captain Stackpole of H.M.S. *Statira*), she is said to have had that number; her broadside would then be 15 long 24's below, 1 long 24, 1 12-pound, and 8 42-pound carronades above. Her *real* broadside weight of metal would thus be about 680 lbs., and she would be superior to the *Macedonian* in the proportion of 5 to 4. But it is possible that Decatur had landed some of his guns in 1813, as James asserts; and though I am not at all sure of this, I have thought it best to be on the safe side in describing his force.

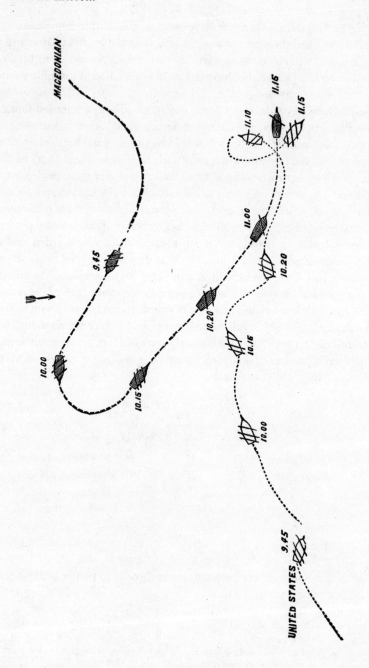

Of course, it would have been almost impossible for the *Macedonian* to conquer with one third less force; but the disparity was by no means sufficient to account for the ninefold greater loss suffered, and the ease and impunity with which the victory was won. The British sailors fought with their accustomed courage, but their gunnery was exceedingly poor; and it must be remembered that though the ship was bravely fought, still the defence was by no means so desparate as that made by the *Essex* or even the *Chesapeake*, as witnessed by their respective losses. The *Macedonian*, moreover, was surrendered when she had suffered less damage than either the *Guerrière* or *Java*. The chief cause of her loss lay in the fact that Captain Carden was a poor commander. The gunnery of the *Java*, *Guerrière*, and *Macedonian* was equally bad; but while Captain Lambert proved himself to be as able as he was gallant, and Captain Dacres did nearly as well, Captain Carden, on the other hand, was first too timid, and then too rash, and showed bad judgment at all times. By continuing his original course he could have closed at once; but he lost his chance by over-anxiety to keep the weather-gage, and was censured by the court-martial accordingly. Then he tried to remedy one error by another, and made a foolishly rash approach. A very able and fair-minded English writer says of this action: "As a display of courage the character of the service was nobly upheld, but we would be deceiving ourselves were we to admit that the comparative expertness of the crews in gunnery was equally satisfactory. Now, taking the difference of effect as given by Captain Carden, we must draw this conclusion—that the comparative loss in killed and wounded (104 to 12), together with the dreadful account he gives of the condition of his own ship, while he admits that the enemy's vessel was in comparatively good order, must have arisen from inferiority in gunnery as well as in force."[1]

On the other hand, the American crew, even according to James, were as fine a set of men as ever were seen on shipboard. Though not one fourth were British by birth, yet many of them had served on board British ships of war, in some cases voluntarily, but much more often because they were impressed. They had been trained at the guns with the greatest care by Lieutenant Allen. And finally Commodore Decatur handled his ship with absolute faultlessness. To sum up: a brave and skilful crew, ably commanded, was matched against an equally brave but unskilful one, with an incompetent leader; and this accounts for the disparity of loss being so much greater than the disparity in force.

At the outset of this battle the position of the parties was just the reverse of that in the case of the *Constitution* and *Guerrière*; the Englishman had the advantage of the wind, but he used it in a very different manner from that in which Captain Hull had done. The latter at once ran down to close, but manœuvred so cautiously that no damage could be done him till he was within pistol shot. Captain Carden did not try to close till after fatal indecision, and then made the attempt so heedlessly that he was cut to pieces before he got to close quarters.

[1] Lord Howard Douglass, "Naval Gunnery," p. 525.

Commodore Decatur, also, manœuvred more skilfully than Captain Dacres, although the difference was less marked between these two. The combat was a plain cannonade; the *States* derived no advantage from the superior number of her men, for they were not needed. The marines in particular had nothing whatever to do, while they had been of the greatest service against the *Guerrière*. The advantage was simply in metal, as 10 is to 7. Lord Howard Douglass' criticisms on these actions seem to me only applicable in part. He says (p. 524): "The Americans would neither approach nor permit us to join in close battle until they had gained some extra-ordinary advantage from the superior faculties of their long guns in distant cannonade, and from the intrepid, uncircumspect, and often very exposed approach of assailants who had long been accustomed to contemn all manœuvring. Our vessels were crippled in distant cannonade from encountering rashly the serious disadvantage of making direct attacks; the uncircumspect gallantry of our commanders led our ships unguardedly into the snares which wary caution had spread."

These criticisms are very just as regards the *Macedonian,* and I fully agree with them (possibly reserving the right to doubt Captain Carden's gallantry, though readily admitting his uncircumspection). But the case of the *Guerrière* differed widely. There the American ship made the attack, while the British at first avoided close combat; and, so far from trying to cripple her adversary by a distant cannonade, the *Constitution* hardly fired a dozen times until within pistol shot. This last point is worth mentioning, because in a work on "Heavy Ordnance," by Captain T. F. Simmons, R. A. (London, 1837), it is stated that the *Guerrière* received her injuries *before* the closing, mentioning especially the "thirty shot below the water-line"; whereas, by the official accounts of both commanders, the reverse was the case. Captain Hull, in his letter, and Lieutenant Morris (in his autobiography), say they only fired a few guns before closing; and Captain Dacres, in his letter, and Captain Brenton, in his "History," say that not much injury was received by the *Guerrière* until about the time the mizzen-mast fell, which was three or four minutes after close action began.

Lieutenant Allen was put aboard the *Macedonian* as prize-master; he secured the fore- and main-masts and rigged a jury mizzen-mast, converting the vessel into a bark. Commodore Decatur discontinued his cruise to convoy his prize back to America; they reached New London Dec. 4th. Had it not been for the necessity of convoying the *Macedonian,* the *States* would have continued her cruise, for the damage she suffered was of the most trifling character.

Captain Carden stated (in Marshall's "Naval Biography") that the *States* measured 1,670 tons, was manned by 509 men, suffered so from shot under water that she had to be pumped out every watch, and that two eighteen-pound shot passed in a horizontal line through her main-masts; all of which statements were highly creditable to the vividness of his imagination. The *States* measured but 1,576 tons (and by English measurement very much less), had 478 men aboard, had not been touched by a shot under water-line, and her lower masts were unwounded. James states that most of her crew were British, which assertion I have already discussed; and that she had but one boy aboard, and that he was seventeen years old,—in which case 29 others, some of whom (as we learn from the "Life of Decatur") were only twelve, must have grown with truly startling rapidity during the hour and a half that the combat lasted.

During the twenty years preceding 1812 there had been almost incessant warfare on the ocean, and although there had been innumerable single conflicts between French and English frigates, there had been but one case in which the French frigate, single-handed, was victorious. This was in the year 1805 when the *Milan* captured the *Cleopatra*. According to Troude, the former threw at a broadside 574 pounds (actual), the latter but 334; and the former lost 35 men out of her crew of 350, the latter 58 out of 200. Or, the forces being as 100 to 58, the loss inflicted was as 100 to 60; while the *States'* force compared to the *Macedonian's* being as 100 to 66, the loss she inflicted was as 100 to 11.

British ships, moreover, had often conquered against odds as great; as, for instance, when the *Sea Horse* captured the great Turkish frigate *Badere-Zaffer;* when the *Astrea* captured the French frigate *Gloire,* which threw at a broadside 286 pounds of shot, while she threw but 174; and when, most glorious of all, Lord Dundonald, in the gallant little *Speedy,* actually captured the Spanish xebec *Gamo,* of over five times her own force! Similarly, the corvette *Comus* captured the Danish frigate *Fredrickscoarn,* the brig *Onyx* captured the Dutch sloop *Manly,* the little cutter *Thorn* captured the French *Courier-National,* and the *Pasley* the Spanish *Virgin;* while there had been many instances of drawn battles between English 12-pound frigates and French or Spanish 18-pounders.

Captain Hull having resigned the command of the *Constitution,* she was given to Captain Bainbridge, of the *Constellation,* who was also entrusted with the command of the *Essex* and *Hornet.* The latter ship was in the port of Boston with the *Constitution,* under the command of Captain Lawrence. The *Essex* was in the Delaware, and accordingly orders were sent to Captain Porter to rendezvous at the Island of San Jago; if that failed several other places were appointed, and if, after a certain time, he did not fall in with his commodore he was to act at his own discretion.

On October 26th the *Constitution* and *Hornet* sailed, touched at the different rendezvous, and on December 13th arrived off San Salvador, where Captain Lawrence found the *Bonne Citoyenne,* 18, Captain Pitt Barnaby Greene. The *Bonne Citoyenne* was armed with 18 32-pound carronades and 2 long nines, and her crew of 150 men was exactly equal in number to that of the *Hornet;* the latter's short weight in metal made her antagonist superior to her in about the same proportion that she herself was subsequently superior to the *Penguin,* or, in other words, the ships were practically equal. Captain Lawrence now challenged Captain Greene to single fight, giving the usual pledges that the *Constitution* should not interfere. The challenge was not accepted for a variety of reasons; among others the *Bonne Citoyenne* was carrying home half a million pounds in specie.[1] Leaving the *Hornet* to blockade her, Commodore Bainbridge ran off to the southward, keeping the land in view.

At 9 A.M., Dec. 29, 1812, while the *Constitution* was running along the coast of Brazil, about thirty miles off shore in latitude 13° 6′ S., and longitude 31° W., two strange sail were made,[2] inshore and to windward. These were H.B.M. frigate *Java*, Captain Lambert, forty-eight days out of Spithead, England, with the captured ship *William* in company. Directing the latter to make for San Salvador, the *Java* bore down in chase of the *Constitution*.[3] The wind was blowing light from the N.N.E., and there was very little sea on. At 10 the *Java* made the private signals, English, Spanish, and Portuguese in succession, none being answered; meanwhile the *Constitution* was standing up toward the *Java* on the starboard tack; a little after 11 she hoisted her private signal, and then, being satisfied that the strange sail was an enemy, she wore and stood off toward the S.E., to draw her antagonist away from the land,[4] which was plainly visible. The *Java* hauled up, and made sail in a parallel course, the *Constitution* bearing about three points on her lee bow. The *Java* gained rapidly, being much the swifter.

At 1.30 the *Constitution* luffed up, shortened her canvas to top-sails, top-gallant sails, jib, and spanker, and ran easily off on the port tack, heading toward the southeast; she carried her commodore's pendant at the main, national ensigns at the mizzen-peak and main top-gallant mast-head, and a Jack at the fore. The *Java* also had taken in the main-sail and royals, and came down in a lasking course on her adversary's weather-quarter,[5] hoisting her ensign at the mizzen-peak, a union Jack at the mizzen top-gallant mast-head, and another lashed to the main-rigging. At 2 P.M., the *Constitution* fired a shot ahead of her, following it quickly by a broadside,[6] and the two ships began at long bowls, the English firing the lee or starboard battery while the Americans replied with their port guns. The cannonade was very spirited on both sides, the ships suffering about equally.

---

[1] Brenton and James both deny that Captain Greene was blockaded by the *Hornet*, and claim that he feared the *Constitution*. James says (p. 275) that the occurrence was one which "the characteristic cunning of Americans turned greatly to their advantage"; and adds that Lawrence only sent the challenge because "it could not be accepted," and so he would "suffer no personal risk." He states that the reason it was sent, as well as the reason that it was refused, was because the *Constitution* was going to remain in the offing and capture the British ship if she proved conqueror. It is somewhat surprising that even James should have had the temerity to advance such arguments. According to his own account (p. 277) the *Constitution* left for Boston on Jan. 6th, and the *Hornet* remained blockading the *Bonne Citoyenne* till the 24th, when the *Montagu*, 74, arrived. During these eighteen days there could have been no possible chance of the *Constitution* or any other ship interfering, and it is ridiculous to suppose that any such fear kept Captain Greene from sailing out to attack his foe. No doubt Captain Greene's course was perfectly justifiable, but it is curious that with all the assertions made by James as to the cowardice of the Americans, this is the only instance throughout the war in which a ship of either party declined a contest with an antagonist of equal force (the cases of Commodore Rodgers and Sir George Collier being evidently due simply to an overestimate of the opposing ships).

[2] Official letter of Commodore Bainbridge, Jan. 3, 1813.

[3] Official letter of Lieutenant Chads, Dec. 31, 1812.

[4] Log of the *Constitution*.

[5] Lieutenant Chads' Address to the Court-martial, April 23, 1813.

[6] Commodore Bainbridge's letter.

The first broadside of the *Java* was very destructive, killing and wounding several of the *Constitution*'s crew. The *Java* kept edging down, and the action continued, with grape and musketry in addition; the swifter British ship soon forereached and kept away, intending to wear across her slower antagonist's bow and rake her; but the latter wore in the smoke, and the two combatants ran off to the westward, the Englishman still a-weather and steering freer than the *Constitution,* which had luffed to close.[1] The action went on at pistol-shot distance. In a few minutes, however, the *Java* again forged ahead, out of the weight of her adversary's fire, and then kept off, as before, to cross her bows; and, as before, the *Constitution* avoided this by wearing, both ships again coming round with their heads to the east, the American still to leeward. The *Java* kept the weather-gage tenaciously, forereaching a little, and whenever the *Constitution* luffed up to close,[2] the former tried to rake her. But her gunnery was now poor, little damage being done by it; most of the loss the Americans suffered was early in the action. By setting her foresail and main-sail the *Constitution* got up close on the enemy's lee beam, her fire being very heavy and carrying away the end of the *Java*'s bowsprit and her jib-boom.[3] The *Constitution* forged ahead and repeated her former manœuvre, wearing in the smoke. The *Java* at once hove in stays, but owing to the loss of head-sail fell off very slowly, and the American frigate poured a heavy raking broadside into her stern, at about two cables' length distance. The *Java* replied with her port guns as she fell off.[4] Both vessels then bore up and ran off free, with the wind on the port quarter; the *Java* being abreast and to windward of her antagonist, both with their heads a little east of south. The ships were less than a cable's length apart, and the *Constitution* inflicted great damage while suffering very little herself. The British lost many men by the musketry of the American topmen, and suffered still more from the round and grape, especially on the forecastle,[5] many marked instances of valor being shown on both sides. The *Java*'s masts were wounded and her rigging cut to pieces, and Captain Lambert then ordered her to be laid aboard the enemy, who was on her lee beam. The helm was put a-weather, and the *Java* came down for the *Constitution*'s main-chains. The boarders and marines gathered in the gangways and on the forecastle, the boatswain having been ordered to cheer them up with his pipe that they might make a clean spring.[6] The Americans, however, raked the British with terrible effect, cutting off their main top-mast above the cap, and their foremast near the cat harpings.[7] The stump of the *Java*'s bowsprit got caught in the *Constitution*'s mizzen-rigging, and before it got clear the British suffered still more.

[1] Log of the *Constitution.*

[2] Log of the *Constitution.*

[3] Lieutenant Chads' letter.

[4] Lieutenant Chads' letter.

[5] Testimony of Christopher Speedy, in minutes of the Court-martial on board H.M.S. *Gladiator,* at Portsmouth, April 23, 1813.

[6] Testimony of James Humble, in *do., do.*

[7] Log of *Constitution.*

Finally the ships separated, the *Java's* bowsprit passing over the taffrail of the *Constitution;* the latter at once kept away to avoid being raked. The ships again got nearly abreast, but the *Constitution,* in her turn, forereached; whereupon Commodore Bainbridge wore, passed his antagonist, luffed up under his quarter, raked him with the starboard guns, then wore, and recommenced the action with his port broadside at about 3.10. Again the vessels were abreast, and the action went on as furiously as ever. The wreck of the top hamper on the *Java* lay over her starboard side, so that every discharge of her guns set her on fire,[1] and in a few minutes her able and gallant commander was mortally wounded by a ball fired by one of the American main-topmen.[2] The command then devolved on the first lieutenant, Chads, himself painfully wounded. The slaughter had been terrible, yet the British fought on with stubborn resolution, cheering lustily. But success was now hopeless, for nothing could stand against the cool precision of the Yankee fire. The stump of the *Java's* foremast was carried away by a double-headed shot, the mizzen-mast fell, the gaff and spanker boom were shot away, also the main-yard, and finally the ensign was cut down by a shot, and all her guns absolutely silenced; when at 4.05 the *Constitution,* thinking her adversary had struck,[3] ceased firing, hauled aboard her tacks, and passed across her adversary's bows to windward, with her top-sails, jib, and spanker set. A few minutes afterward the *Java's* main-mast fell, leaving her a sheer hulk. The *Constitution* assumed a weatherly position, and spent an hour in repairing damages and securing her masts; then she wore and stood toward her enemy, whose flag was again flying, but only for bravado, for as soon as the *Constitution* stood across her forefoot she struck. At 5.25 she was taken possession of by Lieutenant Parker, 1st of the *Constitution,* in one of the latter's only two remaining boats.

The American ship had suffered comparatively little. But a few round shot had struck her hull, one of which carried away the wheel; one 18-pounder went through the mizzen-mast; the foremast, main-top-mast, and a few other spars were slightly wounded, and the running rigging and shrouds were a good deal cut; but in an hour she was again in good fighting trim. Her loss amounted to 8 seamen and 1 marine killed; the 5th lieutenant, John C. Aylwin, and 2 seamen, mortally, Commodore Bainbridge and 12 seamen, severely, and 7 seamen and 2 marines, slightly wounded; in all 12 killed and mortally wounded, and 22 wounded severely and slightly.[4]

"The *Java* sustained unequalled injuries beyond the *Constitution,*" says the British account.[5] These have already been given in detail; she was a riddled and entirely dismasted hulk. Her loss (for discussion of which see farther on) was 48 killed (including Captain Henry Lambert, who died soon after the close of

---

[1] Lieut. Chads' Address.
[2] Surgeon J. C. Jones' Report.
[3] Log of the *Constitution* (as given in Bainbridge's letter).
[4] Report of Surgeon Amos A. Evans.
[5] "Naval Chronicle," xxix, 452.

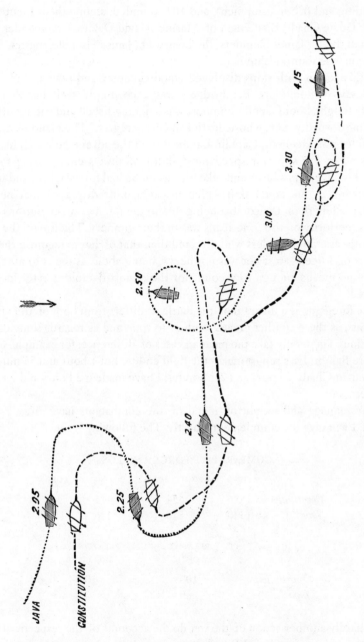

This differs somewhat from the English diagram; the American officers distinctly assert that the *Java* kept the weather-gage in every position.

the action, and five midshipmen), and 102 wounded, among them Lieutenant Henry Ducie Chads, Lieutenant of Marines David Davies, Commander John Marshall, Lieut. James Saunders, the boatswain, James Humble, master, Batty Robinson, and four midshipmen.

In this action both ships displayed equal gallantry and seamanship. "The *Java*," says Commodore Bainbridge, "was exceedingly well handled and bravely fought. Poor Captain Lambert was a distinguished and gallant officer, and a most worthy man, whose death I sincerely regret." The manœuvring on both sides was excellent; Captain Lambert used the advantage which his ship possessed in her superior speed most skilfully, always endeavoring to run across his adversary's bows and rake him when he had forereached, and it was only owing to the equal skill which his antagonist displayed that he was foiled, the length of the combat being due to the number of evolutions. The great superiority of the Americans was in their gunnery. The fire of the *Java* was both less rapid and less well directed than that of her antagonist; the difference of force against her was not heavy, being about as ten is to nine, and was by no means enough to account for the almost fivefold greater loss she suffered.

The foregoing is a diagram of the battle. It differs from both of the official accounts, as these conflict greatly both as to time and as regards some of the evolutions. I generally take the mean in cases of difference; for example, Commodore Bainbridge's report makes the fight endure but 1 hour and 55 minutes, Lieutenant Chads' 2 hours and 25 minutes; I have made it 2 hours and 10 minutes, etc., etc.

The tonnage and weight of metal of the combatants have already been stated; I will give the complements shortly. The following is the

COMPARATIVE FORCE AND LOSS

| | TONS. | WEIGHT METAL. | NO. MEN. | LOSS. |
|---|---|---|---|---|
| *Constitution* | 1576 | 654 | 475 | 34 |
| *Java* | 1340 | 576 | 426 | 150 |

| | RELATIVE FORCE. | RELATIVE LOSS INFLICTED. |
|---|---|---|
| *Constitution* | 100 | 100 |
| *Java* | 89 | 23 |

In hardly another action of the war do the accounts of the respective forces differ so widely; the official British letter makes their total of men at the beginning of the action 377, of whom Commodore Bainbridge officially reports that he paroled 378! The British state their loss in killed and mortally wounded at 24; Commodore Bainbridge reports that the dead alone amounted to nearly 60! Usually I have taken each commander's account of his own force and loss, and I should do so now if it were not that the British accounts differ among themselves, and whenever they relate to the Americans, are flatly contradicted by the affidavits of the latter's officers. The British first handicap themselves by the statement that the surgeon of the *Constitution* was an Irishman and lately an assistant surgeon in the British navy ("Naval Chronicle," xxix, 452); which draws from Surgeon Amos A. Evans a solemn statement in the Boston *Gazette* that he was born in Maryland and was never in the British navy in his life. Then Surgeon Jones of the *Java*, in his official report, after giving his own killed and mortally wounded at 24, says that the Americans lost in all about 60, and that 4 of their amputations perished under his own eyes; whereupon Surgeon Evans makes the statement (*Niles' Register*, vi, p. 35), backed up by affidavits of his brother officers, that in all he had but five amputations, of whom only one died, and that one, a month after Surgeon Jones had left the ship. To meet the assertions of Lieutenant Chads that he began action with but 377 men, the *Constitution's* officers produced the *Java's* muster-roll, dated Nov. 17th, or five days after she had sailed, which showed 446 persons, of whom 20 had been put on board a prize. The presence of this large number of supernumeraries on board is explained by the fact that the *Java* was carrying out Lieutenant-General Hislop, the newly-appointed Governor of Bombay, and his suite, together with part of the crews for the *Cornwallis*, 74, and gun-sloops *Chameleon* and *Icarus*; she also contained stores for those two ships.

Besides conflicting with the American reports, the British statements contradict one another. The official published report gives but two midshipmen as killed; while one of the volumes of the "Naval Chronicle" (vol. xxix, p. 452) contains a letter from one of the *Java's* lieutenants, in which he states that there were five. Finally, Commodore Bainbridge found on board the *Constitution*, after the prisoners had left, a letter from Lieutenant H. D. Cornick, dated Jan. 1, 1813, and addressed to Lieutenant Peter V. Wood, 22d Regiment, foot, in which he states that 65 of their men were killed. James ("Naval Occurrences") gets around this by stating that it was probably a forgery; but, aside from the improbability of Commodore Bainbridge being a forger, this could not be so, for nothing would have been easier than for the British lieutenant to have denied having written it, which he never did. On the other hand, it would be very likely that in the heat of the action, Commodore Bainbridge and the *Java's* own officers should overestimate the latter's loss.[1]

Taking all these facts into consideration, we find 446 men on board the *Java* by her own muster-list; 378 of these were paroled by Commodore Bainbridge at San Salvador; 24 men were acknowledged by the enemy to be killed or mortally wounded; 20 were absent in a prize, leaving 24 unaccounted for, who were undoubtedly slain.

---

[1] For an account of the shameless corruption then existing in the Naval Administration of Great Britain, see Lord Dundonald's "Autobiography of a Seaman." The letters of the commanders were often garbled, as is mentioned by Brenton. Among numerous cases that he gives, may be mentioned the cutting out of the *Chevrette*, where he distinctly says, "our loss was much greater than was ever acknowledged." (Vol. i, p. 505, edition of 1837.)

The British loss was thus 48 men killed and mortally wounded, and 102 wounded severely and slightly. The *Java* was better handled and more desperately defended than the *Macedonian* or even the *Guerrière*, and the odds against her were much smaller; so she caused her opponent greater loss, though her gunnery was no better than theirs.

Lieutenant Parker, prize-master of the *Java*, removed all the prisoners and baggage to the *Constitution*, and reported the prize to be in a very disabled state; owing partly to this, but more to the long distance from home and the great danger there was of recapture, Commodore Bainbridge destroyed her on the 31st, and then made sail for San Salvador. "Our gallant enemy," reports Lieutenant Chads, "has treated us most generously"; and Lieutenant-General Hislop presented the Commodore with a very handsome sword as a token of gratitude for the kindness with which he had treated the prisoners.

Partly in consequence of his frigate's injuries, but especially because of her decayed condition, Commodore Bainbridge sailed from San Salvador on Jan. 6, 1813, reaching Boston Feb. 27th, after his four months' cruise. At San Salvador he left the *Hornet* still blockading the *Bonne Citoyenne*.

In order "to see ourselves as others see us," I shall again quote from Admiral Jurien de la Gravière,[1] as his opinions are certainly well worthy of attention both as to these first three battles, and as to the lessons they teach. "When the American Congress declared war on England in 1812," he says, "it seemed as if this unequal conflict would crush her navy in the act of being born; instead, it but fertilized the germ. It is only since that epoch that the United States has taken rank among maritime powers. Some combats of frigates, corvettes, and brigs, insignificant without doubt as regards material results, sufficed to break the charm which protected the standard of St. George, and taught Europe what she could have already learned from some of our combats, if the louder noise of our defeats had not drowned the glory, that the only invincibles on the sea are good seamen and good artillerists.

"The English covered the ocean with their cruisers when this unknown navy, composed of six frigates and a few small craft hitherto hardly numbered, dared to establish its cruisers at the mouth of the Channel, in the very centre of the British power. But already the *Constitution* had captured the *Guerrière* and *Java*, the *United States* had made a prize of the *Macedonian*, the *Wasp* of the *Frolic*, and the *Hornet* of the *Peacock*. The honor of the new flag was established. England, humiliated, tried to attribute her multiplied reverses to the unusual size of the vessels which Congress had had constructed in 1799, and which did the fighting in 1812. She wished to refuse them the name of frigates, and called them, not without some appearance of reason, disguised line-of-battle ships. Since then all maritime powers have copied these gigantic models, as the result of the war of 1812 obliged England herself to change her naval material; but if they had employed, instead of frigates, cut-down 74's (vaisseaux

---

[1] "Guerres Maritimes," ii, 284 (Paris, 1881).

rasés), it would still be difficult to explain the prodigious success of the Americans. * * *

"In an engagement which terminated in less than half an hour, the English frigate *Guerrière,* completely dismasted, had fifteen men killed, sixty-three wounded, and more than thirty shot below the water-line. She sank twelve hours after the combat. The *Constitution,* on the contrary, had but seven men killed and seven wounded, and did not lose a mast. As soon as she had replaced a few cut ropes and changed a few sails, she was in condition, even by the testimony of the British historian, to take another *Guerrière.* The *United States* took an hour and a half to capture the *Macedonian,* and the same difference made itself felt in the damage suffered by the two ships. The *Macedonian* had her masts shattered, two of her main-deck and all her spar-deck guns disabled; more than a hundred shot had penetrated the hull, and over a third of the crew had suffered by the hostile fire. The American frigate, on the contrary, had to regret but five men killed and seven wounded; her guns had been fired each sixty-six times to the *Macedonian's* thirty-six. The combat of the *Constitution* and the *Java* lasted two hours, and was the most bloody of these three engagements. The *Java* only struck when she had been razed like a sheer hulk; she had twenty-two men killed and one hundred and two wounded.

*　　*　　*

"This war should be studied with unceasing diligence; the pride of two peoples to whom naval affairs are so generally familiar has cleared all the details and laid bare all the episodes, and through the sneers which the victors should have spared, merely out of care for their own glory, at every step can be seen that great truth, that there is only success for those who know how to prepare it.

*　　*　　*

"It belongs to us to judge impartially these marine events, too much exalted perhaps by a national vanity one is tempted to excuse. The Americans showed, in the War of 1812, a great deal of skill and resolution. But if, as they have asserted, the chances had always been perfectly equal between them and their adversaries, if they had only owed their triumphs to the intrepidity of Hull, Decatur, and Bainbridge, there would be for us but little interest in recalling the struggle. We need not seek lessons in courage outside of our own history. On the contrary, what is to be well considered is that the ships of the United States constantly fought with the chances in their favor, and it is on this that the American government should found its true title to glory. * * * The Americans in 1812 had secured to themselves the advantage of a better organization [than the English]."

The fight between the *Constitution* and the *Java* illustrates best the proposition, "that there is only success for those who know how to prepare it." Here the odds in men and metal were only about as 10 to 9 in favor of the victors, and it is safe to say that they might have been reversed without vitally affecting the result. In the fight Lambert handled his ship as skilfully as Bainbridge did his; and the *Java's* men proved by their indomitable courage that they were excellent material. The *Java's* crew was new shipped for the voyage, and had been at sea but six weeks; in the *Constitution*'s first fight her crew had been aboard of her but *five* weeks. So the chances should have been nearly equal, and the difference in fighting capacity that was shown by the enormous disparity in the loss, and still more in the damage inflicted, was due to the fact that the officers of one ship had, and the officers of the other had not, trained their raw crews. The *Constitution*'s men were not "picked," but simply average American sailors, as the *Java*'s were average British sailors. The essential difference was in the training.

During the six weeks the *Java* was at sea her men had fired but six broadsides, of blank cartridges; during the first five weeks the *Constitution* cruised, her crew were incessantly practised at firing with blank cartridges and also at a target.[1] The *Java*'s crew had only been exercised occasionally, even in pointing the guns, and when the captain of a gun was killed the effectiveness of the piece was temporarily ruined, and, moreover, the men did not work together. The *Constitution*'s crew were exercised till they worked like machines, and yet with enough individuality to render it impossible to cripple a gun by killing one man. The unpractised British sailors fired at random; the trained Americans took aim. The British marines had not been taught any thing approximating to skirmishing or sharp-shooting; the Americans had. The British sailors had not even been trained enough in the ordinary duties of seamen; while the Americans in five weeks had been rendered almost perfect. The former were at a loss what to do in an emergency at all out of their own line of work; they were helpless when the wreck fell over their guns, when the Americans would have cut it away in a jiffy. As we learn from Commodore Morris' "Autobiography," each Yankee sailor could, at need, do a little carpentering or sail-mending, and so was more self-reliant. The crew had been trained to act as if guided by one mind, yet each man retained his own individuality. The petty officers were better paid than in Great Britain, and so were of a better class of men, thoroughly self-respecting; the Americans soon got their subordinates in order, while the British did not. To sum up: one ship's crew had been trained practically and thoroughly, while the other crew was not much better off than the day it sailed; and, as far as it goes, this is a good test of the efficiency of the two navies.

———

The U.S. brig *Vixen*, 12, Lieutenant George U. Read, had been cruising off the southern coast; on Nov. 22d she fell in with the *Southampton*, 32, Captain Sir James Lucas Yeo, and was captured after a short but severe trial of speed. Both vessels were wrecked soon afterward.

The *Essex*, 32, Captain David Porter, left the Delaware on Oct. 28th, two days after Commodore Bainbridge had left Boston. She expected to make a very long cruise and so carried with her an unusual quantity of stores and sixty more men than ordinarily, so that her muster-roll contained 319 names. Being deep in the water she reached San Iago after Bainbridge had left. Nothing was

---

[1] In looking through the logs of the *Constitution, Hornet,* etc., we continually find such entries as "beat to quarters, exercised the men at the great guns," "exercised with musketry," "exercised the boarders," "exercised the great guns, blank cartridges, and afterward firing at mark."

met with until after the *Essex* had crossed the equator in latitude 30° W. on Dec. 11th. On the afternoon of the next day a sail was made out to windward, and chased. At nine in the evening it was overtaken, and struck after receiving a volley of musketry which killed one man. The prize proved to be the British packet *Nocton,* of 10 guns and 31 men, with $55,000 in specie aboard. The latter was taken out, and the *Nocton* sent home with Lieutenant Finch and a prize crew of 17 men, but was recaptured by a British frigate.

The next appointed rendezvous was the Island of Fernando de Noronha, where Captain Porter found a letter from Commodore Bainbridge, informing him that the other vessels were off Cape Frio. Thither cruised Porter, but his compatriots had left. On the 29th he captured an English merchant vessel; and he was still cruising when the year closed.

—

The year 1812, on the ocean, ended as gloriously as it had begun. In four victorious fights the disparity in loss had been so great as to sink the disparity of force into insignificance. Our successes had been unaccompanied by any important reverse. Nor was it alone by the victories, but by the cruises, that the year was noteworthy. The Yankee men-of-war sailed almost in sight of the British coast and right in the tract of the merchant fleets and their armed protectors. Our vessels had shown themselves immensely superior to their foes.

The reason of these striking and unexpected successes was that our navy in 1812 was the exact reverse of what our navy is now, in 1882. I am not alluding to the personnel, which still remains excellent; but, whereas we now have a large number of worthless vessels, standing very low down in their respective classes, we then possessed a few vessels, each unsurpassed by any foreign ship of her class. To bring up our navy to the condition in which it stood in 1812 it would not be *necessary* (although in reality both very wise and in the end very economical) to spend any more money than at present; only instead of using it to patch up a hundred antiquated hulks, it should be employed in building half a dozen ships on the most effective model. If in 1812 our ships had borne the same relation to the British ships that they do now, not all the courage and skill of our sailors would have won us a single success. As it was, we could only cope with the lower rates, and had no vessels to oppose to the great "liners"; but to-day there is hardly any foreign ship, no matter how low its rate, that is not superior to the corresponding American ones. It is too much to hope that our political shortsightedness will ever enable us to have a navy that is first-class in point of size; but there certainly seems no reason why what ships we have should not be of the very best quality. The effect of a victory is two-fold, moral and material. Had we been as roughly handled on water as we were on land during the first year of the war, such a succession of disasters would have had a most demoralizing effect on the nation at large. As it was, our victorious sea-fights, while they did not inflict any material damage upon the colossal sea-might of England, had the most important results in the feelings they produced at home and even abroad. Of course they were magnified absurdly by most of our writers at the time; but they do not need to be magnified, for as they are any American can look back upon them with the keenest national pride. For a hundred and thirty years England had had no equal on the sea; and now she suddenly found one in the untried navy of an almost unknown power.

### BRITISH VESSELS CAPTURED OR DESTROYED IN 1812

| NAME. | GUNS. | TONNAGE. | REMARKS. |
|---|---|---|---|
| *Guerrière* | 49 | 1,340 | |
| *Macedonian* | 49 | 1,325 | |
| *Java* | 49 | 1,340 | |
| *Frolic* | 19 | 477 | Recaptured. |
| *Alert* | 20 | 325 | |
| | 186 | 4,807 | |
| | 19 | 477 | Deducting *Frolic.* |
| | 167 | 4,330 | |

### AMERICAN VESSELS CAPTURED OR DESTROYED

| NAME. | GUNS. | TONNAGE. |
|---|---|---|
| *Wasp* | 18 | 450 |
| *Nautilus* | 14 | 185 |
| *Vixen* | 14 | 185 |
| | 46 | 820 |

### VESSELS BUILT IN 1812

| NAME. | RIG. | GUNS. | TONNAGE. | WHERE BUILT. | COST. |
|---|---|---|---|---|---|
| *Nonsuch* | Schooner | 14 | 148 | Charleston | $15,000 |
| *Carolina* | Schooner | 14 | 230 | " | 8,743 |
| *Louisiana* | Ship | 16 | 341 | New Orleans | 15,500 |

### PRIZES MADE[1]

| SHIP. | NO. OF PRIZES. |
|---|---|
| *President* | 7 |
| *United States* | 2 |
| *Constitution* | 9 |
| *Congress* | 2 |
| *Chesapeake* | 1 |
| *Essex* | 11 |
| *Wasp* | 2 |
| *Hornet* | 1 |
| *Argus* | 6 |
| Small Craft | 5 |
| | 46 |

[1] These can only be approximately given; the records are often incomplete or contradictory, especially as regards the small craft. Most accounts do not give by any means the full number.

# IV

# 1812

# ON THE LAKES

PRELIMINARY · The combatants starting nearly on an equality · Difficulties of creating a naval force · Difficulty of comparing the force of the rival squadrons · Meagreness of the published accounts · Unreliability of James · ONTARIO · Extraordinary nature of the American squadron · Canadian squadron forming only a kind of water militia · Sackett's Harbor feebly attacked by Commodore Earle · Commodore Chauncy bombards York · ERIE · Lieutenant Elliott captures the *Detroit* and *Caledonia* · Unsuccessful expedition of Lieutenant Angus.

At the time we are treating of, the State of Maine was so sparsely settled, and covered with such a dense growth of forest, that it was practically impossible for either of the contending parties to advance an army through its territory. A continuation of the same wooded and mountainous district protected the northern parts of Vermont and New Hampshire, while in New York the Adirondack region was an impenetrable wilderness. It thus came about that the northern boundary was formed, for military purposes, by Lake Huron, Lake Erie, the Niagara, Lake Ontario, the St. Lawrence, and, after an interval, by Lake Champlain. The road into the States by the latter ran close along shore, and without a naval force the invader would be wholly unable to protect his flanks, and would probably have his communications cut. This lake, however, was almost wholly within the United States, and did not become of importance till toward the end of the war. Upon it were two American gun-boats, regularly officered and manned, and for such smooth water sufficiently effective vessels.

What was at that time the western part of the northern frontier became the main theatre of military operations, and as it presented largely a water front, a naval force was an indispensable adjunct, the command of the lakes being of the utmost importance. As these lakes were fitted for the manœuvring of ships of the largest size, the operations upon them were of the same nature as those on the ocean, and properly belong to naval and not to military history. But while on the ocean America started with too few ships to enable her really to do any serious harm to her antagonist, on the inland waters the two sides began very nearly on an equality. The chief regular forces either belligerent possessed were on Lake Ontario. Here the United States had a man-of-war brig, the *Oneida*, of 240 tons, carrying 16 24-pound carronades, manned by experienced seamen, and commanded by Lieutenant M. T. Woolsey. Great Britain possessed the *Royal George*, 22, *Prince Regent*, 16, *Earl of Moira*, 14, *Gloucester*, 10, *Seneca*, 8, and *Simco*, 8, all under the command of a Commodore Earle; but though this force was so much the more powerful it was very inefficient, not being considered as belonging to the regular navy, the sailors being undisciplined, and the officers totally without experience, never having been really trained in the British service. From these causes it resulted that the struggle on the lakes was to be a work as much of creating as of using a navy. On the seaboard success came to those who made best use of the ships that had already been built; on the lakes the real contest lay in the building. And building an inland navy was no easy task. The country around the lakes, especially on the south side, was still very sparsely settled, and all the American naval supplies had to be brought from the seaboard cities through the valley of the Mohawk. There was no canal or other means of communication, except very poor roads intermittently relieved by transportation on the Mohawk and on Oneida Lake, when they were navigable. Supplies were thus brought up at an enormous cost, with tedious delays and great difficulty; and bad weather put a stop to all travel. Very little indeed, beyond timber, could be procured at the stations on the lakes. Still a few scattered villages and small towns had grown up on the shores, whose inhabitants were largely engaged in the carrying trade. The vessels used for the purpose were generally small sloops or schooners, swift and fairly good sailers, but very shallow and not fitted for rough weather. The frontiersmen themselves, whether Canadian or American, were bold, hardy seamen, and when properly trained and led made excellent man-of-war's men; but on the American side they were too few in number, and too untrained to be made use of, and the seamen had to come from the coast. But the Canadian shores had been settled longer, the inhabitants were more numerous, and by means of the St. Lawrence the country was easy of access to Great Britain; so that the seat of war, as regards getting naval supplies, and even men, was nearer to Great Britain than to us. Our enemies also possessed in addition to the squadron on Lake Ontario another on Lake Erie, consisting of the *Queen Charlotte*, 17, *Lady Prevost*, 13, *Hunter*, 10, *Caledonia*, 2, *Little Belt*, 2, and *Chippeway*, 2. These two squadrons furnished training schools for some five hundred Canadian seamen, whom a short course of discipline under experienced officers sufficed to render as good men as their British friends or American foes. Very few British seamen ever reached Lake Erie (according to James, not over fifty); but on Lake Ontario, and afterward on Lake Champlain, they formed the bulk of the crews, "picked seamen, sent out by government expressly for service on the Canada lakes."[1] As the contrary has sometimes been asserted it may be as well to mention that Admiral Codrington states that no want of seamen contributed to the

---

[1] James, vi, 353.

British disasters on the lakes, as their sea-ships at Quebec had men drafted from them for that service till their crews were utterly depleted.[1] I am bound to state that while I think that on the ocean our sailors showed themselves superior to their opponents, especially in gun practice, on the lakes the men of the rival fleets were as evenly matched, in skill and courage, as could well be. The difference, when there was any, appeared in the officers, and, above all, in the builders; which was the more creditable to us, as in the beginning we were handicapped by the fact that the British already had a considerable number of war vessels, while we had but one.

The Falls of Niagara interrupt navigation between Erie and Ontario; so there were three independent centres of naval operations on the northern frontier. The first was on Lake Champlain, where only the Americans possessed any force, and, singularly enough, this was the only place where the British showed more enterprise in ship-building than we did. Next came Lake Ontario, where both sides made their greatest efforts, but where the result was indecisive, though the balance of success was slightly inclined toward us. Our naval station was at Sackett's Harbor; that of our foes at Kingston. The third field of operations was Lake Erie and the waters above it. Here both sides showed equal daring and skill in the fighting, and our advantage must be ascribed to the energy and success with which we built and equipped vessels. Originally we had no force at all on these waters, while several vessels were opposed to us. It is a matter of wonder that the British and Canadian governments should have been so supine as to permit their existing force to go badly armed, and so unenterprising as to build but one additional ship, when they could easily have preserved their superiority.

It is very difficult to give a full and fair account of the lake campaigns. The inland navies were created especially for the war, and, after it were allowed to decay, so that the records of the tonnage, armament, and crews are hard to get at. Of course, where everything had to be created, the services could not have the regular character of those on the ocean. The vessels employed were of widely different kinds, and this often renders it almost impossible to correctly estimate the relative force of two opposing squadrons. While the Americans were building their lake navy, they, as make-shifts, made use of some ordinary merchant schooners, which were purchased and fitted up with one or two long, heavy guns each. These gun-vessels had no quarters, and suffered under all the other disadvantages which make a merchant vessel inferior to a regularly constructed man-of-war. The chief trouble was that in a heavy sea they had a strong tendency to capsize, and were so unsteady that the guns could not be aimed when any wind was blowing. Now, if a few of these schooners, mounting long 32's, encountered a couple of man-of-war brigs, armed with carronades, which side was strongest? In smooth water the schooners had the advantage, and in rough weather they were completely at the mercy of the brigs; so that it would be very hard to get at the true worth of such a contest, as

---

[1] Memoirs, i, 322, referring especially to battle of Lake Champlain.

each side would be tolerably sure to insist that the weather was such as to give a great advantage to the other. In all the battles and skirmishes on Champlain, Erie, and Huron, at least there was no room left for doubt as to who were the victors. But on Lake Ontario there was never any decisive struggle, and whenever an encounter occurred, each commodore always claimed that his adversary had "declined the combat" though "much superior in strength." It is, of course, almost impossible to find out which really did decline the combat, for the official letters flatly contradict each other; and it is often almost as difficult to discover where the superiority in force lay, when the fleets differed so widely in character as was the case in 1813. Then Commodore Chauncy's squadron consisted largely of schooners; their long, heavy guns made his total foot up in a very imposing manner, and similar gun-vessels did very good work on Lake Erie; so Commodore Yeo, and more especially Commodore Yeo's admirers, exalted these schooners to the skies, and conveyed the impression that they were most formidable craft, by means of which Chauncy ought to have won great victories. Yet when Yeo captured two of them he refused to let them even cruise with his fleet, and they were sent back to act as coast gun-boats and transports, which certainly would not have been done had they been fitted to render any effectual assistance. Again, one night a squall came on and the two largest schooners went to the bottom, which did not tend to increase the confidence felt in the others. So there can be no doubt that in all but very smooth water the schooners could almost be counted out of the fight. Then the question arises in any given case, was the water smooth? And the testimony is as conflicting as ever.

It is not too easy to reconcile the official letters of the commanders, and it is still harder to get at the truth from either the American or British histories. Cooper is very inexact, and, moreover, paints every thing *couleur de rose,* paying no attention to the British side of the question, and distributing so much praise to everybody that one is at a loss to know where it really belongs. Still, he is very useful, for he lived at the time of the events he narrates, and could get much information about them at first hand, from the actors themselves. James is almost the only British authority on the subject; but he is not nearly as reliable as when dealing with the ocean contests, most of this part of his work being taken up with a succession of acrid soliloquies on the moral defects of the American character. The British records for this extraordinary service on the lakes were not at all carefully kept, and so James is not hampered by the necessity of adhering more or less closely to official documents, but lets his imagination run loose. On the ocean and seaboard his account of the British force can generally be relied upon; but on the lakes his authority is questionable in every thing relating either to friends or foes. This is the more exasperating because it is done wilfully, when, if he had chosen, he could have written an invaluable history; he must often have known the truth when, as a matter of preference, he chose either to suppress or alter it. Thus he ignores all the small "cutting out" expeditions in which the Americans were successful, and where one would like to hear the British side. For example, Captain Yeo captured two schooners, the *Julia* and *Growler,* but Chauncy recaptured both. We have the American account of this recapture in full, but James does not even hint at it, and blandly puts down both vessels in the total "American loss" at the end of his smaller work. Worse still, when the *Growler* again changed hands, he counts it in again, in the total, as if it were an entirely different boat, although he invariably rules out of the American list all recaptured vessels. A more serious perversion of facts are his statements about comparative tonnage. This was at that time measured arbitrarily, the depth of hold being estimated at half the breadth of beam; and the tonnage of our lake vessels was put down exactly as if they were regular ocean cruisers of the same dimensions in length and breadth. But on these inland seas the vessels really did not draw more than half as much water as on the ocean, and the depth would of course be much less. James, in comparing the tonnage, gives that of the Americans as if they were regular ocean ships, but in the case of the British vessels, carefully allows for their shallowness, although professing to treat the two classes in the same way; and thus he makes out a most striking and purely imaginary difference. The best example is furnished by his accounts of the fleets on Lake Erie. The captured vessels were appraised by two captains and the ship-builder, Mr. Henry Eckford; their tonnage being computed precisely as the tonnage of the American vessels. The appraisement was recorded in the Navy Department, and was first made public by Cooper, so that it could not have been done for effect. Thus measured it was found that the tonnage was in round numbers as follows: *Detroit,* 490 tons; *Queen Charlotte,* 400; *Lady Prevost,* 230; *Hunter,* 180; *Little Belt,* 90; *Chippeway,* 70. James makes them measure respectively 305, 280, 120, 74, 54, and 32 tons, but carefully gives the American ships the regular sea tonnage. So also he habitually deducts about 25 per cent. from the real number of men on board the British ships; as regards Lake Erie he contradicts himself so much that he does not need to be exposed from outside sources. But the most glaring and least excusable misstatements are made as to the battle of Lake Champlain, where he gives the American as greatly exceeding the British force. He reaches this conclusion by the most marvellous series of garblings and misstatements. First, he says that the *Confiance* and the *Saratoga* were of nearly equal tonnage. The *Confiance* being captured was placed on our naval lists, where for years she ranked as a 36-gun frigate, while the *Saratoga* ranked among the 24-gun corvettes; and by actual measurement the former was half as large again as the latter. He gives the *Confiance* but 270 men; one of her officers, in a letter published in the *London Naval Chronicle,*[1] gives her over 300; more than that number of dead and prisoners were taken out of her. He misstates the calibre of her guns, and counts out two of them because they were used through the bow-

[1] Vol. xxxii, p. 272. The letter also says that hardly five of her men remained unhurt.

ports; whereas, from the method in which she made her attack, these would have been peculiarly effective. The guns are given accurately by Cooper, on the authority of an officer[1] who was on board the *Confiance* within 15 minutes after the *Linnet* struck, and who was in charge of her for two months.

Then James states that there were but 10 British gallies, while Sir George Prevost's official account, as well as all the American authorities, state the number to be 12. He says that the *Finch* grounded opposite an American battery before the engagement began, while in reality it was an hour afterward, and because she had been disabled by the shot of the American fleet. The gallies were largely manned by Canadians, and James, anxious to put the blame on these rather than the British, says that they acted in the most cowardly way, whereas in reality they caused the Americans more trouble than Downie's smaller sailing vessels did. His account of the armament of these vessels differs widely from the official reports. He gives the *Linnet* and *Chubb* a smaller number of men than the number of prisoners that were actually taken out of them, not including the dead. Even misstating Downie's force in guns, underestimating the number of his men, and leaving out two of his gun-boats, did not content James; and to make the figures show a proper disproportion, he says (vol. vi, p. 504) that he shall exclude the *Finch* from the estimate, because she grounded, and half of the gun-boats, because he does not think they acted bravely. Even were these assertions true, it would be quite as logical for an American writer to put the *Chesapeake*'s crew down as only 200, and say he should exclude the other men from the estimate because they flinched; and to exclude all the guns that were disabled by shot, would be no worse than to exclude the *Finch*. James' manipulation of the figures is a really curious piece of audacity. Naturally, subsequent British historians have followed him without inquiry. James' account of this battle, alone, amply justifies our rejecting his narrative entirely, as far as affairs on the lakes go, whenever it conflicts with any other statement, British or American. Even when it does not conflict, it must be followed with extreme caution, for whenever he goes into figures the only thing certain about them is that they are wrong. He gives no details at all of most of the general actions. Of these, however, we already possess excellent accounts, the best being those in the "Manual of Naval Tactics," by Commander J. H. Ward, U.S.N. (1859), and in Lossing's "Field-Book of the War of 1812," and Cooper's "Naval History." The chief difficulty occurs in connection with matters on Lake Ontario,[2] where I have been obliged to have recourse to a perfect

---

[1] Lieutenant E. A. F. Lavallette.

[2] The accounts of the two commanders on Lake Ontario are as difficult to reconcile as are those of the contending admirals in the battles which the Dutch waged against the English and French during the years 1672–1675. In every one of De Ruyter's last six battles each side regularly claimed the victory, although there can be but little doubt that on the whole the strategical, and probably the tactical, advantage remained with De Ruyter. Every historian ought to feel a sense of the most lively gratitude toward Nelson; in his various encounters he never left any possible room for dispute as to which side had come out first best.

patchwork of authors and even newspapers, for the details, using *Niles' Register* and James as mutual correctives. The armaments and equipments being so irregular I have not, as in other cases, made any allowance for the short weight of the American shot, as here the British may have suffered under a similar disadvantage; and it may be as well to keep in mind that on these inland waters the seamen of the two navies seem to have been as evenly matched in courage and skill as was possible. They were of exactly the same stock, with the sole exception that among and under, but entirely distinct from, the Canadian-English, fought the descendants of the conquered Canadian-French; and even these had been trained by Englishmen, were led by English captains, fought on ships built by English gold, and with English weapons and discipline.

## ON LAKE ONTARIO

There being, as already explained, three independent centres of inland naval operations, the events at each will be considered separately.

At the opening of the war Lieutenant Woolsey, with the *Oneida*, was stationed at Sackett's Harbor, which was protected at the entrance by a small fort with a battery composed of one long 32. The Canadian squadron of six ships, mounting nearly 80 guns, was of course too strong to be meddled with. Indeed, had the *Royal George*, 22, the largest vessel, been commanded by a regular British sea-officer, she would have been perfectly competent to take both the *Oneida* and Sackett's Harbor; but before the Canadian commodore, Earle, made up his mind to attack, Lieut. Woolsey had time to make one or two short cruises, doing some damage among the merchant vessels of the enemy.

On the 19th of July Earle's ships appeared off the Harbor; the *Oneida* was such a dull sailer that it was useless for her to try to escape, so she was hauled up under a bank where she raked the entrance, and her off guns landed and mounted on the shore, while Lieut. Woolsey took charge of the "battery," or long 32, in the fort. The latter was the only gun that was of much use, for after a desultory cannonade of about an hour, Earle withdrew, having suffered very little damage, inflicted none at all, and proved himself and his subordinates to be grossly incompetent.

Acting under orders, Lieut. Woolsey now set about procuring merchant schooners to be fitted and used as gun-vessels until more regular cruisers could be built. A captured British schooner was christened the *Julia*, armed with a long 32 and two 6's, manned with 30 men, under Lieut. Henry Wells, and sent down to Ogdensburg. "On her way thither she encountered and actually beat off, without losing a man, the *Moira*, of 14, and *Gloucester*, of 10 guns."[1] Five other schooners were also purchased; the *Hamilton*, of 10 guns, being the largest, while the other four, the *Governor Tompkins*, *Growler*, *Conquest*, and *Pert*

[1] James, vi, 350.

had but 11 pieces between them. Nothing is more difficult than to exactly describe the armaments of the smaller lake vessels. The American schooners were mere make-shifts, and their guns were frequently changed[1]; as soon as they could be dispensed with they were laid up, or sold, and forgotten.

It was even worse with the British, who manifested the most indefatigable industry in intermittently changing the armament, rig, and name of almost every vessel, and, the records being very loosely kept, it is hard to find what was the force at any one time. A vessel which in one conflict was armed with long 18's, in the next would have replaced some of them with 68-pound carronades; or, beginning life as a ship, she would do most of her work as a schooner, and be captured as a brig, changing her name even oftener than any thing else.

On the first of September Commodore Isaac Chauncy was appointed commander of the forces on the lakes (except of those on Lake Champlain), and he at once bent his energies to preparing an effective flotilla. A large party of ship-carpenters were immediately despatched to the Harbor; and they were soon followed by about a hundred officers and seamen, with guns, stores, etc. The keel of a ship to mount 24 32-pound carronades, and to be called the *Madison,* was laid down, and she was launched on the 26th of November, just when navigation had closed on account of the ice. Late in the autumn, four more schooners were purchased, and named the *Ontario, Scourge, Fair American,* and *Asp,* but these were hardly used until the following spring. The cruising force of the Americans was composed solely of the *Oneida* and the six schooners first mentioned. The British squadron was of nearly double this strength, and had it been officered and trained as it was during the ensuing summer, the Americans could not have stirred out of port. But as it was, it merely served as a kind of water militia, the very sailors, who subsequently did well, being then almost useless, and unable to oppose their well-disciplined foes, though the latter were so inferior in number and force. For the reason that it was thus practically a contest of regulars against militia, I shall not give numerical comparisons of the skirmishes in the autumn of 1812, and shall touch on them but slightly. They teach the old lesson that, whether by sea or land, a small, well-officered, and well-trained force, can not, except very rarely, be resisted by a greater number of mere militia; and that in the end it is true economy to have the regular force prepared beforehand, without waiting until we have been forced to prepare it by the disasters happening to the irregulars. The Canadian seamen behaved badly, but no worse than the American land-forces did at the same time; later, under regular training, both nations retrieved their reputations.

Commodore Chauncy arrived at Sackett's Harbor in October, and appeared on the lake on Nov. 8th, in the *Oneida,* Lieutenant Woolsey, with the six

---

[1] They were always having accidents happen to them that necessitated some alteration. If a boat was armed with a long 32, she rolled too much, and they substituted a 24; if she also had an 18-pound carronade, it upset down the hatchway in the middle of a fight, and made way for a long 12, which burst as soon as it was used, and was replaced by two medium 6's. So a regular gamut of changes would be rung.

schooners *Conquest,* Lieutenant Elliott; *Hamilton,* Lieutenant McPherson; *Tomp-kins,* Lieutenant Brown; *Pert,* Sailing-master Arundel; *Julia,* Sailing-master Trant; *Growler,* Sailing-master Mix. The Canadian vessels were engaged in con-veying supplies from the westward. Commodore Chauncy discovered the *Royal George* off the False Duck Islands, and chased her under the batteries of Kingston, on the 9th. Kingston was too well defended to be taken by such a force as Chauncy's; but the latter decided to make a reconnoissance, to discover the enemy's means of defence and see if it was possible to lay the *Royal George* aboard. At 3 P.M. the attack was made. The *Hamilton* and *Tompkins* were absent chasing, and did not arrive until the fighting had begun. The other four gun-boats, *Conquest, Julia, Pert,* and *Growler,* led, in the order named, to open the at-tack with their heavy guns, and prepare the way for the *Oneida,* which followed. At the third discharge the *Pert's* gun burst, putting her nearly *hors de combat,* badly wounding her gallant commander, Mr. Arundel (who shortly afterward fell overboard and was drowned), and slightly wounding four of her crew. The other gun-boats engaged the five batteries of the enemy, while the *Oneida* pushed on without firing a shot till at 3.40 she opened on the *Royal George,* and after 20 minutes' combat actually succeeded in compelling her opponent, though of double her force, to cut her cables, run in, and tie herself to a wharf, where some of her people deserted her; here she was under the protection of a large body of troops, and the Americans could not board her in face of the land-forces. It soon began to grow dusk, and Chauncy's squadron beat out through the channel, against a fresh head-wind. In this spirited attack the American loss had been confined to half a dozen men, and had fallen almost exclusively on the *Oneida.* The next day foul weather came on, and the squadron sailed for Sackett's Harbor. Some merchant vessels were taken, and the *Simco,* 8, was chased, but unsuccessfully.

The weather now became cold and tempestuous, but cruising continued till the middle of November. The Canadian commanders, however, utterly refused to fight; the *Royal George* even fleeing from the *Oneida,* when the latter was en-tirely alone, and leaving the American commodore in undisputed command of the lake. Four of the schooners continued blockading Kingston till the middle of November; shorly afterward navigation closed.[1]

## LAKE ERIE

On Lake Erie there was no American naval force; but the army had fitted out a small brig, armed with six 6-pounders. This fell into the hands of the British at the capture of Detroit, and was named after that city, so that by the time a force of American officers and seamen arrived at the lake there was not a vessel on it

[1] These preliminary events were not very important, and the historians on both sides agree almost exactly, so that I have not considered it necessary to quote authorities.

for them to serve in, while their foes had eight. But we only have to deal with two of the latter at present. The *Detroit*, still mounting six 6-pounders, and with a crew of 56 men, under the command of Lieutenant of Marines Rolette, of the Royal Navy, assisted by a boatswain and gunner, and containing also 30 American prisoners, and the *Caledonia*, a small brig mounting two 4-pounders on pivots, with a crew of 12 men, Canadian-English, under Mr. Irvine, and having aboard also 10 American prisoners, and a very valuable cargo of furs worth about 200,000 dollars, moved down the lake, and on Oct. 7th anchored under Fort Erie.[1]

Commander Jesse D. Elliott had been sent up to Erie some time before with instructions from Commodore Chauncy to construct a naval force, partly by building two brigs of 300 tons each,[2] and partly by purchasing schooners to act as gun-boats. No sailors had yet arrived; but on the very day on which the two brigs moved down and anchored under Fort Erie, Captain Elliott received news that the first detachment of the promised seamen, 51 in number, including officers,[3] was but a few miles distant. He at once sent word to have these men hurried up, but when they arrived they were found to have no arms, for which application was made to the military authorities. The latter not only gave a sufficiency of sabres, pistols, and muskets to the sailors, but also detailed enough soldiers, under Captain N. Towson and Lieutenant Isaac Roach, to make the total number of men that took part in the expedition 124. This force left Black Rock at one o'clock on the morning of the 8th in two large boats, one under the command of Commander Elliott, assisted by Lieutenant Roach, the other under Sailing-master George Watts and Captain Towson. After two hours' rowing they reached the foe, and the attack was made at three o'clock. Elliott laid his boat alongside the *Detroit* before he was discovered, and captured her after a very brief struggle, in which he lost but one man killed, and Midshipman J. C. Cummings wounded with a bayonet in the leg. The noise of the scuffle roused the hardy provincials aboard the *Caledonia*, and they were thus enabled to make a far more effectual resistance to Sailing-master Watts than the larger vessel had to Captain Elliott. As Watts pulled alongside he was greeted with a volley of musketry, but at once boarded and carried the brig, the twelve Canadians being cut down or made prisoners; one American was killed and four badly wounded. The wind was too light and the current too strong to enable the prizes to beat out and reach the lake, so the cables were cut and they ran down stream. The *Caledonia* was safely beached under the protection of an American battery near Black Rock. The *Detroit*, however, was obliged to anchor but four hundred yards from a British battery, which, together with some flying

[1] Letter of Captain Jesse D. Elliott to Secretary of Navy, Black Rock, Oct. 5, 1812.

[2] That is, of 300 tons actual capacity; measured as if they had been ordinary sea vessels they each tonned 480. Their opponent, the ship *Detroit*, similarly tonned 305, actual measurement, or 490, computing it in the ordinary manner.

[3] The number of men in this expedition is taken from Lossing's "Field-Book of the War of 1812," by Benson L. Lossing, New York, 1869, p. 385, note, where a complete list of the names is given.

artillery, opened on her. Getting all his guns on the port side, Elliott kept up a brisk cannonade till his ammunition gave out, when he cut his cable and soon grounded on Squaw Island. Here the *Detroit* was commanded by the guns of both sides, and which ever party took possession of her was at once driven out by the other. The struggle ended in her destruction, most of her guns being taken over to the American side. This was a very daring and handsome exploit, reflecting great credit on Commander Elliott, and giving the Americans, in the *Caledonia*, the nucleus of their navy on Lake Erie; soon afterward Elliott returned to Lake Ontario, a new detachment of seamen under Commander S. Angus having arrived.

On the 28th of November, the American general, Smith, despatched two parties to make an attack on some of the British batteries. One of these consisted of 10 boats, under the command of Captain King of the 15th infantry, with 150 soldiers, and with him went Mr. Angus with 82 sailors, including officers. The expedition left at one o'clock in the morning, but was discovered and greeted with a warm fire from a field battery placed in front of some British barracks known as the Red House. Six of the boats put back; but the other four, containing about a hundred men, dashed on. While the soldiers were forming line and firing, the seamen rushed in with their pikes and axes, drove off the British, capturing their commander, Lieut. King, of the Royal Army, spiked and threw into the river the guns, and then took the barracks and burned them, after a desperate fight. Great confusion now ensued, which ended in Mr. Angus and some of the seamen going off in the boats. Several had been killed; eight, among whom were Midshipmen Wragg, Dudley, and Holdup, all under 20 years old, remained with the troops under Captain King, and having utterly routed the enemy found themselves deserted by their friends. After staying on the shore a couple of hours some of them found two boats and got over; but Captain King and a few soldiers were taken prisoners. Thirty of the seamen, including nine of the twelve officers, were killed or wounded—among the former being Sailing-masters Sisson and Watts, and among the latter Mr. Angus, Sailing-master Carter, and Midshipmen Wragg, Holdup, Graham, Brailesford, and Irvine. Some twenty prisoners were secured and taken over to the American shore; the enemy's loss was more severe than ours, his resistance being very stubborn, and a good many cannon were destroyed, but the expedition certainly ended most disastrously. The accounts of it are hard to reconcile, but it is difficult to believe that Mr. Angus acted correctly.

Later in the winter Captain Oliver Hazard Perry arrived to take command of the forces on Lake Erie.

# V

# 1813

## ON THE OCEAN

Blockade of the American coast · The *Essex* in the South Pacific · The *Hornet* captures the *Peacock* · American privateers cut out by British boats · Unsuccessful cruise of Commodore Rodgers · The *Chesapeake* is captured by the *Shannon* · Futile gun-boat actions · Defence of Craney Island · Cutting-out expeditions · The *Argus* is captured by the *Pelican* · The *Enterprise* captures the *Boxer* · Summary

By the beginning of the year 1813 the British had been thoroughly aroused by the American successes, and active measures were at once taken to counteract them. The force on the American station was largely increased, and a strict blockade begun, to keep the American frigates in port. The British frigates now cruised for the most part in couples, and orders were issued by the Board of Admiralty that an 18-pounder frigate was not to engage an American 24-pounder. Exaggerated accounts of the American 44's being circulated, a new class of spar-deck frigates was constructed to meet them, rating 50 and mounting 60 guns; and some 74's were cut down for the same purpose.[1] These new ships were all much heavier than their intended opponents.

As New England's loyalty to the Union was, not unreasonably, doubted abroad, her coasts were at first troubled but little. A British squadron was generally kept cruising off the end of Long Island Sound, and another off Sandy Hook. Of course America had no means of raising a blockade, as each squadron contained generally a 74 or a razee, vessels too heavy for any in our navy to cope with. Frigates and sloops kept skirting the coasts of New Jersey, the Carolinas, and Georgia. Delaware Bay no longer possessed the importance it had during the Revolutionary War, and as the only war vessels in it were some miserable gun-boats, the British generally kept but a small force on that station. Chesapeake Bay became the principal scene of their operations; it was there that their main body collected, and their greatest efforts were made. In it a

---

[1] James, vi, p. 206.

number of line-of-battle ships, frigates, sloops, and cutters had been collected, and early in the season Admiral Sir John Warren and Rear-Admiral Cockburn arrived to take command. The latter made numerous descents on the coast, and frequently came into contact with the local militia, who generally fled after a couple of volleys. These expeditions did not accomplish much, beyond burning the houses and driving off the live-stock of the farmers along shore, and destroying a few small towns—one of them, Hampton, being sacked with revolting brutality.[1] The government of the United States was, in fact, supported by the people in its war policy very largely on account of these excesses, which were much exaggerated by American writers. It was really a species of civil war, and in such a contest, at the beginning of this century, it was impossible that some outrages should not take place.

The American frigate *Constellation* had by this time got ready for sea, and, under the command of Captain Stewart, she prepared to put out early in January. As the number of blockaders rendered a fight almost certain within a few days of her departure, her crew were previously brought to the highest state of discipline, the men being exercised with especial care in handling the great guns and in firing at a target.[2] However, she never got out; for when she reached Hampton Roads she fell in with a British squadron of line-of-battle ships and frigates. She kedged up toward Norfolk, and when the tide rose ran in and anchored between the forts; and a few days later dropped down to cover the forts which were being built at Craney Island. Here she was exposed to attacks from the great British force still lying in Hampton Roads, and, fearing they would attempt to carry her by surprise, Captain Stewart made every preparation for defence. She was anchored in the middle of the narrow channel, flanked by gun-boats, her lower ports closed, not a rope left hanging over the sides; the boarding nettings, boiled in half-made pitch till they were as hard as wire, were triced outboard toward the yardarms, and loaded with kentledge to fall on the attacking boats when the tricing lines were cut, while the carronades were loaded to the muzzle with musket balls, and depressed so as to sweep the water near the ship.[3] Twice, a force of British, estimated by their foes to number 2,000 men, started off at night to carry the *Constellation* by surprise; but on each occasion they were discovered and closely watched by her guard-boats, and they never ventured to make the attack. However, she was unable to get to sea, and remained blockaded to the close of the war.

At the beginning of the year several frigates and smaller craft were at sea. The *Chesapeake*, Captain Evans, had sailed from Boston on Dec. 13, 1812.[4] She ran down past Madeira, the Canaries, and Cape de Verde, crossed the equator,

---

[1] James (vi, 340) says: The conduct of the British troops on this occasion was "revolting to human nature" and "disgraceful to the flag."

[2] *Life of Commodore Tatnall*, by C. C. Jones (Savannah, 1878), p. 15.

[3] For an admirable account of these preparations, as well as of the subsequent events, see Cooper, ii, 242.

[4] Statistical "History of the U. S. Navy," by Lieutenant G. E. Emmons.

and for six weeks cruised to the south of the line between longitudes 16° and 25°. Thence she steered to the west, passing near Surinam, over the same spot on which the *Hornet* had sunk the *Peacock* but a day previous. Cruising northward through the West Indies, she passed near the Bermudas, where she was chased by a 74 and a frigate; escaping from them she got into Boston on April 9th, having captured five merchantmen, and chased unsuccessfully for two days a brig-sloop. The term of two years for which her crew were enlisted now being up, they, for the most part, left, in consequence of some trouble about the prize-money. Captain Evans being in ill health, Captain James Lawrence was appointed to command her. He reached Boston about the middle of May[1] and at once set about enlisting a new crew, and tried, with but partial success, to arrange matters with the old sailors, who were now almost in open mutiny.

When the year 1812 had come to an end, the *Essex,* 32, was in the South Atlantic, and Captain Porter shortly afterward ran into St. Catherines to water. Being at a loss where to find his consorts, he now decided to adopt the exceedingly bold measure of doubling Cape Horn and striking at the British whalers in the Pacific. This was practically going into the enemy's waters, the Portuguese and Spanish countries being entirely under the influence of Britain, while there were no stations where Porter could revictual or repair in safety. However, the *Essex* started, doubled the Horn, and on March 13th anchored in the harbor of Valparaiso. Her adventurous cruise in the Pacific was the most striking feature of the war; but as it has been most minutely described by Commodore Porter himself, by his son, Admiral Porter, by Admiral Farragut, and by Cooper, I shall barely touch upon it.

On March 20th the *Essex* captured the Peruvian corsair *Nereyda,* 16, hove her guns and small arms overboard, and sent her into port. She made the island of San Gallan, looked into Callao, and thence went to the Gallipagos, getting every thing she wanted from her prizes. Then she went to Tumbez, and returned to the Gallipagos; thence to the Marquesas, and finally back to Valparaiso again. By this year's campaign in the Pacific, Captain Porter had saved all our ships in those waters, had not cost the government a dollar, living purely on the enemy, and had taken from him nearly 4,000 tons of shipping and 400 men, completely breaking up his whaling trade in the South Pacific.

The cruise was something *sui generis* in modern warfare, recalling to mind the cruises of the early English and Dutch navigators. An American ship was at a serious disadvantage in having no harbor of refuge away from home; while on almost every sea there were British, French, and Spanish ports into which vessels of those nations could run for safety. It was an unprecedented thing for a small frigate to cruise a year and a half in enemy's waters, and to supply herself

---

[1] He was still on the *Hornet* at New York on May 10th, as we know from a letter of Biddle's, written on that date (in letters of "Masters' Commandant," 1813, No. 58), and so could hardly have been with the *Chesapeake* two weeks before he put out; and had to get his crew together and train them during that time.

during that time, purely from captured vessels, with every thing—cordage, sails, guns, anchors, provisions, and medicines, and even money to pay the officers and men! Porter's cruise was the very model of what such an expedition should be, harassing the enemy most effectually at no cost whatever. Had the *Essex* been decently armed with long guns, instead of carronades, the end might have been as successful as it was glorious. The whalers were many of them armed letters-of-marque, and, though of course unable to oppose the frigate, several times smart skirmishes occurred in attacking them with boats, or in captured ships; as when Lieutenant Downs and 20 men in the prize *Georgiana* after a short brush captured the *Hector,* with 25 men, two of whom were killed and six wounded; and when, under similar circumstances, the prize *Greenwich,* of 25 men, captured the *Seringapatam* of 40. The cruise of the *Essex,* the first American man-of-war ever in the Pacific, a year and a half out and many thousand miles away from home, was a good proof of Porter's audacity in planning the trip and his skill and resource in carrying it out.

To return now to the *Hornet.* This vessel had continued blockading the *Bonne Citoyenne* until January 24th, when the *Montagu,* 74, arrived toward evening and chased her into port. As the darkness came on the *Hornet* wore, stood out to sea, passing into the open without molestation from the 74, and then steered toward the northeast, cruising near the coast, and making a few prizes, among which was a brig, the *Resolution,* with $23,000 in specie aboard, captured on February 14th. On the 24th of February, while nearing the mouth of the Demerara River, Captain Lawrence discovered a brig to leeward, and chased her till he ran into quarter less five, when, having no pilot, he hauled off-shore. Just within the bar a man-of-war brig was lying at anchor; and while beating round Caroband Bank, in order to get at her, Captain Lawrence discovered another sail edging down on his weather-quarter.[1] The brig at anchor was the *Espiègle,* of 18 guns, 32-pound carronades, Captain John Taylor[2]; and the second brig seen was the *Peacock,* Captain William Peake,[3] which, for some unknown reason, had exchanged her 32-pound carronades for 24's. She had sailed from the *Espiègle's* anchorage the same morning at 10 o'clock. At 4.20 P.M. the *Peacock* hoisted her colors; then the *Hornet* beat to quarters and cleared for action. Captain Lawrence kept close by the wind, in order to get the weather-gage; when he was certain he could weather the enemy, he tacked, at 5.10, and the *Hornet* hoisted her colors. The ship and the brig now stood for each other, both on the wind, the *Hornet* being on the starboard and the *Peacock* on the port tack, and at 5.25 they exchanged broadsides, at half pistol-shot distance, while going in opposite directions, the Americans using their lee and the British their weather battery. The guns were fired as they bore, and the *Peacock* suffered severely, while her antagonist's hull was uninjured, though she suffered slightly aloft and had her

[1] Letter of Captain Lawrence, March 29, 1813.
[2] James, vi, 278.
[3] *Do.*

pennant cut off by the first shot fired.[1] One of the men in the mizzen-top was killed by a round shot, and two more were wounded on the main-top.[2] As soon as they were clear, Captain Peake put his helm hard up and wore, firing his starboard guns; but the *Hornet* had watched him closely, bore up as quickly, and coming down at 5.35, ran him close aboard on the starboard quarter. Captain Peake fell at this moment, together with many of his crew, and, unable to withstand the *Hornet's* heavy fire, the *Peacock* surrendered at 5.39, just 14 minutes after the first shot; and directly afterward hoisted her ensign union down in the forerigging as a signal of distress. Almost immediately her main-mast went by the board. Both vessels then anchored, and Lieutenant J. T. Shubrick, being sent on board the prize, reported her sinking. Lieutenant D. Connor was then sent in another boat to try to save the vessel; but though they threw the guns overboard, plugged the shot holes, tried the pumps, and even attempted bailing, the water gained so rapidly that the *Hornet's* officers devoted themselves to removing the wounded and other prisoners; and while thus occupied the short tropical twilight left them. Immediately afterward the prize settled, suddenly and easily, in 5½ fathoms water, carrying with her three of the *Hornet's* people and nine of her own, who were rummaging below; meanwhile four others of her crew had lowered her damaged stern boat, and in the confusion got off unobserved and made their way to the land. The foretop still remained above water, and four of the prisoners saved themselves by running up the rigging into it. Lieutenant Connor and Midshipman Cooper (who had also come on board) saved themselves, together with most of their people and the remainder of the *Peacock's* crew, by jumping into the launch, which was lying on the booms, and paddling her toward the ship with pieces of boards in default of oars.

The *Hornet's* complement at this time was 150, of whom she had 8 men absent in a prize and 7 on the sick list,[3] leaving 135 fit for duty in the action[4]; of these one man was killed, and two wounded, all aloft. Her rigging and sails were a good deal cut, a shot had gone through the foremast, and the bowsprit was slightly damaged; the only shot that touched her hull merely glanced athwart her bows, indenting a plank beneath the cat-head. The *Peacock's* crew had amounted to 134, but 4 were absent in a prize, and but 122[5] fit for action; of these she lost her captain, and seven men killed and mortally wounded, and her master, one midshipman, and 28 men severely and slightly wounded,—in all 8 killed and 30 wounded, or about 13 times her antagonist's loss. She suffered under the disadvantage of light metal, having 24's opposed to 32's; but judging from her gunnery this was not much of a loss, as 6-pounders would have inflicted nearly as great damage. She was well handled and bravely fought; but

---

[1] Cooper, p. 200.

[2] See entry in her log for this day (In "Log-Book of *Hornet, Wasp,* and *Argus,* from July 20, 1809, to October 6, 1813,") in the Bureau of Navigation, at Washington.

[3] Letter of Captain Lawrence.

[4] Letter of Lieutenant D. Conner, April 26, 1813.

[5] Letter of Lieutenant F. W. Wright (of the *Peacock*), April 17, 1813.

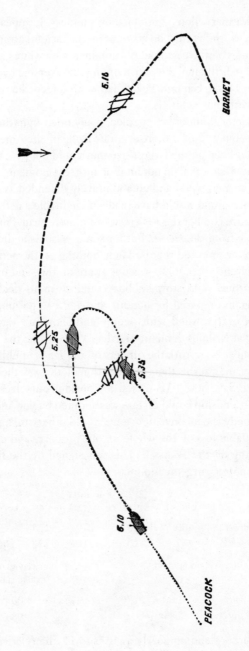

her men showed a marvellous ignorance of gunnery. It appears that she had long been known as "the yacht," on account of the tasteful arrangement of her deck; the breechings of the carronades were lined with white canvas, and nothing could exceed in brilliancy the polish upon the traversing bars and elevating screws.[1] In other words, Captain Peake had confounded the mere *incidents* of good discipline with the essentials.[2]

The *Hornet's* victory cannot be regarded in any other light than as due, *not* to the heavier metal, but to the far more accurate firing of the Americans; "had the guns of the *Peacock* been of the largest size they could not have changed the result, as the weight of shot that do not hit is of no great moment." Any merchant-ship might have been as well handled and bravely defended as she was; and an ordinary letter-of-marque would have made as creditable a defence.

During the entire combat the *Espiègle* was not more than 4 miles distant and was plainly visible from the *Hornet;* but for some reason she did not come out, and her commander reported that he knew nothing of the action till the next day. Captain Lawrence of course was not aware of this, and made such exertions to bend on new sails, stow his boats, and clear his decks that by nine o'clock he was again prepared for action,[3] and at 2 P.M. got under way for the N.W. Being now overcrowded with people and short of water he stood for home, anchoring at Holmes' Hole in Martha's Vineyard on the 19th of March.

On their arrival at New York the officers of the *Peacock* published a card expressing in the warmest terms their appreciation of the way they and their men had been treated. Say they: "We ceased to consider ourselves prisoners; and every thing that friendship could dictate was adopted by you and the officers of the *Hornet* to remedy the inconvenience we would otherwise have experienced from the unavoidable loss of the whole of our property and clothes owing to the sudden sinking of the *Peacock*."[4] This was signed by the first and second lieutenants, the master, surgeon and purser.

|  | TONNAGE. | GUNS. | WEIGHT METAL. | MEN. | LOSS. |
|---|---|---|---|---|---|
| *Hornet* | 480 | 10 | 279 | 135 | 3 |
| *Peacock* | 477 | 10 | 210 | 122 | 38 |

|  | RELATIVE FORCE. | RELATIVE LOSS INFLICTED. |
|---|---|---|
| *Hornet* | 1.00 | 1.00 |
| *Peacock* | .83 | .08 |

That is, the forces standing nearly as 13 is to 11, the relative execution was about as 13 is to 1.

---

[1] James, vi, 280.
[2] Codrington ("Memoirs," i, 310) comments very forcibly on the uselessness of a mere martinet.
[3] Letter of Captain Lawrence.
[4] Quoted in full in "Niles' Register" and Lossing's "Field Book."

The day after the capture Captain Lawrence reported 277 souls aboard, including the crew of the English brig *Resolution* which he had taken, and of the American brig *Hunter,* prize to the *Peacock*. As James, very ingeniously, tortures these figures into meaning what they did not, it may be well to show exactly what the 277 included. Of the *Hornet's* original crew of 150, 8 were absent in a prize, 1 killed, and 3 drowned, leaving (including 7 sick) 138; of the *Peacock's* original 134, 4 were absent in a prize, 5 killed, 9 drowned, and 4 escaped, leaving (including 8 sick and 3 mortally wounded) 112; there were also aboard 16 other British prisoners, and the *Hunter's* crew of 11 men—making just 277.[1] According to Lieutenant Connor's letter, written in response to one from Lieutenant Wright, there were in reality 139 in the *Peacock's* crew when she began action; but it is, of course, best to take each commander's account of the number of men on board his ship that were fit for duty.

On Jan. 17th the *Viper,* 12, Lieutenant J. D. Henly, was captured by the British frigate *Narcissus,* 32, Captain Lumly.

———

On Feb. 8th, while a British squadron, consisting of the four frigates *Belvidera* (Captain Richard Byron), *Maidstone, Junon,* and *Statira,* were at anchor in Lynhaven Bay, a schooner was observed in the northeast standing down Chesapeake Bay.[2] This was the *Lottery,* letter-of-marque, of six 12-pounder carronades and 25 men, Captain John Southcomb, bound from Baltimore to Bombay. Nine boats, with 200 men, under the command of Lieutenant Kelly Nazer were sent against her, and, a calm coming on, overtook her. The schooner opened a well-directed fire of round and grape, but the boats rushed forward and boarded her, not carrying her till after a most obstinate struggle, in which Captain Southcomb and 19 of his men, together with 13 of the assailants, were killed or wounded. The best war ship of a regular navy might be proud of the discipline and courage displayed by the captain and crew of the little *Lottery*. Captain Byron on this, as well as on many another occasion, showed himself to be as humane as he was brave and skilful. Captain Southcomb, mortally wounded, was taken on board Byron's frigate, where he was treated with the greatest attention and most delicate courtesy, and when he died his body was sent ashore with every mark of the respect due to so brave an officer. Captain Stewart (of the *Constellation*) wrote Captain Byron a letter of acknowledgment for his great courtesy and kindness.[3]

On March 16th a British division of five boats and 105 men, commanded by Lieutenant James Polkinghorne, set out to attack the privateer schooner *Dolphin* of 12 guns and 70 men, and the letters-of-marque, *Racer, Arab,* and *Lynx,* each of six guns and 30 men. Lieutenant Polkinghorne, after pulling 15 miles, found the

[1] The 277 men were thus divided into: *Hornet's* crew, 138; *Peacock's* crew, 112; *Resolution's* crew, 16; *Hunter's* crew, 11. James quotes "270" men, which he divides as follows: *Hornet* 160, *Peacock* 101, *Hunter,* 9,—leaving out the *Resolution's* crew, 11 of the *Peacock's,* and 2 of the *Hunter's.*

[2] James, vi, 325.

[3] The correspondence between the two captains is given in full in "Niles' Register," which also contains fragmentary notes on the action, principally as to the loss incurred.

four schooners all prepared to receive him, but in spite of his great inferiority in force he dashed gallantly at them. The *Arab* and *Lynx* surrendered at once; the *Racer* was carried after a sharp struggle in which Lieutenant Polkinghorne was wounded, and her guns turned on the *Dolphin*. Most of the latter's crew jumped overboard; a few rallied round their captain, but they were at once scattered as the British seamen came aboard. The assailants had 13, and the privateersmen 16 men killed and wounded in the fight. It was certainly one of the most brilliant and daring cutting-out expeditions that took place during the war, and the victors well deserved their success. The privateersmen (according to the statement of the *Dolphin's* master, in "Niles' Register") were panic-struck, and acted in any thing but a brave manner. All irregular fighting-men do their work by fits and starts. No regular cruisers could behave better than did the privateers *Lottery, Chasseur,* and *General Armstrong;* none would behave as badly as the *Dolphin, Lynx,* and *Arab.* The same thing appears on shore. Jackson's irregulars at New Orleans did as well, or almost as well, as Scott's troops at Lundy's Lane; but Scott's troops would never have suffered from such a panic as overcame the militia at Bladensburg.

On April 9th the schooner *Norwich,* of 14 guns and 61 men, Sailing-master James Monk, captured the British privateer *Caledonia,* of 10 guns and 41 men, after a short action in which the privateer lost 7 men.

On April 30th Commodore Rodgers, in the *President,* 44, accompanied by Captain Smith in the *Congress,* 38, sailed on his third cruise.[1] On May 2d he fell in with and chased the British sloop *Curlew,* 18, Captain Michael Head, but the latter escaped by knocking away the wedges of her masts and using other means to increase her rate of sailing. On the 8th, in latitude 39° 30' N., long. 60° W., the *Congress* parted company, and sailed off toward the southeast, making four prizes, of no great value, in the North Atlantic[2]; when about in long. 35° W. she steered south, passing to the south of the line. But she never saw a man-of-war, and during the latter part of her cruise not a sail of any kind; and after crusing nearly eight months returned to Portsmouth Harbor on Dec. 14th, having captured but four merchant-men. Being unfit to cruise longer, owing to her decayed condition, she was disarmed and laid up; nor was she sent to sea again during the war.[3]

Meanwhile Rodgers cruised along the eastern edge of the Grand Bank until he reached latitude 48°, without meeting any thing, then stood to the southeast, and cruised off the Azores till June 6th. Then he crowded sail to the northeast after a Jamaica fleet of which he had received news, but which he failed to over-

---

[1] Letter of Commodore Rodgers, Sept. 30, 1813.

[2] Letter of Captain Smith, Dec. 15, 1813.

[3] James states that she was "blockaded" in port by the *Tenedos,* during part of 1814; but was too much awed by the fate of the *Chesapeake* to come out during the "long blockade" of Captain Parker. Considering the fact that she was too decayed to put to sea, had no guns aboard, no crew, and was, in fact, laid up, the feat of the *Tenedos* was not very wonderful; a row-boat could have "blockaded" her quite as well. It is worth noticing, as an instance of the way James alters a fact by suppressing half of it.

take, and on June 13th, in lat. 46°, long. 28°, he gave up the chase and shaped his course toward the North Sea, still without any good luck befalling him. On June 27th he put into North Bergen in the Shetlands for water, and thence passed the Orkneys and stretched toward the North Cape, hoping to intercept the Archangel fleet. On July 19th, when off the North Cape, in lat. 71° 52′ N., long. 20° 18′ E., he fell in with two sail of the enemy, who made chase; after four days' pursuit the commodore ran his opponents out of sight. According to his letter the two sail were a line-of-battle ship and a frigate; according to James they were the 12-pounder frigate *Alexandria*, Captain Cathcart, and *Spitfire*, 16, Captain Ellis. James quotes from the logs of the two British ships, and it would seem that he is correct, as it would not be possible for him to falsify the logs so utterly. In case he is true, it was certainly carrying caution to an excessive degree for the commodore to retreat before getting some idea of what his antagonists really were. His mistaking them for so much heavier ships was a precisely similar error to that made by Sir George Collier and Lord Stuart at a later date about the *Cyane* and *Levant*. James wishes to prove that each party perceived the force of the other, and draws a contrast (p. 312) between the "gallantry of one party and pusillanimity of the other." This is nonsense, and, as in similar cases, James over-reaches himself by proving too much. If he had made an 18-pounder frigate like the *Congress* flee from another 18-pounder, his narrative would be within the bounds of possibility and would need serious examination. But the little 12-pounder *Alexandria*, and the ship-sloop with her 18-pound carronades, would not have stood the ghost of a chance in the contest. Any man who would have been afraid of them would also have been afraid of the *Little Belt*, the sloop Rodgers captured before the war. As for Captains Cathcart and Ellis, had they known the force of the *President*, and chased her with a view of attacking her, their conduct would have only been explicable on the ground that they were afflicted with emotional insanity.

The *President* now steered southward and got into the mouth of the Irish Channel; on August 2d she shifted her berth and almost circled Ireland; then steered across to Newfoundland, and worked south along the coast. On Sept. 23d, a little south of Nantucket, she decoyed under her guns and captured the British schooner *Highflyer*, 6, Lieut. William Hutchinson, and 45 men; and went into Newport on the 27th of the same month, having made some 12 prizes.

On May 24th Commodore Decatur in the *United States*, which had sent ashore six carronades, and now mounted but 48 guns, accompanied by Captain Jones in the *Macedonian*, 38, and Captain Biddle in the *Wasp*, 20, left New York, passing through Hell Gate, as there was a large blockading force off the Hook. Opposite Hunter's Point the main-mast of the *States* was struck by lightning, which cut off the broad pendant, shot down the hatchway into the doctor's cabin, put out his candle, ripped up the bed, and entering between the skin and ceiling of the ship tore off two or three sheets of copper near the water-line, and disappeared without leaving a trace! The *Macedonian*, which was close behind, hove all aback, in expectation of seeing the *States* blown up.

At the end of the sound Commodore Decatur anchored to watch for a chance of getting out. Early on June 1st he started; but in a couple of hours met the British Captain R. D. Oliver's squadron, consisting of a 74, a razee, and a frigate. These chased him back, and all his three ships ran into New London. Here, in the mud of the Thames River, the two frigates remained blockaded till the close of the war; but the little sloop slipped out later, to the enemy's cost.

We left the *Chesapeake*, 38, being fitted out at Boston by Captain James Lawrence, late of the *Hornet*. Most of her crew, as already stated, their time being up, left, dissatisfied with the ship's ill luck, and angry at not having received their due share of prize-money. It was very hard to get sailors, most of the men preferring to ship in some of the numerous privateers where the discipline was less strict and the chance of prize-money much greater. In consequence of this an unusually large number of foreigners had to be taken, including about forty British and a number of Portuguese. The latter were peculiarly troublesome; one of their number, a boatswain's mate, finally almost brought about a mutiny among the crew, which was only pacified by giving the men prize-checks. A few of the *Constitution*'s old crew came aboard, and these, together with some of the men who had been on the *Chesapeake* during her former voyage, made an excellent nucleus. Such men needed very little training at either guns or sails; but the new hands were unpractised, and came on board so late that the last draft that arrived still had their hammocks and bags lying in the boats stowed over the booms when the ship was captured. The officers were largely new to the ship, though the first lieutenant, Mr. A. Ludlow, had been the third in her former cruise; the third and fourth lieutenants were not regularly commissioned as such, but were only midshipmen acting for the first time in higher positions. Captain Lawrence himself was of course new to all, both officers and crew.[1] In other words, the *Chesapeake* possessed good material, but in an exceedingly unseasoned state.

Meanwhile the British frigate *Shannon*, 38, Captain Philip Bowes Vere Broke, was cruising off the mouth of the harbor. To give some idea of the reason why she proved herself so much more formidable than her British sister frigates it may be well to quote, slightly condensing, from James:

"There was another point in which the generality of British crews, as compared with any one American crew, were miserably deficient; that is, skill in the art of gunnery. While the American seamen were constantly firing at marks, the British seamen, except in particular cases, scarcely did so once in a year; and some ships could be named on board which not a shot had been fired in this way for upward of three years. Nor was the fault wholly the captain's. The instructions under which he was bound to act forbade him to use, during the first

---

[1] On the day on which he sailed to attack the *Shannon*, Lawrence writes to the Secretary of the Navy as follows: "Lieutenant Paige is so ill as to be unable to go to sea with the ship. At the urgent request of Acting-Lieutenant Pierce I have granted him, also, permission to go on shore; one inducement for my granting his request was his being at variance with every officer in his mess." "Captains' Letters," vol. 29, No. 1, in the Naval Archives at Washington. Neither officers nor men had shaken together.

six months after the ship had received her armament, more shots per month than amounted to a third in number of the upper-deck guns; and, after these six months, only half the quantity. Many captains never put a shot in the guns till an enemy appeared; they employed the leisure time of the men in handling the sails and in decorating the ship." Captain Broke was not one of this kind. "From the day on which he had joined her, the 14th of September, 1806, the *Shannon* began to feel the effect of her captain's proficiency as a gunner and zeal for the service. The laying of the ship's ordnance so that it may be correctly fired in a horizontal direction is justly deemed a most important operation, as upon it depends in a great measure the true aim and destructive effect of the shot; this was attended to by Captain Broke in person. By draughts from other ships, and the usual means to which a British man-of-war is obliged to resort, the *Shannon* got together a crew; and in the course of a year or two, by the paternal care and excellent regulations of Captain Broke, the ship's company became as pleasant to command as it was dangerous to meet." The *Shannon's* guns were all carefully sighted, and, moreover, "every day, for about an hour and a half in the forenoon, when not prevented by chase or the state of the weather, the men were exercised at training the guns, and for the same time in the afternoon in the use of the broadsword, pike, musket, etc. Twice a week the crew fired at targets, both with great guns and musketry; and Captain Broke, as an additional stimulus beyond the emulation excited, gave a pound of tobacco to every man that put a shot through the bull's eye." He would frequently have a cask thrown overboard and suddenly order some one gun to be manned to sink the cask. In short, the *Shannon* was very greatly superior, thanks to her careful training, to the average British frigate of her rate, while the *Chesapeake*, owing to her having a raw and inexperienced crew, was decidedly inferior to the average American frigate of the same strength.

In force the two frigates compared pretty equally,[1] the American being the superior in just about the same proportion that the *Wasp* was to the *Frolic*, or, at a later date, the *Hornet* to the *Penguin*. The *Chesapeake* carried 50 guns (26 in broadside), 28 long 18's on the gun-deck, and on the spar-deck two long 12's, one long 18, eighteen 32-pound carronades, and one 12-pound carronade (which was not used in the fight however). Her broadside, allowing for the short weight of metal was 542 lbs.; her complement, 379 men. The *Shannon* carried 52 guns (26 in broadside), 28 long 18's on the gun-deck, and on the spar-deck four long 9's, one long 6, 16 32-pound carronades, and three 12-pound carronades (two of which were not used in the fight). Her broadside was 550 lbs.; her crew consisted of 330 men, 30 of whom were raw hands. Early on the morning of June 1st, Captain Broke sent in to Captain Lawrence, by an American prisoner, a letter of challenge, which for courteousness, manliness, and candor is the very model of what such an epistle should be. Before it reached Boston, however, Captain Lawrence had weighed anchor, to attack the *Shannon*,

[1] Taking each commander's account for his own force.

which frigate was in full sight in the offing. It has been often said that he engaged against his judgment, but this may be doubted. His experience with the
*Bonne Citoyenne, Espiègle,* and *Peacock* had not tended to give him a very high idea
of the navy to which he was opposed, and there is no doubt that he was confident of capturing the *Shannon.*[1] It was most unfortunate that he did not receive
Broke's letter, as the latter in it expressed himself willing to meet Lawrence in
any latitude and longitude he might appoint; and there would thus have been
some chance of the American crew having time enough to get into shape.

At midday of June 1, 1812, the *Chesapeake* weighed anchor, stood out of
Boston Harbor, and at 1 P.M. rounded the Light-house. The *Shannon* stood off
under easy sail, and at 3.40 hauled up and reefed top-sails. At 4 P.M. she again
bore away with her foresail brailed up, and her main top-sail braced flat and
shivering, that the *Chesapeake* might overtake her. An hour later, Boston Light-
house bearing west distant about six leagues, she again hauled up, with her head
to the southeast, and lay to under top-sails, top-gallant sails, jib, and spanker.
Meanwhile, as the breeze freshened the *Chesapeake* took in her studding-sails,
top-gallant sails, and royals, got her royal yards on deck, and came down very
fast under top-sails and jib. At 5.30, to keep under command and be able to wear
if necessary, the *Shannon* filled her main top-sail and kept a close luff, and then
again let the sail shiver. At 5.25 the *Chesapeake* hauled up her foresail, and, with
three ensigns flying, steered straight for the *Shannon*'s starboard quarter. Broke
was afraid that Lawrence would pass under the *Shannon*'s stern, rake her, and
engage her on the quarter; but either overlooking or waiving this advantage, the
American captain luffed up within 50 yards upon the *Shannon*'s starboard quarter, and squared his main-yard. On board the *Shannon* the captain of the 14th
gun, William Mindham, had been ordered not to fire till it bore into the second
main-deck port forward; at 5.50 it was fired, and then the other guns in quick
succession from aft forward, the *Chesapeake* replying with her whole broadside.
At 5.53 Lawrence, finding he was forging ahead, hauled up a little. The *Chesapeake*'s broadsides were doing great damage, but she herself was suffering even
more than her foe; the men in the *Shannon*'s tops could hardly see the deck of
the American frigate through the cloud of splinters, hammocks, and other
wreck that was flying across it. Man after man was killed at the wheel; the
fourth lieutenant, the master, and the boatswain were slain; and at 5.56, having
had her jib sheet and foretop-sail tie shot away, and her spanker brails loosened
so that the sail blew out, the *Chesapeake* came up into the wind somewhat, so as
to expose her quarter to her antagonist's broadside, which beat in her stern-
ports and swept the men from the after guns. One of the arm chests on the

[1] In his letter written just before sailing (already quoted on p. 100) he says: "An English frigate is now
in sight from our deck. * * * I am in hopes to give a good account of her before night." My account of
the action is mainly taken from James' "Naval History" and Brighton's "Memoir of Admiral Broke" (according to which the official letter of Captain Broke was tampered with); see also the letter of Lieut.
George Budd, June 15, 1813; the report of the Court of Inquiry, Commodore Bainbridge presiding, and
the Court-martial held on board frigate *United States,* April 15, 1814, Commodore Decatur presiding.

quarter-deck was blown up by a hand-grenade thrown from the *Shannon.*[1] The *Chesapeake* was now seen to have stern-way on and to be paying slowly off; so the *Shannon* put her helm a-starboard and shivered her mizzen top-sail, so as to keep off the wind and delay the boarding. But at that moment her jib stay was shot away, and her head-sails becoming becalmed, she went off very slowly. In consequence, at 6 P.M. the two frigates fell aboard, the *Chesapeake's* quarter pressing upon the *Shannon's* side just forward the starboard main-chains, and the frigates were kept in this position by the fluke of the *Shannon's* anchor catching in the *Chesapeake's* quarter port.

The *Shannon's* crew had suffered severely, but not the least panic or disorder existed among them. Broke ran forward, and seeing his foes flinching from the quarter-deck guns, he ordered the ships to be lashed together, the great guns to cease firing, and the boarders to be called. The boatswain, who had fought in Rodney's action, set about fastening the vessels together, which the grim veteran succeeded in doing, though his right arm was literally hacked off by a blow from a cutlass. All was confusion and dismay on board the *Chesapeake.* Lieutenant Ludlow had been mortally wounded and carried below; Lawrence himself, while standing on the quarter-deck, fatally conspicuous by his full-dress uniform and commanding stature, was shot down, as the vessels closed, by Lieutenant Law of the British marines. He fell dying, and was carried below, exclaiming: "Don't give up the ship"—a phrase that has since become proverbial among his countrymen. The third lieutenant, Mr. W. S. Cox, came on deck, but, utterly demoralized by the aspect of affairs, he basely ran below without staying to rally the men, and was court-martialled afterward for so doing. At 6.02 Captain Broke stepped from the *Shannon's* gangway rail on to the muzzle of the *Chesapeake's* aftermost carronade, and thence over the bulwark on to her quarter-deck, followed by about 20 men. As they came aboard, the *Chesapeake's* foreign mercenaries and the raw natives of the crew deserted their quarters; the Portuguese boatswain's mate removed the gratings of the berth-deck, and he ran below, followed by many of the crew, among them one of the midshipmen named Deforest. On the quarter-deck almost the only man that made any resistance was the chaplain, Mr. Livermore, who advanced, firing his pistol at Broke, and in return nearly had his arm hewed off by a stroke from the latter's broad Toledo blade. On the upper deck the only men who behaved well were the marines, but of their original number of 44 men, 14, including Lieutenant

---

[1] This explosion may have had more effect than is commonly supposed in the capture of the *Chesapeake.* Commodore Bainbridge, writing from Charleston, Mass., on June 2, 1813 (see "Captains' Letters," vol. xxix, No. 10), says: "Mr. Knox, the pilot on board, left the *Chesapeake* at 5 P.M. * * * At 6 P.M., Mr. Knox informs me, the fire opened, and at 12 minutes past six both ships were laying alongside one another as if in the act of boarding; at that moment an explosion took place on board the *Chesapeake,* which spread a fire on her upper deck from the foremast to the mizzen-mast, as high as her tops, and enveloped both ships in smoke for several minutes. After it cleared away they were seen separate, with the British flag hoisted on board the *Chesapeake* over the American." James denies that the explosion was caused by a hand-grenade, though he says there were some of these aboard the *Shannon.* It is a point of no interest.

James Broom and Corporal Dixon, were dead, and 20, including Sergeants Twin and Harris, wounded, so that there were left but one corporal and nine men, several of whom had been knocked down and bruised, though reported unwounded. There was thus hardly any resistance, Captain Broke stopping his men for a moment till they were joined by the rest of the boarders under Lieutenants Watt and Falkiner. The *Chesapeake's* mizzen-topmen began firing at the boarders, mortally wounding a midshipman, Mr. Samwell, and killing Lieutenant Watt; but one of the *Shannon's* long nines was pointed at the top and cleared it out, being assisted by the English main-topmen, under Midshipman Coshnahan. At the same time the men in the *Chesapeake's* main-top were driven out of it by the fire of the *Shannon's* foretopmen, under Midshipman Smith. Lieutenant George Budd, who was on the main-deck, now for the first time learned that the English had boarded, as the upper-deck men came crowding down, and at once called on his people to follow him; but the foreigners and novices held back, and only a few of the veterans followed him up. As soon as he reached the spar-deck, Budd, followed by only a dozen men, attacked the British as they came along the gangways, repulsing them for a moment, and killing the British purser, Aldham, and captain's clerk, Dunn; but the handful of Americans were at once cut down or dispersed, Lieutenant Budd being wounded and knocked down the main hatchway. "The enemy," writes Captain Broke, "fought desperately, but in disorder." Lieutenant Ludlow, already mortally wounded, struggled up on deck, followed by two or three men, but was at once disabled by a sabre cut. On the forecastle a few seamen and marines turned to bay. Captain Broke was still leading his men with the same brilliant personal courage he had all along shown. Attacking the first American, who was armed with a pike, he parried a blow from it, and cut down the man; attacking another he was himself cut down, and only saved by the seaman Mindham, already mentioned, who slew his assailant. One of the American marines, using his clubbed musket, killed an Englishman, and so stubborn was the resistance of the little group that for a moment the assailants gave back, having lost several killed and wounded; but immediately afterward they closed in and slew their foes to the last man. The British fired a volley or two down the hatchway, in response to a couple of shots fired up; all resistance was at an end, and at 6.05, just fifteen minutes after the first gun had been fired, and not five after Captain Broke had come aboard, the colors of the *Chesapeake* were struck. Of her crew of 379 men, 61 were killed or mortally wounded, including her captain, her first and fourth lieutenants, the lieutenant of marines, the master (White), boatswain (Adams), and three midshipmen, and 85 severely and slightly wounded, including both her other lieutenants, five midshipmen, and the chaplain; total, 148; the loss falling almost entirely upon the American portion of the crew.

Of the *Shannon's* men, 33 were killed outright or died of their wounds, including her first lieutenant, purser, captain's clerk, and one midshipman, and 50 wounded, including the captain himself and the boatswain; total, 83.

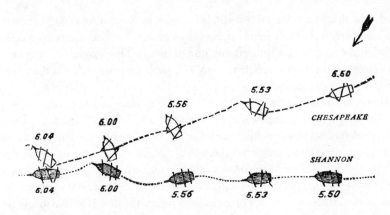

The *Chesapeake* was taken into Halifax, where Captain Lawrence and Lieutenant Ludlow were both buried with military honors. Captain Broke was made a baronet, very deservedly, and Lieutenants Wallis and Falkiner were both made commanders.

The British writers accuse some of the American crew of treachery; the Americans, in turn, accuse the British of revolting brutality. Of course in such a fight things are not managed with urbane courtesy, and, moreover, writers are prejudiced. Those who would like to hear one side are referred to James; if they wish to hear the other, to the various letters from officers published in "Niles' Register," especially vol. v, p. 142.

Neither ship had lost a spar, but all the lower masts, especially the two mizzen-masts, were badly wounded. The Americans at that period were fond of using bar shot, which were of very questionable benefit, being useless against a ship's hull, though said to be sometimes of great help in unrigging an antagonist from whom one was desirous of escaping, as in the case of the *President* and *Endymion*.

| "CHESAPEAKE" STRUCK BY | "SHANNON" STRUCK BY |
|---|---|
| 29 eighteen-pound shot, | 12 eighteen-pound shot, |
| 25 thirty-two-pound shot, | 13 thirty-two-pound shot, |
| 2 nine-pound shot, | 14 bar shot, |
| 306 grape, | 119 grape, |
| 362 shot. | 158 shot. |

It is thus seen that the *Shannon* received from shot alone only about half the damage the *Chesapeake* did; the latter was thoroughly beaten at the guns, in spite of what some American authors say to the contrary. And her victory was not in the slightest degree to be attributed to, though it may have been slightly hastened by, accident. Training and discipline won the victory, as often before; only in this instance the training and discipline were against us.

It is interesting to notice that the *Chesapeake* battered the *Shannon*'s hull far more than either the *Java*, *Guerrière*, or *Macedonian* did the hulls of their opponents, and that she suffered less in return (not in *loss* but in *damage*) than they did. The *Chesapeake* was a better fighter than either the *Java, Guerrière,* or *Macedonian,* and could have captured any one of them. The *Shannon* of course did less damage than any of the American 44's, probably just about in the proportion of the difference in force.

Almost all American writers have treated the capture of the *Chesapeake* as if it was due simply to a succession of unfortunate accidents; for example, Cooper, with his usual cheerful optimism, says that the incidents of the battle, excepting its short duration, are "altogether the results of the chances of war," and that it was mainly decided by "fortuitous events as unconnected with any particular merit on the one side as they are with any particular demerit on the other."[1] Most naval men consider it a species of treason to regard the defeat as due to any thing but extraordinary ill fortune. And yet no disinterested reader can help acknowledging that the true reason of the defeat was the very simple one that the *Shannon* fought better than the *Chesapeake.* It has often been said that up to the moment when the ships came together the loss and damage suffered by each were about the same. This is not true, and even if it was, would not affect the question. The heavy loss on board the *Shannon* did not confuse or terrify the thoroughly trained men with their implicit reliance on their leaders; and the experienced officers were ready to defend any point that was menaced. An equal or greater amount of loss aboard the *Chesapeake* disheartened and confused the raw crew, who simply had not had the time or chance to become well disciplined. Many of the old hands, of course, kept their wits and their pluck, but the novices and the disaffected did not. Similarly with the officers; some, as the Court of Inquiry found, had not kept to their posts, and all being new to each other and the ship, could not show to their best. There is no doubt that the *Chesapeake* was beaten at the guns before she was boarded. Had the ships not come together, the fight would have been longer, the loss greater, and more nearly equal; but the result would have been the same. Cooper says that the enemy entered with great caution, and so slowly that twenty resolute men could have repulsed him. It was no proof of caution for Captain Broke and his few followers to leap on board, unsupported, and then they only waited for the main body to come up; and no twenty men could have repulsed such boarders as followed Broke. The fight was another lesson, with the parties reversed, to the effect that want of training and discipline is a bad handicap. Had the *Chesapeake*'s crew been in service as many months as the *Shannon*'s had been years, such a captain as Lawrence would have had his men perfectly in hand; they would not have been cowed by their losses, nor some of the officers too demoralized to act properly, and the material advantages which the *Chesapeake* possessed, although not very great, would probably have been enough to give her a good chance of victory. It is well worth noticing that the

[1] The worth of such an explanation is very aptly gauged in General Alexander S. Webb's "The Peninsula; McClellan's Campaign of 1862" (New York, 1881), p. 35, where he speaks of "those unforeseen or uncontrollable agencies which are vaguely described as the 'fortune of war,' but which usually prove to be the superior ability or resources of the antagonist."

only thoroughly disciplined set of men aboard (all, according to James himself, by the way, native Americans), namely, the marines, did excellently, as shown by the fact that three fourths of their number were among the killed and wounded. The foreigners aboard the *Chesapeake* did not do as well as the Americans, but it is nonsense to ascribe the defeat in any way to them; it was only rendered rather more disastrous by their actions. Most of the English authors give very fair accounts of the battle, except that they hardly allude to the peculiar disadvantages under which the *Chesapeake* suffered when she entered into it. Thus, James thinks the *Java* was unprepared because she had only been to sea six weeks; but does not lay any weight on the fact that the *Chesapeake* had been out only as many hours.

Altogether the best criticism on the fight is that written by M. de la Gravière.[1] "It is impossible to avoid seeing in the capture of the *Chesapeake* a new proof of the enormous power of a good organization, when it has received the consecration of a few years' actual service on the sea. On this occasion, in effect, two captains equally renowned, the honor of two navies, were opposed to each other on two ships of the same tonnage and number of guns. Never had the chances seemed better balanced, but Sir Philip Broke had commanded the *Shannon* for nearly seven years, while Captain Lawrence had only commanded the *Chesapeake* for a few days. The first of these frigates had cruised for eighteen months on the coast of America; the second was leaving port. One had a crew long accustomed to habits of strict obedience; the other was manned by men who had just been engaged in mutiny. The Americans were wrong to accuse fortune on this occasion. Fortune was not fickle, she was merely logical. The *Shannon* captured the *Chesapeake* on the first of June, 1813, but on the 14th of September, 1806, the day when he took command of his frigate, Captain Broke had begun to prepare the glorious termination to this bloody affair."

Hard as it is to breathe a word against such a man as Lawrence, a very Bayard of the seas, who was admired as much for his dauntless bravery as he was loved for his gentleness and uprightness, it must be confessed that he acted rashly. And after he had sailed, it was, as Lord Howard Douglass has pointed out, a tactical error, however chivalric, to neglect the chance of luffing across the *Shannon*'s stern to rake her; exactly as it was a tactical error of his equally chivalrous antagonist to have let him have such an opportunity. Hull would not have committed either error, and would, for the matter of that, have been an overmatch for either commander. But it must always be remembered that Lawrence's encounters with the English had not been such as to give him a high opinion of them. The only foe he had fought had been inferior in strength, it is true, but had hardly made any effective resistance. Another sloop, of equal, if not superior force, had tamely submitted to blockade for several days, and had absolutely refused to fight. And there can be no doubt that the *Chesapeake,* unprepared though she was, would have been an overmatch for the *Guerrière, Macedonian,* or *Java.* Altogether it is hard to blame Lawrence for going out, and in every other respect his actions never have

[1] "Guerres Maritimes," ii, 272.

been, nor will be, mentioned, by either friend or foe, without the warmest respect. But that is no reason for insisting that he was ruined purely by an adverse fate. We will do far better to recollect that as much can be learned from reverses as from victories. Instead of flattering ourselves by saying the defeat was due to chance, let us try to find out what the real cause was, and then take care that it does not have an opportunity to act again. A little less rashness would have saved Lawrence's life and his frigate, while a little more audacity on one occasion would have made Commodore Chauncy famous for ever. And whether a lesson is to be learned or not, a historian should remember that his profession is not that of a panegyrist. The facts of the case unquestionably are that Captain Broke, in fair fight, within sight of the enemy's harbor, proved conqueror over a nominally equal and in reality slightly superior force; and that this is the only single-ship action of the war in which the victor was weaker in force than his opponent. So much can be gathered by reading only the American accounts. Moreover accident had little or nothing to do with the gaining of the victory. The explanation is perfectly easy; Lawrence and Broke were probably exactly equal in almost every thing that goes to make up a first-class commander, but one had trained his crew for seven years, and the other was new to the ship, to the officers, and to the men, and the last to each other. The *Chesapeake*'s crew must have been of fine material, or they would not have fought so well as they did.

So much for the American accounts. On the other hand, the capture of the *Chesapeake* was, and is, held by many British historians to "conclusively prove" a good many different things; such as, that if the odds were anything like equal, a British frigate could always whip an American, that in a hand-to-hand conflict such would invariably be the case, etc.; and as this was the only single-ship action of the war in which the victor was the inferior in force, most British writers insist that it reflected more honor on them than all the frigate actions of 1812 put together did on the Americans.

These assertions can be best appreciated by reference to a victory won by the French in the year of the Battle of the Nile. On the 14th of December, 1798, after two hours' conflict, the French 24-gun corvette *Bayonnaise* captured, by boarding, the English 32-gun frigate *Ambuscade*. According to James the *Ambuscade* threw at a broadside 262 pounds of shot, and was manned by 190 men, while the *Bayonnaise* threw 150 pounds, and had on board supernumeraries and passenger soldiers enough to make in all 250 men. According to the French historian Rouvier[1] the broadside force was 246 pounds against 80 pounds; according to Troude[2] it was 276 pounds against 112. M. Léon Guérin, in his voluminous but exceedingly prejudiced and one-sided work,[3] makes the difference even greater. At any rate the English vessel was vastly the superior in

---

[1] "Histoire des Marins Français sous la République," par Charles Rouvier, Lieutenant de Vaisseau, Paris, 1868.

[2] "Batailles Navales."

[3] "Histoire Maritime de France" (par Léon Guerin, Historien titulaire de la Marine, Membre de la Legion d'Honneur), vi, 142 (Paris, 1852).

force, and was captured by boarding, after a long and bloody conflict in which she lost 46, and her antagonist over 50, men. During all the wars waged with the Republic and the Empire, no English vessel captured a French one as much superior to itself as the *Ambuscade* was to the *Bayonnaise,* precisely as in the war of 1812 no American vessel captured a British opponent as much superior to itself as the *Chesapeake* was to the *Shannon.* Yet no sensible man can help acknowledging, in spite of these and a few other isolated instances, that at that time the French were inferior to the English, and the latter to the Americans.

It is amusing to compare the French histories of the English with the English histories of the Americans, and to notice the similarity of the arguments they use to detract from their opponents' fame. Of course I do not allude to such writers as Lord Howard Douglass or Admiral de la Gravière, but to men like William James and Léon Guérin, or even O. Troude. James is always recounting how American ships ran away from British ones, and Guérin tells as many anecdotes of British ships who fled from French foes. James reproaches the Americans for adopting a "Parthian" mode of warfare, instead of "bringing to in a bold and becoming manner." Precisely the same reproaches are used by the French writers, who assert that the English would not fight "fairly," but acquired an advantage by manœuvring. James lays great stress on the American long guns; so does Lieutenant Rouvier on the British carronades. James always tells how the Americans avoided the British ships, when the crews of the latter demanded to be led aboard; Troude says the British always kept at long shot, while the French sailors "demandèrent, à grands cris, l' abordage." James says the Americans "hesitated to grapple" with their foes "unless they possessed a twofold superiority"; Guérin that the English "never dared attack" except when they possessed "une supériorité énorme." The British sneer at the "mighty dollar"; the French at the "eternal guinea." The former consider Decatur's name as "sunk" to the level of Porter's or Bainbridge's; the latter assert that the "presumptuous Nelson" was inferior to any of the French admirals of the time preceding the Republic. Says James: "The Americans only fight well when they have the superiority of force on their side"; and Lieutenant Rouvier: "Never have the English vanquished us with an undoubted inferiority of force."

———

On June 12, 1813, the small cutter *Surveyor,* of 6 12-pound carronades, was lying in York River, in the Chesapeake, under the command of Mr. William S. Travis; her crew consisted of but 15 men.[1] At nightfall she was attacked by the boats of the *Narcissus* frigate, containing about 50 men, under the command of Lieutenant John Creerie.[2] None of the carronades could be used; but Mr. Travis made every preparation that he could for defence. The Americans waited till the British were within pistol shot before they opened their fire; the latter dashed gallantly on, however, and at once carried the cutter. But though

[1] Letter of W. S. Travis, June 16, 1813.
[2] James, vi, 334.

brief, the struggle was bloody; 5 of the Americans were wounded, and of the British 3 were killed and 7 wounded. Lieutenant Creerie considered his opponents to have shown so much bravery that he returned Mr. Travis his sword, with a letter as complimentary to him as it was creditable to the writer.[1]

———

As has been already mentioned, the Americans possessed a large force of gunboats at the beginning of the war. Some of these were fairly sea-worthy vessels, of 90 tons burden, sloop- or schooner-rigged, and armed with one or two long, heavy guns, and sometimes with several light carronades to repel boarders.[2] Gun-boats of this kind, together with the few small cutters owned by the government, were serviceable enough. They were employed all along the shores of Georgia and the Carolinas, and in Long Island Sound, in protecting the coasting trade by convoying parties of small vessels from one port to another, and preventing them from being molested by the boats of any of the British frigates. They also acted as checks upon the latter in their descents upon the towns and plantations, occasionally capturing their boats and tenders, and forcing them to be very cautious in their operations. They were very useful in keeping privateers off the coast, and capturing them when they came too far in. The exploits of those on the southern coast will be mentioned as they occurred. Those in Long Island Sound never came into collision with the foe, except for a couple of slight skirmishes at very long range; but in convoying little fleets of coasters, and keeping at bay the man-of-war boats sent to molest them, they were invaluable; and they also kept the Sound clear of hostile privateers.

Many of the gun-boats were much smaller than those just mentioned, trusting mainly to their sweeps for motive power, and each relying for offence on one long pivot gun, a 12- or 18-pounder. In the Chesapeake there was quite a large number of these small gallies, with a few of the larger kind, and here it was thought that by acting together in flotillas the gun-boats might in fine weather do considerable damage to the enemy's fleet by destroying detached vessels, instead of confining themselves to the more humble tasks in

---

[1] The letter, dated June 13th, is as follows: "Your gallant and desperate attempt to defend your vessel against more than double your number, on the night of the 12th instant, excited such admiration on the part of your opponents as I have seldom witnessed, and induced me to return you the sword you had so nobly used, in testimony of mine. Our poor fellows have suffered severely, occasioned chiefly, if not solely, by the precautions you had taken to prevent surprise. In short, I am at a loss which to admire most, the previous arrangement aboard the *Surveyor*, or the determined manner in which her deck was disputed inch by inch. I am, sir," etc.

[2] According to a letter from Captain Hugh G. Campbell (in the Naval Archives, "Captains' Letters," 1812, vol. ii, Nos. 21 and 192), the crews were distributed as follows: ten men and a boy to a long 32, seven men and a boy to a long 9, and five men and a boy to a carronade, exclusive of petty officers. Captain Campbell complains of the scarcity of men, and rather naively remarks that he is glad the marines have been withdrawn from the gun-boats, as this may make the commanders of the latter keep a brighter lookout than formerly.

which their brethren elsewhere were fairly successful. At this period Denmark, having lost all her larger ships of war, was confining herself purely to gun-brigs. These were stout little crafts, with heavy guns, which, acting together, and being handled with spirit and skill, had on several occasions in calm weather captured small British sloops, and had twice so injured frigates as to make their return to Great Britain necessary; while they themselves had frequently been the object of successful cutting-out expeditions. Congress hoped that our gun-boats would do as well as the Danish; but for a variety of reasons they failed utterly in every serious attack that they made on a man-of-war, and were worse than useless for all but the various subordinate employments above mentioned. The main reason for this failure was in the gun-boats themselves. They were utterly useless except in perfectly calm weather, for in any wind the heavy guns caused them to career over so as to make it difficult to keep them right side up, and impossible to fire. Even in smooth water they could not be fought at anchor, requiring to be kept in position by means of sweeps; and they were very unstable, the recoil of the guns causing them to roll so as to make it difficult to aim with any accuracy after the first discharge, while a single shot hitting one put it *hors de combat*. This last event rarely happened, however, for they were not often handled with any approach to temerity, and, on the contrary, usually made their attacks at a range that rendered it as impossible to inflict as to receive harm. It does not seem as if they were very well managed; but they were such ill-conditioned craft that the best officers might be pardoned for feeling uncomfortable in them. Their operations throughout the war offer a painfully ludicrous commentary on Jefferson's remarkable project of having our navy composed exclusively of such craft.

The first aggressive attempt made with the gun-boats was characteristically futile. On June 20th 15 of them, under Captain Tarbell, attacked the *Junon*, 38, Captain Sanders, then lying becalmed in Hampton Roads, with the *Barossa*, 36, and *Laurestinus*, 24, near her. The gun-boats, while still at very long range, anchored, and promptly drifted round so that they couldn't shoot. Then they got under way, and began gradually to draw nearer to the *Junon*. Her defence was very feeble; after some hasty and ill-directed vollies she endeavored to beat out of the way. But meanwhile, a slight breeze having sprung up, the *Barossa*, Captain Sherriff, approached near enough to take a hand in the affair, and at once made it evident that she was a more dangerous foe than the *Junon*, though a lighter ship. As soon as they felt the effects of the breeze the gun-boats became almost useless, and, the *Barossa*'s fire being animated and well aimed, they withdrew. They had suffered nothing from the *Junon*, but during the short period she was engaged, the *Barossa* had crippled one boat and slightly damaged another; one man was killed and two wounded. The *Barossa* escaped unscathed and the *Junon* was but slightly injured. Of the combatants, the *Barossa* was the only one that came off with credit, the *Junon* behaving, if any thing, rather worse than the gun-boats. There was no longer any doubt as to the amount of reliance to be placed on the latter.[1]

On June 20, 1813, a British force of three 74's, one 64, four frigates, two sloops, and three transports was anchored off Craney Island. On the northwest side of this island was a battery of 18-pounders, to take charge of which Captain Cassin, commanding the naval forces at Norfolk, sent ashore one hundred sailors of the *Constellation,* under the command of Lieutenants Neale, Shubrick, and Saunders, and fifty marines under Lieutenant Breckenbridge.[2] On the morning of the 22d they were attacked by a division of 15 boats, containing 700 men,[3] seamen, marines, chasseurs, and soldiers of the 102d regiment, the whole under the command of Captain Pechell, of the *San Domingo,* 74. Captain Hanchett led the attack in the *Diadem*'s launch. The battery's guns were not fired till the British were close in, when they opened with destructive effect. While still some seventy yards from the guns the *Diadem*'s launch grounded, and the attack was checked. Three of the boats were now sunk by shot, but the water was so shallow that they remained above water; and while the fighting was still at its height, some of the *Constellation*'s crew, headed by Midshipman Tatnall, waded out and took possession of them.[4] A few of their crew threw away their arms and came ashore with their captors; others escaped to the remaining boats, and immediately afterward the flotilla made off in disorder having lost 91 men. The three captured barges were large, strong boats, one called the *Centipede* being fifty feet long, and more formidable than many of the American gun-vessels. The *Constellation*'s men deserve great credit for their defence, but the British certainly did not attack with their usual obstinacy. When the foremost boats were sunk, the water was so shallow and the bottom so good that the Americans on shore, as just stated, at once waded out to them; and if in the heat of the fight Tatnall and his seamen could get *out* to the boats, the 700 British ought to have been able to get *in* to the battery, whose 150 defenders would then have stood no chance.[5]

---

[1] Though the flotilla men did nothing in the boats, they acted with the most stubborn bravery at the battle of Bladensburg. The British Lieutenant Graig, himself a spectator, thus writes of their deeds on that occasion ("Campaign at Washington," p. 119). "Of the sailors, however, it would be injustice not to speak in the terms which their conduct merits. They were employed as gunners, and not only did they serve their guns with a quickness and precision which astonished their assailants, but they stood till some of them were actually bayoneted with fuses in their hands; nor was it till their leader was wounded and taken, and they saw themselves deserted on all sides by the soldiers, that they quitted the field." Certainly such men could not be accused of lack of courage. Something else is needed to account for the failure of the gun-boat system.

[2] Letter of Captain John Cassin, June 23, 1813.

[3] James, vi, 337.

[4] "Life of Commodore Josiah Tatnall," by Charles C. Jones, Jr. (Savannah, 1878), p. 17.

[5] James comments on this repulse as "a defeat as discreditable to those that caused it as honorable to those that suffered in it." "Unlike most other nations, the Americans in particular, the British, when engaged in expeditions of this nature, always rest their hopes of success upon valor rather than on numbers." These comments read particularly well when it is remembered that the assailants outnumbered the assailed in the proportion of 5 to 1. It is monotonous work to have to supplement a history by a run-

On July 14, 1813, the two small vessels *Scorpion* and *Asp*, the latter commanded by Mr. Sigourney, got under way from out of the Yeocomico Creek,[1] and at 10 A.M. discovered in chase the British brig-sloops *Contest*, Captain James Rattray, and *Mohawk*, Captain Henry D. Byng.[2] The *Scorpion* beat up the Chesapeake, but the dull-sailing *Asp* had to reenter the creek; the two brigs anchored off the bar and hoisted out their boats, under the command of Lieutenant Rodger C. Curry; whereupon the *Asp* cut her cable and ran up the creek some distance. Here she was attacked by three boats, which Mr. Sigourney and his crew of twenty men, with two light guns, beat off; but they were joined by two others, and the five carried the *Asp*, giving no quarter. Mr. Sigourney and 10 of his men were killed or wounded, while the British also suffered heavily, having 4 killed and 7 (including Lieutenant Curry) wounded. The surviving Americans reached the shore, rallied under Midshipman H. McClintock (second in command), and when the British retired after setting the *Asp* on fire, at once boarded her, put out the flames, and got her in fighting order; but they were not again molested.

On July 29th, while the *Junon*, 38, Captain Sanders, and *Martin*, 18, Captain Senhouse, were in Delaware Bay, the latter grounded on the outside of Crow's Shoal; the frigate anchored within supporting distance, and while in this position the two ships were attacked by the American flotilla in those waters, consisting of eight gun-boats, carrying each 25 men and one long 32, and two heavier block-sloops,[3] commanded by Lieutenant Samuel Angus. The flotilla kept at such a distance that an hour's cannonading did no damage whatever to anybody; and during that time gun-boat No. 121, Sailing-master Shead, drifted a mile and a half away from her consorts. Seeing this the British made a dash at her, in 7 boats, containing 140 men, led by Lieutenant Philip Westphal. Mr. Shead anchored and made an obstinate defence, but at the first discharge the gun's pintle gave way, and the next time it was fired the gun-carriage was almost torn to pieces. He kept up a spirited fire of small arms, in reply to the boat-carronades and musketry of the assailants; but the latter advanced steadily and carried the gun-boat by boarding, 7 of her people being wounded, while 7 of the British were killed and 13 wounded.[4] The defence of No. 121 was very creditable, but otherwise the honor of the day was certainly with the British; whether because the gun-boats were themselves so worthless or because they were not handled boldly enough, they did

---

ning commentary on James' mistakes and inventions; but it is worth while to prove once for all the utter unreliability of the author who is accepted in Great Britain as the great authority about the war. Still, James is no worse than his compeers. In the American Coggeshall's "History of Privateers," the misstatements are as gross and the sneers in as poor taste—the British, instead of the Americans, being the objects.

[1] Letter of Midshipman McClintock, July 15, 1813.
[2] James, vi, 343.
[3] Letter of Lieutenant Angus, July 30, 1813.
[4] Letter of Mr. Shead, Aug. 5, 1813.

no damage, even to the grounded sloop, that would seem to have been at their mercy.[1]

On June 18th the American brig-sloop *Argus*, commanded by Lieutenant William Henry Allen, late first of the *United States*, sailed from New York for France, with Mr. Crawford, minister for that country, aboard, and reached L'Orient on July 11th, having made one prize on the way. On July 14th she again sailed, and cruised in the chops of the Channel, capturing and burning ship after ship, and creating the greatest consternation among the London merchants; she then cruised along Cornwall and got into St. George's Channel, where the work of destruction went on. The labor was very severe and harassing, the men being able to get very little rest.[2] On the night of August 13th, a brig laden with wine from Oporto was captured and burnt, and unluckily many of the crew succeeded in getting at some of the cargo. At 5 A.M. on the 14th a large brig-of-war was discovered standing down under a cloud of canvas.[3] This was the British brig-sloop *Pelican*, Captain John Fordyce Maples, which, from information received at Cork three days previous, had been cruising especially after the *Argus*, and had at last found her; St. David's Head bore east five leagues (lat. 52° 15′ N. and 5° 50′ W.).

The small, fine-lined American cruiser, with her lofty masts and long spars, could easily have escaped from her heavier antagonist; but Captain Allen had no such intention, and, finding he could not get the weather-gage, he shortened sail and ran easily along on the starboard tack, while the *Pelican* came down on him with the wind (which was from the south) nearly aft. At 6 A.M. the *Argus* wore and fired her port guns within grape distance, the *Pelican* responding with her starboard battery, and the action began with great spirit on both sides.[4] At 6.04 a round shot carried off Captain Allen's leg, inflicting a mortal wound, but he stayed on deck till he fainted from loss of blood. Soon the British fire carried away the main-braces, main-spring-stay, gaff, and try-sail mast of the *Argus*; the first lieutenant, Mr. Watson, was wounded in the head by a grape-shot and carried below; the second lieutenant, Mr. U. H. Allen (no relation of the captain), continued to fight the ship with great skill. The *Pelican*'s fire continued very heavy, the *Argus* losing her spritsail-yard and most of the standing rigging on the port side of the foremast. At 6.14 Captain Maples bore up to pass astern of his antagonist, but Lieutenant Allen luffed into the wind and threw the main-top-sail aback, getting into a beautiful raking position[5]; had the men at

---

[1] The explanation possibly lies in the fact that the gun-boats had worthless powder. In the Naval Archives there is a letter from Mr. Angus ("Masters' Commandant Letters," 1813, No. 3; see also No. 91), in which he says that the frigate's shot passed over them, while theirs could not even reach the sloop. He also encloses a copy of a paper, signed by the other gun-boat officers, which runs: "We, the officers of the vessels comprising the Delaware flotilla, protest against the powder as being unfit for service."

[2] Court of Inquiry into loss of *Argus*, 1815.

[3] Letter of Lieutenant Watson, March 2, 1815.

[4] Letter of Captain Maples to Admiral Thornborough, Aug. 14, 1813.

[5] Letter of Lieutenant Watson.

the guns done their duty as well as those on the quarter-deck did theirs, the issue of the fight would have been very different; but, as it was, in spite of her favorable position, the raking broadside of the *Argus* did little damage. Two or three minutes afterward the *Argus* lost the use of her after-sails through having her preventer-main-braces and top-sail tie shot away, and fell off before the wind, when the *Pelican* at 6.18 passed her stern, raking her heavily, and then ranged up on her starboard quarter. In a few minutes the wheel-ropes and running-rigging of every description were shot away, and the *Argus* became utterly unmanageable. The *Pelican* continued raking her with perfect impunity, and at 6.35 passed her broadside and took a position on her starboard bow, when at 6.45 the brigs fell together, and the British "were in the act of boarding when the *Argus* struck her colors,"[1] at 6.45 A.M. The *Pelican* carried, besides her regular armament, two long 6's as stern-chasers, and her broadside weight of metal was thus:[2]

$$1 \times 6$$
$$1 \times 6$$
$$1 \times 12$$
$$8 \times 32$$

or 280 lbs. against the *Argus*':

$$1 \times 12$$
$$9 \times 24$$

or, subtracting as usual 7 per cent. for light weight of metal, 210 lbs. The *Pelican*'s crew consisted of but 116 men, according to the British account, though the American reports make it much larger. The *Argus* had started from New York with 137 men, but having manned and sent in several prizes, her crew amounted, as near as can be ascertained, to 104. Mr. Low in his "Naval History," published just after the event, makes it but 99. James makes it 121; as he placed the crew of the *Enterprise* at 125, when it was really 102; that of the *Hornet* at 162, instead of 135; of the *Peacock* at 185, instead of 166; of the *Nautilus* at 106 instead of 95, etc., etc., it is safe to presume that he has overestimated it by at least 20, which brings the number pretty near to the American accounts. The *Pelican* lost but two men killed and five wounded. Captain Maples had a narrow escape, a spent grape-shot striking him in the chest with some force, and then falling on the deck. One shot had passed through the boatswain's and one through the carpenter's cabin; her sides were filled with grape-shot, and her rigging and sails much injured; her foremast, main-top-mast, and royal masts were slightly wounded, and two of her carronades dismounted.

[1] Letter of Captain Maples.
[2] James, vi, 320.

The injuries of the *Argus* have already been detailed; her hull and lower masts were also tolerably well cut up. Of her crew, Captain Allen, two midshipmen, the carpenter, and six seamen were killed or mortally wounded; her first lieutenant and 13 seamen severely and slightly wounded: total, 10 killed and 14 wounded.

In reckoning the comparative force, I include the Englishman's six-pound stern-chaser, which could not be fired in broadside with the rest of the guns, because I include the *Argus'* 12-pound bow-chaser, which also could not be fired in broadside, as it was crowded into the bridle-port. James, of course, carefully includes the latter, though leaving out the former.

COMPARISON

| | TONS. | NO. GUNS. | WEIGHT METAL. | MEN. | LOSS. |
|---|---|---|---|---|---|
| *Argus* | 298 | 10 | 210 | 104 | 24 |
| *Pelican* | 467 | 11 | 280 | 116 | 7 |

| | COMPARATIVE FORCE. | COMPARATIVE LOSS INFLICTED. |
|---|---|---|
| *Argus* | .82 | .29 |
| *Pelican* | 1.00 | 1.00 |

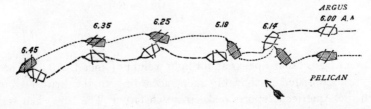

Of all the single-ship actions fought in the war this is the least creditable to the Americans. The odds in force, it is true, were against the *Argus,* about in the proportion of 10 to 8, but this is neither enough to account for the loss inflicted being as 10 to 3, nor for her surrendering when she had been so little ill used. It was not even as if her antagonist had been an unusually fine vessel of her class. The *Pelican* did not do as well as either the *Frolic* previously, or the *Reindeer* afterward, though perhaps rather better than the *Avon, Penguin,* or *Peacock.* With a comparatively unmanageable antagonist, in smooth water, she ought to have sunk her in three quarters of an hour. But the *Pelican's* not having done particularly well merely makes the conduct of the Americans look worse; it is just the reverse of the *Chesapeake's* case, where, paying the highest credit to the British, we still thought the fight no discredit to us. Here we can indulge no such reflection. The officers did well, but the crew did not. Cooper says: "The enemy was so much heavier that it may be doubted whether the *Argus* would have captured her antagonist under any ordinary circumstances." This I doubt; such a crew as the *Wasp's* or *Hornet's* probably would have been successful. The trouble with the guns of the *Argus* was not so much that they were too small, as that they did not hit; and this seems all the more incomprehensible when it is remembered that Captain Allen is the very man to whom Commodore Decatur, in his official letter, attributed the skilful gun-practice of the crew of the frigate *United States.* Cooper says that the powder was bad; and it has also been said that the men of the *Argus* were over-fatigued and were drunk, in which case they ought not to have been brought into action. Besides unskilfulness, there is another very serious count against the crew. Had the *Pelican* been some distance from the *Argus,* and in a position where she could pour in her fire with perfect impunity to herself, when the surrender took place, it would have been more justifiable. But, on the contrary, the vessels were touching, and the British boarded just as the colors were hauled down; it was certainly very disgraceful that the Americans did not rally to repel them, for they had still four fifths of their number absolutely untouched. They certainly *ought* to have succeeded, for boarding is a difficult and dangerous experiment; and if they had repulsed their antagonists they might in turn have carried the *Pelican.* So that, in summing up the merits of this action, it is fair to say that both sides showed skilful seamanship and unskilful gunnery; that the British fought bravely and that the Americans did not.

It is somewhat interesting to compare this fight, where a weaker American sloop was taken by a stronger British one, with two or three others, where both the comparative force and the result were reversed. Comparing it, therefore, with the actions between the *Hornet* and *Peacock* (British), the *Wasp* and *Avon,* and the *Peacock* (American) and *Epervier,* we get four actions, in one of which, the first-named, the British were victorious, and in the other three the Americans.

| | COMPARATIVE FORCE. | COMPARATIVE LOSS INFLICTED. | PER CENT. LOSS. |
|---|---|---|---|
| *Pelican* (British) | 1.00 | 1.00 | .06 |
| *Argus* (American) | .82 | .29 | .23 |
| *Hornet* (American) | 1.00 | 1.00 | .02 |
| *Peacock* (British) | .83 | .07 | .31 |
| *Wasp* (American) | 1.00 | 1.00 | .02 |
| *Avon* (British) | .80 | .07 | .33 |
| *Peacock* (American) | 1.00 | 1.00 | .01 |
| *Epervier* (British) | .81 | .08 | .20 |

It is thus seen that in these sloop actions the superiority of force on the side of the victor was each time about the same. The *Argus* made a much more effectual resistance than did either the *Peacock, Avon,* or *Epervier,* while the *Pelican* did her work in poorer form than either of the victorious American sloops; and, on the other hand, the resistance of the *Argus* did not by any means show as much bravery as was shown in the defence of the *Peacock* or *Avon*, although rather more than in the case of the *Epervier*.

This is the only action of the war where it is almost impossible to find out the cause of the inferiority of the beaten crew. In almost all other cases we find that one crew had been carefully drilled, and so proved superior to a less-trained antagonist; but it is incredible that the man, to whose exertions when first lieutenant of the *States* Commodore Decatur ascribes the skilfulness of that ship's men, should have neglected to train his own crew; and this had the reputation of being composed of a fine set of men. Bad powder would not account for the surrender of the *Argus* when so little damaged. It really seems as if the men *must* have been drunk or over-fatigued, as has been so often asserted. Of course drunkenness would account for the defeat, although not in the least altering its humiliating character.

"Et tu quoque" is not much of an argument; still it may be as well to call to mind here two engagements in which British sloops suffered much more discreditable defeats than the *Argus* did. The figures are taken from James; as given by the French historians they make even a worse showing for the British.

A short time before our war the British brig *Carnation*, 18, had been captured, by boarding, by the French brig *Palinure*, 16, and the British brig *Alacrity*, 18, had been captured, also by boarding, by the corvette *Abeille*, 20.

The following was the comparative force, etc., of the combatants:

|  | WEIGHT METAL. | NO. CREW. | LOSS. |
|---|---|---|---|
| *Carnation* | 262 | 117 | 40 |
| *Palinure* | 174 | 100 | 20 |
| *Alacrity* | 262 | 100 | 18 |
| *Abeille* | 260 | 130 | 19 |

In spite of the pride the British take in their hand-to-hand prowess both of these ships were captured by boarding. The *Carnation* was captured by a much smaller force, instead of by a much larger one, as in the case of the *Argus;* and if the *Argus* gave up before she had suffered greatly, the *Alacrity* surrendered when she had suffered still less. French historians asserted that the capture of the two brigs proved that "French valor could conquer British courage"; and a similar opinion was very complacently expressed by British historians after the defeat of the *Argus.* All that the three combats really "proved" was, that in eight encounters between British and American sloops the Americans were defeated once; and in a far greater number of encounters between French and British sloops the British were defeated twice. No one pretends that either navy was invincible; the question is, which side averaged best?

---

At the opening of the war we possessed several small brigs; these had originally been fast, handy little schooners, each armed with 12 long sixes, and with a crew of 60 men. As such they were effective enough; but when afterward changed into brigs, each armed with a couple of extra guns, and given 40 additional men, they became too slow to run, without becoming strong enough to fight. They carried far too many guns and men for their size, and not enough to give them a chance with any respectable opponent; and they were almost all ignominiously captured. The single exception was the brig *Enterprise*. She managed to escape capture, owing chiefly to good luck, and once fought a victorious engagement, thanks to the fact that the British possessed a class of vessels even worse than our own. She was kept near the land and finally took up her station off the eastern coast, where she did good service in chasing away or capturing the various Nova Scotian or New Brunswick privateers, which were smaller and less formidable vessels than the privateers of the United States, and not calculated for fighting.

By crowding guns into her bridle-ports, and over-manning herself, the *Enterprise*, now under the command of Lieutenant William Burrows, mounted 14 eighteen-pound carronades and 2 long 9's, with 102 men. On September 5th, while standing along shore near Penguin Point, a few miles to the eastward of Portland, Me., she discovered, at anchor inside, a man-of-war brig[1] which proved to be H.M.S. *Boxer*, Captain Samuel Blyth, of 12 carronades, eighteen-pounders and two long sixes, with but 66 men aboard, 12 of her crew being absent.[2] The *Boxer* at once hoisted three British ensigns and bore up for the *Enterprise*, then standing in on the starboard tack; but when the two brigs were still 4 miles apart it fell calm. At midday a breeze sprang up from the southwest, giving the American the weather-gage, but the latter manœuvred for some time to windward to try the comparative rates of sailing of the vessels. At 3 P.M. Lieutenant Burrows hoisted three ensigns, shortened sail, and edged away toward the enemy, who came gallantly on. Captain Blyth had nailed his colors to the mast, telling his men they should never be struck while he had life in his body.[3] Both crews cheered loudly as they neared each other, and at 3.15, the two brigs being on the starboard tack not a half pistol-shot apart, they opened fire, the American using the port, and the English the starboard, battery. Both broadsides were very destructive, each of the commanders falling at the very beginning of the action. Captain Blyth was struck by an eighteen-pound shot while he was standing on the quarter-deck; it passed completely through his body, shattering his left arm and killing him on the spot. The command, thereupon, devolved on Lieutenant David McCreery. At almost the same time his equally gallant antagonist fell. Lieutenant Burrows, while encouraging his men, laid hold of a gun-tackle fall to help the crew of a carronade run out the gun; in doing so he raised one leg against the bulwark, when a canister shot struck his thigh, glancing into his body and inflicting a fearful wound.[4] In spite of the pain he refused to be carried

[1] Letter from Lieutenant Edward R. McCall to Commodore Hull, September 5, 1813.

[2] James, "Naval Occurrences," 264. The American accounts give the *Boxer* 104 men, on very insufficient grounds. Similarly James gives the *Enterprise* 123 men. Each side will be considered authority for its own force and loss.

[3] "Naval Chronicle," vol. xxxii, p. 462.

[4] Cooper, "Naval History," vol. ii, p. 259.

below, and lay on the deck, crying out that the colors must never be struck. Lieutenant Edward McCall now took command. At 3.30 the *Enterprise* ranged ahead, rounded to on the starboard tack, and raked the *Boxer* with the starboard guns. At 3.35 the *Boxer* lost her main-top-mast and top-sail yard, but her crew still kept up the fight bravely, with the exception of four men who deserted their quarters and were afterward court-martialed for cowardice.[1] The *Enterprise* now set her fore-sail and took position on the enemy's starboard bow, delivering raking fires; and at 3.45 the latter surrendered, when entirely unmanageable and defenceless. Lieutenant Burrows would not go below until he had received the sword of his adversary, when he exclaimed, "I am satisfied, I die contented."

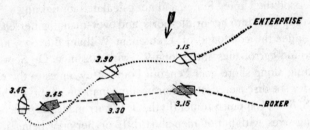

Both brigs had suffered severely, especially the *Boxer*, which had been hulled repeatedly, had three eighteen-pound shot through her foremast, her top-gallant forecastle almost cut away, and several of her guns dismounted. Three men were killed and seventeen wounded, four mortally. The *Enterprise* had been hulled by one round and many grape; one 18-pound ball had gone through her foremast, and another through her main-mast, and she was much cut up aloft. Two of her men were killed and ten wounded, two of them (her commander and Midshipman Kervin Waters) mortally. The British court-martial attributed the defeat of the *Boxer* "to a superiority in the enemy's force, principally in the number of men, as well as to a greater degree of skill in the direction of her fire, and to the destructive effects of the first broadside." But the main element was the superiority in force, the difference in loss being very nearly proportional to it; both sides fought with equal bravery and equal skill. This fact was appreciated by the victors, for at a naval dinner given in New York shortly afterward, one of the toasts offered was: "The crew of the *Boxer*, enemies by law, but by gallantry brothers." The two commanders were both buried at Portland, with all the honors of war. The conduct of Lieutenant Burrows needs no comment. He was an officer greatly beloved and respected in the service. Captain Blyth, on the other side, had not only shown himself on many occasions to be a man of distinguished personal courage, but was equally noted for his gentleness and humanity. He had been one of Captain Lawrence's pall-bearers, and but a month previous to his death had received a public note of thanks from an American colonel, for an act of great kindness and courtesy.[2]

[1] Minutes of court-martial held aboard H.M.S. *Surprise*, January 8, 1814.
[2] "Naval Chronicle," xxxii, 466.

The *Enterprise,* under Lieut.-Com. Renshaw, now cruised off the southern coast, where she made several captures. One of them was a heavy British privateer, the *Mars,* of 14 long nines and 75 men, which struck after receiving a broadside that killed and wounded 4 of her crew. The *Enterprise* was chased by frigates on several occasions; being once forced to throw overboard all her guns but two, and escaping only by a shift in the wind. Afterward, as she was unfit to cruise, she was made a guard-ship at Charlestown; for the same reason the *Boxer* was not purchased into the service.

———

On October 4th some volunteers from the Newport flotilla captured, by boarding, the British privateer *Dart,*[1] after a short struggle in which two of the assailants were wounded and several of the privateersmen, including the first officer, were killed.

On December 4th, Commodore Rodgers, still in command of the *President,* sailed again from Providence, Rhode Island. On the 25th, in lat. 19° N. and long. 35° W., the *President,* during the night, fell in with two frigates, and came so close that the head-most fired at her, when she made off. These were thought to be British, but were in reality the two French 40-gun frigates *Nymphe* and *Meduse,* one month out of Brest. After this little encounter Rodgers headed toward the Barbadoes, and cruised to windward of them.

———

On the whole the ocean warfare of 1813 was decidedly in favor of the British, except during the first few months. The *Hornet*'s fight with the *Peacock* was an action similar to those that took place in 1812, and the cruise of Porter was unique in our annals, both for the audacity with which it was planned, and the success with which it was executed. Even later in the year the *Argus* and the *President* made bold cruises in sight of the British coasts, the former working great havoc among the merchant-men. But by that time the tide had turned strongly in favor of our enemies. From the beginning of summer the blockade was kept up so strictly that it was with difficulty any of our vessels broke through it; they were either chased back or captured. In the three actions that occurred, the British showed themselves markedly superior in two, and in the third the combatants fought equally well, the result being fairly decided by the fuller crew and slightly heavier metal of the *Enterprise.* The gun-boats, to which many had looked for harbor defence, proved nearly useless, and were beaten off with ease whenever they made an attack.

The lessons taught by all this were the usual ones. Lawrence's victory in the *Hornet* showed the superiority of a properly trained crew to one that had not been properly trained; and his defeat in the *Chesapeake* pointed exactly the same way, demonstrating in addition the folly of taking a raw levy out of port, and, before they have had the slightest chance of getting seasoned, pitting them against skilled veterans. The victory of the *Enterprise* showed the wisdom of having the odds in men and metal in our favor, when our antagonist was other-

[1] Letter of Mr. Joseph Nicholson, Oct. 5, 1813.

wise our equal; it proved, what hardly needed proving, that, whenever possible, a ship should be so constructed as to be superior in force to the foes it would be likely to meet. As far as the capture of the *Argus* showed any thing, it was the advantage of heavy metal and the absolute need that a crew should fight with pluck. The failure of the gun-boats *ought* to have taught the lesson (though it did not) that too great economy in providing the means of defence may prove very expensive in the end, and that good officers and men are powerless when embarked in worthless vessels. A similar point was emphasized by the strictness of the blockade, and the great inconvenience it caused; namely, that we ought to have had ships powerful enough to break it.

We had certainly lost ground during this year; fortunately we regained it during the next two.

### BRITISH VESSELS SUNK OR TAKEN

| NAME. | GUNS. | TONNAGE. |
|-------|-------|----------|
| Peacock | 20 | 477 |
| Boxer | 14 | 181 |
| Highflyer | 6 | 96 |
| | 40 | 754 |

### AMERICAN VESSELS SUNK OR TAKEN

| NAME. | GUNS. | TONNAGE. |
|-------|-------|----------|
| Chesapeake | 50 | 1,265 |
| Argus | 20 | 298 |
| Viper | 10 | 148 |
| | 80 | 1,711 |

### VESSELS BUILT OR PURCHASED

| NAME. | RIG. | GUNS. | TONNAGE. | WHERE BUILT. | COST. |
|-------|------|-------|----------|--------------|-------|
| Rattlesnake | Brig | 14 | 278 | Medford, Pa. | $18,000 |
| Alligator | Schooner | 4 | 80 | | |
| Asp | Sloop | 3 | 56 | | 2,600 |

### PRIZES MADE

| NAME OF SHIP. | NO. OF PRIZE. |
|---------------|---------------|
| President | 13 |
| Congress | 4 |
| Chesapeake | 6 |
| Essex | 14 |
| Hornet | 3 |
| Argus | 21 |
| Small craft | 18 |
| | 79 |

# VI

# 1813

## ON THE LAKES

## ONTARIO

Winter had almost completely stopped preparations on the American side. Bad weather put an end to all communication with Albany or New York, and so prevented the transit of stores, implements, etc. It was worse still with the men, for the cold and exposure so thinned them out that the new arrivals could at first barely keep the ranks filled. It was, moreover, exceedingly difficult to get seamen to come from the coast to serve on the lakes, where work was hard, sickness prevailed, and there was no chance of prize-money. The British government had the great advantage of being able to move its sailors where it pleased, while in the American service, at that period, the men enlisted for particular ships, and the only way to get them for the lakes at all was by inducing portions of crews to volunteer to follow their officers thither.[1] However, the work went on in spite of interruptions. Fresh gangs of shipwrights arrived, and, largely owing to the energy and capacity of the head builder, Mr. Henry Eckford (who did as much as any naval officer in giving us an effective force on Ontario), the *Madison* was equipped, a small despatch sloop, *The Lady of the Lake* prepared,

---

[1] Cooper, ii, 357. One of James' most comical misstatements is that on the lakes the American sailors were all "picked men." On p. 367, for example, in speaking of the battle of Lake Erie he says: "Commodore Perry had picked crews to all his vessels." As a matter of fact Perry had once sent in his resignation solely on account of the very poor quality of his crews, and had with difficulty been induced to withdraw it. Perry's crews were of hardly average excellence, but then the average American sailor was a very good specimen.

and a large new ship, the *General Pike*, 28, begun, to mount 13 guns in each broadside and 2 on pivots.

Meanwhile Sir George Prevost, the British commander in Canada, had ordered two 24-gun ships to be built, and they were begun; but he committed the mistake of having one laid down in Kingston and the other in York, at the opposite end of the lake. Earle, the Canadian commodore, having proved himself so incompetent, was removed; and in the beginning of May Captain Sir James Lucas Yeo arrived, to act as commander-in-chief of the naval forces, together with four captains, eight lieutenants, twenty-four midshipmen, and about 450 picked seamen, sent out by the home government especially for service on the Canada lakes.[1]

The comparative force of the two fleets or squadrons it is hard to estimate. I have already spoken of the difficulty in finding out what guns were mounted on any given ship at a particular time, and it is even more perplexing with the crews. A schooner would make one cruise with but thirty hands; on the next it would appear with fifty, a number of militia having volunteered as marines. Finding the militia rather a nuisance, they would be sent ashore, and on her third cruise the schooner would substitute half a dozen frontier seamen in their place. It was the same with the larger vessels. The *Madison* might at one time have her full complement of 200 men; a month's sickness would ensue, and she would sail with but 150 effectives. The *Pike*'s crew of 300 men at one time would shortly afterward be less by a third in consequence of a draft of sailors being sent to the upper lakes. So it is almost impossible to be perfectly accurate; but, making a comparison of the various authorities from Lieutenant Emmons to James, the following tables of the forces may be given as very nearly correct. In broadside force I count every pivot gun, and half of those that were not on pivots.

This is not materially different from James' account (p. 356), which gives Chauncy 114 guns, 1,193 men, and 2,121 tons. The *Lady of the Lake*, however, was never intended for any thing but a despatch boat, and the *Scourge* and *Hamilton* were both lost before Chauncy actually came into collision with Yeo. Deducting these, in order to compare the two foes, Chauncy had left 11 vessels of 2,265 tons, with 865 men and 92 guns throwing a broadside of 1,230 pounds.

This differs but slightly from James, who gives Yeo 92 guns throwing a broadside of 1,374 pounds, but only 717 men. As the evidence in the court-martial held on Captain Barclay, and the official accounts (on both sides) of Macdonough's victory, convict him of very much underrating the force in men of the British on Erie and Champlain, it can be safely assumed that he has underestimated the force in men on Lake Ontario. By comparing the tonnage he gives to Barclay's and Downie's squadrons with what it really was, we can correct his account of Yeo's tonnage.

[1] James, vi, 353.

## CHAUNCY'S SQUADRON

| NAME. | RIG. | TONNAGE. | CREW. | BROADSIDE METAL; LBS. | ARMAMENT. |
|---|---|---|---|---|---|
| Pike, | ship | 875 | 300 | 360 | 28 long 24's |
| Madison, | " | 593 | 200 | 364 | 24 short 32's |
| Oneida, | brig | 243 | 100 | 172 | 16 " 24's |
| Hamilton, | schooner | 112 | 50 | 80 | 1 long 32 / 1 " 24 / 8 " 6's |
| Scourge, | " | 110 | 50 | 80 | 1 " 32 / 8 short 12's |
| Conquest, | " | 82 | 40 | 56 | 1 long 32 / 1 " 12 / 4 " 6's |
| Tompkins, | " | 96 | 40 | 62 | 1 " 32 / 1 " 12 / 6 " 6's |
| Julia, | " | 82 | 35 | 44 | 1 " 32 / 1 " 12 |
| Growler, | " | 81 | 35 | 44 | 1 " 32 / 1 " 12 |
| Ontario, | " | 53 | 35 | 44 | 1 long 32 / 1 " 12 |
| Fair American, | " | 53 | 30 | 36 | 1 " 24 / 1 " 12 |
| Pert, | " | 50 | 25 | 24 | 1 " 24 |
| Asp, | " | 57 | 25 | 24 | 1 " 24 |
| Lady of the Lake, | " | 89 | 15 | 9 | 1 " 9 |
| 14 | | 2,576 | 980 | 1,399 | 112 |

## YEO'S SQUADRON

| NAME. | RIG. | TONNAGE. | CREW. | BROADSIDE METAL; LBS. | ARMAMENT. |
|---|---|---|---|---|---|
| Wolfe, | ship | 637 | 220 | 392 | 1 long 24 / 8 " 18's / 4 short 68's / 10 " 32's |
| Royal George, | " | 510 | 200 | 360 | 3 long 18's / 2 short 68's / 16 " 32's |
| Melville, | brig | 279 | 100 | 210 | 2 long 18's / 12 short 32's |
| Moira, | " | 262 | 100 | 153 | 2 long 9's / 12 short 24's |
| Sydney Smith, | schooner | 216 | 80 | 172 | 2 long 12's / 10 short 32's |
| Beresford, | " | 187 | 70 | 87 | 1 long 24 / 1 " 9 / 6 short 18's |
| 6 | | 2,091 | 770 | 1,374 | 92 |

The above figures would apparently make the two squadrons about equal, Chauncy having 95 men more, and throwing at a broadside 144 pounds shot less than his antagonist. But the figures do not by any means show all the truth. The Americans greatly excelled in the number and calibre of their long guns. Compared thus, they threw at one discharge 694 pounds of long-gun metal and 536 pounds of carronade metal; while the British only threw from their long guns 180 pounds, and from their carronades 1,194. This unequal distribution of metal was very much in favor of the Americans. Nor was this all. The *Pike*, with her 15 long 24's in battery, was an overmatch for any one of the enemy's vessels, and bore the same relation to them that the *Confiance*, at a later date, did to Macdonough's squadron. She should certainly have been a match for the *Wolfe* and *Melville* together, and the *Madison* and *Oneida* for the *Royal George* and *Sydney Smith*. In fact, the three heavy American vessels ought to have been an overmatch for the four heaviest of the British squadron, although these possessed the nominal superiority. And in ordinary cases the eight remaining American gun-vessels would certainly seem to be an overmatch for the two British schooners, but it is just here that the difficulty of comparing the forces comes in. When the water was very smooth and the wind light, the long 32's and 24's of the Americans could play havoc with the British schooners, at a distance which would render the carronades of the latter useless. But the latter were built for war, possessed quarters and were good cruisers, while Chauncy's schooners were merchant vessels, without quarters, crank, and so loaded down with heavy metal that whenever it blew at all hard they could with difficulty be kept from upsetting, and ceased to be capable even of defending themselves. When Sir James Yeo captured two of them he would not let them cruise with his other vessels at all, but sent them back to act as gun-boats, in which capacity they were serving when recaptured; this is a tolerable test of their value compared to their opponents. Another disadvantage that Chauncy had to contend with, was the difference in the speed of the various vessels. The *Pike* and *Madison* were fast, weatherly ships; but the *Oneida* was a perfect slug, even going free, and could hardly be persuaded to beat to windward at all. In this respect Yeo was much better off; his six ships were regular men-of-war, with quarters, all of them seaworthy, and fast enough to be able to act with uniformity, and not needing to pay much regard to the weather. His force could act as a unit; but Chauncy's could not. Enough wind to make a good working breeze for his larger vessels put all his smaller ones *hors de combat;* and in weather that suited the latter, the former could not move about at all. When speed became necessary the two ships left the brig hopelessly behind, and either had to do without her, or else perhaps let the critical moment slip by while waiting for her to come up. Some of the schooners sailed quite as slowly; and finally it was found out that the only way to get all the vessels into action at once was to have one half the fleet tow the other half. It was certainly difficult to keep the command of the lake when, if it came on to blow, the commodore had to put into port under penalty of seeing a quarter of his fleet founder before his eyes. These conflicting considerations render it hard to pass judgment; but on the whole it would seem as if Chauncy was the superior in force, for even if his schooners were not counted, his three square-rigged vessels were at least a match for the four square-rigged British vessels, and the two British schooners would not have counted very much in such a conflict. In calm weather he was certainly the superior. This only solves one of the points in which the official letters of the two commanders differ: after every meeting each one insists that he was inferior in force, that the weather suited his antagonist, and that the latter ran away, and got the worst of it; all of which will be considered further on.

In order to settle toward which side the balance of success inclined, we must remember that there were two things the combatants were trying to do, viz.:

(1) To damage the enemy directly by capturing or destroying his vessels. This was the only object we had in view in sending out ocean cruisers, but on the lakes it was subordinated to:—

(2) Getting the control of the lake, by which invaluable assistance could be rendered to the army. The most thorough way of accomplishing this, of course, was by destroying the enemy's squadron; but it could also be done by building ships too powerful for him to face, or by beating him in some engagement which, although not destroying his fleet, would force him to go into port. If one side was stronger, then the weaker party by skilful manœuvring might baffle the foe, and rest satisfied by keeping the sovereignty of the lake disputed; for, as long as one squadron was not undisputed master it could not be of much assistance in transporting troops, attacking forts, or otherwise helping the military.

In 1813 the Americans gained the first point by being the first to begin operations. They were building a new ship, afterward the *Pike*, at Sackett's Harbor; the British were building two new ships, each about two thirds the force of the *Pike*, one at Toronto (then called *York*), one at Kingston. Before these were built the two fleets were just on a par; the destruction of the *Pike* would give the British the supremacy; the destruction of either of the British ships, provided the *Pike* were saved, would give the Americans the supremacy. Both sides had already committed faults. The Americans had left Sackett's Harbor so poorly defended and garrisoned that it invited attack, while the British had fortified Kingston very strongly, but had done little for York, and, moreover, ought not to have divided their forces by building ships in different places.

Commodore Chauncy's squadron was ready for service on April 19th, and on the 25th he made sail with the *Madison*, Lieutenant-Commander Elliott, floating his own broad pennant, *Oneida*, Lieutenant Woolsey, *Hamilton*, Lieutenant McPherson, *Scourge*, Mr. Osgood, *Tompkins*, Lieutenant Brown, *Conquest*, Lieutenant Pettigrew, *Growler*, Mr. Mix, *Julia*, Mr. Trant, *Asp*, Lieutenant Smith, *Pert*, Lieutenant Adams, *American*, Lieutenant Chauncy, *Ontario*, Mr. Stevens, *Lady of the Lake*, Mr. Hinn, and *Raven*, transport, having on board General Dearborn and 1,700 troops, to attack York, which was garrisoned by about 700 British regulars and Canadian militia under Major-General Sheafe. The new 24-gun ship was almost completed, and the *Gloucester* 10-gun brig was in port;

the guns of both vessels were used in defence of the port. The fleet arrived before York early on April 27th, and the debarkation began at about 8 A.M. The schooners beat up to the fort under a heavy cannonade, and opened a spirited fire from their long guns; while the troops went ashore under the command of Brigadier-General Pike. The boats were blown to leeward by the strong east wind, and were exposed to a galling fire, but landed the troops under cover of the grape thrown by the vessels. The schooners now beat up to within a quarter of a mile from the principal work, and opened heavily upon it, while at the same time General Pike and the main body of the troops on shore moved forward to the assault, using their bayonets only. The British regulars and Canadian militia, outnumbered three to one (including the American sailors) and with no very good defensive works, of course had to give way, having lost heavily, especially from the fire of the vessels. An explosion immediately afterward killed or wounded 250 of the victors, including General Pike. The Americans lost, on board the fleet, 4 killed, including midshipmen Hatfield and Thompson, and 8 wounded[1]; and of the army,[2] 14 killed and 32 wounded by the enemy's fire, and 52 killed and 180 wounded by the explosion: total loss, 288. The British regulars lost 130 killed and wounded, including 40 by the explosion[3]; together with 50 Canadians and Indians, making a total of 180, besides 290 prisoners. The 24-gun ship was burned, her guns taken away, and the *Gloucester* sailed back to Sackett's Harbor with the fleet. Many military and naval stores were destroyed, and much more shipped to the Harbor. The great fault that the British had committed was in letting the defences of so important a place remain so poor, and the force in it so small. It was impossible to resist very long when Pike's troops were landed, and the fleet in position. On the other hand, the Americans did the work in good style; the schooners were finely handled, firing with great precision and completely covering the troops, who, in turn, were disembarked and brought into action very handsomely.

After being detained in York a week by bad weather the squadron got out, and for the next fortnight was employed in conveying troops and stores to General Dearborn. Then it was determined to make an attack on Fort George, where the British General Vincent was stationed with from 1,000[4] to 1,800[5] regulars, 600 militia, and about 100 Indians. The American troops numbered about 4,500, practically under the command of Colonel Scott. On May 26th Commodore Chauncy carefully reconnoitred the place to be attacked, and in the night made soundings along the coast, and laid buoys so as to direct the small vessels, who were to do the fighting. At 3 A.M. on the 27th the signal was made to weigh, the heavy land artillery being on the *Madison,* and the other troops on the *Oneida,* the

---

[1] Letter of Commodore Chauncy, April 28, 1813.
[2] James, "Military Occurrences" (London, 1818) vol. i, p. 151.
[3] Lossing's "Field-Book of the War of 1812," p. 581. The accounts vary somewhat.
[4] James, "Military Occurrences," i, p. 151.
[5] Lossing, 596.

*Lady of the Lake,* and in batteaux, many of which had been captured at York. The *Julia, Growler,* and *Ontario* moved in and attacked a battery near the light-house, opening a cross-fire which silenced it. The troops were to be disembarked farther along the lake, near a battery of one long 24, managed by Canadian militia. The *Conquest* and *Tompkins* swept in under fire to this battery, and in 10 minutes killed or drove off the artillerymen, who left the gun spiked, and then opened on the British. "The American ships with their heavy discharges of round and grape too well succeeded in thinning the British ranks."[1] Meanwhile the troop-boats, under Captain Perry and Colonel Scott dashed in, completely covered by a heavy fire of grape directed point-blank at the foe by the *Hamilton, Scourge,* and *Asp.* "The fire from the American shipping committed dreadful havoc among the British, and rendered their efforts to oppose the landing of the enemy ineffectual."[2] Colonel Scott's troops, thus protected, made good their landing and met the British regulars; but the latter were so terribly cut up by the tremendous discharges of grape and canister from the schooners, that in spite of their gallantry and discipline they were obliged to retreat, blowing up and abandoning the fort. One sailor was killed and two wounded[3]; seventeen soldiers were killed and forty-five wounded[4]; making the total American loss sixty-five. Of the British regulars 52 were killed, 44 wounded, and 262 "wounded and missing,"[5] in addition to about forty Canadians and Indians *hors de combat* and nearly 500 militia captured; so that in this very brilliant affair the assailants suffered hardly more than a fifth of the loss in killed and wounded that the assailed did; which must be attributed to the care with which Chauncy had reconnoitred the ground and prepared the attack, the excellent handling of the schooners, and the exceedingly destructive nature of their fire. The British batteries were very weak, and, moreover, badly served. Their regular troops fought excellently; it was impossible for them to stand against the fire of the schooners, which should have been engaged by the batteries on shore; and they were too weak in numbers to permit the American army to land and then attack it when away from the boats. The Americans were greatly superior in force, and yet deserve very much credit for achieving their object so quickly, with such slight loss to themselves, and at such a heavy cost to the foe. The effect of the victory was most important, the British evacuating the whole Niagara frontier, and leaving the river in complete possession of the Americans for the time being. This offered the opportunity for despatching Captain Perry up above the falls to take out one captured brig (the *Caledonia*) and four purchased schooners, which had been lying in the river unable to get past the British batteries into Lake Erie. These five vessels were now carried into that lake, being tracked up against the current by oxen, to become a most important addition to the American force upon it.

---

[1] James, "Military Occurrences," i, p. 151.
[2] *Loc. cit.*
[3] Letter of Commodore Chauncy, May 29, 1813.
[4] Letter of General Dearborn, May 27, 1813.
[5] Letter of Brig.-Gen. Vincent, May 28, 1813.

While Chauncy's squadron was thus absent at the west end of the lake the *Wolfe*, 24, was launched and equipped at Kingston, making the British force on the lake superior to that of the Americans. Immediately Sir George Prevost, and Sir James Lucas Yeo, the commanders-in-chief of the land and water forces in the Canadas, decided to strike a blow at Sackett's Harbor and destroy the *General Pike*, 28, thus securing to themselves the superiority for the rest of the season. Accordingly they embarked on May 27th, in the *Wolfe*, *Royal George*, *Moira*, *Prince Regent*, *Simco*, and *Seneca*, with a large number of gun-boats, barges, and batteaux; and on the next day saw and attacked a brigade of 19 boats transporting troops to Sackett's Harbor, under command of Lieutenant Aspinwall. Twelve boats were driven ashore, and 70 of the men in them captured; but Lieutenant Aspinwall and 100 men succeeded in reaching the Harbor, bringing up the total number of regulars there to 500 men, General Brown having been summoned to take the chief command. About 400 militia also came in, but were of no earthly service. There were, however, 200 Albany volunteers, under Colonel Mills, who could be relied on. The defences were miserably inadequate, consisting of a battery of one long gun and a block-house.

On the 29th Sir George Prevost and 800 regulars landed, being covered by the gun-boats under Sir James Lucas Yeo. The American militia fled at once, but the regulars and volunteers held their ground in and around the block-house. "At this point the further energies of the [British] troops became unavailing. The [American] block-house and stockade could not be carried by assault nor reduced by field-pieces, had we been provided with them; the fire of the gun-boats proved insufficient to attain that end; light and adverse winds continued, and our larger vessels were still far off."[1] The British reëmbarked precipitately. The American loss amounted to 23 killed and 114 wounded; that of the British to 52 killed and 211 wounded,[2] most of the latter being taken prisoners. During the fight some of the frightened Americans set fire to the store-houses, the *Pike* and the *Gloucester;* the former were consumed, but the flames were extinguished before they did any damage to either of the vessels. This attack differed especially from those on Fort George and York, in that the attacking force was relatively much weaker; still it ought to have been successful. But Sir George could not compare as a leader with Col. Scott or Gen. Pike; and Sir James did not handle the gun-boats by any means as well as the Americans did their schooners in similar attacks. The admirers of Sir James lay the blame on Sir George, and *vice versa;* but in reality neither seems to have done particularly well. At any rate the affair was the reverse of creditable to the British.

The British squadron returned to Kingston, and Chauncy, having heard that they were out, came down the lake and went into port about June 2d. So far the Americans had had all the success, and had controlled the lake; but now Yeo's

---

[1] Letter of Adj.-Gen. Baynes, May 30, 1813.
[2] James, "Military Occurrences," p. 173.

force was too formidable to be encountered until the *Pike* was built, and the supremacy passed undisputed into his hands, while Chauncy lay in Sackett's Harbor. Of course with the *Pike* soon to be built, Yeo's uncontested superiority could be of but short duration; but he used his time most actively. He sailed from Kingston on the 3d of June, to coöperate with the British army at the head of the lake, and intercept all supplies going to the Americans. On the 8th he discovered a small camp of the latter near Forty Mile Creek, and attacked it with the *Beresford, Sydney Smith,* and gun-boats, obliging the Americans to leave their camp, while their equipages, provisions, stores, and batteaux fell into the hands of the British, whose troops occupied the post, thus assisting in the series of engagements which ended in the humiliating repulse of General Wilkinson's expedition into Canada. On the 13th two schooners and some boats bringing supplies to the Americans were captured, and on the 16th a depôt of provisions at the Genesee River shared the same fate. On the 19th a party of British soldiers were landed by the fleet at Great Sodas, and took off 600 barrels of flour. Yeo then returned to Kingston, where he anchored on the 27th having done good service in assisting the land forces.[1] As a small compensation, on the 18th of the same month the *Lady of the Lake,* Lieut. Wolcott Chauncy, captured off Presque Isle the British schooner *Lady Murray,* containing 1 ensign, 15 soldiers, and 6 sailors, together with stores and ammunition.[2]

During the early part of July neither squadron put out in force; although on the first of the month Commodore Yeo made an abortive attempt to surprise Sackett's Harbor, but abandoned it when it was discovered. Meanwhile the Americans were building a new schooner, the *Sylph,* and the formidable corvette *Pike* was made ready to sail by July 21st. On the same day the entire American squadron, or fleet, sailed up to the head of the lake, and reached Niagara on the 27th. Here Col. Scott and some of his regulars were embarked, and on the 30th a descent was made upon York, where 11 transports were destroyed, 5 cannon, a quantity of flour, and some ammunition carried off, and the barracks burned. On the 3d of August the troops were disembarked at the Niagara, and 111 officers and men were sent up to join Perry on Lake Erie. As this left the squadron much deranged 150 militia were subsequently lent it by General Boyd, but they proved of no assistance (beyond swelling the number of men Yeo captured in the *Growler* and *Julia* from 70 individuals to 80), and were again landed.

Commodore Yeo sailed with his squadron from Kingston on Aug. 2d, and on the 7th the two fleets for the first time came in sight of one another, the Americans at anchor off Fort Niagara, the British six miles to windward, in the W.N.W. Chauncy's squadron contained one corvette, one ship sloop, one brig sloop, and ten schooners, manned by about 965 men, and throwing at a broadside 1,390 lbs. of shot, nearly 800 of which were from long guns. Yeo's included two ship

[1] Letter of Sir James Lucas Yeo to Mr. Croker, June 29, 1813.
[2] Letter of Lieut. Wolcott Chauncy to Com. Chauncy, June 18, 1813.

sloops, two brig sloops, and two schooners, manned by 770 men, and throwing at a broadside 1,374 lbs., but 180 being from long guns. But Yeo's vessels were all built with bulwarks, while ten of Chauncy's had none; and, moreover, his vessels could all sail and manœuvre together, while, as already remarked, one half of the American fleet spent a large part of its time towing the other half. The *Pike* would at ordinary range be a match for the *Wolfe* and *Melville* together; yet in actual weight of metal she threw less than the former ship alone. In calm weather the long guns of the American schooners gave them a great advantage; in rough weather they could not be used at all. Still, on the whole, it could fairly be said that Yeo was advancing to attack a superior fleet.

All through the day of the 7th the wind blew light and variable, and the two squadrons went through a series of manœuvres, nominally to bring on an action. As each side flatly contradicts the other it is hard to tell precisely what the manœuvres were; each captain says the other avoided him and that *he* made all sail in chase. At any rate it was just the weather for Chauncy to engage in.

That night the wind came out squally; and about 1 A.M. on the morning of the 8th a heavy gust struck the *Hamilton* and *Scourge,* forcing them to career over till the heavy guns broke loose, and they foundered, but 16 men escaping,— which accident did not open a particularly cheerful prospect to the remainder of the schooners. Chauncy's force was, by this accident, reduced to a numerical equality with Yeo's, having perhaps a hundred more men,[1] and throwing 144 lbs. less shot at a broadside. All through the two succeeding days the same manœuvring went on; the question as to which avoided the fight is simply one of veracity between the two commanders, and of course each side, to the end of time, will believe its own leader. But it is not of the least consequence, as neither accomplished any thing.

On the 10th the same tedious evolutions were continued, but at 7 P.M. the two squadrons were tolerably near one another, Yeo to windward, the breeze being fresh from the S.W. Commodore Chauncy formed his force in two lines on the port tack, while Commodore Yeo approached from behind and to windward, in single column, on the same tack. Commodore Chauncy's weather line was formed of the *Julia, Growler, Pert, Asp, Ontario,* and *American,* in that order, and the lee line of the *Pike, Oneida, Madison, Tompkins,* and *Conquest.* Chauncy formed his weather line of the smaller vessels, directing them, when the British should engage, to edge away and form to leeward of the second line, expecting that Sir James would follow them down. At 11 the weather line opened fire at very long range; at 11.15 it was returned, and the action became general and harmless; at

---

[1] This estimate as to men is a mere balancing of probabilities. If James underestimates the British force on Ontario as much as he has on Erie and Champlain, Yeo had as many men as his opponent. Chauncy, in one of his letters (preserved with the other manuscript letters in the Naval Archives), says: "I enclose the muster-rolls of all my ships," but I have not been able to find them, and in any event the complements were continually changing completely. The point is not important, as each side certainly had plenty of men on this occasion.

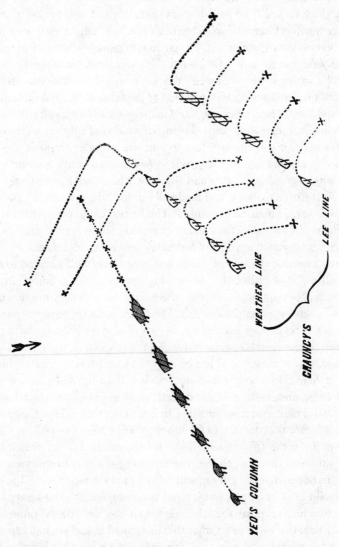

The ships are shown just before the weather line bore up; the dotted lines show the courses the vessels kept, and the crosses indicate their positions shortly after the *Julia* and *Growler* had tacked, and after Chauncy's lee line had "kept off two points."

11.30 the weather line bore up and passed to leeward, except the *Julia* and *Growler,* which tacked. The British ships kept their luff and cut off the two that had tacked; while Commodore Chauncy's lee line "edged away two points, to lead the enemy down, not only to engage him to more advantage, but to lead him from the *Julia* and *Growler*."[1] Of course the enemy did not come down, and the *Julia* and *Growler* were not saved. Yeo kept on till he had cut off the two schooners, fired an ineffectual broadside at the other ships, and tacked after the *Growler* and *Julia*. Then, when too late, Chauncy tacked also, and stood after him. The schooners, meanwhile, kept clawing to windward till they were overtaken, and, after making a fruitless effort to run the gauntlet through the enemy's squadron by putting before the wind, were captured. Yeo's account is simple: "Came within gunshot of *Pike* and *Madison,* when they immediately bore up, fired their stern-chase guns, and made all sail for Niagara, leaving two of their schooners astern, which we captured."[2] The British had acted faultlessly, and the honor and profit gained by the encounter rested entirely with them. On the contrary, neither Chauncy nor his subordinates showed to advantage.

Cooper says that the line of battle was "singularly well adapted to draw the enemy down," and "admirable for its advantages and ingenuity." In the first place it is an open question whether the enemy needed drawing down; on this occasion he advanced boldly enough. The formation may have been ingenious, but it was the reverse of advantageous. It would have been far better to have had the strongest vessels to windward, and the schooners, with their long guns, to leeward, where they would not be exposed to capture by any accident happening to them. Moreover, it does not speak well for the discipline of the fleet, that two commanders should have directly disobeyed orders. And when the two schooners did tack, and it was evident that Sir James would cut them off, it was an extraordinary proceeding for Chauncy to "edge away two points * * * to lead the enemy from the *Growler* and *Julia*." It is certainly a novel principle, that if part of a force is surrounded the true way to rescue it is to run away with the balance, in hopes that the enemy will follow. Had Chauncy tacked at once, Sir James would have been placed between two fires, and it would have been impossible for him to capture the schooners. As it was, the British commander had attacked a superior force in weather that just suited it, and yet had captured two of its vessels without suffering any injury beyond a few shot holes in the sails. The action, however, was in no way decisive. All next day, the 11th, the fleets were in sight of one another, the British to windward, but neither attempted to renew the engagement. The wind grew heavier, and the villainous little American schooners showed such strong tendencies to upset, that two had to run into Niagara Bay to anchor. With the rest Chauncy ran down the lake to Sackett's Harbor, which he reached on the 13th, provisioned his squadron for five weeks, and that same evening proceeded up the lake again.

---

[1] Letter of Commodore Isaac Chauncy, Aug. 13, 1813.
[2] Letter of Sir James Lucas Yeo, Aug. 10, 1813.

The advantage in this action had been entirely with the British, but it is simple nonsense to say, as one British historian does, that "on Lake Ontario, therefore, we at last secured a decisive predominance, which we maintained until the end of the war."[1] This "decisive" battle left the Americans just as much in command of the lake as the British; and even this very questionable "predominance" lasted but six weeks, after which the British squadron was blockaded in port most of the time. The action has a parallel in that fought on the 22d of July, 1805, by Sir Robert Calder's fleet of 15 sail of the line against the Franco-Spanish fleet of 20 sail of the line, under M. Villeneuve.[2] The two fleets engaged in a fog, and the English captured two ships, when both sides drew off, and remained in sight of each other the next day without either renewing the action. "A victory therefore it was that Sir Robert Calder had gained, but not a 'decisive' nor a 'brilliant' victory."[3] This is exactly the criticism that should be passed on Sir James Lucas Yeo's action of the 10th of August.

From the 13th of August to the 10th of September both fleets were on the lake most of the time, each commodore stoutly maintaining that he was chasing the other; and each expressing in his letters his surprise and disgust that his opponent should be afraid of meeting him "though so much superior in force." The facts are of course difficult to get at, but it seems pretty evident that Yeo was determined to engage in heavy, and Chauncy in light, weather; and that the party to leeward generally made off. The Americans had been re-inforced by the *Sylph* schooner, of 300 tons and 70 men, carrying four long 32's on pivots, and six long 6's. Theoretically her armament would make her formidable; but practically her guns were so crowded as to be of little use, and the next year she was converted into a brig, mounting 24-pound carronades.

On the 11th of September a partial engagement, at very long range, in light weather, occurred near the mouth of the Genesee River; the Americans suffered no loss whatever, while the British had one midshipman and three seamen killed and seven wounded, and afterward ran into Amherst Bay. One of their brigs, the *Melville,* received a shot so far under water that to get at and plug it, the guns had to be run in on one side and out on the other. Chauncy describes it as a running fight of 3½ hours, the enemy then escaping into Amherst Bay.[4] James (p. 38) says that "At sunset a breeze sprang up from the westward, when Sir James steered for the American fleet; but the American commodore avoided

---

[1] "History of the British Navy," by Charles Duke Yonge (London 1866), vol. iii, p. 24. It is apparently not a work of any authority, but I quote it as showing probably the general feeling of British writers about the action and its results, which can only proceed from extreme partisanship and ignorance of the subject.

[2] "Batailles Navales de la France," par O. Troude, iii, 352. It seems rather ridiculous to compare these lake actions, fought between small flotillas, with the gigantic contests which the huge fleets of Europe waged in contending for the supremacy of the ocean; but the difference is one of degree and not of kind, and they serve well enough for purposes of illustration or comparison.

[3] James' "Naval History," iv, 14.

[4] Letter to the Secretary of the Navy, Sept. 13, 1813.

a close action, and thus the affair ended." This is a good sample of James' trust-worthiness; his account is supposed to be taken from Commodore Yeo's letter,[1] which says: "At sunset a breeze sprang up from the westward, when I steered for the False Duck Islands, under which the enemy could not keep the weather-gage, but be obliged to meet us on equal terms. This, however, he carefully avoided doing." In other words Yeo did *not* steer *for* but *away from* Chauncy. Both sides admit that Yeo got the worst of it and ran away, and it is only a question as to whether Chauncy followed him or not. Of course in such light weather Chauncy's long guns gave him a great advantage. He had present 10 vessels; the *Pike, Madison, Oneida, Sylph, Tompkins, Conquest, Ontario, Pert, American,* and *Asp,* throwing 1,288 lbs. of shot, with a total of 98 guns. Yeo had 92 guns, throwing at a broadside 1,374 lbs. Nevertheless, Chauncy told but part of the truth in writing as he did: "I was much disappointed at Sir James refusing to fight me, as he was so much superior in point of force, both in guns and men, having up-ward of 20 guns more than we have, and heaves a greater weight of shot." His inferiority in long guns placed Yeo at a great disadvantage in such a very light wind; but in his letter he makes a marvellous admission of how little able he was to make good use of even what he had. He says: "I found it impossible to bring them to close action. We remained in this mortifying situation five hours, having only six guns in all the squadron that would reach the enemy (not a car-ronade being fired)." Now according to James himself ("Naval Occurrences," p. 297) he had in his squadron 2 long 24's, 13 long 18's, 2 long 12's, and 3 long 9's, and, in a fight of five hours, at very long range, in smooth water, it was a proof of culpable incompetency on his part that he did not think of doing what Elliott and Perry did in similar circumstances on Lake Erie—substitute all his long guns for some of the carronades on the engaged side. Chauncy could place in broadside 7 long 32's, 18 long 24's, 4 long 12's, 8 long 6's; so he could oppose 37 long guns, throwing 752 lbs. of shot, to Yeo's 20 long guns, throwing 333 lbs. of shot. The odds were thus more than two to one against the British in any case; and their commander's lack of resource made them still greater. But it proved a mere skirmish, with no decisive results.

The two squadrons did not come in contact again till on the 28th, in York Bay. The Americans had the weather-gage, the wind being fresh from the east. Yeo tacked and stretched out into the lake, while Chauncy steered directly for his centre. When the squadrons were still a league apart the British formed on the port tack, with their heavy vessels ahead; the Americans got on the same tack and edged down toward them, the *Pike* ahead, towing the *Asp;* the *Tompkins,* under Lieut. Bolton Finch, next; the *Madison* next, being much retarded by having a schooner in tow; then the *Sylph,* with another schooner in tow, the *Oneida,* and the two other schooners. The British, fearing their sternmost vessels would be cut off, at 12.10 came round on the starboard tack, beginning with the *Wolfe,* Commodore Yeo, and *Royal George,* Captain William Howe Mulcaster,

---

[1] Letter to Admiral Warren, Sept. 12, 1813.

which composed the van of the line. They opened with their starboard guns as soon as they came round. When the *Pike* was a-beam of the *Wolfe*, which was past the centre of the British line, the Americans bore up in succession for their centre.

The *Madison* was far back, and so was the *Sylph*, neither having cast off their tows; so the whole brunt of the action fell on the *Pike, Asp,* and *Tompkins*. The latter kept up a most gallant and spirited fire till her foremast was shot away. But already the *Pike* had shot away the *Wolfe*'s main-top-mast and main-yard, and

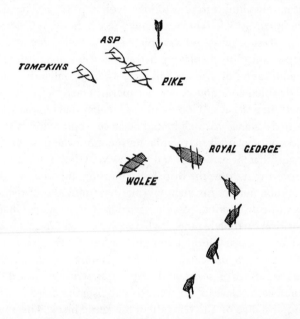

inflicted so heavy a loss upon her that Commodore Yeo, not very heroically, put dead before the wind, crowding all the canvas he could on her forward spars, and she ran completely past all her own vessels, who of course crowded sail after her. The retreat of the commodore was most ably covered by the *Royal George*, under Captain Mulcaster, who was unquestionably the best British officer on the lake. He luffed up across the commodore's stern, and delivered broadsides in a manner that won the admiration even of his foes. The *Madison* and *Sylph*, having the schooners in tow, could not overtake the British ships, though the *Sylph* opened a distant fire; the *Pike* kept on after them, but did not cast off the *Asp*, and so did not gain; and at 3.15 the pursuit was relinquished,[1] when the enemy were running into the entirely undefended port of Burlington Bay, whence escape would have been impossible. The *Tompkins* had lost her foremast, and the *Pike* her foretop-gallant mast, with her bowsprit and mainmast wounded; and of her crew five men were killed or wounded, almost all by the guns of the *Royal George*. These were the only injuries occasioned by the

---

[1] Letter of Commodore Chauncy, Sept. 28, 1813.

enemy's fire, but the *Pike*'s starboard bow-chaser burst, killing or wounding 22 men, besides blowing up the top-gallant forecastle, so that the bow pivot gun could not be used. Among the British ships, the *Wolfe* lost her main-top-mast, mizzen-top-mast, and main-yard, and the *Royal George* her foretop-mast; both suffered a heavy loss in killed and wounded, according to the report of the British officers captured in the transports a few days afterward.

As already mentioned, the British authorities no longer published accounts of their defeats, so Commodore Yeo's report on the action was not made public. Brenton merely alludes to it as follows (vol. ii, p. 503): "The action of the 28th of September, 1813, in which Sir James Yeo in the *Wolfe* had his main- and mizzen-top-masts shot away, and was obliged to put before the wind, gave Mulcaster an opportunity of displaying a trait of valor and seamanship which elicited the admiration of friends and foes, when he gallantly placed himself between his disabled commodore and a superior enemy." James speaks in the vaguest terms. He first says, "Commodore Chauncy, having the weather-gage, kept his favorite distance," which he did because Commodore Yeo fled so fast that he could not be overtaken; then James mentions the injuries the *Wolfe* received, and says that "it was these and not, as Mr. Clark says, 'a manœuvre of the commodore's' that threw the British in confusion." In other words, it was the commodore's shot and not his manœuvring that threw the British into confusion—a very futile distinction. Next he says that "Commodore Chauncy would not venture within carronade range," whereas he *was* within carronade range of the *Wolfe* and *Royal George,* but the latter did not wait for the *Madison* and *Oneida* to get within range with *their* carronades. The rest of his article is taken up with exposing the absurdities of some of the American writings, miscalled histories, which appeared at the close of the war. His criticisms on these are very just, but afford a funny instance of the pot calling the kettle black. This much is clear, that the British were beaten and forced to flee, when but part of the American force was engaged. But in good weather the American force was so superior that being beaten would have been no disgrace to Yeo, had it not been for the claims advanced both by himself and his friends, that on the whole he was victorious over Chauncy. The *Wolfe* made any thing but an obstinate fight, leaving almost all the work to the gallant Mulcaster, in the *Royal George,* who shares with Lieutenant Finch of the *Tompkins* most of the glory of the day. The battle, if such it may be called, completely established Chauncy's supremacy, Yeo spending most of the remainder of the season blockaded in Kingston. So Chauncy gained a victory which established his control over the lakes; and, moreover, he gained it by fighting in succession, almost single-handed, the two heaviest ships of the enemy. But gaining the victory was only what should have been expected from a superior force. The question is, did Chauncy use his force to the best advantage? And it can not be said that he did. When the enemy bore up it was a great mistake not to cast off the schooners which were being towed. They were small craft, not of much use in the fight, and they entirely prevented the *Madison* from taking any part in the contest, and kept the *Sylph* at a great distance;

and by keeping the *Asp* in tow the *Pike,* which sailed faster than any of Yeo's ships, was distanced by them. Had she left the *Asp* behind and run in to engage the *Royal George* she could have mastered, or at any rate disabled, her; and had the swift *Madison* cast off her tow she could also have taken an effective part in the engagement. If the *Pike* could put the British to flight almost single-handed, how much more could she not have done when assisted by the *Madison* and *Oneida?* The cardinal error, however, was made in discontinuing the chase. The British were in an almost open road-stead, from which they could not possibly escape. Commodore Chauncy was afraid that the wind would come up to blow a gale, and both fleets would be thrown ashore; and, moreover, he expected to be able to keep a watch over the enemy, and to attack him at a more suitable time. But he utterly failed in this last; and had the American squadron cast off their tows and gone boldly in, they certainly ought to have been able to destroy or capture the entire British force before a gale could blow up. Chauncy would have done well to keep in mind the old adage, so peculiarly applicable to naval affairs: "L'audace! toujours l'audace! et encore l'audace!" Whether the fault was his or that of his subordinates, it is certain that while the victory of the 28th of September definitely settled the supremacy of the lake in favor of the Americans, yet this victory was by no means so decided as it should have been, taking into account his superiority in force and advantage in position, and the somewhat spiritless conduct of his foe.

Next day a gale came on to blow, which lasted till the evening of the 31st. There was no longer any apprehension of molestation from the British, so the troop transports were sent down the lake by themselves, while the squadron remained to watch Yeo. On Oct. 2d he was chased, but escaped by his better sailing; and next day false information induced Chauncy to think Yeo had eluded him and passed down the lake, and he accordingly made sail in the direction of his supposed flight. On the 5th, at 3 P.M., while near the False Ducks, seven vessels were made out ahead, which proved to be British gun-boats, engaged in transporting troops. All sails were made after them; one was burned, another escaped, and five were captured, the *Mary, Drummond, Lady Gore, Confiance,* and *Hamilton,*[1]—the two latter being the rechristened *Julia* and *Growler.* Each gun-vessel had from one to three guns, and they had aboard in all 264 men, including seven naval (three royal and four provincial) and ten military officers. These prisoners stated that in the action of the 28th the *Wolfe* and *Royal George* had lost very heavily.

After this Yeo remained in Kingston, blockaded there by Chauncy for most of the time; on Nov. 10th he came out and was at once chased back into port by Chauncy, leaving the latter for the rest of the season entirely undisturbed. Accordingly, Chauncy was able to convert his small schooners into transports. On the 17th these transports were used to convey 1,100 men of the army of General Harrison from the mouth of the Genesee to Sackett's Harbor, while

---

[1] Letter of Commodore Chauncy, Oct. 8, 1813.

Chauncy blockaded Yeo in Kingston. The duty of transporting troops and stores went on till the 27th, when every thing had been accomplished; and a day or two afterward navigation closed.

As between the Americans and British, the success of the season was greatly in favor of the former. They had uncontested control over the lake from April 19th to June 3d, and from Sept. 28th to Nov. 29th, in all 107 days; while their foes only held it from June 3d to July 21st, or for 48 days; and from that date to Sept. 28th, for 69 days, the two sides were contending for the mastery. York and Fort George had been taken, while the attack on Sackett's Harbor was repulsed. The Americans lost but two schooners, both of which were recaptured; while the British had one 24-gun ship nearly ready for launching destroyed, and one 10-gun brig taken, and the loss inflicted upon each other in transports, gun-boats, store-houses, stores, etc., was greatly in favor of the former. Chauncy's fleet, moreover, was able to co-operate with the army for over twice the length of time Yeo's could (107 days to 48).

It is more difficult to decide between the respective merits of the two com-manders. We had shown so much more energy than the Anglo-Canadians that at the beginning of the year we had overtaken them in the building race, and the two fleets were about equally formidable. The *Madison* and *Oneida* were not quite a match for the *Royal George* and *Sydney Smith* (opposing 12 32-pound and 8 24-pound carronades to 2 long 18's, 1 long 12, 1 68-pound and 13 32-pound carronades); and our ten gun-schooners would hardly be considered very much of an overmatch for the *Melville, Moira,* and *Beresford.* Had Sir James Yeo been as bold and energetic as Barclay or Mulcaster he would certainly not have per-mitted the Americans, when the forces were so equal, to hold uncontested sway over the lake, and by reducing Fort George, to cause disaster to the British land forces. It would certainly have been better to risk a battle with equal forces, than to wait till each fleet received an additional ship, which rendered Chauncy's squadron the superior by just about the superiority of the *Pike* to the *Wolfe.* Again, Yeo did not do particularly well in the repulse before Sackett's Harbor; in the skirmish off Genesee River he showed a marked lack of re-source; and in the action of the 28th of September (popularly called the "Burlington Races" from the celerity of his retreat) he evinced an amount of caution that verged toward timidity, in allowing the entire brunt of the fighting to fall on Mulcaster in the *Royal George,* a weaker ship than the *Wolfe.* On the other hand, he gave able co-operation to the army while he possessed control of the lake; he made a most gallant and successful attack on a superior force on the 10th of August; and for six weeks subsequently by skilful manœuvring he prevented this same superior force from acquiring the uncontested mastery. It was no disgrace to be subsequently blockaded; but it is very ludicrous in his ad-mirers to think that he came out first best.

Chauncy rendered able and invaluable assistance to the army all the while that he had control of the water; his attacks on York and Fort George were managed with consummate skill and success, and on the 28th of September he practically defeated the opposing force with his own ship alone. Nevertheless he can by no means be said to have done the best he could with the materials he had. His stronger fleet was kept two months in check by a weaker British fleet. When he first encountered the foe, on August 10th, he ought to have inflicted such a check upon him as would at least have confined him to port and given the Americans immediate superiority on the lake; instead of which he suffered a mortifying, although not at all disastrous, defeat, which allowed the British to contest the supremacy with him for six weeks longer. On the 28th of September, when he only gained a rather barren victory, it was nothing but excessive caution that prevented him from utterly destroying his foe. Had Perry on that day commanded the American fleet there would have been hardly a British ship left on Ontario. Chauncy was an average commander; and the balance of success inclined to the side of the Americans only because they showed greater energy and skill in ship-building, the crews and commanders on both sides being very nearly equal.

## LAKE ERIE

Captain Oliver Hazard Perry had assumed command of Erie and the upper lakes, acting under Commodore Chauncy. With intense energy he at once began creating a naval force which should be able to contend successfully with the foe. As already said, the latter in the beginning had exclusive control of Lake Erie; but the Americans had captured the *Caledonia*, brig, and purchased three schooners, afterward named the *Somers, Tigress*, and *Ohio*, and a sloop, the *Trippe*. These at first were blockaded in the Niagara, but after the fall of Fort George and retreat of the British forces, Captain Perry was enabled to get them out, tracking them up against the current by the most arduous labor. They ran up to Presque Isle (now called Erie), where two 20-gun brigs were being constructed under the directions of the indefatigable captain. Three other schooners, the *Ariel, Scorpion*, and *Porcupine*, were also built.

The harbor of Erie was good and spacious, but had a bar on which there was less than seven feet of water. Hitherto this had prevented the enemy from getting in; now it prevented the two brigs from getting out. Captain Robert Heriot Barclay had been appointed commander of the British forces on Lake Erie; and he was having built at Amherstburg a 20-gun ship. Meanwhile he blockaded Perry's force, and as the brigs could not cross the bar with their guns in, or except in smooth water, they of course could not do so in his presence. He kept a close blockade for some time; but on the 2d of August he disappeared. Perry at once hurried forward every thing; and on the 4th, at 2 P.M., one brig, the *Lawrence*, was towed to that point of the bar where the water was deepest. Her guns were whipped out and landed on the beach, and the brig got over the bar by a hastily improvised "camel."

"Two large scows, prepared for the purpose, were hauled along-side, and the work of lifting the brig proceeded as fast as possible. Pieces of massive timber had been run through the forward and after ports, and when the scows were sunk to the water's edge, the ends of the timbers were blocked up, supported by these floating foundations. The plugs were now put in the scows, and the water was pumped out of them. By this process the brig was lifted quite two feet, though when she was got on the bar it was found that she still drew too much water. It became necessary, in consequence, to cover up every thing, sink the scows anew, and block up the timbers afresh. This duty occupied the whole night."[1]

Just as the *Lawrence* had passed the bar, at 8 A.M. on the 5th, the enemy reappeared, but too late; Captain Barclay exchanged a few shots with the schooners and then drew off. The *Niagara* crossed without difficulty. There were still not enough men to man the vessels, but a draft arrived from Ontario, and many of the frontiersmen volunteered, while soldiers also were sent on board. The squadron sailed on the 18th in pursuit of the enemy, whose ship was now ready. After cruising about some time the *Ohio* was sent down the lake, and the other ships went into Put-in Bay. On the 9th of September Captain Barclay put out from Amherstburg, being so short of provisions that he felt compelled to risk an action with the superior force opposed. On the 10th of September his squadron was discovered from the mast-head of the *Lawrence* in the northwest. Before going into details of the action we will examine the force of the two squadrons, as the accounts vary considerably.

The tonnage of the British ships, as already stated, we know exactly, they having been all carefully appraised and measured by the builder Mr. Henry Eckford, and two sea-captains. We also know the dimensions of the American ships. The *Lawrence* and *Niagara* measured 480 tons apiece. The *Caledonia,* brig, was about the size of the *Hunter,* or 180 tons. The *Tigress, Somers,* and *Scorpion* were subsequently captured by the foe and were then said to measure, respectively, 96, 94, and 86 tons; in which case they were larger than similar boats on Lake Ontario. The *Ariel* was about the size of the *Hamilton;* the *Porcupine* and *Trippe* about the size of the *Asp* and *Pert.* As for the guns, Captain Barclay in his letter gives a complete account of those on board his squadron. He has also given a complete account of the American guns, which is most accurate, and, if any thing, underestimates them. At least Emmons in his "History" gives the *Trippe* a long 32, while Barclay says she had only a long 24; and Lossing in his "Field-Book" says (but I do not know on what authority) that the *Caledonia* had 3 long 24's, while Barclay gives her 2 long 24's and one 32-pound carronade; and that the *Somers* had two long 32's, while Barclay gives her one long 32 and one 24-pound carronade. I shall take Barclay's account, which corresponds with that of Emmons; the only difference being that Emmons puts a 24-pounder on the *Scorpion* and a 32 on the *Trippe,* while Barclay reverses this. I

---

[1] Cooper, ii, 389. Perry's letter of Aug. 5th is very brief.

shall also follow Emmons in giving the *Scorpion* a 32-pound carronade instead of a 24.

It is more difficult to give the strength of the respective crews. James says the Americans had 580, all "picked men." They were just as much picked men as Barclay's were, and no more; that is, the ships had "scratch" crews. Lieutenant Emmons gives Perry 490 men; and Lossing says he "had upon his muster-roll 490 names." In vol. xiv, p. 566, of the American State Papers, is a list of the prize-monies owing to each man (or to the survivors of the killed), which gives a grand total of 532 men, including 136 on the *Lawrence* and 155 on the *Niagara,* 45 of whom were volunteers—frontiersmen. Deducting these we get 487 men, which is pretty near Lieutenant Emmons' 490. Possibly Lieutenant Emmons did not include these volunteers; and it may be that some of the men whose names were down on the prize list had been so sick that they were left on shore. Thus Lieutenant Yarnall testified before a Court of Inquiry in 1815, that there were but 131 men and boys of every description on board the *Lawrence* in the action; and the *Niagara* was said to have had but 140. Lieutenant Yarnall also said that "but 103 men on board the *Lawrence* were fit for duty"; as Captain Perry in his letter said that 31 were unfit for duty, this would make a total of 134. So I shall follow the prize-money list; at any rate the difference in number is so slight as to be immaterial. Of the 532 men whose names the list gives, 45 were volunteers, or landsmen, from among the surrounding inhabitants; 158 were marines or soldiers (I do not know which, as the list gives marines, soldiers, and privates, and it is impossible to tell which of the two former heads include the last); and 329 were officers, seamen, cooks, pursers, chaplains, and supernumeraries. Of the total number, there were on the day of action, according to Perry's report, 116 men unfit for duty, including 31 on board the *Lawrence,* 28 on board the *Niagara,* and 57 on the small vessels.

All the later American writers put the number of men in Barclay's fleet precisely at "502," but I have not been able to find out the original authority. James ("Naval Occurrences," p. 289) says the British had but 345, consisting of 50 seamen, 85 Canadians, and 210 soldiers. But the letter of Adjutant-General E. Bayne, Nov. 24, 1813, states that there were 250 soldiers aboard Barclay's squadron, of whom 23 were killed, 49 wounded, and the balance (178) captured; and James himself on a previous page (284) states that there were 102 Canadians on Barclay's vessels, not counting the *Detroit,* and we know that Barclay originally joined the squadron with 19 sailors from the Ontario fleet, and that subsequently 50 sailors came up from the *Dover.* James gives at the end of his "Naval Occurrences" some extracts from the court-martial held on Captain Barclay. Lieut. Thomas Stokes, of the *Queen Charlotte,* there testified that he had on board "between 120 and 130 men, officers and all together," of whom "16 came up from the *Dover* three days before." James, on p. 284, says her crew already consisted of 110 men; adding these 16 gives us 126 (almost exactly "between 120 and 130"). Lieutenant Stokes also testified that the *Detroit* had more men on account of being a larger and heavier vessel; to give her 150 is perfectly safe, as her heavier guns and larger size would at least need 24 men more than the *Queen Charlotte*. James gives the *Lady Prevost* 76, *Hunter* 39, *Little Belt* 15, and *Chippeway* 13 men, Canadians and soldiers, a total of 143; supposing that the number of British sailors placed on them was proportional to the amount placed on board the *Queen Charlotte*, we could add 21. This would make a grand total of 440 men, which must certainly be near the truth. This number is corroborated otherwise: General Bayne, as already quoted, says that there were aboard 250 soldiers, of whom 72 were killed or wounded. Barclay reports a total loss of 135, of whom 63 must therefore have been sailors or Canadians, and if the loss suffered by these bore the same proportion to their whole number as in the case of the soldiers, there ought to have been 219 sailors and Canadians, making in all 469 men. It can thus be said with certainty that there were between 440 and 490 men aboard, and I shall take the former number, though I have no doubt that this is too small. But it is not a point of very much importance, as the battle was fought largely at long range, where the number of men, provided there were plenty to handle the sails and guns, did not much matter. The following statement of the comparative force must therefore be very nearly accurate:

PERRY'S SQUADRON

| NAME. | RIG. | TONS. | TOTAL CREW. | CREW FIT FOR DUTY. | BROADSIDE; LBS. | ARMAMENT. |
|---|---|---|---|---|---|---|
| *Lawrence,* | brig | 480 | 136 | 105 | 300 | 2 long 12's / 18 short 32's |
| *Niagara,* | " | 480 | 155 | 127 | 300 | 2 long 12's / 18 short 32's |
| *Caledonia,* | " | 180 | 53 | | 80 | 2 long 24's / 1 short 32 |
| *Ariel,* | schooner | 112 | 36 | | 48 | 4 long 12's |
| *Scorpion,* | " | 86 | 35 | | 64 | 1 " 32 / 1 short 32 |
| | | | | 184 | 56 | 1 long 24 / 1 short 32 |
| *Somers,* | " | 94 | 30 | | | |
| *Porcupine,* | " | 83 | 25 | | 32 | 1 long 32 |
| *Tigress,* | " | 96 | 27 | | 32 | 1 " 32 |
| *Trippe,* | sloop | 60 | 35 | | 24 | 1 " 24 |
| 9 vessels, | | 1,671 | 532 | (416) | 936 lbs. | |

During the action, however, the *Lawrence* and *Niagara* each fought a long 12 instead of one of the carronades on the engaged side, making a broadside of 896 lbs., 288 lbs. being from long guns.

ed up on deck to lend a feeble hand in placing the last guns. Perry himself
the last effective heavy gun, assisted only by the purser and chaplain. A
who did not possess his indomitable spirit would have then struck. Instead,
ver, although failing in the attack so far, Perry merely determined to win
w methods, and remodelled the line accordingly. Mr. Turner, in the *Cale-*
when ordered to close, had put his helm up, run down on the opposing
nd engaged at very short range, though the brig was absolutely without
rs. The *Niagara* had thus become the next in line astern of the *Lawrence,*
e sloop *Trippe,* having passed the three schooners in front of her, was next
. The *Niagara* now, having a breeze, steered for the head of Barclay's line,
g over a quarter of a mile to windward of the *Lawrence,* on her port beam.
as almost uninjured, having so far taken very little part in the combat, and
Perry shifted his flag. Leaping into a row boat, with his brother and four
n, he rowed to the fresh brig, where he arrived at 2.30, and at once sent
astern to hurry up the three schooners. The *Trippe* was now very near
ledonia. The *Lawrence,* having but 14 sound men left, struck her colors, but
not be taken possession of before the action re-commenced. She drifted
, the *Caledonia* passing between her and her foes. At 2.45, the schooners
g closed up, Perry, in his fresh vessel, bore up to break Barclay's line.
e British ships had fought themselves to a standstill. The *Lady Prevost* was
ed and sagged to leeward, though ahead of the others. The *Detroit* and
*Charlotte* were so disabled that they could not effectually oppose fresh an-
ists. There could thus be but little resistance to Perry, as the *Niagara* stood
, and broke the British line, firing her port guns into the *Chippeway, Little Belt,*
*ady Prevost,* and the starboard ones into the *Detroit, Queen Charlotte,* and
, raking on both sides. Too disabled to tack, the *Detroit* and *Charlotte* tried to
the latter running up to leeward of the former; and, both vessels having
brace and almost every stay shot away, they fell foul. The *Niagara* luffed
rt their bows, within half pistol-shot, keeping up a terrific discharge of
guns and musketry, while on the other side the British vessels were raked by
ledonia and the schooners so closely that some of their grape shot, passing
he foe, rattled through Perry's spars. Nothing further could be done, and
ay's flag was struck at 3 P.M., after three and a quarter hours' most gallant and
rate fighting. The *Chippeway* and *Little Belt* tried to escape, but were over-
and brought to respectively by the *Trippe* and *Scorpion,* the commander of
ter, Mr. Stephen Champlin, firing the last, as he had the first, shot of the
. "Captain Perry has behaved in the most humane and attentive manner, not
o myself and officers, but to all the wounded," writes Captain Barclay.
e American squadron had suffered severely, more than two thirds of the
lling upon the *Lawrence,* which was reduced to the condition of a perfect
, her starboard bulwarks being completely beaten in. She had, as already
, 22 men killed, including Lieutenant of Marines Brooks and Midship-
Lamb; and 61 wounded, including Lieutenant Yarnall, Midshipman (act-
cond lieutenant) Forrest, Sailing-Master Taylor, Purser Hambleton, and

## BARCLAY'S SQUADRON

| NAME. | RIG. | TONS. | CREW. | BROADSIDE; LBS. | ARMAMENT. |
|-------|------|-------|-------|-----------------|-----------|
| *Detroit,* | ship | 490 | 150 | 138 | 1 long 18<br>2 " 24's<br>6 " 12's<br>8 " 9's<br>1 short 24<br>1 " 18 |
| *Queen Charlotte,* | " | 400 | 126 | 189 | 1 long 12<br>2 " 9's<br>14 short 24's |
| *Lady Prevost,* | schooner | 230 | 86 | 75 | 1 long 9<br>2 " 6's<br>10 short 12's |
| *Hunter,* | brig | 180 | 45 | 30 | 4 long 6's<br>2 " 4's<br>2 " 2's<br>2 short 12's |
| *Chippeway,* | schooner | 70 | 15 | 9 | 1 long 9 |
| *Little Belt,* | sloop | 90 | 18 | 18 | 1 " 12<br>2 " 6's |
| 6 vessels, | | 1,460 | 440 | 459 lbs. | |

These six vessels thus threw at a broadside 459 lbs., of which 195 were from
long guns.

The superiority of the Americans in long-gun metal was therefore nearly as
three is to two, and in carronade metal greater than two to one. The chief fault
to be found in the various American accounts is that they sedulously conceal
the comparative weight of metal, while carefully specifying the number of
guns. Thus, Lossing says: "Barclay had 35 long guns to Perry's 15, and possessed
greatly the advantage in action at a distance"; which he certainly did not. The
tonnage of the fleets is not so very important; the above tables are probably
pretty nearly right. It is, I suppose, impossible to tell exactly the number of
men in the two crews. Barclay almost certainly had more than the 440 men I
have given him, but in all likelihood some of them were unfit for duty, and the
number of his effectives was most probably somewhat less than Perry's. As the
battle was fought in such smooth water, and part of the time at long range, this,
as already said, does not much matter. The *Niagara* might be considered a
match for the *Detroit,* and the *Lawrence* and *Caledonia* for the five other British
vessels; so the Americans were certainly very greatly superior in force.

At daylight on Sept. 10th Barclay's squadron was discovered in the N.W., and
Perry at once got under weigh; the wind soon shifted to the N.E., giving us the
weather-gage, the breeze being very light. Barclay lay to in a close column,
heading to the S.W. in the following order: *Chippeway,* Master's Mate J. Camp-

bell; *Detroit*, Captain R. H. Barclay; *Hunter*, Lieutenant G. Bignell; *Queen Char-lotte*, Captain R. Finnis; *Lady Prevost*, Lieutenant Edward Buchan; and *Little Belt*, by whom commanded is not said. Perry came down with the wind on his port beam, and made the attack in column ahead, obliquely. First in order came the *Ariel*, Lieut. John H. Packet, and *Scorpion*, Sailing-Master Stephen Champlin, both being on the weather bow of the *Lawrence*, Captain O. H. Perry; next came the *Caledonia*, Lieut. Daniel Turner; *Niagara*, Captain Jesse D. Elliott; *Somers*, Lieutenant A. H. M. Conklin; *Porcupine*, Acting Master George Serrat; *Tigress*, Sailing-Master Thomas C. Almy, and *Trippe*, Lieutenant Thomas Holdup.[1]

As, amid light and rather baffling winds, the American squadron approached the enemy, Perry's straggling line formed an angle of about fifteen degrees with the more compact one of his foes. At 11.45 the *Detroit* opened the action by a shot from her long 24, which fell short; at 11.50 she fired a second which went crashing through the *Lawrence*, and was replied to by the *Scorpion*'s long 32. At 11.55 the *Lawrence*, having shifted her port bow-chaser, opened with both the long 12's, and at meridian began with her carronades, but the shot from the latter all fell short. At the same time the action became general on both sides, though the rearmost American vessels were almost beyond the range of their own guns, and quite out of range of the guns of their antagonists. Meanwhile the *Lawrence* was already suffering considerably as she bore down on the enemy. It was twenty minutes before she succeeded in getting within good carronade range, and during that time the action at the head of the line was between the long guns of the *Chippeway* and *Detroit*, throwing 123 pounds, and those of the *Scorpion*, *Ariel*, and *Lawrence*, throwing 104 pounds. As the enemy's fire was directed almost exclusively at the *Lawrence* she suffered a great deal. The *Caledonia*, *Niagara*, and *Somers* were meanwhile engaging, at long range, the *Hunter* and *Queen Charlotte*, opposing from their long guns 96 pounds to the 39 pounds of their antagonists, while from a distance the three other American gun-vessels engaged the *Prevost* and *Little Belt*. By 12.20 the *Lawrence* had worked down to close quarters, and at 12.30 the action was going on with great fury between her and her antagonists, within canister range. The raw and inexperienced American crews committed the same fault the British so often fell into on the ocean, and overloaded their carronades. In consequence, that of the *Scorpion* upset down the hatchway in the middle of the action, and the sides of the *Detroit* were dotted with marks from shot that did not penetrate. One of the *Ariel*'s long 12's also burst. Barclay fought the *Detroit* exceedingly well, her guns being most excellently aimed, though they actually had to be discharged by flashing pistols at the

[1] The accounts of the two commanders tally almost exactly. Barclay's letter is a model of its kind for candor and generosity. Letter of Captain R. H. Barclay to Sir James, Sept. 2, 1813; of Lieutenant Inglis to Captain Barclay, Sept. 10th; of Captain Perry to the Secretary of the Navy, Sept. 10th and Sept. 13th, and to General Harrison, Sept. 11th and Sept. 13th. I have relied mainly on Lossing's "Field-Book of the War of 1812" (especially for the diagrams furnished him by Commodore Champlin), on Commander Ward's "Naval Tactics," p. 76, and on Cooper's "Naval History." Extracts from the court-martial on Captain Barclay are given in James' "Naval Occurrences," lxxxiii.

touchholes, so deficient was the ship's equipment. Meanw[...] down too, but the *Niagara* was wretchedly handled, Ellio[...] which prevented the use either of his carronades or of t[...] *lotte*, his antagonist; the latter, however, suffered greatly [...] the opposing schooners, and lost her gallant command[...] first lieutenant, Mr. Stokes, who were killed early in the a[...] mand, Provincial Lieutenant Irvine, perceiving that he co[...] the *Hunter* and joined in the attack on the *Lawrence*, at cl[...] *gara*, the most efficient and best-manned of the Americ[...] most kept out of the action by her captain's misconduct. [...] the fight went on at long range between the *Somers*, *Tigre*[...] on one side, and *Little Belt* and *Lady Prevost* on the other; t[...] a very noble fight, although her 12-pound carronades ren[...] less against the long guns of the Americans. She was gr[...] mander, Lieutenant Buchan, was dangerously, and her [...] Mr. Roulette, severely wounded, and she began falling gr[...]

The fighting at the head of the line was fierce and b[...] nary degree. The *Scorpion*, *Ariel*, *Lawrence*, and *Caledonia*[...] with the most determined courage, were opposed to [...] *Queen Charlotte*, and *Hunter*, which were fought to the f[...] close quarters the two sides engaged on about equal term[...] superior in weight of metal, and inferior in number of [...] had received such damage in working down as to make [...] On each side almost the whole fire was directed at the op[...] vessels; in consequence the *Queen Charlotte* was almost di[...] was also frightfully shattered, especially by the raking fire[...] first lieutenant, Mr. Garland, being mortally wounded, a[...] severely injured that he was obliged to quit the deck, l[...] command of Lieutenant George Inglis. But on board the[...] gone even worse, the combined fire of her adversar[...] grimmest carnage on her decks. Of the 103 men who wer[...] began the action, 83, or over four fifths, were killed or wo[...] shallow, and the ward-room, used as a cockpit, to whic[...] taken, was mostly above water, and the shot came through[...] and wounding many men under the hands of the surgeo[...]

The first lieutenant, Yarnall, was three times wounde[...] through all; the only other lieutenant on board, Brooks[...] mortally wounded. Every brace and bowline was shot awa[...] completely dismantled; her hull was shattered to pieces, [...] pletely through it, and the guns on the engaged side we[...] mounted. Perry kept up the fight with splendid courage. A[...] one, the commodore called down through the skylight fo[...] assistants; and this call was repeated and obeyed till no[...] asked, "Can any of the wounded pull a rope?" and th[...]

Midshipmen Swartout and Claxton. The *Niagara* lost 2 killed and 25 wounded (almost a fifth of her effectives), including among the latter the second lieutenant, Mr. Edwards, and Midshipman Cummings. The *Caledonia* had 3, the *Somers* 2, and *Trippe* 2, men wounded. The *Ariel* had 1 killed and 3 wounded; the *Scorpion* 2 killed, including Midshipman Lamb. The total loss was 123; 27 were killed and 96 wounded, of whom 3 died.

The British loss, falling most heavily on the *Detroit* and *Queen Charlotte*, amounted to 41 killed (including Capt. S. J. Garden, R.N., and Captain R. A. Finnis), and 94 wounded (including Captain Barclay and Lieutenants Stokes, Buchan, Roulette, and Bignall): in all 135. The first and second in command on every vessel were killed or wounded, a sufficient proof of the desperate nature of the defence.

The victory of Lake Erie was most important, both in its material results and in its moral effect. It gave us complete command of all the upper lakes,

The following diagrams will serve to explain the movements.

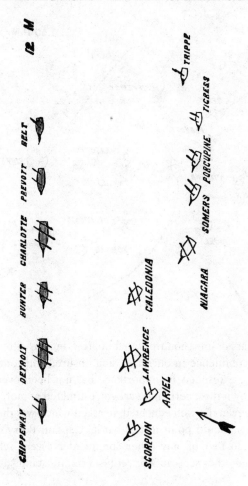

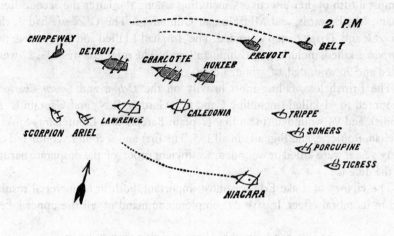

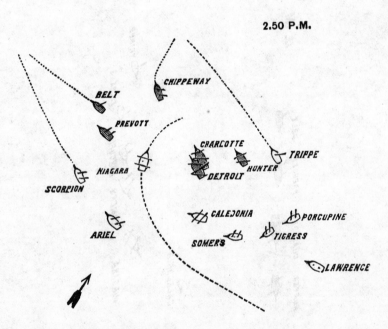

prevented any fears of invasion from that quarter, increased our prestige with the foe and our confidence in ourselves, and ensured the conquest of upper Canada; in all these respects its importance has not been overrated. But the "glory" acquired by it most certainly *has* been estimated at more than its worth. Most Americans, even the well educated, if asked which was the most glorious victory of the war, would point to this battle. Captain Perry's name is more widely known than that of any other commander. Every school-boy reads about *him*, if of no other sea-captain; yet he certainly stands on a lower grade

than either Hull or Macdonough, and not a bit higher than a dozen others. On
Lake Erie our seamen displayed great courage and skill; but so did their antagonists. The simple truth is, that, where on both sides the officers and men were
equally brave and skilful, the side which possessed the superiority in force, in
the proportion of three to two, could not well help winning. The courage with
which the *Lawrence* was defended has hardly ever been surpassed, and may
fairly be called heroic; but equal praise belongs to the men on board the *Detroit,*
who had to discharge the great guns by flashing pistols at the touchholes, and
yet made such a terribly effective defence. Courage is only one of the many elements which go to make up the character of a first-class commander; something more than bravery is needed before a leader can be really called great.

There happened to be circumstances which rendered the bragging of our
writers over the victory somewhat plausible. Thus they could say with an appearance of truth that the enemy had 63 guns to our 54, and outnumbered us.
In reality, as well as can be ascertained from the conflicting evidence, he was inferior in number; but a few men more or less mattered nothing. Both sides had
men enough to work the guns and handle the ships, especially as the fight was
in smooth water, and largely at long range. The important fact was that though
we had nine guns less, yet, at a broadside, they threw half as much metal again
as those of our antagonist. With such odds in our favor it would have been a
disgrace to have been beaten. The water was too smooth for our two brigs to
show at their best; but this very smoothness rendered our gun-boats more
formidable than any of the British vessels, and the British testimony is unanimous, that it was to them the defeat was primarily due. The American fleet
came into action in worse form than the hostile squadron, the ships straggling
badly, either owing to Perry having formed his line badly, or else to his having
failed to train the subordinate commanders how to keep their places. The *Niagara* was not fought well at first, Captain Elliott keeping her at a distance that
prevented her from doing any damage to the vessels opposed, which were battered to pieces by the gun-boats without the chance of replying. It certainly
seems as if the small vessels at the rear of the line should have been closer up,
and in a position to render more effectual assistance; the attack was made in too
loose order, and, whether it was the fault of Perry or of his subordinates, it fails
to reflect credit on the Americans. Cooper, as usual, praises all concerned; but
in this instance not with very good judgment. He says the line-of-battle was
highly judicious, but this may be doubted. The weather was peculiarly suitable
for the gun-boats, with their long, heavy guns; and yet the line-of-battle was so
arranged as to keep them in the rear, and let the brunt of the assault fall on the
*Lawrence,* with her short carronades. Cooper again praises Perry for steering for
the head of the enemy's line, but he could hardly have done any thing else. In
this battle the firing seems to have been equally skilful on both sides, the *Detroit*'s long guns being peculiarly well served; but the British captains manœuvred better than their foes at first, and supported one another better, so that the
disparity in damage done on each side was not equal to the disparity in force.

The chief merit of the American commander and his followers was indomitable courage, and determination not to be beaten. This is no slight merit; but it may well be doubted if it would have ensured victory had Barclay's force been as strong as Perry's. Perry made a headlong attack; his superior force, whether through his fault or his misfortune can hardly be said, being brought into action in such a manner that the head of the line was crushed by the inferior force opposed. Being literally hammered out of his own ship, Perry brought up its powerful twin-sister, and the already shattered hostile squadron was crushed by sheer weight. The manœuvres which marked the close of the battle, and which ensured the capture of all the opposing ships, were unquestionably very fine.

The British ships were fought as resolutely as their antagonists, not being surrendered till they were crippled and helpless, and almost all the officers, and a large proportion of the men placed *hors de combat*. Captain Barclay handled his ships like a first-rate seaman. It was impossible to arrange them so as to be superior to his antagonist, for the latter's force was of such a nature that in smooth water his gun-boats gave him a great advantage, while in any sea his two brigs were more than a match for the whole British squadron. In short, our victory was due to our heavy metal. As regards the honor of the affair, in spite of the amount of boasting it has given rise to, I should say it was a battle to be looked upon as in an equally high degree creditable to both sides. Indeed, if it were not for the fact that the victory was so complete, it might be said that the length of the contest and the trifling disparity in loss reflected rather the most credit on the British. Captain Perry showed indomitable pluck, and readiness to adapt himself to circumstances; but his claim to fame rests much less on his actual victory than on the way in which he prepared the fleet that was to win it. Here his energy and activity deserve all praise, not only for his success in collecting sailors and vessels and in building the two brigs, but above all for the manner in which he succeeded in getting them out on the lake. On *that* occasion he certainly out-generalled Barclay; indeed the latter committed an error that the skill and address he subsequently showed could not retrieve. But it will always be a source of surprise that the American public should have so glorified Perry's victory over an inferior force, and have paid comparatively little attention to Macdonough's victory, which really was won against decided odds in ships, men, and metal.

There are always men who consider it unpatriotic to tell the truth, if the truth is not very flattering; but, aside from the morality of the case, we never can learn how to produce a certain effect unless we know rightly what the causes were that produced a similar effect in times past. Lake Erie teaches us the advantage of having the odds on our side; Lake Champlain, that, even if they are not, skill can still counteract them. It is amusing to read some of the pamphlets written "in reply" to Cooper's account of this battle, the writers apparently regarding him as a kind of traitor for hinting that the victory was not "Nelsonic," "unsurpassed," etc. The arguments are stereotyped: Perry had 9 fewer guns, and also fewer men than the foe. This last point is the only one respecting which there is any doubt. Taking sick and well together, the Americans unquestionably had the greatest number in crew; but a quarter of them were sick. Even deducting these they were still, in all probability, more numerous than their foes.

But it is really not a point of much consequence, as both sides had enough, as stated, to serve the guns and handle the ships. In sea-fights, after there are enough hands for those purposes additional ones are not of so much advantage. I have in all my accounts summed up as accurately as possible the contending forces, because it is so customary with British writers to follow James' minute and inaccurate statements, that I thought it best to give every thing exactly; but it was really scarcely necessary, and, indeed, it is impossible to compare forces numerically. Aside from a few exceptional cases, the number of men, after a certain point was reached, made little difference. For example, the *Java* would fight just as effectually with 377 men, the number James gives her, as with 426, the number I think she really had. Again, my figures make the *Wasp* slightly superior in force to the *Frolic,* as she had 25 men the most; but in reality, as the battle was fought under very short sail, and decided purely by gunnery, the difference in number of crew was not of the least consequence. The *Hornet* had nine men more than the *Penguin,* and it would be absurd to say that this gave her much advantage. In both the latter cases, the forces were practically equal, although, numerically expressed, the odds were in favor of the Americans. The exact reverse is the case in the last action of the *Constitution.* Here, the *Levant* and *Cyane* had all the men they required, and threw a heavier broadside than their foe. Expressed in numbers, the odds against them were not great, but numbers could not express the fact that carronades were opposed to long guns, and two small ships to one big one. Again, though in the action on Lake Champlain numbers do show a slight advantage both in weight of metal and number of men on the British side, they do not make the advantage as great as it really was, for they do not show that the British possessed a frigate with a main-deck battery of 24-pounders, which was equal to the two chief vessels of the Americans, exactly as the *Constitution* was superior to the *Cyane* and *Levant.*[1] And on

---

[1] It must always be remembered that these rules cut both ways. British writers are very eloquent about the disadvantage in which carronades placed the *Cyane* and *Levant,* but do not hint that the *Essex* suffered from a precisely similar cause, in addition to her other misfortunes; either they should give the *Constitution* more credit or the *Phœbe* less. So the *Confiance,* throwing 480 pounds of metal at a broadside, was really equal to both the *Eagle* and *Saratoga,* who jointly threw 678. From her long guns she threw 384 pounds, from her carronades 96. Their long guns threw 168, their carronades 510. Now the 32-pound carronade mounted on the spar-deck of a 38-gun frigate, was certainly much less formidable than the long 18 on the main-deck; indeed, it probably ranked more nearly with a long 12, in the ordinary chances of war (and it must be remembered that Downie was the attacking party and chose his own position, so far as Macdonough's excellent arrangements would let him). So that in comparing the forces, the carronades should not be reckoned for more than half the value of the long guns, and we get, as a mere approximation, 384 + 48 = 432, against 168 + 255 = 423. At any rate, British writers, as well as Americans, should remember that if the *Constitution* was greatly superior to her two foes, then the *Confiance* was certainly equal to the *Eagle* and *Saratoga;* and *vica versa.*

the same principles I think that every fair-minded man must admit the great superiority of Perry's fleet over Barclay's, though the advantage was greater in carronades than in long guns.

But to admit this by no means precludes us from taking credit for the victory. Almost all the victories gained by the English over the Dutch in the 17th century were due purely to great superiority in force. The cases have a curious analogy to this lake battle. Perry won with 54 guns against Barclay's 63; but the odds were largely in his favor. Blake won a doubtful victory on the 18th of February, 1653, with 80 ships against Tromp's 70; but the English vessels were twice the size of the Dutch, and in number of men and weight of metal greatly their superior. The English were excellent fighters, but no better than the Dutch, and none of their admirals of that period deserve to rank with De Ruyter. Again, the great victory of La Hogue was won over a very much smaller French fleet, after a day's hard fighting, which resulted in the capture of *one* vessel! This victory was most exultingly chronicled, yet it was precisely as if Perry had fought Barclay all day and only succeeded in capturing the *Little Belt*. Most of Lord Nelson's successes were certainly won against heavy odds by his great genius and the daring skill of the captains who served under him; but the battle of the Baltic, as far as the fighting went, reflected as much honor on the defeated Danes as on the mighty sea-chief who conquered them. Many a much-vaunted victory, both on sea and land, has really reflected less credit on the victors than the battle of Lake Erie did on the Americans. And it must always be remembered that a victory, honorably won, if even over a weaker foe, *does* reflect credit on the nation by whom it is gained. It was creditable to us as a nation that our ships were better made and better armed than the British frigates, exactly as it was creditable to them that a few years before their vessels had stood in the same relation to the Dutch ships.[1] It was greatly to our credit that we had been enterprising enough to fit out such an effective little flotilla on Lake Erie, and for this Perry deserves the highest praise.[2]

Before leaving the subject it is worth while making a few observations on the men who composed the crews. James, who despised a Canadian as much as he hated an American, gives as one excuse for the defeat, the fact that most of Barclay's crew were Canadians, whom he considers to be "sorry substitutes." On each side the regular sailors, from the seaboard, were not numerous enough to permit the battle to be fought purely by them. Barclay took a number of soldiers of the regular army, and Perry a number of militia, aboard; the former had a few Indian sharp-shooters, the latter quite a number of negroes. A great

[1] After Lord Duncan's victory at Camperdown, James chronicled the fact that all the captured line-of-battle ships were such poor craft as not to be of as much value as so many French frigates. This at least showed that the Dutch sailors must have done well to have made such a bloody and obstinate fight as they did, with the materials they had. According to his own statements the loss was about proportional to the forces in action. It was another parallel to Perry's victory.

[2] Some of my countrymen will consider this but scant approbation, to which the answer must be that a history is not a panegyric.

many men in each fleet were lake sailors, frontiersmen, and these were the especial objects of James' contempt; but it may be doubted if they, thoroughly
accustomed to lake navigation, used to contests with Indians and whites, naturally forced to be good sailors, and skilful in the use of rifle and cannon, were
not, when trained by good men and on their own waters, the very best possible
material. Certainly the battle of Lake Erie, fought mainly by Canadians, was
better contested than that of Lake Champlain, fought mainly by British.

The difference between the American and British seamen on the Atlantic
was small, but on the lakes what little there was disappeared. A New Englander
and an Old Englander differed little enough, but they differed more than a
frontiersman born north of the line did from one born south of it. These last
two resembled one another more nearly than either did the parent. There had
been no long-established naval school on the lakes, and the British sailors that
came up there were the best of their kind; so the combatants were really so
evenly matched in courage, skill, and all other fighting qualities, as to make it
impossible to award the palm to either for these attributes. The dogged obstinacy of the fighting, the skilful firing and manœuvring, and the daring and
coolness with which cutting-out expeditions were planned and executed, were
as marked on one side as the other. The only un-English element in the contest
was the presence among the Canadian English of some of the descendants of
the Latin race from whom they had conquered the country. Otherwise the men
were equally matched, but the Americans owed their success—for the balance
of success was largely on their side—to the fact that their officers had been
trained in the best and most practical, although the smallest, navy of the day.
The British sailors on the lakes were as good as our own, but no better. None of
their commanders compare with Macdonough.

Perry deserves all praise for the manner in which he got his fleet ready; his
victory over Barclay was precisely similar to the quasi-victories of Blake over
the Dutch, which have given that admiral such renown. Blake's success in attacking Spanish and Algerian forts is his true title to fame. In his engagements
with the Dutch fleets (as well as in those of Monk, after him) his claim to merit
is no greater and no less than Perry's. Each made a headlong attack, with furious, stubborn courage, and by dint of sheer weight crushed or disabled a
greatly inferior foe. In the fight that took place on Feb. 18, 1653, De Ruyter's
ship carried but 34 guns,[1] and yet with it he captured the *Prosperous* of 54;
which vessel was stronger than any in the Dutch fleet. The fact that Blake's battles were generally so indecisive must be ascribed to the fact that his opponents
were, though inferior in force, superior in skill. No decisive defeat was inflicted
on the Dutch until Tromp's death. Perry's operations were on a very small, and
Blake's on a very large, scale; but whereas Perry left no antagonists to question

---

[1] "La Vie et Les Actions Memorables de Lt.-Amiral Michel De Ruyter" (Amsterdam, 1677), p. 23. By
the way, why is Tromp always called Van Tromp by English writers? It would be quite as correct for a
Frenchman to speak of MacNelson.

his claim to victory, Blake's successes were sufficiently doubtful to admit of his antagonists in almost every instance claiming that *they* had won, or else that it was a draw. Of course it is absurd to put Perry and Blake on a par, for one worked with a fleet forty times the strength of the other's flotilla; but the way in which the work was done was very similar. And it must always be remembered that when Perry fought this battle he was but 27 years old; and the commanders of his other vessels were younger still.

## CHAMPLAIN

The commander on this lake at this time was Lieutenant Thomas Macdonough, who had superseded the former commander, Lieutenant Sydney Smith,—whose name was a curious commentary on the close inter-relationship of the two contesting peoples. The American naval force now consisted of two sloops, the *Growler* and *Eagle,* each mounting 11 guns, and six galleys, mounting one gun each. Lieutenant Smith was sent down with his two sloops to harass the British gun-boats, which were stationed round the head of Sorel River, the outlet to Lake Champlain. On June 3d he chased three gun-boats into the river, the wind being aft, up to within sight of the fort of Isle-aux-noix. A strong British land-force, under Major-General Taylor, now came up both banks of the narrow stream, and joined the three gun-boats in attacking the sloops. The latter tried to beat up the stream, but the current was so strong and the wind so light that no headway could be made. The gun-boats kept out of range of the sloop's guns, while keeping up a hot fire from their long 24's, to which no reply could be made; but the galling fire of the infantry who lined the banks was responded to by showers of grape. After three hours' conflict, at 12.30, a 24-pound shot from one of the galleys struck the *Eagle* under her starboard quarter, and ripped out a whole plank under water. She sank at once, but it was in such shoal water that she did not settle entirely, and none of the men were drowned. Soon afterward the *Growler* had her forestay and main-boom shot away, and, becoming unmanageable, ran ashore and was also captured. The *Growler* had 1 killed and 8 wounded, the *Eagle* 11 wounded; their united crews, including 34 volunteers, amounted to 112 men. The British gun-boats suffered no loss; of the troops on shore three were wounded, one dangerously, by grape.[1] Lieutenant Smith had certainly made a very plucky fight, but it was a great mistake to get cooped up in a narrow channel, with wind and current dead against him. It was a very creditable success to the British, and showed the effectiveness of well-handled gun-boats under certain circumstances. The possession of these two sloops gave the command of the lake to the British. Macdonough at once set about building others, but with all his energy the materials at hand were so deficient

---

[1] Letter from Major-General Taylor (British) to Major-General Stone, June 3, 1813. Lossing says the loss of the British was "probably at least one hundred,"—on what authority, if any, I do not know.

that he could not get them finished in time. On July 31st, 1,000 British troops, under Col. J. Murray, convoyed by Captain Thomas Everard, with the sloops *Chubb* and *Finch* (late *Growler* and *Eagle*) and three gun-boats, landed at Plattsburg and destroyed all the barracks and stores both there and at Saranac. For some reason Colonel Murray left so precipitately that he overlooked a picket of 20 of his men, who were captured; then he made descents on two or three other places, and returned to the head of the lake by Aug. 3d. Three days afterward, on Aug. 6th, Macdonough completed his three sloops, the *President, Montgomery,* and *Preble,* of 7 guns each, and also six gun-boats; which force enabled him to prevent any more plundering expeditions taking place that summer, and to convoy Hampton's troops when they made an abortive effort to penetrate into Canada by the Sorel River on Sept. 21st.

### BRITISH LOSS ON THE LAKES DURING 1813

| NAME. | TONS. | GUNS. | REMARKS. |
|---|---|---|---|
| *Ship,* | 600 | 24 | Burnt on stocks. |
| *Gloucester,* | 180 | 10 | Taken at York. |
| *Mary,* | 80 | 3 | Burnt. |
| *Drummond,* | 80 | 3 | Captured. |
| *Lady Gore,* | 80 | 3 | " |
| *Schooner,* | 80 | 3 | " |
| *Detroit,* | 490 | 19 | " |
| *Queen Charlotte,* | 400 | 17 | " |
| *Lady Prevost,* | 230 | 13 | " |
| *Hunter,* | 180 | 10 | " |
| *Chippeway,* | 70 | 1 | " |
| *Little Belt,* | 90 | 3 | " |
| 12 vessels, | 2,560 | 109 | |

### AMERICAN LOSS.[1]

| NAME. | TONS. | GUNS. | REMARKS. |
|---|---|---|---|
| *Growler,* | 112 | 11 | Captured. |
| *Eagle,* | 110 | 11 | " |
| 2 vessels, | 222 | 22 | |

[1] Excluding the *Growler* and *Julia,* which were recaptured.

# VII

# 1814

# ON THE OCEAN

During this year the blockade of the American coast was kept up with ever in-creasing rigor. The British frigates hovered like hawks off every seaport that was known to harbor any fighting craft; they almost invariably went in couples, to support one another and to lighten, as far as was possible, the severity of their work. On the northern coasts in particular, the intense cold of the furious winter gales rendered it no easy task to keep the assigned stations; the ropes were turned into stiff and brittle bars, the hulls were coated with ice, and many, both of men and officers, were frost-bitten and crippled. But no stress of weather could long keep the stubborn and hardy British from their posts. With ceaseless vigilance they traversed continually the allotted cruising grounds, capturing the privateers, harrying the coasters, and keeping the more powerful ships confined to port; "no American frigate could proceed singly to sea with-out imminent risk of being crushed by the superior force of the numerous British squadrons."[1] But the sloops of war, commanded by officers as skilful as they were daring, and manned by as hardy seamen as ever sailed salt water, could often slip out; generally on some dark night, when a heavy gale was blow-ing, they would make the attempt, under storm canvas, and with almost invari-able success. The harder the weather, the better was their chance; once clear of the coast the greatest danger ceased, though throughout the cruise the most untiring vigilance was needed. The new sloops that I have mentioned as being built proved themselves the best possible vessels for this kind of work; they

---

[1] Captain Broke's letter of challenge to Captain Lawrence.

were fast enough to escape from most cruisers of superior force, and were over-matches for any British flush-decked ship, that is, for any thing below the rank of the frigate-built corvettes of the *Cyane*'s class. The danger of recapture was too great to permit of the prizes being sent in, so they were generally destroyed as soon as captured; and as the cruising grounds were chosen right in the track of commerce, the damage done and consternation caused were very great.

Besides the numerous frigates cruising along the coast in couples or small squadrons, there were two or three places that were blockaded by a heavier force. One of these was New London, before which cruised a squadron under the direction of Sir Thomas Hardy, in the 74-gun ship *Ramillies*. Most of the other cruising squadrons off the coast contained razees or two-deckers. The boats of the *Hogue*, 74, took part in the destruction of some coasters and fishing-boats at Pettipauge in April; and those of the *Superb*, 74, shared in a similar expedition against Wareham in June.[1] The command on the coast of North America was now given to Vice-Admiral Sir Alexander Cochrane. The main British force continued to lie in the Chesapeake, where about 50 sail were collected. During the first part of this year these were under the command of Sir Robert Barrie, but in May he was relieved by Rear-Admiral Cockburn.[2]

The *President*, 44, Commodore Rodgers, at the beginning of 1814 was still out, cruising among the Barbadoes and West Indies, only making a few prizes of not much value. She then turned toward the American coast, striking soundings near St. Augustine, and thence proceeding north along the coast to Sandy Hook, which was reached on Feb. 18th. The light was passed in the night, and shortly afterward several sail were made out, when the *President* was at once cleared for action.[3] One of these strange sail was the *Loire*, 38 (British), Capt. Thomas Brown, which ran down to close the *President*, unaware of her force; but on discovering her to be a 44, hauled to the wind and made off.[4] The *President* did not pursue, another frigate and a gun-brig being in sight.[5] This rencontre gave rise to nonsensical boastings on both sides; one American writer calls the *Loire* the *Plantagenet*, 74; James, on the other hand, states that the *President* was afraid to engage the 38-gun frigate, and that the only reason the latter declined the combat was because she was short of men. The best answer to this is a quotation from his own work (vol. vi, p. 402), that "the admiralty had issued an order that no 18-pounder frigate was voluntarily to engage one of the 24-pounder frigates of America." Coupling this order with the results of the combats that had already taken place between frigates of these classes, it can always be safely set down as sheer bravado when any talk is made of an American 44 refusing to give battle to a British 38; and it is even more absurd to say that a

[1] James, vi, 474.
[2] James, vi, 437.
[3] Letter of Commodore Rodgers, Feb. 20, 1814.
[4] James, vi, 412.
[5] "Naval Monument," p. 235.

British line-of-battle ship would hesitate for a minute about engaging *any* frigate.

On Jan. 1st, the *Constitution,* which had been lying in Boston harbor undergoing complete repairs, put out to sea under the command of Capt. Charles Stewart. The British 38-gun frigate *Nymphe* had been lying before the port, but she disappeared long before the *Constitution* was in condition, in obedience to the order already mentioned. Capt. Stewart ran down toward the Barbadoes, and on the 14th of February captured and destroyed the British 14-gun schooner *Pictou,* with a crew of 75 men. After making a few other prizes and reaching the coast of Guiana she turned homeward, and on the 23d of the same month fell in, at the entrance to the Mona passage, with the British 36-gun frigate *Pique* (late French *Pallas*), Captain Maitland. The *Constitution* at once made sail for the *Pique,* steering free;[1] the latter at first hauled to the wind and waited for her antagonist, but when the latter was still 3 miles distant she made out her force and immediately made all sail to escape; the *Constitution,* however, gained steadily till 8 P.M., when the night and thick squally weather caused her to lose sight of the chase. Captain Maitland had on board the prohibitory order issued by the admiralty,[2] and acted correctly. His ship was altogether too light for his antagonist. James, however, is not satisfied with this, and wishes to prove that *both* ships were desirous of avoiding the combat. He says that Capt. Stewart came near enough to count "13 ports and a bridle on the *Pique*'s main-deck," and "saw at once that she was of a class inferior to the *Guerrière* or *Java,*" but "thought the *Pique*'s 18's were 24's, and therefore did not make an effort to bring her to action." He portrays very picturesquely the grief of the *Pique*'s crew when they find they are not going to engage; how they come aft and request to be taken into action; how Captain Maitland reads them his instructions, but "fails to persuade them that there had been any necessity of issuing them"; and, finally, how the sailors, overcome by woe and indignation, refuse to take their supper-time grog,—which was certainly remarkable. As the *Constitution* had twice captured British frigates "with impunity," according to James himself, is it likely that she would now shrink from an encounter with a ship which she "saw at once was of an inferior class" to those already conquered? Even such abject cowards as James' Americans would not be guilty of so stupid an action. Of course neither Capt. Stewart nor any one else supposed for an instant that a 36-gun frigate was armed with 24-pounders.

It is worth while mentioning as an instance of how utterly untrustworthy James is in dealing with American affairs, that he says (p. 476) the *Constitution* had now "what the Americans would call a bad crew," whereas, in her previous battles, all her men had been "picked." Curiously enough, this is the exact reverse of the truth. In no case was an American ship manned with a "picked" crew, but the nearest approach to such was the crew the *Constitution* carried in

[1] Letter of Capt. Stewart, April 8, 1814.
[2] James, vi, 477.

this and the next cruise, when "she probably possessed as fine a crew as ever manned a frigate. They were principally New England men, and it has been said of them that they were almost qualified to fight the ship without her officers."[1] The statement that such men, commanded by one of the bravest and most skilful captains of our navy, would shrink from attacking a greatly inferior foe, is hardly worth while denying; and, fortunately, such denial is needless, Captain Stewart's account being fully corroborated in the "Memoir of Admiral Durham," written by his nephew, Captain Murray, London, 1846.

The *Constitution* arrived off the port of Marblehead on April 3d, and at 7 A.M. fell in with the two British 38-gun frigates *Junon*, Captain Upton, and *Tenedos*, Captain Parker. "The American frigate was standing to the westward with the wind about north by west and bore from the two British frigates about northwest by west. The *Junon* and *Tenedos* quickly hauled up in chase, and the *Constitution* crowded sail in the direction of Marblehead. At 9.30, finding the *Tenedos* rather gaining upon her, the *Constitution* started her water and threw overboard a quantity of provisions and other articles. At 11.30 she hoisted her colors, and the two British frigates, who were now dropping slowly in the chase, did the same. At 1.30 P.M. the *Constitution* anchored in the harbor of Marblehead. Captain Parker was anxious to follow her into the port, which had no defences; but the *Tenedos* was recalled by a signal from the *Junon*."[2] Shortly afterward the *Constitution* again put out, and reached Boston unmolested.

On Jan. 29, 1814, the small U. S. coasting schooner *Alligator*, of 4 guns and 40 men, Sailing-master R. Basset, was lying at anchor in the mouth of Stone River, S.C., when a frigate and a brig were perceived close inshore near the breakers. Judging from their motions that they would attempt to cut him out when it was dark, Mr. Basset made his preparations accordingly.[3] At half-past seven six boats were observed approaching cautiously under cover of the marsh, with muffled oars; on being hailed they cheered and opened with boat carronades and musketry, coming on at full speed; whereupon the *Alligator* cut her cable and made sail, the wind being light from the southwest; while the crew opened such a heavy fire on the assailants, who were then not thirty yards off, that they stopped the advance and fell astern. At this moment the *Alligator* grounded, but the enemy had suffered so severely that they made no attempt to renew the attack, rowing off down stream. On board the *Alligator* two men were killed and two wounded, including the pilot, who was struck down by a grape-shot while standing at the helm; and her sails and rigging were much cut. The extent of the enemy's loss was never known; next day one of his cutters was picked up at North Edisto, much injured and containing the bodies of an officer and a seaman.[4] For his skill and gallantry Mr. Basset was promoted to a lieutenancy, and

---

[1] Cooper, ii, 463.
[2] James, vi, 479.
[3] Letter of Sailing-master Basset, Jan. 31, 1814.
[4] Letter from Commander J. H. Dent, Feb. 21, 1814.

for a time his exploit put a complete stop to the cutting-out expeditions along that part of the coast. The *Alligator* herself sank in a squall on July 1st, but was afterward raised and refitted.

It is much to be regretted that it is almost impossible to get at the British account of any of these expeditions which ended successfully for the Americans; all such cases are generally ignored by the British historians; so that I am obliged to rely solely upon the accounts of the victors, who, with the best intentions in the world, could hardly be perfectly accurate.

At the close of 1813 Captain Porter was still cruising in the Pacific.

Early in January the *Essex,* now with 255 men aboard, made the South American coast, and on the 12th of that month anchored in the harbor of Valparaiso. She had in company a prize, re-christened the *Essex Junior,* with a crew of 60 men, and 20 guns, 10 long sixes and 10 eighteen-pound carronades. Of course she could not be used in a combat with regular cruisers.

On Feb. 8th, the British frigate *Phœbe,* 36, Captain James Hilyar, accompanied by the *Cherub,* 18, Captain Thomas Tudor Tucker, the former carrying 300 and the latter 140 men,[1] made their appearance, and apparently proposed to take the *Essex* by a *coup de main.* They hauled into the harbor on a wind, the *Cherub* falling to leeward; while the *Phœbe* made the port quarter of the *Essex,* and then, putting her helm down, luffed up on her starboard bow, but 10 or 15 feet distant. Porter's crew were all at quarters, the powder-boys with slow matches ready to discharge the guns, the boarders standing by, cutlass in hand, to board in the smoke; every thing was cleared for action on both frigates. Captain Hilyar now probably saw that there was no chance of carrying the *Essex* by surprise, and, standing on the after-gun, he inquired after Captain Porter's health; the latter returned the inquiry, but warned Hilyar not to fall foul. The British captain then braced back his yards, remarking that if he did fall aboard it would be purely accidental. "Well," said Porter, "you have no business where you are; if you touch a rope-yarn of this ship I shall board instantly."[2] The *Phœbe,* in her then position, was completely at the mercy of the American ships, and Hilyar, greatly agitated, assured Porter that he meant nothing hostile; and the *Phœbe* backed down, her yards passing over those of the *Essex* without touching a rope, and anchored half a mile astern. Shortly afterward the two captains met on shore, when Hilyar thanked Porter for his behavior, and, on his inquiry, assured him that after thus owing his safety to the latter's forbearance, Porter need be under no apprehension as to his breaking the neutrality.

The British ships now began a blockade of the port. On Feb. 27th, the *Phœbe* being hove to close off the port, and the *Cherub* a league to leeward, the former fired a weather-gun; the *Essex* interpreting this as a challenge, took the crew of the *Essex Junior* aboard and went out to attack the British frigate. But the latter

---

[1] They afterward took on board enough men from British merchant-vessels to raise their complements respectively to 320 and 180.

[2] "Life of Farragut," p. 33.

did not await the combat; she bore up, set her studding-sails, and ran down to the *Cherub*. The American officers were intensely irritated over this, and American writers have sneered much at "a British 36 refusing combat with an American 32." But the armaments of the two frigates were so wholly dissimilar that it is hard to make comparison. When the fight really took place, the *Essex* was so crippled and the water so smooth that the British ships fought at their own distance, and as they had long guns to oppose to Porter's carronades, this really made the *Cherub* more nearly suited to contend with the *Essex* than the latter was to fight the *Phœbe*. But when the *Essex* in fairly heavy weather, with the crew of the *Essex Junior* aboard, was to windward, the circumstances were very different; she carried as many men and guns as the *Phœbe*, and in close combat, or in a hand-to-hand struggle, could probably have taken her. Still, Hilyar's conduct in avoiding Porter except when the *Cherub* was in company was certainly over-cautious, and very difficult to explain in a man of his tried courage.

On March 27th Porter decided to run out of the harbor on the first opportunity, so as to draw away his two antagonists in chase, and let the *Essex Junior* escape. This plan had to be tried sooner than was expected. The two vessels were always ready, the *Essex* only having her proper complement of 255 men aboard. On the next day, the 28th, it came on to blow from the south, when the *Essex* parted her port cable and dragged the starboard anchor to leeward, so she got under way, and made sail; by several trials it had been found that she was faster than the *Phœbe*, and that the *Cherub* was very slow indeed, so Porter had little anxiety about his own ship, only fearing for his consort. The British vessels were close in with the weather-most point of the bay, but Porter thought he could weather them, and hauled up for that purpose. Just as he was rounding the outermost point, which, if accomplished, would have secured his safety, a heavy squall struck the *Essex*, and when she was nearly gunwale under, the main-top-mast went by the board. She now wore and stood in for the harbor, but the wind had shifted, and on account of her crippled condition she could not gain it; so she bore up and anchored in a small bay, three miles from Valparaiso, and half a mile from a detached Chilian battery of one gun, the *Essex* being within pistol-shot of the shore.[1] The *Phœbe* and *Cherub* now bore down upon her, covered with ensigns, union-jacks, and motto flags; and it became evident that Hilyar did not intend to keep his word, as soon as he saw that Porter was disabled. So the *Essex* prepared for action, though there could be no chance whatever of success. Her flags were flying from every mast, and every thing was made ready as far as was possible. The attack was made before springs could be got on her cables. She was anchored so near the shore as to preclude the possibility of Captain Hilyar's passing ahead of her[2]; so his two ships came cautiously down, the *Cherub* taking her position on the starboard bow of the

---

[1] Letter of Captain David Porter, July 3, 1814.
[2] Letter of Captain James Hilyar, March 30, 1814.

*Essex,* and the *Phœbe* under the latter's stern. The attack began at 4 P.M.[1] Some of the bow-guns of the American frigate bore upon the *Cherub,* and, as soon as she found this out, the sloop ran down and stationed herself near the *Phœbe.* The latter had opened with her broadside of long 18's, from a position in which not one of Porter's guns could reach her. Three times springs were got on the cables of the *Essex,* in order to bring her round till her broadside bore; but in each instance they were shot away, as soon as they were hauled taut. Three long 12's were got out of the stern-ports, and with these an animated fire was kept up on the two British ships, the aim being especially to cripple their rigging. A good many of Porter's crew were killed during the first five minutes, before he could bring any guns to bear; but afterward he did not suffer much, and at 4.20, after a quarter of an hour's fight between the three long 12's of the *Essex,* and the whole 36 broadside guns of the *Phœbe* and *Cherub,* the latter were actually driven off. They wore, and again began with their long guns; but, these producing no visible effect, both of the British ships hauled out of the fight at 4.30. "Having lost the use of main-sail, jib, and main-stay, appearances looked a little inauspicious," writes Captain Hilyar. But the damages were soon repaired, and his two ships stood back for the crippled foe. Both stationed themselves on her port-quarter, the *Phœbe* at anchor, with a spring, firing her broadside, while the *Cherub* kept under way, using her long bow-chasers. Their fire was very destructive, for they were out of reach of the *Essex's* carronades, and not one of her long guns could be brought to bear on them. Porter now cut his cable, at 5.20, and tried to close with his antagonists. After many ineffectual efforts sail was made. The flying-jib halyards were the only serviceable ropes uncut. That sail was hoisted, and the foretop-sail and foresail let fall, though the want of sheets and tacks rendered them almost useless. Still the *Essex* drove down on her assailants, and for the first time got near enough to use her carronades; for a minute or two the firing was tremendous, but after the first broadside the *Cherub* hauled out of the fight in great haste, and during the remainder of the action confined herself to using her bow-guns from a distance. Immediately afterward the *Phœbe* also edged off, and by her superiority of sailing, her foe being now almost helpless, was enabled to choose her own distance, and again opened from her long 18's, out of range of Porter's carronades.[2] The carnage on board the *Essex* had now made her decks look like shambles. One gun was manned three times, fifteen men being slain at it; its captain alone escaped without a wound. There were but one or two instances of flinching; the wounded, many of whom were killed by flying splinters while under the hands

---

[1] Mean time. Porter says 3.54; Hilyar, a few minutes past 4. The former says the first attack lasted half an hour; the latter, but 10 minutes. I accordingly make it 20.

[2] American writers often sneer at Hilyar for keeping away from the *Essex,* and out of reach of her short guns; but his conduct was eminently proper in this respect. It was no part of his duty to fight the *Essex* at the distance which *best* suited her; but, on the contrary, at that which *least* suited her. He, of course, wished to win the victory with the least possible loss to himself, and acted accordingly. His conduct in the action itself could not be improved upon.

of the doctors, cheered on their comrades, and themselves worked at the guns like fiends as long as they could stand. At one of the bow-guns was stationed a young Scotchman, named Bissly, who had one leg shot off close by the groin. Using his handkerchief as a tourniquet, he said, turning to his American ship-mates: "I left my own country and adopted the United States, to fight for her. I hope I have this day proved myself worthy of the country of my adoption. I am no longer of any use to you or to her, so good-by!" With these words he leaned on the sill of the port, and threw himself overboard.[1] Among the very few men who flinched was one named William Roach; Porter sent one of his midshipmen to shoot him, but he was not to be found. He was discovered by a man named William Call, whose leg had been shot off and was hanging by the skin, and who dragged the shattered stump all round the bag-house, pistol in hand, trying to get a shot at him. Lieut. J. G. Cowell had his leg shot off above the knee, and his life might have been saved had it been amputated at once; but the surgeons already had rows of wounded men waiting for them, and when it was proposed to him that he should be attended to out of order, he replied: "No, doctor, none of that; fair play's a jewel. One man's life is as dear as another's; I would not cheat any poor fellow out of his turn." So he stayed at his post, and died from loss of blood.

Finding it hopeless to try to close, the *Essex* stood for the land, Porter intending to run her ashore and burn her. But when she had drifted close to the bluffs the wind suddenly shifted, took her flat aback and paid her head off shore, exposing her to a raking fire. At this moment Lieutenant Downes, commanding the *Junior*, pulled out in a boat, through all the fire, to see if he could do any thing. Three of the men with him, including an old boatswain's mate, named Kingsbury, had come out expressly "to share the fate of their old ship"; so they remained aboard, and, in their places, Lieutenant Downes took some of the wounded ashore, while the *Cherub* kept up a tremendous fire upon him. The shift of the wind gave Porter a faint hope of closing; and once more the riddled hulk of the little American frigate was headed for her foes. But Hilyar put his helm up to avoid close quarters; the battle was his already, and the cool old captain was too good an officer to leave any thing to chance. Seeing he could not close, Porter had a hawser bent on the sheet-anchor and let go. This brought the ship's head round, keeping her stationary; and from such of her guns as were not dismounted and had men enough left to man them, a broadside was fired at the *Phœbe*. The wind was now very light, and the *Phœbe*, whose main- and mizzen-masts and main-yard were rather seriously wounded, and who had suffered a great loss of canvas and cordage aloft, besides receiving a number of shot between wind and water,[2] and was thus a good deal crippled, began to drift slowly

---

[1] This and most of the other anecdotes are taken from the invaluable "Life of Farragut," pp. 37–46.

[2] Captain Hilyar's letter. James says the *Phœbe* had 7 shot between wind and water, and one below the water-line. Porter says she had 18 12-pound shot below the water-line. The latter statement must have been an exaggeration; and James is probably farther wrong still.

to leeward. It was hoped that she would drift out of gun-shot, but this last chance was lost by the parting of the hawser, which left the *Essex* at the mercy of the British vessels. Their fire was deliberate and destructive, and could only be occasionally replied to by a shot from one of the long 12's of the *Essex*. The ship caught fire, and the flames came bursting up the hatchway, and a quantity of powder exploded below. Many of the crew were knocked overboard by shot, and drowned; others leaped into the water, thinking the ship was about to blow up, and tried to swim to the land. Some succeeded; among them was one man who had sixteen or eighteen pieces of iron in his leg, scales from the muzzle of his gun. The frigate had been shattered to pieces above the water-line, although from the smoothness of the sea she was not harmed enough below it to reduce her to a sinking condition.[1] The carpenter reported that he alone of his crew was fit for duty; the others were dead or disabled. Lieutenant Wilmer was knocked overboard by a splinter, and drowned; his little negro boy, "Ruff," came up on deck, and, hearing of the disaster, deliberately leaped into the sea and shared his master's fate. Lieutenant Odenheimer was also knocked overboard, but afterward regained the ship. A shot, glancing upward, killed four of the men who were standing by a gun, striking the last one in the head and scattering his brains over his comrades. The only commissioned officer left on duty was Lieutenant Decatur McKnight. The sailing-master, Barnwell, when terribly wounded, remained at his post till he fainted from loss of blood. Of the 255 men aboard the *Essex* when the battle began, 58 had been killed, 66 wounded, and 31 drowned ("missing"), while 24 had succeeded in reaching shore. But 76 men were left unwounded, and many of these had been bruised or otherwise injured. Porter himself was knocked down by the windage of a passing shot. While the young midshipman, Farragut, was on the ward-room ladder, going below for gun-primers, the captain of the gun directly opposite the hatchway was struck full in the face by an 18-pound shot, and tumbled back on him. They fell down the hatch together, Farragut being stunned for some minutes. Later, while standing by the man at the wheel, an old quartermaster named Francis Bland, a shot coming over the fore-yard took off the quartermaster's right leg, carrying away at the same time one of Farragut's coat tails. The old fellow was helped below, but he died for lack of a tourniquet, before he could be attended to.

Nothing remained to be done, and at 6.20 the *Essex* surrendered and was taken possession of. The *Phœbe* had lost 4 men killed, including her first lieutenant, William Ingram, and 7 wounded; the *Cherub*, 1 killed, and 3, including Captain Tucker, wounded. Total, 5 killed and 10 wounded.[2] The difference in loss was natural, as, owing to their having long guns and the choice of position, the British had been able to fire ten shot to the Americans' one.

---

[1] An exactly analogous case to that of the British sloop *Reindeer*.

[2] James says that most of the loss was occasioned by the first three broadsides of the *Essex*; this is not surprising, as in all she hardly fired half a dozen, and the last were discharged when half of the guns had been disabled, and there were scarcely men enough to man the remainder. Most of the time her resistance was limited to firing such of her six long guns as would bear.

The conduct of the two English captains in attacking Porter as soon as he was disabled, in neutral waters, while they had been very careful to abstain from breaking the neutrality while he was in good condition, does not look well; at the best it shows that Hilyar had only been withheld hitherto from the attack by timidity, and it looks all the worse when it is remembered that Hilyar owed his ship's previous escape entirely to Porter's forbearance on a former occasion when the British frigate was entirely at his mercy, and that the British captain had afterward expressly said that he would not break the neutrality. Still, the British in this war did not act very differently from the way we ourselves did on one or two occasions in the Civil War,—witness the capture of the *Florida*. And after the battle was once begun the sneers which most of our historians, as well as the participators in the fight, have showered upon the British captains for not foregoing the advantages which their entire masts and better artillery gave them by coming to close quarters, are decidedly foolish. Hilyar's conduct during the battle, as well as his treatment of the prisoners afterward, was perfect, and as a minor matter it may be mentioned that his official letter is singularly just and fair-minded. Says Lord Howard Douglass[1]: "The action displayed all that can reflect honor on the science and admirable conduct of Captain Hilyar and his crew, which, without the assistance of the *Cherub*, would have insured the same termination. Captain Porter's sneers at the respectful distance the *Phœbe* kept are in fact acknowledgments of the ability with which Captain Hilyar availed himself of the superiority of his arms; it was a brilliant affair." While endorsing this criticism, it may be worth while to compare it with some of the author's comments upon the other actions, as that between Decatur and the *Macedonian*. To make the odds here as great against Carden as they were against Porter, it would be necessary to suppose that the *Macedonian* had lost her main-top-mast, had but six long 18's to oppose to her antagonist's 24's, and that the latter was assisted by the corvette *Adams*; so that as a matter of fact Porter fought at fully double or treble the disadvantage Carden did, and, instead of surrendering when he had lost a third of his crew, fought till three fifths of his men were dead or wounded, and, moreover, inflicted greater loss and damage on his antagonists than Carden did. If, then, as Lord Douglass says, the defence of the *Macedonian* brilliantly upheld the character of the British navy for courage, how much more did that of the *Essex* show for the American navy; and if Hilyar's conduct was "brilliant," that of Decatur was more so.

This was an action in which it is difficult to tell exactly how to award praise. Captain Hilyar deserves it, for the coolness and skill with which he made his approaches and took his positions so as to destroy his adversary with least loss to himself, and also for the precision of his fire. The *Cherub*'s behavior was more remarkable for extreme caution than for any thing else. As regards the mere fight, Porter certainly did every thing a man could do to contend successfully with the overwhelming force opposed to him, and the few guns that were available were served with the utmost precision. As an exhibition of dogged courage it has never

---

[1] "Naval Gunnery," p. 149.

been surpassed since the time when the Dutch captain, Klæsoon, after fighting two long days, blew up his disabled ship, devoting himself and all his crew to death, rather than surrender to the hereditary foes of his race, and was bitterly avenged afterward by the grim "sea-beggars" of Holland; the days when Drake singed the beard of the Catholic king, and the small English craft were the dread and scourge of the great floating castles of Spain. Any man reading Farragut's account is forcibly reminded of some of the deeds of "derring do" in that, the heroic age of the Teutonic navies. Captain Hilyar in his letter says: "The defence of the *Essex*, taking into consideration our superiority of force and the very discouraging circumstance of her having lost her main-top-mast and being twice on fire, did honor to her brave defenders, and most fully evinced the courage of Captain Porter and those under his command. Her colors were not struck until the loss in killed and wounded was so awfully great and her shattered condition so seriously bad as to render all further resistance unavailing."[1] He also bears very candid testimony to the defence of the *Essex* having been effective enough to at one time render the result doubtful, saying: "Our first attack * * * produced no visible effect. Our second * * * was not more successful; and having lost the use of our main-sail, jib, and main-stay, appearances looked a little inauspicious." Throughout the war no ship was so desperately defended as the *Essex*, taking into account the frightful odds against which she fought, which always enhances the merit of a defence. The *Lawrence*, which suffered even more, was backed by a fleet; the *Frolic* was overcome by an equal foe; and the *Reindeer* fought at far less of a disadvantage, and suffered less. None of the frigates, British or American, were defended with any thing like the resolution she displayed.

---

[1] James (p. 419) says: "The *Essex*, as far as is borne out by proof (the only safe way where an American is concerned), had 24 men killed and 45 wounded. But Capt. Porter, thinking by exaggerating his loss to prop up his fame, talks of 58 killed and mortally wounded, 39 severely, 27 slightly," etc., etc. This would be no more worthy of notice than any other of his falsifications, were it not followed by various British writers. Hilyar states that he has 161 prisoners, has found 23 dead, that 3 wounded were taken off, between 20 and 30 reached the shore, and that the "remainder are either killed or wounded." It is by wilfully preserving silence about this last sentence that James makes out his case. It will be observed that Hilyar enumerates 161 + 23 + 3 + 25 (say) or 212, and says the remainder were either killed or wounded; Porter having 255 men at first, this remainder was 43. Hilyar stating that of his 161 prisoners, 42 were wounded, his account thus gives the Americans 111 killed and wounded. James' silence about Hilyar's last sentence enables him to make the loss but 69, and his wilful omission is quite on a par with the other meannesses and falsehoods which utterly destroy the reliability of his work. By Hilyar's own letter it is thus seen that Porter's loss in killed and wounded was certainly 111, perhaps 116, or if Porter had, as James says, 265 men, 126. There still remain some discrepancies between the official accounts, which can be compared in tabular form:

| HILYAR. | | | PORTER. |
|---|---|---|---|
| Prisoners unwounded, | 119 | 75 | prisoners unwounded. |
| " wounded, | 42 | 27 | " slightly wounded. |
| Taken away wounded, | 3 | 39 | " severely " |
| Those who reached shore, | 25 | 58 | killed. |
| Remainder killed or wounded, | 43 | 31 | missing. |
| Killed, | 23 | 25 | reached shore. |
| | 255 | 255 | |

But it is perhaps permissible to inquire whether Porter's course, after the accident to his top-mast occurred, was altogether the best that could have been taken. On such a question no opinion could have been better than Farragut's, although of course his judgment was *ex post facto*, as he was very young at the time of the fight.

"In the first place, I consider our original and greatest error was in attempting to regain the anchorage; being greatly superior in sailing powers we should have borne up and run before the wind. If we had come in contact with the *Phœbe* we should have carried her by boarding; if she avoided us, as she might have done by her greater ability to manœuvre, then we should have taken her fire and passed on, leaving both vessels behind until we had replaced our topmast, by which time they would have been separated, as unless they did so it would have been no chase, the *Cherub* being a dull sailer.

"Secondly, when it was apparent to everybody that we had no chance of success under the circumstances, the ship should have been run ashore, throwing her broadside to the beach to prevent raking, and fought as long as was consistent with humanity, and then set on fire. But having determined upon anchoring we should have bent a spring on to the ring of the anchor, instead of to the cable, where it was exposed, and could be shot away as fast as put on."

But it must be remembered that when Porter decided to anchor near shore, in neutral water, he could not anticipate Hilyar's deliberate and treacherous breach of faith. I do not allude to the mere disregard of neutrality. Whatever international moralists may say, such disregard is a mere question of expediency. If the benefits to be gained by attacking a hostile ship in neutral waters are such as to counterbalance the risk of incurring the enmity of the neutral power, why then the attack ought to be made. Had Hilyar, when he first made his appearance off Valparaiso, sailed in with his two ships, the men at quarters and guns out, and at once attacked Porter, considering the destruction of the *Essex* as outweighing the insult to Chili, why his behavior would have been perfectly justifiable. In fact this is unquestionably what he intended to do; but he suddenly found himself in such a position, that in the event of hostilities, *his* ship would be the captured one, and he owed his escape purely to Porter's overforbearance, under great provocation. Then he gave his word to Porter that he would not infringe on the neutrality; and he never dared to break it, until he saw Porter was disabled and almost helpless! This may seem strong language to use about a British officer, but it is justly strong. Exactly as any outsider must consider Warrington's attack on the British brig *Nautilus* in 1815, as a piece of

---

The explanation probably is that Hilyar's "42 wounded" do not include Porter's "27 slightly wounded," and that his "161 prisoners" include Porter's "25 who reached shore," and his "25 who reached shore" comes under Porter's "31 missing." This would make the accounts nearly tally. At any rate in Porter's book are to be found the names of all his killed, wounded, and missing; and their relatives received pensions from the American government, which, if the returns were false, would certainly have been a most elaborate piece of deception. It is far more likely that Hilyar was mistaken; or he may have counted in the *Essex Junior's* crew, which would entirely account for the discrepancies. In any event it must be remembered that he makes the American killed and wounded 111 (Porter, 124), and *not* 69, as James says. The latter's statement is wilfully false, as he had seen Hilyar's letter.

needless cruelty; so any outsider must consider Hilyar as having most treach-erously broken faith with Porter.

After the fight Hilyar behaved most kindly and courteously to the prisoners; and, as already said, he fought his ship most ably, for it would have been quixotic to a degree to forgo his advantages. But previous to the battle his con-duct had been over-cautious. It was to be expected that the *Essex* would make her escape as soon as practicable, and so he should have used every effort to bring her to action. Instead of this he always declined the fight when alone; and he owed his ultimate success to the fact that the *Essex* instead of escaping, as she could several times have done, stayed, hoping to bring the *Phœbe* to action single-handed. It must be remembered that the *Essex* was almost as weak com-pared to the *Phœbe*, as the *Cherub* was compared to the *Essex*. The latter was just about midway between the British ships, as may be seen by the following com-parison. In the action the *Essex* fought all six of her long 12's, and the *Cherub* both her long 9's, instead of the corresponding broadside carronades which the ships regularly used. This gives the *Essex* a better armament than she would have had fighting her guns as they were regularly used; but it can be seen how great the inequality still was. It must also be kept in mind, that while in the bat-tles between the American 44's and British 38's, the short weight 24-pounders of the former had in reality no greater range or accuracy than the full weight 18's of their opponents, in this case the *Phœbe*'s full weight 18's had a very much greater range and accuracy than the short weight 12's of the *Essex*.

### COMPARATIVE FORCE

| | MEN. | BROADSIDE GUNS. | WEIGHT. | TOTAL. |
|---|---|---|---|---|
| *Phœbe,* | 320 | 13 long 18's | 234 lbs. | |
| | | 1 " 12 | 12 " | |
| | | 1 " 9 | 9 " | (255) |
| | | 7 short 32's | 224 " | |
| | | 1 " 18 | 18 " | (242) |
| | | 23 guns, | 497 lbs. | |
| *Cherub,* | 180 | 2 long 9's | 18 lbs. | (18) |
| | | 2 short 18's | 36 " | |
| | | 9 " 32's | 288 " | (324) |
| | | 13 guns, | 342 lbs. | |
| | 500 men, | 36 guns, | 839 lbs., metal. | |
| | | | $\left\{ \begin{array}{l} 273 \text{ long.} \\ 566 \text{ short.} \end{array} \right\}$ | |
| *Essex,* | 255 | 6 long 12's | 66 lbs. | $\left\{ \begin{array}{l} \text{Taking 7 per cent.} \\ \text{off for short} \\ \text{weight.} \end{array} \right.$ |
| | | 17 short 32's | 504 " | |
| | 255 men, | 23 guns, | 570 lbs. | |

All accounts agree as to the armament of the *Essex*. I have taken that of the *Phœbe* and *Cherub* from James; but Captain Porter's official letter, and all the other American accounts make the *Phœbe's* broadside 15 long 18's and 8 short 32's, and give the *Cherub*, in all, 18 short 32's, 8 short 24's, and two long nines. This would make their broadside 904 lbs., 288 long, 616 short. I would have no doubt that the American accounts were right if the question rested solely on James' veracity; but he probably took his figures from official sources. At any rate, remembering the difference between long guns and carronades, it appears that the *Essex* was really nearly intermediate in force between the *Phœbe* and the *Cherub*. The battle being fought, with a very trifling exception, at long range, it was in reality a conflict between a crippled ship throwing a broadside of 66 lbs. of metal, and two ships throwing 273 lbs., who by their ability to manœuvre could choose positions where they could act with full effect, while their antagonist could not return a shot. Contemporary history does not afford a single instance of so determined a defence against such frightful odds.

The official letters of Captains Hilyar and Porter agree substantially in all respects; the details of the fight, as seen in the *Essex*, are found in the "Life of Farragut." But although the British captain does full justice to his foe, British historians have universally tried to belittle Porter's conduct. It is much to be regretted that we have no British account worth paying attention to of the proceedings before the fight, when the *Phœbe* declined single combat with the *Essex*. James, of course, states that the *Phœbe* did *not* decline it, but he gives no authority, and his unsupported assertion would be valueless even if uncontradicted. His account of the action is grossly inaccurate as he has inexcusably garbled Hilyar's report. One instance of this I have already mentioned, as regards Hilyar's account of Porter's loss. Again, Hilyar distinctly states that the *Essex* was twice on fire, yet James (p. 418) utterly denies this, thereby impliedly accusing the British captain of falsehood. There is really no need of the corroboration of Porter's letter, but he has it most fully in the "Life of Farragut," p. 37: "The men came rushing up from below, many with their clothes burning, which were torn from them as quickly as possible, and those for whom this could not be done were told to jump overboard and quench the flames. * * * One man swam to shore with scarcely a square inch of his body which had not been burned, and, although he was deranged for some days, he ultimately recovered, and afterward served with me in the West Indies." The third unfounded statement in James' account is that buckets of spirits were found in all parts of the main deck of the *Essex*, and that most of the prisoners were drunk. No authority is cited for this, and there is not a shadow of truth in it. He ends by stating that "few even in his own country will venture to speak well of Captain David Porter." After these various paragraphs we are certainly justified in rejecting James' account *in toto*. An occasional mistake is perfectly excusable, and gross ignorance of a good many facts does not invalidate a man's testimony with regard to some others with which he is acquainted; but a wilful and systematic perversion of the truth in a number of cases throws a very strong doubt on a historian's remaining statements, unless they are supported by unquestionable authority.

But if British historians have generally given Porter much less than his due, by omitting all reference to the inferiority of his guns, his lost top-mast, etc., it is no worse than Americans have done in similar cases. The latter, for example, will make great allowances in the case of the *Essex* for her having carronades only, but utterly fail to allude to the *Cyane* and *Levant* as having suffered under the same disadvantage. They should remember that the rules cut both ways.

The *Essex* having suffered chiefly above the water-line, she was repaired sufficiently in Valparaiso to enable her to make the voyage to England, where she was added to the British navy. The *Essex Junior* was disarmed and the American prisoners embarked in her for New York, on parole. But Lieutenant McKnight, Chaplain Adams, Midshipman Lyman, and 11 seamen were exchanged on the spot for some of the British prisoners on board the *Essex Junior.* McKnight and Lyman accompanied the *Phœbe* to Rio Janeiro, where they embarked on a Swedish vessel, were taken out of her by the *Wasp,* Captain Blakely, and were lost with the rest of the crew of that vessel. The others reached New York in safety. Of the prizes made by the *Essex,* some were burnt or sunk by the Americans, and some retaken by the British. And so, after nearly two years' uninterrupted success, the career of the *Essex* terminated amid disasters of all kinds. But at least her officers and crew could reflect that they had afforded an example of courage in adversity that it would be difficult to match elsewhere.

—

The first of the new heavy sloops of war that got to sea was the *Frolic,* Master Commandant Joseph Bainbridge, which put out early in February. Shortly afterward she encountered a large Carthagenian privateer, which refused to surrender and was sunk by a broadside, nearly a hundred of her crew being drowned. Before daylight on the 20th of April, lat. 24°12′ N., long. 81°25′ W., she fell in with the British 36-gun frigate *Orpheus,* Capt. Pigot, and the 12-gun schooner *Shelburne,* Lieut. Hope, both to leeward. The schooner soon weathered the *Frolic,* but of course was afraid to close, and the American sloop continued beating to windward, in the effort to escape, for nearly 13 hours; the water was started, the anchors cut away, and finally the guns thrown overboard—a measure by means of which both the *Hornet,* the *Rattlesnake,* and the *Adams* succeeded in escaping under similar circumstances,—but all was of no avail, and she was finally captured. The court of inquiry honorably acquitted both officers and crew. As was to be expected James considers the surrender a disgraceful one, because the guns were thrown overboard. As I have said, this was a measure which had proved successful in several cases of a like nature; the criticism is a piece of petty meanness. Fortunately we have Admiral Codrington's dictum on the surrender ("Memoirs," vol. 1, p. 310), which he evidently considered as perfectly honorable.

A sister ship to the *Frolic,* the *Peacock,* Capt. Lewis Warrington, sailed from New York on March 12th, and cruised southward; on the 28th of April, at seven in the morning, lat. 17° 47′ N., long. 80° 7′ W., several sail were made to wind-ward.[1] These were a small convoy of merchant-men, bound for the Bermudas, under the protection of the 18-gun brig-sloop *Epervier,* Capt. Wales, 5 days out of Havana, and with $118,000 in specie on board.[2] The *Epervier* when discov-ered was steering north by east, the wind being from the eastward; soon after-ward the wind veered gradually round to the southward, and the *Epervier* hauled up close on the port tack, while the convoy made all sail away, and the *Peacock* came down with the wind on her starboard quarter. At 10 A.M. the ves-sels were within gun-shot, and the *Peacock* edged away to get in a raking broad-side, but the *Epervier* frustrated this by putting her helm up until close on her adversary's bow, when she rounded to and fired her starboard guns, receiving in return the starboard broadside of the *Peacock* at 10.20 A.M. These first broad-sides took effect aloft, the brig being partially dismantled, while the *Peacock's* fore-yard was totally disabled by two round shot in the starboard quarter, which deprived the ship of the use of her fore-sail and fore-top-sail, and compelled her to run large. However, the *Epervier* eased away[3] when abaft her foe's beam, and ran off alongside of her (using her port guns, while the American still had the starboard battery engaged) at 10.35. The *Peacock's* fire was now very hot, and directed chiefly at her adversary's hull, on which it told heavily, while she did not suffer at all in return. The *Epervier* coming up into the wind, owing some-what to the loss of head-sail, Capt. Wales called his crew aft to try boarding, but they refused, saying "she's too heavy for us,"[4] and then, at 11.05 the colors were hauled down.

Except the injury to her fore-yard, the *Peacock's* damages were confined to the loss of a few top-mast and top-gallant backstays, and some shot-holes through her sails. Of her crew, consisting, all told, of 166 men and boys,[5] only two were wounded, both slightly. The *Epervier,* on the other hand, had 45 shot-holes in her hull, 5 feet of water in her hold, main-top-mast over the side, main-mast nearly in two, main-boom shot away, bowsprit wounded severely, and most of the fore-rigging and stays shot away; and of her crew of 128 men (according to the list of prisoners given by Captain Warrington; James says 118, but he is not backed up by any official report) 9 were killed and mortally wounded, and 14 severely and slightly wounded. Instead of two long sixes for bow-chasers, and a shifting carronade, she had two 18-pound carronades (ac-cording to the American prize-lists;[6] Capt. Warrington says 32's). Otherwise she

---

[1] Official letter of Capt. Warrington, April 29, 1814.

[2] James, vi, 424.

[3] According to some accounts she at this time tacked.

[4] James, "Naval Occurrences," p. 243.

[5] "Niles' Register," vi, 196, says only 160; the above is taken from Warrington's letter of June 1st, pre-served with the other manuscript letters in the Naval Archives. The crew contained about 10 boys, was not composed of picked men, and did not number 185—*vide* James.

[6] American State Papers, vol. xiv, p. 427.

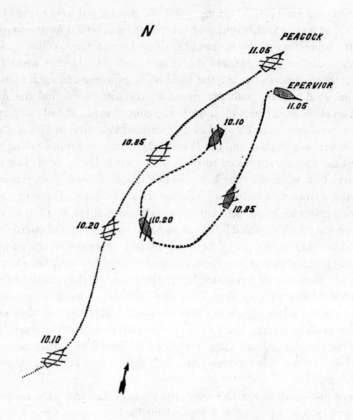

was armed as usual. She was, like the rest of her kind, very "tubby," being as broad as the *Peacock,* though 10 feet shorter on deck. Allowing, as usual, 7 per cent. for short weight of the American shot, we get the

### COMPARATIVE FORCE

| | TONS. | NO. BROADSIDE GUNS. | WEIGHT METAL. | CREW. | LOSS. |
|---|---|---|---|---|---|
| *Peacock* | 509 | 11 | 315 | 166 | 2 |
| *Epervier* | 477 | 9 | 274 | 128 | 23 |

That is, the relative force being as 12 is to 10, the relative execution done was as 12 is to 1, and the *Epervier* surrendered before she had lost a fifth of her crew. The case of the *Epervier* closely resembles that of the *Argus.* In both cases the officers behaved finely; in both cases, too, the victorious foe was heavier, in about the same proportion, while neither the crew of the *Argus,* nor the crew of the *Epervier* fought with the determined bravery displayed by the combatants in almost every other struggle of the war. But it must be added that the *Epervier* did worse than the *Argus,* and the *Peacock* (American) better than the *Pelican.* The gunnery of the *Epervier* was extraordinarily poor; "the most disgraceful part of the affair was that our ship was cut to pieces and the enemy hardly scratched."[1] James states that after the first two or three broadsides several carronades became unshipped, and that the others were dismounted by the fire of the *Peacock;* that the men had not been exercised at the guns; and, most important of all, that the crew (which contained "several foreigners," but was chiefly British; as the *Argus'* was chiefly American) was disgracefully bad. The *Peacock,* on the contrary, showed skilful seamanship as well as excellent gunnery. In 45 minutes after the fight was over the fore-yard had been sent down and fished, the foresail set up, and every thing in complete order again;[2] the prize was got in sailing order by dark, though great exertions had to be made to prevent her sinking. Mr. Nicholson, first of the *Peacock,* was put in charge as prize-master. The next day the two vessels were abreast of Amelia Island, when two frigates were discovered in the north, to leeward. Capt. Warrington at once directed the prize to proceed to St. Mary's, while he separated and made sail on a wind to the south, intending to draw the frigates after him, as he was confident that the *Peacock,* a very fast vessel, could outsail them.[3] The plan succeeded perfectly, the brig reaching Savannah on the first of May, and the ship three days afterward. The *Epervier* was purchased for the U.S. navy, under the same name and rate. The *Peacock* sailed again on June 4th,[4] going first northward to the Grand Banks, then to the Azores; then she stationed herself in the mouth of the Irish Channel, and afterward cruised off Cork, the mouth of the Shannon, and the north of Ireland, capturing several very valuable prizes and creating great consternation. She then changed her station, to elude the numerous vessels that had been sent after her, and sailed southward, off Cape Ortegal, Cape Finisterre, and finally among the Barbadoes, reaching New York Oct. 29th. During this cruise she encountered no war vessel smaller than a frigate; but captured 14 sail of merchant-men, some containing valuable cargoes, and manned by 148 men.

On April 29th, H.M.S. schooner *Ballahou,* 6, Lieut. King, while cruising off the American coast was captured by the *Perry,* privateer, a much heavier vessel, after an action of 10 minutes' duration.

———

The general peace prevailing in Europe allowed the British to turn their energies altogether to America; and in no place was this increased vigor so much felt as in Chesapeake Bay where a great number of line-of-battle ships, frigates, sloops, and transports had assembled, in preparation for the assault on Washington and Baltimore. The defence of these waters was confided to Capt. Joshua Barney,[5] with a flotilla of gun-boats. These consisted of three or four

[1] "Memoirs of Admiral Codrington," i, 322.
[2] Letter of Capt. Warrington, April 29, 1814.
[3] Letter of Capt. Warrington, May 4, 1814.
[4] Letter of Capt. Warrington, Oct. 30, 1814.
[5] He was born at Baltimore, July 6, 1759; James, with habitual accuracy, calls him an Irishman. He makes Decatur, by the way, commit the geographical solecism of being born in "Maryland, Virginia."

sloops and schooners, but mainly of barges, which were often smaller than the ship's boats that were sent against them. These gun-boats were manned by from 20 to 40 men each, and each carried, according to its size, one or two long 24-, 18-, or 12-pounders. They were bad craft at best; and, in addition, it is difficult to believe that they were handled to the fullest advantage.

On June 1st Commodore Barney, with the block sloop *Scorpion* and 14 smaller "gun-boats," chiefly row galleys, passed the mouth of the Patuxent, and chased the British schooner *St. Lawrence* and seven boats, under Captain Barrie, until they took refuge with the *Dragon*, 74, which in turn chased Barney's flotilla into the Patuxent, where she blockaded it in company with the *Albion*, 74. They were afterward joined by the *Loire*, 38, *Narcissus*, 32, and *Jasseur*, 18, and Commodore Barney moved two miles up St. Leonard's Creek, while the frigates and sloop blockaded its mouth. A deadlock now ensued; the gun-boats were afraid to attack the ships, and the ships' boats were just as afraid of the gun-boats. On the 8th, 9th, and 11th skirmishes occurred; on each occasion the British boats came up till they caught sight of Barney's flotilla, and were promptly chased off by the latter, which, however, took good care not to meddle with the larger vessels. Finally, Colonel Wadsworth, of the artillery, with two long 18-pounders, assisted by the marines, under Captain Miller, and a few regulars, offered to cooperate from the shore while Barney assailed the two frigates with the flotilla. On the 26th the joint attack took place most successfully; the *Loire* and *Narcissus* were driven off, although not much damaged, and the flotilla rowed out in triumph, with a loss of but 4 killed and 7 wounded. But in spite of this small success, which was mainly due to Colonel Wadsworth, Commodore Barney made no more attempts with his gun-boats. The bravery and skill which the flotilla men showed at Bladensburg prove conclusively that their ill success on the water was due to the craft they were in, and not to any failing of the men. At the same period the French gun-boats were even more unsuccessful, but the Danes certainly did very well with theirs.

Barney's flotilla in the Patuxent remained quiet until August 22d, and then was burned when the British advanced on Washington. The history of this advance, as well as of the unsuccessful one on Baltimore, concerns less the American than the British navy, and will be but briefly alluded to here. On August 20th Major-General Ross and Rear-Admiral Cockburn, with about 5,000 soldiers and marines, moved on Washington by land; while a squadron, composed of the *Seahorse*, 38, *Euryalus*, 36, bombs *Devastation*, *Ætna*, and *Meteor*, and rocket-ship *Erebus*, under Captain James Alexander Gordon, moved up the Potomac to attack Fort Washington, near Alexandria; and Sir Peter Parker, in the *Menelaus*, 38, was sent "to create a diversion" above Baltimore. Sir Peter's "diversion" turned out most unfortunately for him: for, having landed to attack 120 Maryland militia, under Colonel Reade, he lost his own life, while fifty of his followers were placed *hors de combat* and the remainder chased back to the ship by the victors, who had but three wounded.

The American army, which was to oppose Ross and Cockburn, consisted of some seven thousand militia, who fled so quickly that only about 1,500 British had time to become engaged. The fight was really between these 1,500 British regulars and the American flotilla men. These consisted of 78 marines, under Captain Miller, and 370 sailors, some of whom served under Captain Barney, who had a battery of two 18's and three 12's, while the others were armed with muskets and pikes, and acted with the marines. Both sailors and marines did nobly, inflicting most of the loss the British suffered, which amounted to 256 men, and in return lost over a hundred of their own men, including the two captains, who were wounded and captured, with the guns.[1] Ross took Washington and burned the public buildings; and the panic-struck Americans foolishly burned the *Columbia,* 44, and *Argus,* 18, which were nearly ready for service.

Captain Gordon's attack on Fort Washington was conducted with great skill and success. Fort Washington was abandoned as soon as fired upon, and the city of Alexandria surrendered upon most humiliating conditions. Captain Gordon was now joined by the *Fairy,* 18, Captain Baker, who brought him orders to return from Vice-Admiral Cochrane; and the squadron began to work down the river, which was very difficult to navigate. Commodore Rodgers, with some of the crew of the two 44's, *Guerrière* and *Java,* tried to bar their progress, but had not sufficient means. On September 1st an attempt was made to destroy the *Devastation* by fire-ships, but it failed; on the 4th the attempt was repeated by Commodore Rodgers, with a party of some forty men, but they were driven off and attacked by the British boats, under Captain Baker, who in turn was repulsed with the loss of his second lieutenant killed, and some twenty-five men killed or wounded. The squadron also had to pass and silence a battery of light field-pieces on the 5th, where they suffered enough to raise their total loss to seven killed and thirty-five wounded. Gordon's inland expedition was thus concluded most successfully, at a very trivial cost; it was a most venturesome feat, reflecting great honor on the captains and crews engaged in it.

Baltimore was threatened actively by sea and land early in September. On the 13th an indecisive conflict took place between the British regulars and American militia, in which the former came off with the honor, and the latter with the profit. The regulars held the field, losing 350 men, including General Ross; the militia retreated in fair order with a loss of but 200. The water attack was also unsuccessful. At 5 A.M. on the 13th the bomb vessels *Meteor, Ætna, Terror, Volcano,* and *Devastation,* the rocket-ship *Erebus,* and the frigates *Severn, Euryalus, Havannah,* and *Hebrus* opened on Fort McHenry, some of the other fortifications being occasionally fired at. A furious but harmless cannonade was kept up between the forts and ships until 7 A.M. on the 14th, when the British fleet and army retired.

---

[1] The optimistic Cooper thinks that two regular regiments would have given the Americans this battle—which is open to doubt.

I have related these events out of their natural order because they really had very little to do with our navy, and yet it is necessary to mention them in order to give an idea of the course of events. The British and American accounts of the various gun-boat attacks differ widely; but it is very certain that the gun-boats accomplished little or nothing of importance. On the other hand, their loss amounted to nothing, for many of those that were sunk were afterward raised, and the total tonnage of those destroyed would not much exceed that of the British barges captured by them from time to time or destroyed by the land batteries.

—

The purchased brig *Rattlesnake,* 16, had been cruising in the Atlantic with a good deal of success; but in lat. 40° N., long. 33° W., was chased by a frigate from which Lieutenant Renshaw, the brig's commander, managed to escape only by throwing overboard all his guns except two long nines; and on June 22d he was captured by the *Leander,* 50, Captain Sir George Ralph Collier, K.C.B.

The third of the new sloops to get to sea was the *Wasp,* 22, Captain John-ston Blakely, which left Portsmouth on May 1st, with a very fine crew of 173 men, almost exclusively New Englanders; there was said not to have been a single foreign seaman on board. It is, at all events, certain that during the whole war no vessel was ever better manned and commanded than this daring and resolute cruiser. The *Wasp* slipped unperceived through the blockading frigates, and ran into the mouth of the English Channel, right in the thick of the English cruisers; here she remained several weeks, burning and scuttling many ships. Finally, on June 28th, at 4 A.M., in lat. 48° 36′ N., long. 11° 15′ W.,[1] while in chase of two merchant-men, a sail was made on the weather-beam. This was the British brig-sloop *Reindeer,* 18, Captain William Manners,[2] with a crew of 118, as brave men as ever sailed or fought on the narrow seas. Like the *Peacock* (British) the *Reindeer* was only armed with 24-pounders, and Captain Manners must have known well that he was to do battle with a foe heavier than himself; but there was no more gallant seaman in the whole British navy, fertile as it was in men who cared but little for odds of size or strength. As the day broke, the *Reindeer* made sail for the *Wasp,* then lying in the west-southwest.

The sky was overcast with clouds, and the smoothness of the sea was hardly disturbed by the light breeze that blew out of the northeast. Captain Blakely hauled up and stood for his antagonist, as the latter came slowly down with the wind nearly aft, and so light was the weather that the vessels kept almost on even keels. It was not till quarter past one that the *Wasp*'s drum rolled out its loud challenge as it beat to quarters, and a few minutes afterward the ship put about and stood for the foe, thinking to weather him; but at 1.50 the brig also tacked and stood away, each of the cool and skilful captains being bent on keep-

---

[1] Letter of Captain Blakely, July 8, 1814.
[2] James, vi, 429.

ing the weather-gage. At half past two the *Reindeer* again tacked, and, taking in her stay-sails, stood for the *Wasp,* who furled her royals; and, seeing that she would be weathered, at 2.50, put about in her turn and ran off, with the wind a little forward the port beam, brailing up the mizzen, while the *Reindeer* hoisted her flying-jib, to close, and gradually came up on the *Wasp's* weather-quarter. At 17 minutes past three, when the vessels were not sixty yards apart, the British opened the conflict, firing the shifting 12-pound carronade, loaded with round and grape. To this the Americans could make no return, and it was again loaded and fired, with the utmost deliberation; this was repeated five times, and would have been a trying ordeal to a crew less perfectly disciplined than the *Wasp's*. At 3.26 Captain Blakely, finding his enemy did not get on his beam, put his helm a-lee and luffed up, firing his guns from aft forward as they bore. For ten minutes the ship and the brig lay abreast, not twenty yards apart, while the cannonade was terribly destructive. The concussion of the explosions almost deadened what little way the vessels had on, and the smoke hung over them like a pall. The men worked at the guns with desperate energy, but the odds in weight of metal (3 to 2) were too great against the *Reindeer,* where both sides played their parts so manfully. Captain Manners stood at his post, as resolute as ever, though wounded again and again. A grape-shot passed through both his thighs, bringing him to the deck; but, maimed and bleeding to death, he sprang to his feet, cheering on the seamen. The vessels were now almost touching, and putting his helm aweather, he ran the *Wasp* aboard on her port[1] quarter, while the boarders gathered forward, to try it with the steel. But the Carolina captain had prepared for this with cool confidence; the marines came aft; close under the bulwarks crouched the boarders, grasping in their hands the naked cutlasses, while behind them were drawn up the pikemen. As the vessels came grinding together the men hacked and thrust at one another through the open port-holes, while the black smoke curled up from between the hulls. Then through the smoke appeared the grim faces of the British sea-dogs, and the fighting was bloody enough; for the stubborn English stood well in the hard hand play. But those who escaped the deadly fire of the top-men, escaped only to be riddled through by the long Yankee pikes; so, avenged by their own hands, the foremost of the assailants died, and the others gave back. The attack was foiled, though the *Reindeer's* marines kept answering well the American fire. Then the English captain, already mortally wounded, but with the indomitable courage that nothing but death could conquer, cheering and rallying his men, himself sprang, sword in hand, into the rigging, to lead them on; and they followed him with a will. At that instant a ball from the *Wasp's* main-top crashed through his skull, and, still clenching in his right hand the sword he had shown he could wear so worthily, with his face to the foe, he fell back on his own deck dead, while above him yet floated the flag for which he had given his life. No

[1] Letter of Captain Blakely, July 8, 1814. Cooper says starboard; it is a point of little importance; all accounts agree as to the *relative* positions of the craft.

Norse Viking, slain over shield, ever died better. As the British leader fell and his men recoiled, Captain Blakely passed the word to board; with wild hurrahs the boarders swarmed over the hammock nettings, there was a moment's furious struggle, the surviving British were slain or driven below, and the captain's clerk, *the highest officer left,* surrendered the brig, at 3.44, just 27 minutes after the *Reindeer* had fired the first gun, and just 18 after the *Wasp* had responded.

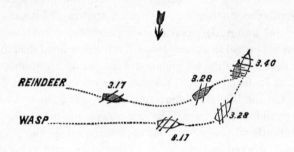

Both ships had suffered severely in the short struggle; but, as with the *Shannon* and *Chesapeake,* the injuries were much less severe aloft than in the hulls. All the spars were in their places. The *Wasp*'s hull had received 6 round, and many grape; a 24-pound shot had passed through the foremast; and of her crew of 173, 11 were killed or mortally wounded, and 15 wounded severely or slightly. The *Reindeer* was completely cut to pieces in a line with her ports; her upper works, boats, and spare spars being one entire wreck. Of her crew of 118 men, 33 were killed outright or died later, and 34 were wounded, nearly all severely.

COMPARATIVE FORCE

|  | TONS. | BROADSIDE GUNS. | WEIGHT METAL. | NO. MEN. | LOSS. |
|---|---|---|---|---|---|
| *Wasp,* | 509 | 11 | 315 | 173 | 26 |
| *Reindeer,* | 477 | 10 | 210 | 118 | 67 |

It is thus seen that the *Reindeer* fought at a greater disadvantage than any other of the various British sloops that were captured in single action during the war; and yet she made a better fight than any of them (though the *Frolic,* and the *Frolic* only, was defended with the same desperate courage); a pretty sure proof that heavy metal is not the only factor to be considered in accounting for the American victories. "It is difficult to say which vessel behaved the best in this short but gallant combat."[1] I doubt if the war produced two better single-ship commanders than Captain Blakely and Captain Manners; and an equal meed of praise attaches to both crews. The British could rightly say that they yielded purely to heavy odds in men and metal; and the Americans, that the difference in execution was fully proportioned to the difference in force. It is

[1] Cooper, ii, 287.

difficult to know which to admire most, the wary skill with which each captain manœuvred before the fight, the perfect training and discipline that their crews showed, the decision and promptitude with which Captain Manners tried to retrieve the day by boarding, and the desperate bravery with which the attempt was made; or the readiness with which Captain Blakely made his preparations, and the cool courage with which the assault was foiled. All people of the English stock, no matter on which side of the Atlantic they live, if they have any pride in the many feats of fierce prowess done by the men of their blood and race, should never forget this fight; although we cannot but feel grieved to find that such men—men of one race and one speech; brothers in blood, as well as in bravery—should ever have had to turn their weapons against one another.

The day after the conflict the prize's foremast went by the board, and, as she was much damaged by shot, Captain Blakely burned her, put a portion of his wounded prisoners on board a neutral, and with the remainder proceeded to France, reaching l'Orient on the 8th day of July.

On July 4th Sailing-master Percival and 30 volunteers of the New York flotilla[1] concealed themselves on board a fishing-smack, and carried by surprise the *Eagle* tender, which contained a 32-pound howitzer and 14 men, 4 of whom were wounded.

On July 12th, while off the west coast of South Africa, the American brig *Syren* was captured after a chase of 11 hours by the *Medway*, 74, Capt. Brine. The chase was to windward during the whole time, and she made every effort to escape, throwing overboard all her boats, anchors, cables, and spare spars.[2] Her commander, Captain Parker, had died, and she was in charge of Lieut. N. J. Nicholson. By a curious coincidence, on the same day, July 12th, H.M. cutter *Landrail*, 4,[3] of 20 men, Lieut. Lancaster, was captured by the American privateer *Syren*, a schooner mounting 1 long heavy gun, with a crew of 70 men; the *Landrail* had 7, and the *Syren* 3 men wounded.

On July 14th Gun-boat No. 88, Sailing-master George Clement, captured after a short skirmish the tender of the *Tenedos* frigate, with her second lieutenant, 2 midshipmen, and 10 seamen.[4]

The *Wasp* stayed in l'Orient till she was thoroughly refitted, and had filled, in part, the gaps in her crew, from the American privateers in port. On Aug. 27th, Captain Blakely sailed again, making two prizes during the next three days. On Sept. 1st she came up to a convoy of 10 sail under the protection of the *Armada*, 74, all bound for Gibraltar; the swift cruiser hovered round the merchant-men like a hawk, and though chased off again and again by the line-of-battle ship, always returned the instant the pursuit stopped, and finally actually succeeded in cutting off and capturing one ship, laden with iron and brass

[1] Letter of Com. J. Lewis, July 6, 1814.
[2] Letter of Capt. Brine to Vice-Admiral Tyler, July 12, 1814.
[3] James, vi, 436; his statement is wrong as regards the privateer.
[4] Letter of Capt. Isaac Hull, July 15, 1814.

cannon, muskets, and other military stores of great value. At half past six on the evening of the same day, in lat. 47° 30′ N., long. 11° W., while running almost free, four sail, two on the starboard bow, and two on the port, rather more to leeward, were made out.[1] Capt. Blakely at once made sail for the most weatherly of the four ships in sight, though well aware that more than one of them might prove to be hostile cruisers, and they were all of unknown force. But the determined Carolinian was not one to be troubled by such considerations. He probably had several men less under his command than in the former action, but had profited by his experience with the *Reindeer* in one point, having taken aboard her 12-pounder boat carronade, of whose efficacy he had had very practical proof.

The chase, the British brig-sloop *Avon,* 18, Captain the Honorable James Arbuthnot,[2] was steering almost southwest; the wind, which was blowing fresh from the southeast, being a little abaft the port beam. At 7.00 the *Avon* began making night signals with the lanterns, but the *Wasp,* disregarding these, came steadily on; at 8.38 the *Avon* fired a shot from her stern-chaser,[3] and shortly afterward another from one of her lee or starboard guns. At 20 minutes past 9, the *Wasp* was on the port or weather-quarter of the *Avon,* and the vessels interchanged several hails; one of the American officers then came forward on the forecastle and ordered the brig to heave to, which the latter declined doing, and set her port foretop-mast studding sail. The *Wasp* then, at 9.29, fired the 12-pound carronade into her, to which the *Avon* responded with her stern-chaser and the aftermost port guns. Capt. Blakely then put his helm up, for fear his adversary would try to escape, and ran to leeward of her, and then ranged up alongside, having poured a broadside into her quarter. A close and furious engagement began, at such short range that the only one of the *Wasp*'s crew who was wounded, was hit by a wad; four round shot struck her hull, killing two men, and she suffered a good deal in her rigging. The men on board did not know the name of their antagonist; but they could see through the smoke and the gloom of the night, as her black hull surged through the water, that she was a large brig; and aloft, against the sky, the sailors could be discerned, clustering in the tops.[4] In spite of the darkness the *Wasp*'s fire was directed with deadly precision; the *Avon*'s gaff was shot away at almost the first broadside, and most of her main-rigging and spars followed suit. She was hulled again and again, often below water-line; some of her carronades were dismounted, and finally the main-mast went by the board. At 10.00, after 31 minutes of combat, her fire had been completely silenced and Captain Blakely hailed to know if she had struck. No answer being received, and the brig firing a few random shot, the action recommenced; but at 10.12 the *Avon* was again hailed, and this time answered that she had struck. While lowering away a boat to take possession,

---

[1] Official letter of Capt. Blakely, Sept. 8, 1814.

[2] James, vi, 432.

[3] James, vi, 432.

[4] Captain Blakely's letter.

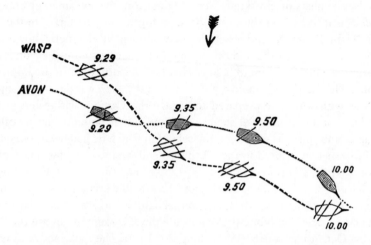

another sail (H.B.M. brig-sloop *Castilian*, 18, Captain Braimer) was seen astern. The men were again called to quarters, and every thing put in readiness as rapidly as possible; but at 10.36 two more sail were seen (one of which was H.B.M. *Tartarus*, 20[1]). The braces being cut away, the *Wasp* was put before the wind until new ones could be rove. The *Castilian* pursued till she came up close, when she fired her lee guns into, or rather over, the weather-quarter of the *Wasp*, cutting her rigging slightly. Repeated signals of distress having now been made by the *Avon* (which had lost 10 men killed and 32 wounded), the *Castilian* tacked and stood for her, and on closing found out she was sinking. Hardly had her crew being taken out when she went down.

Counting the *Wasp*'s complement as full (though it was probably two or three short), taking James' statement of the crew of the *Avon* as true, including the boat carronades of both vessels, and considering the *Avon*'s stern-chaser to have been a six-pounder, we get the

### COMPARATIVE FORCE

| | TONS. | NO. GUNS. | WEIGHT METAL. | NO. MEN. | LOSS. |
|---|---|---|---|---|---|
| *Wasp,* | 509 | 12 | 327 | 160 | 3 |
| *Avon,* | 477 | 11 | 280 | 117 | 42 |

It is self-evident that in the case of this action the odds, 14 to 11, are neither enough to account for the loss inflicted being as 14 to 1, nor for the rapidity with which, during a night encounter, the *Avon* was placed in a sinking condition. "The gallantry of the *Avon*'s officers and crew cannot for a moment be questioned; but the gunnery of the latter appears to have been not one whit better than, to the discredit of the British navy, had frequently before been dis-

[1] "Niles' Register," vi, 216.

played in combats of this kind. Nor, judging from the specimen given by the *Castilian,* is it likely that she would have performed any better."[1] On the other hand, "Capt. Blakely's conduct on this occasion had all the merit shown in the previous action, with the additional claim of engaging an enemy under circumstances which led him to believe that her consorts were in the immediate vicinity. The steady, officer-like way in which the *Avon* was destroyed, and the coolness with which he prepared to engage the *Castilian* within ten minutes after his first antagonist had struck, are the best encomiums on this officer's character and spirit, as well as on the school in which he had been trained."[2]

The *Wasp* now cruised to the southward and westward, taking and scuttling one or two prizes. On Sept. 21st, lat. 33° 12′ N., long. 14° 56′ W., she captured the brig *Atalanta,* 8, with 19 men, which proved a valuable prize, and was sent in with one of the midshipmen, Mr. Geisinger, aboard, as prize-master, who reached Savannah in safety on Nov. 4th. Meanwhile the *Wasp* kept on toward the southeast. On Oct. 9th, in lat. 18° 35′ N., long. 30° 10′ W., she spoke and boarded the Swedish brig *Adonis,* and took out of her Lieut. McKnight and Mr. Lyman, a master's mate, both late of the *Essex,* on their way to England from Brazil.

This was the last that was ever heard of the gallant but ill-fated *Wasp.* How she perished none ever knew; all that is certain is that she was never seen again. She was as good a ship, as well manned, and as ably commanded as any vessel in our little navy; and it may be doubted if there was at that time any foreign sloop of war of her size and strength that could have stood against her in fair fight.

As I have said, the *Wasp* was manned almost exclusively by Americans. James says they were mostly Irish; the reason he gives for the assertion being that Capt. Blakely spent the first 16 months of his life in Dublin. This argument is quite on a par with another piece of logic which I cannot resist noticing. The point he wishes to prove is that Americans are cowards. Accordingly, on p. 475: "On her capstan the *Constitution* now mounted a piece resembling 7 musket barrels, fixed together with iron bands. It was discharged by one lock, and each barrel threw 25 balls. * * * What could have impelled the Americans to invent such extraordinary implements of war but fear, down-right fear?" Then a little further on: "The men were provided with leather boarding-caps, fitted with bands of iron, * * * another strong symptom of fear!" Now, such a piece of writing as this is simply evidence of an unsound mind; it is not so much malicious as idiotic. I only reproduce it to help prove what I have all along insisted on, that any of James' unsupported statements about the Americans, whether respecting the tonnage of the ships or the courage of the crews, are not worth the paper they are written on; on all points connected purely with the British navy, or which can be checked off by official documents or ships' logs, or where there would be no particular object in falsifying, James is an invaluable assistant, from the diligence and painstaking care he shows, and the thoroughness and minuteness with which he goes into details.

---

[1] James, vi, 435.
[2] Cooper, ii, 291.

A fair-minded and interesting English critic,[1] whose remarks are generally very just, seems to me to have erred somewhat in commenting on this last sloop action. He says that the *Avon* was first crippled by dismantling shot from *long guns.* Now, the *Wasp* had but *one* long gun on the side engaged, and, moreover, began the action with the shortest and lightest of her carronades. Then he continues that the *Avon,* like the *Peacock,* "was hulled so low that the shot-holes could not be got at, and yielded to this fatal circumstance only." It certainly cannot be said when a brig has been dismasted, has had a third of her crew placed *hors de combat,* and has been rendered an unmanageable hulk, that she yields *only* because she has received a few shot below the water-line. These shot-holes undoubtedly hastened the result, but both the *Peacock* and the *Avon* would have surrendered even if they had remained absolutely water-tight.

———

The *Adams,* 28, had been cut down to a sloop of war at Washington, and then lengthened into a flush-decked, heavy corvette, mounting on each side 13 medium 18's, or columbiads, and 1 long 12, with a crew of 220 men, under the command of Capt. Charles Morris, late first lieut. of the *Constitution.*[2] She slipped out of the Potomac and past the blockaders on Jan. 18th, and cruised eastward to the African coast and along it from Cape Mount to Cape Palmas, thence to the Canaries and Cape de Verd. She returned very nearly along the Equator, thence going toward the West Indies. The cruise was unlucky, but a few small prizes, laden with palm-oil and ivory, being made. In hazy weather, on March 25th, a large Indiaman (the *Woodbridge*) was captured; but while taking possession the weather cleared up, and Capt. Morris found himself to leeward of 25 sail, two of which, a two-decker and a frigate, were making for him, and it took him till the next day to shake them off. He entered Savannah on May 1st and sailed again on the 8th, standing in to the Gulf Stream, between Makanilla and Florida, to look out for the Jamaica fleet. He found this fleet on the 24th, but the discovery failed to do him much good, as the ships were under the convoy of a 74, two frigates, and three brigs. The *Adams* hovered on their skirts for a couple of days, but nothing could be done with them, for the merchant-men sailed in the closest possible order and the six war vessels exercised the greatest vigilance. So the corvette passed northward to the Newfoundland Banks, where she met with nothing but fogs and floating ice, and then turned her prow toward Ireland. On July 4th she made out and chased two sail, who escaped into the mouth of the Shannon. After this the *Adams,* heartily tired of fogs and cold, stood to the southward and made a few prizes; then, in lat. 44° N., long. 10° W., on July 15th, she stumbled across the 18-pounder 36-gun frigate *Tigris,* Capt. Henderson. The frigate was to leeward, and a hard chase ensued. It was only by dint of cutting away her anchors and throwing overboard some of her guns that the *Adams* held her own till sunset, when it fell calm. Capt Morris

---

[1] Lord Howard Douglass, "Treatise on Naval Gunnery," p. 416.
[2] "Autobiography of Commodore Morris," Annapolis, 1880, p. 172.

and his first lieutenant, Mr. Wadsworth, had been the first and second lieutenants of *Old Ironsides* in Hull's famous cruise, and they proved that they had
not forgotten their early experience, for they got out the boats to tow, and employed their time so well that by sunrise the frigate was two leagues astern. After
18 hours' more chase the *Adams* dropped her. But in a day or two she ran across
a couple more, one of which, an old bluff-bows, was soon thrown out; but the
other was very fast, and kept close on the corvette's heels. As before, the frigate
was to leeward. The *Adams* had been built by contract; one side was let to a sub-
contractor of economical instincts, and accordingly turned out rather shorter
than the other; the result was, the ship sailed a good deal faster on one tack than
on the other. In this chase she finally got on her good tack in the night, and so escaped.[1] Capt. Morris now turned homeward. During his two cruises he had
made but 10 prizes (manned by 161 men), none of very great value. His luck
grew worse and worse. The continual cold and damp produced scurvy, and soon
half of his crew were prostrated by the disease; and the weather kept on foggy
as ever. Off the Maine coast a brig-sloop (the *Rifleman,* Capt. Pearce) was discovered and chased, but it escaped in the thick weather. The fog grew heavier,
and early on the morning of Aug. 17th the *Adams* struck land—literally struck
it, too, for she grounded on the Isle of Haute, and had to throw over provisions,
spare spars, etc., before she could be got off. Then she entered the Penobscot,
and sailed 27 miles up it to Hampden. The *Rifleman* meanwhile conveyed intelligence of her whereabouts to a British fleet, consisting of two line-of-battle
ships, three frigates, three sloops, and ten troop transports, under the joint command of Rear-Admiral Griffeth and Lieutenant-General Sherbrooke.[2]

This expedition accordingly went into the Penobscot and anchored off Cas-
tine. Captain Morris made every preparation he could to defend his ship, but
his means were very limited; seventy of his men were dead or disabled by the
scurvy; the remainder, many of them also diseased, were mustered out, to the
number of 130 officers and seamen (without muskets) and 20 marines. He was
joined, however, by 30 regulars, and later by over 300 militia armed with squir-
rel guns, ducking- and fowling-pieces, etc.,—in all between 500 and 550 men,[3]
only 180 of whom, with 50 muskets among them, could be depended upon. On
Sept. 3d the British advanced by land and water, the land-force being under
the direction of Lieutenant-Colonel John, and consisting of 600 troops, 80
marines, and 80 seamen.[4] The flotilla was composed of barges, launches, and
rocket-boats, under the command of Captain Barry of the *Dragon,* 74. In all
there were over 1,500 men. The seamen of the *Adams,* from the wharf, opened
fire on the flotilla, which returned it with rockets and carronades; but the ad-

[1] This statement is somewhat traditional; I have also seen it made about the *John Adams.* But some old
officers have told me positively that it occurred to the *Adams* on this cruise.

[2] James, vi, 479.

[3] "Autobiography of Commodore Morris."

[4] James, vi, 481. Whenever militia are concerned James has not much fear of official documents and
lets his imagination run riot; he here says the Americans had 1,400 men, which is as accurate as he gen-

vance was checked. Meanwhile the British land-forces attacked the militia, who acted up to the traditional militia standard, and retreated with the utmost promptitude and celerity, omitting the empty formality of firing. This left Captain Morris surrounded by eight times his number, and there was nothing to do but set fire to the corvette and retreat. The seamen, marines, and regulars behaved well, and no attempt was made to molest them. None of Captain Morris' men were hit; his loss was confined to one sailor and one marine who were too much weakened by scurvy to retreat with the others, who marched to Portland, 200 miles off. The British lost ten men killed or wounded.

———

On Sept. 9th Gun-boats No. 160 and 151, commanded by Mr. Thomas M. Pendleton, captured off Sapoleo Bar, Ga., the British privateer *Fortune of War,* armed with two heavy pivot guns, and 35 men. She made a brief resistance, losing two of her men.[1]

On Sept. 15th the British 20-gun ship-sloops *Hermes* and *Carron,* and 18-gun brig-sloops *Sophie* and *Childers,* and a force of 200 men on shore,[2] attacked Fort Bowyer, on Mobile Point, but were repulsed without being able to do any damage whatever to the Americans. The *Hermes* was sunk and the assailants lost about 80 men.

On the 26th of September, while the privateer-schooner *General Armstrong,* of New York, Captain Samuel C. Reid, of one long 24, eight long 9's, and 90 men, was lying at anchor in the road of Fayal, a British squadron, composed of the *Plantagenet,* 74, Captain Robert Floyd, *Rota,* 38, Captain Philip Somerville, and *Carnation,* 18, Captain George Bentham, hove in sight.[3] One or more boats were sent in by the British, to reconnoitre the schooner, as they asserted, or, according to the American accounts, to carry her by a *coup de main.* At any rate, after repeatedly warning them off, the privateer fired into them, and they withdrew. Captain Reid then anchored, with springs on his cables, nearer shore, to await the expected attack, which was not long deferred. At 8 P.M. four boats from the *Plantagenet* and three from the *Rota,* containing in all 180 men,[4] under the command of Lieutenant William Matterface, first of the *Rota,* pulled in toward the road, while the *Carnation* accompanied them to attack the schooner if she got under way. The boats pulled in under cover of a small reef of rocks, where they lay for some time, and about midnight made the attack. The Americans opened with the pivot gun, and immediately afterward with their long 9's, while the boats replied with their carronades, and, pulling spiritedly on amidst a terrific fire of musketry from

---

erally is in writing about this species of force. His aim being to overestimate the number of the Americans in the various engagements, he always supplies militia *ad libitum,* to make up any possible deficiency.

[1] Letter from Commodore H. E. Campbell, St. Mary's, Sept. 12, 1814.

[2] James, vi, 527.

[3] Letter of Captain S. C. Reid, Oct. 7, 1814; and of John B. Dabney, Consul at Fayal, Oct. 5, 1814.

[4] James, vi, 509: Both American accounts say 12 boats, with 400 men, and give the British loss as 250. According to my usual rule, I take each side's statement of its own force and loss.

both sides, laid the schooner aboard on her bow and starboard quarter. The struggle was savage enough, the British hacking at the nettings and trying to clamber up on deck, while the Americans fired their muskets and pistols in the faces of their assailants and thrust the foremost through with their long pikes. The boats on the quarter were driven off; but on the forecastle all three of the American lieutenants were killed or disabled, and the men were giving back when Captain Reid led all the after-division up and drove the British back into their boats. This put an end to the assault. Two boats were sunk, most of the wounded being saved as the shore was so near; two others were captured, and but three of the scattered flotilla returned to the ships. Of the Americans, 2 were killed, including the second lieutenant, Alexander O. Williams, and 7 were wounded, including the first and third lieutenants, Frederick A. Worth and Robert Johnson. Of the British, 34 were killed and 86 were wounded; among the former being the *Rota*'s first and third lieutenants, William Matterface and Charles R. Norman, and among the latter her second lieutenant and first lieutenant of marines, Richard Rawle and Thomas Park. The schooner's long 24 had been knocked off its carriage by a carronade shot, but it was replaced and the deck cleared for another action. Next day the *Carnation* came in to destroy the privateer, but was driven off by the judicious use the latter made of her "Long Tom." But affairs being now hopeless, the *General Armstrong* was scuttled and burned, and the Americans retreated to the land. The British squadron was bound for New Orleans, and on account of the delay and loss that it suffered, it was late in arriving, so that this action may be said to have helped in saving the Crescent City. Few regular commanders could have done as well as Captain Reid.

On October 6th, while Gun-boat No. 160 was convoying some coasters from Savannah, it was carried by a British tender and nine boats.[1] The gun-vessel was lying at anchor about eight leagues from St. Mary's, and the boats approached with muffled oars early in the morning. They were not discovered till nearly aboard, but the defence though short was spirited, the British losing about 20 men. Of the gun-boat's 30 men but 16 were fit for action; those, under Sailing-master Thomas Paine, behaved well. Mr. Paine, especially, fought with the greatest gallantry; his thigh was broken by a grape-shot at the very beginning, but he hobbled up on his other leg to resist the boarders, fighting till he was thrust through by a pike and had received two sabre cuts. Any one of his wounds would have been enough to put an ordinary man *hors de combat*.

On October 11th, another desperate privateer battle took place. The brigantine *Prince-de-Neufchatel*, Captain Ordronaux, of New York, was a superbly built vessel of 310 tons, mounting 17 guns, and originally possessing a crew of 150 men.[2] She had made a very successful cruise, having on board goods to the amount of $300,000, but had manned and sent in so many prizes that only 40 of her crew were left on board, while 37 prisoners were confined in the hold. One

---

[1] Letter from Commander H. C. Campbell, Oct. 12, 1814.
[2] "History of American Privateers," by George Coggeshall, p. 241, New York, 1876.

of her prizes was in company, but had drifted off to such a distance that she was unable to take part in the fight. At mid-day, on the 11th of October, while off Nantucket, the British frigate *Endymion,* 40, Captain Henry Hope, discovered the privateer and made sail in chase.[1] At 8.30 P.M., a calm having come on, the frigate despatched 5 boats, containing 111 men,[2] under the command of the first lieutenant, Abel Hawkins, to take the brigantine; while the latter triced up the boarding nettings, loaded the guns with grape and bullets, and prepared herself in every way for the coming encounter. She opened fire on the boats as they drew near, but they were soon alongside, and a most desperate engagement ensued. Some of the British actually cut through the nettings and reached the deck, but were killed by the privateersmen; and in a few minutes one boat was sunk, three others drifted off, and the launch, which was under the brigantine's stern, was taken possession of. The slaughter had been frightful, considering the number of the combatants. The victorious privateersmen had lost 7 killed, 15 badly and 9 slightly wounded, leaving but 9 untouched! Of the *Endymion's* men, James says 28, including the first lieutenant and a midshipman, were killed, and 37, including the second lieutenant and a master's mate, wounded: "besides which the launch was captured and the crew made prisoners." I do not know if this means 37 wounded, *besides* the wounded in the launch, or not[3]; of the prisoners captured 18 were wounded and 10 unhurt, so the loss was either 28 killed, 55 wounded, and 10 unhurt prisoners; or else 28 killed, 37 wounded, and 10 prisoners; but whether the total was 93 or 75 does not much matter. It was a most desperate conflict, and, remembering how short-handed the brigantine was, it reflected the highest honor on the American captain and his crew.

After their repulse before Baltimore the British concentrated their forces for an attack upon New Orleans. Accordingly a great fleet of line-of-battle ships, frigates, and smaller vessels, under Vice-Admiral Cochrane, convoying a still larger number of store-ships and transports, containing the army of General Packenham, appeared off the Chandeleur Islands on Dec. 8th. The American navy in these parts consisted of the ship *Louisiana* and schooner *Carolina* in the Mississippi River, and in the shallow bayous a few gun-boats, of course without quarters, low in the water, and perfectly easy of entrance. There were also a few tenders and small boats. The British frigates and sloops anchored off the broad, shallow inlet called Lake Borgne on the 12th; on this inlet there were 5 gun-boats and 2 small tenders, under the command of Lieut. Thomas Catesby Jones. It was impossible for the British to transport their troops across Lake Borgne, as contemplated, until this flotilla was destroyed. Accordingly, on the night of the 12th, 42 launches, armed with 24-, 18-, and 12-pounder carronades, and 3 unarmed

---

[1] James, vi, p. 527.

[2] According to Captain Ordronaux; James does not give the number, but says 28 were killed, 37 wounded, and the crew of the launch captured. Ten of the latter were unwounded, and 18 wounded. I do not know if he included these last among his "37 wounded."

[3] I think James does not include the wounded in the launch, as he says 28 wounded were sent aboard the *Saturn*; this could hardly have included the men who had been captured.

gigs, carrying 980 seamen and marines, under the orders of Capt. Lockyer,[1] pushed off from the *Armide,* 38, in three divisions; the first under the command of Capt. Lockyer, the second under Capt. Montresor, and the third under Capt. Roberts.[2] Lieut. Jones was at anchor with his boats at the Malheureux Islands, when he discovered, on the 13th, the British flotilla advancing toward Port Christian. He at once despatched the *Seahorse* of one 6-pounder and 14 men, under Sailing-master William Johnston, to destroy the stores at Bay St. Louis. She moored herself under the bank, where she was assisted by two 6-pounders. There the British attacked her with seven of their smaller boats, which were repulsed after sustaining for nearly half an hour a very destructive fire.[3] However, Mr. Johnston had to burn his boat to prevent it from being taken by a larger force. Meanwhile Lieut. Jones got under way with the five gun-vessels, trying to reach Les Petites Coquilles, near a small fort at the mouth of a creek. But as the wind was light and baffling, and the current very strong, the effort was given up, and the vessels came to anchor off Malheureux Island passage at 1 A.M. on the 14th.[4] The other tender, the *Alligator,* Sailing-master Sheppard, of one 4-pounder and 8 men, was discovered next morning trying to get to her consorts, and taken with a rush by Capt. Roberts and his division. At daybreak Lieut. Jones saw the British boats about nine miles to the eastward, and moored his 5-gun vessel abreast in the channel, with their boarding nettings triced up, and every thing in readiness; but the force of the current drifted two of them, Nos. 156 and 163, a hundred yards down the pass and out of line, No. 156 being the head-most of all. Their exact force was as follows: No. 156, Lieut. Jones, 41 men and 5 guns (1 long 24 and 4 12-pound carronades); No. 163, Sailing-master Geo. Ulrick, 21 men, 3 guns (1 long 24 and 2 12-pound carronades); No. 162, Lieut. Robert Speddes, 35 men, 5 guns (1 long 24 and 4 light sixes); No. 5, Sailing-master John D. Ferris, 36 men, 5 guns (1 long 24, 4 12-pound carronades); No. 23, Lieut. Isaac McKeever, 39 men and 5 guns (1 long 32 and 4 light sixes). There were thus, in all, 182 men and a broadside of 14 guns, throwing 212 pounds of shot. The British forces amounted, as I have said, to 980 men, and (supposing they had equal numbers of 24's, 18's, and 12's) the flotilla threw seven hundred and fifty-eight pounds of shot. The odds of course were not as much against the Americans as these figures would make them, for they were stationary, and had some long, heavy guns and boarding nettings; on the other hand the fact that two of their vessels had drifted out of line was a very serious misfortune. At any rate, the odds were great enough, considering that he had British sailors to deal with, to make it any thing but a cheerful look-out for Lieut. Jones; but nowise daunted by the almost certain prospect of defeat the American officers and seamen prepared very coolly for the fight. In this connection it should be remembered that simply to run the boats on shore would have permitted the men to escape, if they had chosen to do so.

---

[1] James, vi, 521.
[2] Letter of Capt. Lockyer to Vice-Admiral Cochrane, Dec. 18, 1814.
[3] James, vi, 521.
[4] Official letter of Lieut. Jones, March 12, 1815.

Captain Lockyer acted as coolly as his antagonist. When he had reached a point just out of gun-shot, he brought the boats to a grapnel, to let the sailors eat breakfast and get a little rest after the fatigue of their long row. When his men were rested and in good trim he formed the boats in open order, and they pulled gallantly on against the strong current. At 10.50 the Americans opened fire from their long guns, and in about 15 minutes the cannonade became general on both sides. At 11.50[1] Captain Lockyer's barge was laid alongside No. 156, and a very obstinate struggle ensued, "in which the greater part of the officers and crew of the barge were killed or wounded,"[2] including among the latter the gallant captain himself, severely, and his equally gallant first lieutenant, Mr. Pratt, of the *Seahorse* frigate, mortally. At the same time Lieut. Tatnall (of the *Tonnant*) also laid his barge aboard the gun-boat, only to have it sunk; another shared the same fate; and the assailants were for the moment repulsed. But at this time Lieut. Jones who had shown as much personal bravery during the assault, as forethought in preparing for it, received a dangerous and disabling wound, while many of his men received the same fate; the boarding nettings, too, had all been cut or shot away. Several more barges at once assailed the boats, the command of which had devolved on a young midshipman, Mr. George Parker; the latter, fighting as bravely as his commander, was like him severely wounded, whereupon the boat was carried at 12.10. Its guns were turned on No. 163, and this, the smallest of the gun-boats, was soon taken; then the British dashed at No. 162 and carried it, after a very gallant defence, in which Lieut. Speddes was badly wounded. No. 5 had her long 24 dismounted by the recoil, and was next carried; finally, No. 23, being left entirely alone, hauled down her flag at 12.30.[3] The Americans had lost 6 killed and 35 wounded; the British 17 killed and 77 (many mortally) wounded. The greater part of the loss on both sides occurred in boarding No. 156, and also the next two gun-boats.

I have in this case, as usual, taken each commander's account of his own force and loss. Lieut. Jones states the British force to have been 1,000, which tallies almost exactly with their own account; but believes that they lost 300 in killed and wounded. Captain Lockyer, on the other hand, gives the Americans 225 men and three additional light guns. But on the main points the two accounts agree perfectly. The victors certainly deserve great credit for the perseverance, gallantry, and dash they displayed; but still more belongs to the vanquished for the cool skill and obstinate courage with which they fought, although with the certainty of ultimate defeat before them,—which is always the severest test of bravery. No comment is needed to prove the effectiveness of their resistance. Even James says that the Americans made an obstinate struggle, that Lieut. Jones displayed great personal bravery, and that the British loss was very severe.

On the night of Dec. 23d Gen. Jackson beat up the quarters of the British encamped on the bank of the Mississippi. The attack was opened by Capt. Patter-

---

[1] Lieut. Jones' letter.

[2] Captain Lockyer's letter.

[3] Minutes of the Court of Inquiry, held May 15, 1851.

son in the schooner *Carolina,* 14; she was manned by 70 men, and mounted on each side six 12-pound carronades and one long 12. Dropping down the stream unobserved, till opposite the bivouac of the troops and so close to the shore that his first command to fire was plainly heard by the foe, Patterson opened a slaughtering cannonade on the flank of the British, and kept it up without suffering any loss in return, as long as the attack lasted. But on the 27th the British had their revenge, attacking the little schooner as she lay at anchor, unable to ascend the current on account of the rapid current and a strong head-wind. The assailants had a battery of 5 guns, throwing hot shot and shell, while the only gun of the schooner's that would reach was the long 12. After half an hour's fighting the schooner was set on fire and blown up; the crew escaped to the shore with the loss of 7 men killed and wounded. The only remaining vessel, exclusive of some small, unarmed row-boats, was the *Louisiana,* 16, carrying on each side eight long 24's. She was of great assistance in the battle of the 28th, throwing during the course of the cannonade over 800 shot, and suffering very little in return.[1] Afterward the American seamen and marines played a most gallant part in all the engagements on shore; they made very efficient artillerists.

## SUMMARY

The following vessels were got ready for sea during this year:[2]

| NAME. | RIG. | WHERE BUILT. | COST. | MEN. | GUNS. | TONS. | REMARKS. |
|---|---|---|---|---|---|---|---|
| *Wasp,* | Ship | Newburyport | $77,459.60 | 160 | 22 | 509 | Built |
| *Frolic,* | " | Boston | 72,094.82 | " | " | " | " |
| *Peacock,* | " | New York | 75,644.36 | " | " | " | " |
| *Ontario,* | " | Baltimore | 59,343.69 | " | " | " | " |
| *Erie,* | " | " | 56,174.36 | " | " | " | " |
| *Tom Bowline,* | Schooner | Portsmouth | 13,000.00 | 90 | 12 | 260 | Purchased |
| *Lynx,* | " | Washington | | 50 | 6 | | Built |
| *Epervier,* | Brig | England | 50,000.00 | 130 | 18 | 477 | Captured |
| *Flambeau,* | " | Baltimore | 14,000.00 | 90 | 14 | 300 | Purchased |
| ⎰ *Spark,* | " | " | 17,389.00 | " | " | " | " |
| ⎱ *Firefly,* | " | " | 17,435.00 | " | " | 333 | " |
| ⎰ *Torch,* | Schooner | " | 13,000.00 | 60 | 12 | 260 | " |
| ⎱ *Spitfire,* | " | " | 20,000.00 | " | " | 286 | " |
| ⎱ *Eagle,* | " | N.O. | | " | " | 270 | " |
| ⎰ *Prometheus,* | " | Philadelphia | 20,000.00 | " | " | 290 | " |
| ⎱ *Chippeway,* | Brig | R.I. | 52,000.00 | 90 | 14 | 390 | " |
| ⎰ *Saranac,* | " | Middleton | 26,000.00 | " | " | 360 | " |
| ⎱ *Boxer,* | " | " | 26,000.00 | " | " | 370 | " |
| *Despatch,* | Schooner | | | 23 | 2 | 52 | |

[1] Cooper, ii, p. 320.
[2] Am. State Papers, xiv, p. 828; also Emmons' statistical "History."

The first 5 small vessels that are bracketed were to cruise under Commodore Porter; the next 4 under Commodore Perry; but the news of peace arrived before either squadron put to sea. Some of the vessels under this catalogue were really almost ready for sea at the end of 1813; and some that I have included in the catalogue of 1815 were almost completely fitted at the end of 1814,—but this arrangement is practically the best.

### LIST OF VESSELS LOST TO THE BRITISH

#### 1. DESTROYED BY BRITISH ARMIES.

| NAME. | TONS. | GUNS. | |
|---|---|---|---|
| *Columbia,* | 1,508 | 52 | Destroyed to prevent |
| *Adams,* | 760 | 28 | them falling into hands |
| *Argus,* | 509 | 22 | of enemy. |
| *Carolina,* | 230 | 14 | Destroyed by battery. |
| | 3,007 | 116 | |

#### 2. CAPTURED, ETC., BY BRITISH NAVY ON OCEAN.

| NAME. | TONS. | GUNS. | |
|---|---|---|---|
| *Essex,* | 860 | 46 | Captured by frigate and corvette. |
| *Frolic,* | 509 | 22 | " by frigate and schooner. |
| *Rattlesnake,* | 258 | 16 | " by frigate. |
| *Syren,* | 250 | 16 | " by seventy-four. |
| | 1,877 | 100 | |

Total, 4,884 tons. 216 guns.

There were also a good many gun-boats, which I do not count, because, as already said, they were often not as large as the barges that were sunk and taken in attacking them, as at Craney Island, etc.

### LIST OF VESSELS TAKEN FROM BRITISH

#### 1. CAPTURED BY AMERICAN PRIVATEERS.

| NAME. | TONS. | GUNS. |
|---|---|---|
| *Ballahou,* | 86 | 4 |
| *Landrail,* | 76 | 4 |

#### 2. CAPTURED, ETC., BY AMERICAN NAVY ON OCEAN.

| NAME. | TONS. | GUNS. | |
|---|---|---|---|
| *Epervier* | 477 | 18 | Captured by sloop *Peacock*. |
| *Avon,* | 477 | 20 | Sunk " " *Wasp*. |
| *Reindeer,* | 477 | 19 | " " " " |
| *Pictou,* | 300 | 14 | Captured by frigate. |

#### 3. SUNK IN ATTACKING FORT.

| NAME. | TONS. | GUNS. |
|---|---|---|
| *Hermes,* | 500 | 22 |
| | 2,393 | 101 |

Taking into account the losses on the lakes, there was not very much difference in the amount of damage done to each combatant by the other; but both as regards the material results and the moral effects, the balance inclined largely to the Americans. The chief damage done to our navy was by the British land-forces, and consisted mainly in forcing us to burn an unfinished frigate and sloop. On the ocean our three sloops were captured in each case by an overwhelming force, against which no resistance could be made, and the same was true of the captured British schooner. The *Essex* certainly gained as much honor as her opponents. There were but three single ship actions, in all of which the Americans were so superior in force as to give them a very great advantage; nevertheless, in two of them the victory was won with such perfect impunity and the difference in the loss and damage inflicted was so very great, that I doubt if the result would have been affected if the odds had been reversed. In the other case, that of the *Reindeer,* the defeated party fought at a still greater disadvantage, and yet came out of the conflict with full as much honor as the victor. No man with a particle of generosity in his nature can help feeling the most honest admiration for the unflinching courage and cool skill displayed by Capt. Manners and his crew. It is worthy of notice (remembering the sneers of so many of the British authors at the "wary circumspection" of the Americans) that Capt. Manners, who has left a more honorable name than any other British commander of the war, excepting Capt. Broke, behaved with the greatest caution as long as it would serve his purpose, while he showed the most splendid personal courage afterward. It is this combination of courage and skill that made him so dangerous an antagonist; it showed that the traditional British bravery was not impaired by refusing to adhere to the traditional British tactics of rushing into a fight "bull-headed." Needless exposure to danger denotes not so much pluck as stupidity. Capt. Manners had no intention of giving his adversary any advantage he could prevent. No one can help feeling regret that he was killed; but if he was to fall, what more glorious death could he meet? It must be remembered that while paying all homage to Capt. Manners, Capt. Blakely did equally well. It was a case where the victory between two combatants, equal in courage and skill, was decided by superior weight of metal and number of men.

### PRIZES MADE

| NAME OF SHIP. | NUMBER OF PRIZES. |
|---|---|
| *President* | 3 |
| *Constitution* | 6 |
| *Adams* | 10 |
| *Frolic* | 2 |
| *Wasp* | 15 |
| *Peacock* | 15 |
| *Hornet* | 1 |
| Small craft | 35 |
| | 87 |

# VIII

# 1814

# ON THE LAKES

## ONTARIO

The winter was spent by both parties in preparing more formidable fleets for the ensuing summer. All the American schooners had proved themselves so unfit for service that they were converted into transports, except the *Sylph*, which was brig-rigged and armed like the *Oneida*. Sackett's Harbor possessed but slight fortifications, and the Americans were kept constantly on the alert, through fear lest the British should cross over. Commodore Chauncy and Mr. Eckford were as unremitting in their exertions as ever. In February two 22-gun brigs, the *Jefferson* and *Jones*, and one large frigate of 50 guns, the *Superior*, were laid: afterward a deserter brought in news of the enormous size of one of the new British frigates, and the *Superior* was enlarged to permit her carrying 62 guns. The *Jefferson* was launched on April 7th, the *Jones* on the 10th; and the *Superior* on May 2d,—an attempt on the part of the British to blow her up having been foiled a few days before. Another frigate, the *Mohawk*, 42, was at once begun. Neither guns nor men for the first three ships had as yet arrived, but they soon began to come in, as the roads got better and the streams opened. Chauncy and Eckford, besides building ships that were literally laid down in the forest, and seeing that they were armed with heavy guns, which, as well as all their stores, had to be carried overland hundreds of miles through the wilderness, were obliged to settle quarrels that occurred among the men, the most serious being one that arose from a sentinel's accidentally killing a ship-wright, whose companions instantly struck work in a body. What was more serious, they had to contend with such constant and virulent sickness that it almost assumed the proportions of a plague. During the winter it was seldom that two thirds of the force were fit for duty, and nearly a sixth of the whole number of men in the port died before navigation opened.[1]

Meanwhile Yeo had been nearly as active at Kingston, laying down two frigates and a huge line-of-battle ship, but his shipwrights did not succeed in getting the latter ready much before navigation closed. The *Prince Regent*, 58, and *Princess Charlotte*, 42, were launched on April 15th. I shall anticipate somewhat by giving tabular lists of the comparative forces, after the two British frigates, the two American frigates, and the two American brigs had all been equipped and manned. Commodore Yeo's original six cruisers had been all renamed, some of them re-armed, and both the schooners changed into brigs. The *Wolfe, Royal George, Melville, Moira, Beresford,* and *Sydney Smith,* were now named respectively *Montreal, Niagara, Star, Charwell, Netly,* and *Magnet.* On the American side there had been but slight changes, beyond the alteration of the *Sylyh* into a brig armed like the *Oneida.* Of the *Superior's* 62 guns, 4 were very shortly sent on shore again.

### CHAUNCY'S SQUADRON

| NAME. | RIG. | TONNAGE. | CREW. | BROADSIDE METAL. | ARMAMENT. |
|---|---|---|---|---|---|
| Superior, | ship, | 1,580 | 500 | 1,050 lbs. | 30 long 32's<br>2 " 24's<br>26 short 42's |
| Mohawk, | " | 1,350 | 350 | 554 " | 26 long 24's<br>2 " 18's<br>14 short 32's |
| Pike, | " | 875 | 300 | 360 " | 26 long 24's<br>2 " 24's |
| Madison, | " | 593 | 200 | 364 " | 2 long 12's<br>22 short 32's |
| Jones, | brig, | 500 | 160 | 332 " | 2 long 12's<br>20 short 32's |
| Jefferson, | " | 500 | 160 | 332 " | 2 long 12's<br>20 short 32's |
| Sylph, | " | 300 | 100 | 180 " | 2 long 12's<br>14 short 24's |
| Oneida, | " | 243 | 100 | 180 " | 2 long 12's<br>14 short 24's |
| 8 vessels, | | 5,941 | 1,870 | 3,352 lbs. | 228 guns. |

This is considerably less than James makes it, as he includes all the schooners, which were abandoned as cruisers, and only used as transports or gun-boats. Similarly Sir James had a large number of gun-boats, which are not

[1] Cooper mentions that in five months the *Madison* buried a fifth of her crew.

included in his cruising force. James thus makes Chauncy's force 2,321 men, and a broadside of 4,188 lbs.

YEO'S SQUADRON

| NAME. | RIG. | TONNAGE. | CREW. | BROADSIDE METAL. | ARMAMENT. |
|---|---|---|---|---|---|
| *Prince Regent,* | ship, | 1,450 | 485 | 872 lbs. | 32 long 24's<br>4 short 68's<br>22 " 32's |
| *Princess Charlotte,* | " | 1,215 | 315 | 604 " | 26 long 24's<br>2 short 68's<br>14 " 32's |
| *Montreal,* | " | 637 | 220 | 258 " | 7 long 24's<br>18 " 18's |
| *Niagara,* | " | 510 | 200 | 332 " | 2 long 12's<br>20 short 32's |
| *Charwell,* | brig, | 279 | 110 | 236 " | 2 long 12's<br>14 short 32's |
| *Star,* | " | 262 | 110 | 236 " | 2 long 12's<br>14 short 32's |
| *Netly,* | " | 216 | 100 | 180 " | 2 long 12's<br>14 short 24's |
| *Magnet,* | " | 187 | 80 | 156 " | 2 long 12's<br>12 short 24's |
| 8 vessels, | | 4,756 | 1,620 | 2,874 lbs. | 209 guns. |

This tallies pretty well with James' statement, which (on p. 488) is 1,517 men, and a broadside of 2,752 lbs. But there are very probably errors as regards the armaments of the small brigs, which were continually changed. At any rate the American fleet was certainly the stronger, about in the proportion of six to five. The disproportion was enough to justify Sir James in his determination not to hazard a battle, although the odds were certainly not such as British commanders had been previously accustomed to pay much regard to. Chauncy would have acted exactly as his opponent did, had he been similarly placed. The odds against the British commodore were too great to be overcome, where the combatants were otherwise on a par, although the refusal to do battle against them would certainly preclude Yeo from advancing any claims to *superiority* in skill or courage. The *Princess Charlotte* and *Niagara* were just about equal to the *Mohawk* and *Madison,* and so were the *Charwell* and *Netly* to the *Oneida* and *Sylph;* but both the *Star* and *Magnet* together could hardly have matched either the *Jones* or the *Jefferson,* while the main-deck 32's of the *Superior* gave her a great advantage over the *Prince Regent's* 24's, where the crews were so equal; and the *Pike* was certainly too heavy for the *Montreal.* A decided superiority in the effectiveness of both crews and captains could alone have warranted Sir James Lucas Yeo in engaging, and this superiority he certainly did not possess.

This year the British architects outstripped ours in the race for supremacy, and Commodore Yeo put out of port with his eight vessels long before the Americans were ready. His first attempt was a successful attack on Oswego. This town is situated some 60 miles distant from Sackett's Harbor, and is the first port on the lake which the stores, sent from the seaboard to Chauncy, reached. Accordingly it was a place of some little importance, but was very much neglected by the American authorities. It was insufficiently garrisoned, and was defended only by an entirely ruined fort of 6 guns, two of them dismounted. Commodore Yeo sailed from Kingston to attack it on the 3d of May, having on board his ships a detachment of 1,080 troops. Oswego was garrisoned by less than 300 men,[1] chiefly belonging to a light artillery regiment, with a score or two of militia; they were under the command of Colonel Mitchell. The recaptured schooner *Growler* was in port, with 7 guns destined for the Harbor; she was sunk by her commander, but afterward raised and carried off by the foe.

On the 5th Yeo appeared off Oswego and sent in Captain Collier and 13 gun-boats to draw the fort's fire; after some firing between them and the four guns mounted in the fort (two long 24's, one long 12, and one long 6), the gun-boats retired. The next day the attack was seriously made. The *Princess Charlotte, Montreal,* and *Niagara* engaged the batteries, while the *Charwell* and *Star* scoured the woods with grape to clear them of the militia.[2] The debarkation of the troops was superintended by Captain O'Connor, and until it was accomplished the *Montreal* sustained almost the whole fire of the fort, being set on fire three times, and much cut up in hull, masts, and rigging.[3] Under this fire 800 British troops were landed, under Lieutenant-Colonel Fischer, assisted by 200 seamen, armed with long pikes, under Captain Mulcaster. They moved gallantly up the hill, under a heavy fire, and carried the fort by assault; Mitchell then fell back unmolested to the Falls, about 12 miles above the town, where there was a large quantity of stores. But he was not again attacked. The Americans lost 6 men killed, including Lieutenant Blaeny, 38 wounded, and 25 missing, both of these last falling into the enemy's hands. The British lost 22 soldiers, marines, and seamen (including Captain Hollaway) killed, and 73 (including the gallant Captain Mulcaster dangerously, and Captain Popham slightly) wounded,[4] the total loss being 95—nearly a third of the American force engaged. General Drummond, in his official letter, reports that "the fort being everywhere almost open, the whole of the garrison * * * effected their escape, except about 60 men, half of them wounded." No doubt the fort's being "everywhere almost open" afforded excellent opportunities for retreat; but it was not much of a recommendation of it as a structure intended for defence.

[1] General order of Gen. Jacob Brown, by R. Jones, Ass. Adj.-General, May 12, 1814.

[2] Letter of General Gordon Drummond, May 7, 1814.

[3] Letter of Sir James Lucas Yeo, May 17, 1814.

[4] Letter of Lieut.-Col. V. Fischer, May 17, 1814. James says "18 killed and 64 wounded," why, I do not know; the official report of Col. Fischer, as quoted, says: "Of the army, 19 killed and 62 wounded; of the navy, 3 killed and 11 wounded."

The British destroyed the four guns in the battery, and raised the *Growler* and carried her off, with her valuable cargo of seven long guns. They also carried off a small quantity of ordnance stores and some flour, and burned the barracks; otherwise but little damage was done, and the Americans reoccupied the place at once. It certainly showed great lack of energy on Commodore Yeo's part that he did not strike a really important blow by sending an expedition up to destroy the quantity of stores and ordnance collected at the Falls. But the attack itself was admirably managed. The ships were well placed, and kept up so heavy a fire on the fort as to effectually cover the debarkation of the troops, which was very cleverly accomplished; and the soldiers and seamen behaved with great gallantry and steadiness, their officers leading them, sword in hand, up a long, steep hill, under a destructive fire. It was similar to Chauncy's attacks on York and Fort George, except that in this case the assailants suffered a much severer loss compared to that inflicted on the assailed. Colonel Mitchell managed the defence with skill, doing all he could with his insufficient materials.

After returning to Kingston, Yeo sailed with his squadron for Sackett's Harbor, where he appeared on May 19th and began a strict blockade. This was especially troublesome because most of the guns and cables for the two frigates had not yet arrived, and though the lighter pieces and stores could be carried over land, the heavier ones could only go by water, which route was now made dangerous by the presence of the blockading squadron. The very important duty of convoying these great guns was entrusted to Captain Woolsey, an officer of tried merit. He decided to take them by water to Stony Creek, whence they might be carried by land to the Harbor, which was but three miles distant; and on the success of his enterprise depended Chauncy's chances of regaining command of the lake. On the 28th of May, at sunset, Woolsey left Oswego with 19 boats, carrying 21 long 32's, 10 long 24's, three 42-pound carronades, and 10 cables—one of the latter, for the *Superior,* being a huge rope 22 inches in circumference and weighing 9,600 pounds. The boats rowed all through the night, and at sunrise on the 29th 18 of them found themselves off the Big Salmon River, and, as it was unsafe to travel by daylight, Woolsey ran up into Big Sandy Creek, 8 miles from the Harbor. The other boat, containing two long 24's and a cable, got out of line, ran into the British squadron, and was captured. The news she brought induced Sir James Yeo at once to send out an expedition to capture the others. He accordingly despatched Captains Popham and Spilsbury in two gun-boats, one armed with one 68-pound and one 24-pound carronade, and the other with a long 32, accompanied by three cutters and a gig, mounting between them two long 12's and two brass 6's, with a total of 180 men.[1] They rowed up to Sandy Creek and lay off its mouth all the night, and began ascending it shortly after daylight on the 30th. Their force, however, was absurdly inadequate for the accomplishment of their object. Captain Woolsey

---

[1] James, vi, 487; while Cooper says 186, James says the British loss was 18 killed and 50 wounded; Major Appling says "14 were killed, 28 wounded, and 27 marines and 106 sailors captured."

had been reinforced by some Oneida Indians, a company of light artillery, and some militia, so that his only care was, not to repulse, but to capture the British party entire, and even this did not need any exertion. He accordingly despatched Major Appling down the river with 120 riflemen[1] and some Indians to lie in ambush.[2] When going up the creek the British marines, under Lieutenant Cox, were landed on the left bank, and the small-arm men, under Lieutenant Brown, on the right bank; while the two captains rowed up the stream between them, throwing grape into the bushes to disperse the Indians. Major Appling waited until the British were close up, when his riflemen opened with so destructive a volley as to completely demoralize and "stampede" them, and their whole force was captured with hardly any resistance, the Americans having only one man slightly wounded. The British loss was severe,—18 killed and 50 dangerously wounded, according to Captain Popham's report, as quoted by James; or "14 killed and 28 wounded," according to Major Appling's letter. It was a very clever and successful ambush.

On June 6th Yeo raised the blockade of the Harbor, but Chauncy's squadron was not in condition to put out till six weeks later, during which time nothing was done by either fleet, except that two very gallant cutting-out expeditions were successfully attempted by Lieutenant Francis H. Gregory, U.S.N. On June 16th he left the Harbor, accompanied by Sailing-masters Vaughan and Dixon and 22 seamen, in three gigs, to intercept some of the enemy's provision schooners; on the 19th he was discovered by the British gun-boat *Black Snake*, of one 18-pound carronade and 18 men, commanded by Captain H. Landon. Lieutenant Gregory dashed at the gun-boat and carried it without the loss of a man; he was afterward obliged to burn it, but he brought the prisoners, chiefly royal marines, safely into port. On the 1st of July he again started out, with Messrs. Vaughan and Dixon, and two gigs. The plucky little party suffered greatly from hunger, but on the 5th he made a sudden descent on Presque Isle, and burned a 14-gun schooner just ready for launching; he was off before the foe could assemble, and reached the Harbor in safety next day.

On July 31st Commodore Chauncy sailed with his fleet; some days previously the larger British vessels had retired to Kingston, where a 100-gun two-decker was building. Chauncy sailed up to the head of the lake, where he intercepted the small brig *Magnet*. The *Sylph* was sent in to destroy her, but her crew ran her ashore and burned her. The *Jefferson*, *Sylph*, and *Oneida* were left to watch some other small craft in the Niagara; the *Jones* was kept cruising between the Harbor and Oswego, and with the four larger vessels Chauncy blockaded Yeo's four large vessels lying in Kingston. The four American vessels were in the aggregate of 4,398 tons, manned by rather more than 1,350 men, and presenting in broadside 77 guns, throwing 2,328 lbs. of shot. The four British

---

[1] Letter from Major D. Appling, May 30, 1814.

[2] Letter of Capt. M. T. Woolsey, June 1, 1814. There were about 60 Indians; in all, the American force amounted to 180 men. James adds 30 riflemen, 140 Indians, and "a large body of militia and cavalry,"—none of whom were present.

vessels measured in all *about* 3,812 tons, manned by 1,220 men, and presenting in broadside 74 guns, throwing 2,066 lbs. of shot. The former were thus superior by about 15 per cent., and Sir James Yeo very properly declined to fight with the odds against him—although it was a nicer calculation than British commanders had been accustomed to enter into.

Major-General Brown had written to Commodore Chauncy on July 13th: "I do not doubt my ability to meet the enemy in the field and to march in any direction over his country, your fleet carrying for me the necessary supplies. We can threaten Forts George and Niagara, and carry Burlington Heights and York, and proceed direct to Kingston and carry that place. For God's sake let me see you: Sir James will not fight." To which Chauncy replied: "I shall afford every assistance in my power to co-operate with the army whenever it can be done without losing sight of the great object for the attainment of which this fleet has been created,—the capture or destruction of the enemy's fleet. But that I consider the primary object. * * * We are intended to seek and fight the enemy's fleet, and I shall not be diverted from my efforts to effectuate it by any sinister attempt to render us subordinate to, or an appendage of, the army." That is, by any "sinister attempt" to make him co-operate intelligently in a really well-concerted scheme of invasion. In further support of these noble and independent sentiments, he writes to the Secretary of the Navy on August 10th.[1] "I told (General Brown) that I should not visit the head of the lake unless the enemy's fleet did so. * * * To deprive the enemy of an apology for not meeting me, I have sent ashore four guns from the *Superior* to reduce her armament in number to an equality with the *Prince Regent*'s, yielding the advantage of their 68-pounders. The *Mohawk* mounts two guns less than the *Princess Charlotte*, and the *Montreal* and *Niagara* are equal to the *Pike* and *Madison*." He here justifies his refusal to co-operate with General Brown by saying that he was of only equal force with Sir James, and that he has deprived the latter of "an apology" for not meeting him. This last was not at all true. The *Mohawk* and *Madison* were just about equal to the *Princess Charlotte* and *Niagara*; but the *Pike* was half as strong again as the *Montreal*; and Chauncy could very well afford to "yield the advantage of their 68-pounders," when in return Sir James had to yield the advantage of Chauncy's long 32's and 42-pound carronades. The *Superior* was a 32-pounder frigate, and, even without her four extra guns, was about a fourth heavier than the *Prince Regent* with her 24-pounders. Sir James was not acting more warily than Chauncy had acted during June and July, 1813. Then he had a fleet which tonned 1,701, was manned by 680 men, and threw at a broadside 1,099 lbs. of shot; and he declined to go out of port or in any way try to check the operation of Yeo's fleet which tonned 2,091, was manned by 770 men, and threw at a broadside 1,374 lbs. of shot. Chauncy then acted perfectly proper, no doubt, but he could not afford to sneer at Yeo for behaving in the same way. Whatever either commander might write, in reality he well knew that his offi-

---

[1] See Niles, vii, 12, and other places (under "Chauncy" in index).

cers and crews were, man for man, just about on a par with those of his antagonists, and so, after the first brush or two, he was exceedingly careful to see that
the odds were not against him. Chauncy, in his petulant answers to Brown's letter, ignored the fact that his superiority of force would prevent his opponent
from giving battle, and would, therefore, prevent any thing more important
than a blockade occurring.

His ideas of the purpose for which his command had been created were erroneous and very hurtful to the American cause. That purpose was not, except
incidentally, "the destruction of the enemy's fleet"; and, if it was, he entirely
failed to accomplish it. The real purpose was to enable Canada to be successfully invaded, or to assist in repelling an invasion of the United States. These
services could only be efficiently performed by acting in union with the land-
forces, for his independent action could evidently have little effect. The only
important services he had performed had been in attacking Forts George and
York, where he *had* been rendered "subordinate to, and an appendage of, the
army." His only chance of accomplishing any thing lay in similar acts of
coöperation, and he refused to do these. Had he acted as he ought to have done,
and assisted Brown to the utmost, he would certainly have accomplished much
more than he did, and might have enabled Brown to assault Kingston, when
Yeo's fleet would of course have been captured. The insubordination, petty
stickling for his own dignity, and lack of appreciation of the necessity of acting in concert that he showed, were the very faults which proved most fatal to
the success of our various land commanders in the early part of the war. Even
had Chauncy's assistance availed nothing, he could not have accomplished less
than he did. He remained off Kingston blockading Yeo, being once or twice
blown off by gales. He sent Lieutenant Gregory, accompanied by Midshipman
Hart and six men, in to reconnoitre on August 25th; the lieutenant ran across
two barges containing 30 men, and was captured after the midshipman had
been killed and the lieutenant and four men wounded. On September 21st he
transported General Izard and 3,000 men from Sackett's Harbor to the Genesee; and then again blockaded Kingston until the two-decker was nearly completed, when he promptly retired to the Harbor.

The equally cautious Yeo did not come out on the lake till Oct. 15th; he did
not indulge in the empty and useless formality of blockading his antagonist,
but assisted the British army on the Niagara frontier till navigation closed,
about Nov. 21st. A couple of days before, Midshipman McGowan headed an
expedition to blow up the two-decker (named the *St. Lawrence*) with a torpedo,
but was discovered by two of the enemy's boats, which he captured and
brought in; the attempt was abandoned, because the *St. Lawrence* was found not
to be lying in Kingston.

For this year the material loss again fell heaviest on the British, amounting
to one 14-gun brig burned by her crew, one 10-gun schooner burned on the
stocks, three gun-boats, three cutters, and one gig captured; while in return the
Americans lost one schooner loaded with seven guns, one boat loaded with two,

and a gig captured and four guns destroyed at Oswego. In men the British loss was heavier still relatively to that of the Americans, being in killed, wounded, and prisoners about 300 to 80. But in spite of this loss and damage, which was too trivial to be of any account to either side, the success of the season was with the British, inasmuch as they held command over the lake for more than four months, during which time they could coöperate with their army; while the Americans held it for barely two months and a half. In fact the conduct of the two fleets on Lake Ontario during the latter part of the war was almost farcical. As soon as one, by building, acquired the superiority, the foe at once retired to port, where he waited until *he* had built another vessel or two, when he came out, and the other went into port in turn. Under such circumstances it was hopeless ever to finish the contest by a stand-up sea-fight, each commander calculating the chances with mathematical exactness. The only hope of destroying the enemy's fleet was by coöperating with the land-forces in a successful attack on his main post, when he would be forced to be either destroyed or to fight—and this coöperation Chauncy refused to give. He seems to have been an excellent organizer, but he did not use (certainly not in the summer of 1813) his materials by any means to the best advantage. He was hardly equal to his opponent, and the latter seems to have been little more than an average officer. Yeo blundered several times, as in the attack on Sackett's Harbor, in not following up his advantage at Oswego, in showing so little resource in the action off the Genesee, etc., and he was not troubled by any excess of daring; but during the period when he was actually cruising against Chauncy on the lake he certainly showed to better advantage than the American did. With an inferior force he won a partial victory over his opponent off Niagara, and then kept him in check for six weeks; while Chauncy, with his superior force, was not only partially defeated once, but, when he did gain a partial victory, failed to take advantage of it.

In commenting upon the timid and dilatory tactics of the two commanders on Ontario, however, it must be remembered that the indecisive nature of the results attained had been often paralleled by the numerous similar encounters that took place on the ocean during the wars of the preceding century. In the War of the American Revolution, the English fought some 19 fleet actions with the French, Dutch, and Spaniards; one victory was gained over the French, and one over the Spaniards, while the 17 others were all indecisive, both sides claiming the victory, and neither winning it. Of course, some of them, though indecisive as regards loss and damage, were strategetical victories: thus, Admiral Arbuthnot beat back Admiral Barras off the Chesapeake, in March of 1781; and near the same place in September of the same year the French had their revenge in the victory (one at least in its results) of the Conte de Grasse over Sir Thomas Graves. In the five desperate and bloody combats which De Suffrein waged with Sir Edward Hughes in the East Indies, the laurels were very evenly divided. These five conflicts were not rendered indecisive by any over-wariness in manœuvring, for De Suffrein's attacks were carried out with as much boldness as skill, and his stubborn antagonist was never inclined to baulk him of a fair battle; but the two hardy fighters were so evenly matched that they would pound one another till each was helpless to inflict injury. Very different were the three consecutive battles that took place in the same waters, on the 25th of April, 1758, the 3d of August, 1758, and on the 10th of September, 1759, between Pocock and d'Aché,[1] where, by skilful manœuvring, the French admiral saved his somewhat inferior force from capture, and the English admiral gained indecisive victories. M. Rivière, after giving a most just and impartial account of the battles, sums up with the following excellent criticism.[2]

"It is this battle, won by Hawke, the 20th of November, 1757, and the combats of Pocock and d'Aché, from which date two distinct schools in the naval affairs of the 18th century: one of these was all for promptness and audacity, which were regarded as the indispensable conditions for victory; the other, on the contrary, praised skilful delays and able evolutions, and created success by science united to prudence. * * * But these two schools were true only according to circumstances, not absolutely. When two fleets of equal worth are facing one another, as in the War of the American Revolution, then tactics should come into play, and audacity would often be mere foolhardiness. If it happens, on the other hand, as in the Republic, or during the last years of Louis XV, that an irresolute fleet, without organization, has to contend with a fleet prepared in every way, then, on the part of this last, audacity is wisdom and prudence would be cowardice, for it would give an enemy who distrusts himself time to become more hardy. The only school always true is that one which, freed from all routine, produces men whose genius will unite in one, in knowing how to apply them appropriately, the audacity which will carry off victory, and the prudence which knows how to obtain it in preparing for it."

These generalizations are drawn from the results of mighty battles, but they apply just as well to the campaigns carried on on a small scale, or even to single-ship actions. Chauncy, as already said, does not deserve the praise which most American historians, and especially Cooper, have lavished on him as well as on all our other officers of that period. Such indiscriminate eulogy entirely detracts from the worth of a writer's favorable criticisms. Our *average* commander was, I firmly believe, at that time superior to the average commander of any other nation; but to get at this average we must include Chauncy, Rodgers, and Angus, as well as Hull, Macdonough, Perry, Porter, Bainbridge, Biddle, Lawrence, and Warrington.

Sir James Yeo did to the full as well as his opponent, and like him was a good organizer; but he did little enough. His campaigns must be considered as being conducted well or ill according as he is believed to have commanded better men than his opponent, or not. If, as many British writers contend, his crews were an

---

[1] "La Marine Française sous le Règne de Louis XV," par Henri Rivière, Lieutenant de Vaisseau, Chevalier de la Légion d' Honneur. (Paris et Toulon, 1859), pp. 385 and 439.

[2] *Ibid.*, p. 425. I pay more attention to the sense than to the letter in my translation.

overmatch for the Americans, man for man, even to a slight degree, then Yeo's conduct was very cowardly; if, on the contrary, the officers and men of the two fleets were on a par, then he acted properly and outgeneralled his opponent. It is to be regretted that most of the histories written on the subject, on either side of the Atlantic, should be of the "hurrah" order of literature, with no attempt whatever to get at the truth, but merely to explain away the defeats or immensely exaggerate the victories suffered or gained by their own side.

## ERIE AND THE UPPER LAKES

Hitherto the vessels on these lakes (as well as on Ontario) had been under the command of Commodore Chauncy; but they were now formed into a separate department, under Captain Arthur Sinclair. The Americans had, of course, complete supremacy, and no attempt was seriously made to contest it with them; but they received a couple of stinging, if not very important, defeats. It is rather singular that here the British, who began with a large force, while there was none whatever to oppose it, should have had it by degrees completely annihilated; and should have then, and not till then, when apparently rendered harmless, have turned round and partially revenged themselves by two cutting-out expeditions which were as boldly executed as they were skilfully planned.

Captain Sinclair sailed into Lake Huron with the *Niagara, Caledonia, Ariel, Scorpion,* and *Tigress,* and on July 20th burnt the fort and barracks of St. Joseph, which were abandoned by their garrison. On Aug. 4th he arrived off the fort of Machilimacinac (Mackinaw), which was situated on such an eminence that the guns of the vessels could not reach it. Accordingly, the troops under Col. Croghan were landed, covered by the fire of the schooners, very successfully; but when they tried to carry the fort they were driven back with the loss of 70 men. Thence Sinclair sailed to the Nattagawassa Creek, attacked and destroyed a block-house three miles up it, which mounted three light guns, and also a schooner called the *Nancy;* but the commander of the schooner, Lieutenant Worsely, with his crew, escaped up the river. Captain Sinclair then departed for Lake Erie, leaving the *Scorpion,* Lieutenant Turner, and *Tigress,* Sailing-master Champlin, to blockade the Nattagawassa. News was received by the British from a party of Indians that the two American vessels were five leagues apart, and it was at once resolved to attempt their capture. On the first of September, in the evening, four boats started out, one manned by 20 seamen, under Lieutenant Worsley, the three others by 72 soldiers under Lieutenants Bulger, Armstrong, and Raderhurst of the army—in all 92 men and two guns, a 6- and a 3-pounder. A number of Indians accompanied the expedition but took no part in the fighting. At sunset on the 2d the boats arrived at St. Mary's Strait, and spent 24 hours in finding out where the American schooners were. At 6 P.M. on the 3d, the nearest vessel, the *Tigress,* was made out, six miles off, and they pulled for her. It was very dark, and they were not discovered till they had come within fifty yards, when Champlin at once fired his long 24 at them; before it could be reloaded the four boats had dashed up, those of Lieutenants Worsely and Armstrong placing themselves on the starboard, and those of Lieutenants Bulger and Raderhurst on the port side. There was a short, sharp struggle, and the schooner was carried. Of her crew of 28 men, 3 were killed and five, including Mr. Champlin, dangerously wounded. The assailants lost three seamen killed, Lieutenant Bulger, seven soldiers and several seamen wounded.[1] "The defence of this vessel," writes Lieut. Bulger, "did credit to her officers, who were all severely wounded." Next day the prisoners were sent on shore; and on the 5th the *Scorpion* was discovered working up to join her consort, entirely ignorant of what had happened. She anchored about 2 miles from the *Tigress;* and next morning at 6 o'clock the latter slipped her cable and ran down under the jib and foresail, the American ensign and pendant still flying. When within 10 yards of the *Scorpion,* the concealed soldiers jumped up, poured a volley into her which killed 2 and wounded 2 men, and the next moment carried her, her surprised crew of 30 men making no resistance. The whole affair reflected great credit on the enterprise and pluck of the British without being discreditable to the Americans. It was like Lieut. Elliott's capture of the *Detroit* and *Caledonia.*

Meanwhile a still more daring cutting-out expedition had taken place at the foot of Lake Erie. The three American schooners, *Ohio, Somers,* and *Porcupine,* each with 30 men, under Lieut. Conkling, were anchored just at the outlet of the lake, to cover the flank of the works at Fort Erie. On the night of August 12th, Capt. Dobbs, of the *Charwell,* and Lieut. Radcliffe, of the *Netly,* with 75 seamen and marines from their two vessels, which were lying off Fort Erie, resolved to attempt the capture of the schooners. The seamen carried the captain's gig upon their shoulders from Queenstown to Frenchman's Creek, a distance of 20 miles; thence, by the aid of some militia, 5 batteaux as well as the gig were carried 8 miles across the woods to Lake Erie, and the party (whether with or without the militia I do not know) embarked in them. Between 11 and 12 the boats were discovered a short distance ahead of the *Somers* and hailed. They answered "provision boats," which deceived the officer on deck, as such boats had been in the habit of passing and repassing continually during the night. Before he discovered his mistake the boats drifted across his hawse, cut his cables, and ran him aboard with a volley of musketry, which wounded two of his men, and before the others could get on deck the schooner was captured. In another moment the British boats were alongside the *Ohio,* Lieut. Conkling's vessel. Here the people had hurried on deck, and there was a moment's sharp struggle, in which the assailants lost Lieut. Radcliffe and one seaman killed and six seamen and marines wounded; but on board the *Ohio* Lieut. Conkling and Sailing-master M. Cally were shot down, one seaman killed, and four wounded, and Captain Dobbs carried her, sword in hand. The *Porcupine* was not molested, and made no effort to

---

[1] Letter of Lieutenant A. H. Bulger, Sept. 7, 1814. James says only 3 killed and 8 wounded; but Lieutenant Bulger distinctly says, in addition, "and several seamen wounded."

interfere with the British in their retreat; so they drifted down the rapids with their two prizes and secured them below. The boldness of this enterprise will be appreciated when it is remembered that but 75 British seamen (unless there were some militia along), with no artillery, attacked and captured two out of three fine schooners, armed each with a long 32 or 24, and an aggregate of 90 men; and that this had been done in waters where the gig and five batteaux of the victors were the only British vessels afloat.

## CHAMPLAIN

This lake, which had hitherto played but an inconspicuous part, was now to become the scene of the greatest naval battle of the war. A British army of 11,000 men under Sir George Prevost undertook the invasion of New York by advancing up the western bank of Lake Champlain. This advance was impracticable unless there was a sufficiently strong British naval force to drive back the American squadron at the same time. Accordingly, the British began to construct a frigate, the *Confiance*, to be added to their already existing force, which consisted of a brig, two sloops, and 12 or 14 gun-boats. The Americans already possessed a heavy corvette, a schooner, a small sloop, and 10 gun-boats or row-galleys; they now began to build a large brig, the *Eagle*, which was launched about the 16th of August. Nine days later, on the 25th, the *Confiance* was launched. The two squadrons were equally deficient in stores, etc.; the *Confiance* having locks to her guns, some of which could not be used, while the American schooner *Ticonderoga* had to fire her guns by means of pistols flashed at the touchholes (like Barclay on Lake Erie). Macdonough and Downie were hurried into action before they had time to prepare themselves thoroughly; but it was a disadvantage common to both, and arose from the nature of the case, which called for immediate action. The British army advanced slowly toward Plattsburg, which was held by General Macomb with less than 2,000 effective American troops. Captain Thomas Macdonough, the American commodore, took the lake a day or two before his antagonist, and came to anchor in Plattsburg harbor. The British fleet, under Captain George Downie, moved from Isle-aux-Noix on Sept. 8th, and on the morning of the 11th sailed into Plattsburg harbor.

The American force consisted of the ship *Saratoga*, Captain T. Macdonough, of about 734 tons,[1] carrying eight long 24-pounders, six 42-pound and twelve 32-pound carronades; the brig *Eagle*, Captain Robert Henly, of about 500 tons, carrying eight long 18's and twelve 32-pound carronades; schooner *Ticonderoga*,

---

[1] In the Naval Archives ("Masters'-Commandant Letters," 1814, 1, No. 134) is a letter from Macdonough in which he states that the *Saratoga* is intermediate in size between the *Pike*, of 875, and the *Madison*, of 593 tons; this would make her 734. The *Eagle* was very nearly the size of the *Lawrence* or *Niagara*, on Lake Erie. The *Ticonderoga* was originally a small steamer, but Commodore Macdonough had her schooner-rigged, because he found that her machinery got out of order on almost every trip that she took. Her tonnage is only approximately known, but she was of the same size as the *Linnet*.

Lieut.-Com. Stephen Cassin, of about 350 tons carrying eight long 12-pounders, four long 18-pounders, and five 32-pound carronades; sloop *Preble*, Lieutenant Charles Budd, of about 80 tons, mounting seven long 9's; the row-galleys *Borer, Centipede, Nettle, Allen, Viper,* and *Burrows,* each of about 70 tons, and mounting one long 24- and one short 18-pounder; and the row-galleys *Wilmer, Ludlow, Aylwin,* and *Ballard,* each of about 40 tons, and mounting one long 12. James puts down the number of men on board the squadron as 950,—merely a guess, as he gives no authority. Cooper says "about 850 men, including officers, and a small detachment of soldiers to act as marines." Lossing (p. 866, note 1) says 882 in all. Vol. xiv of the "American State Papers" contains on p. 572 the prize-money list presented by the purser, George Beale, Jr. This numbers the men (the dead being represented by their heirs or executors) up to 915, including soldiers and seamen, but many of the numbers are omitted, probably owing to the fact that their owners, though belonging on board, happened to be absent on shore, or in the hospital; so that the actual number of names tallies very closely with that given by Lossing; and accordingly I shall take that.[1] The total number of men in the galleys (including a number of soldiers, as there were not enough sailors) was 350. The exact proportions in which this force was distributed among the gun-boats can not be told, but it may be roughly said to be 41 in each large galley and 26 in each small one. The complement of the *Saratoga* was 210, of the *Eagle,* 130, of the *Ticonderoga,* 100, and of the *Preble,* 30; but the first three had also a few soldiers distributed between them. The following list is probably pretty accurate as to the aggregate; but there may have been a score or two fewer men on the gun-boats, or more on the larger vessels.

MACDONOUGH'S FORCE

| NAME. | TONS. | CREW. | BROADSIDE. | METAL, FROM LONG OR SHORT GUNS. | |
|---|---|---|---|---|---|
| *Saratoga,* | 734 | 240 | 414 lbs. | long, | 96 |
| | | | | short, | 318 |
| *Eagle,* | 500 | 150 | 264 " | long, | 72 |
| | | | | short, | 192 |
| *Ticonderoga,* | 350 | 112 | 180 " | long, | 84 |
| | | | | short, | 96 |
| *Preble,* | 80 | 30 | 36 " | long, | 36 |
| Six gun-boats, | 420 | 246 | 252 " | long, | 144 |
| | | | | short, | 108 |
| Four gun-boats, | 160 | 104 | 48 " | long, | 48 |

[1] In the Naval Archives are numerous letters from Macdonough, in which he states continually that, as fast as they arrive, he substitutes sailors for the soldiers with which the vessels were originally manned. Men were continually being sent ashore on account of sickness. In the Bureau of Navigation is the log-book of "sloop-of-war *Surprise,* Captain Robert Henly" (*Surprise* was the name the *Eagle* originally went by). It mentions from time to time that men were buried and sent ashore to the hospital (five being sent ashore on September 2d); and finally mentions that the places of the absent were partially filled by a draft of 21 soldiers, to act as marines. The notes on the day of battle are very brief.

In all, 14 vessels of 2,244 tons and 882 men, with 86 guns throwing at a broadside 1,194 lbs. of shot, 480 from long, and 714 from short guns.

The force of the British squadron in guns and ships is known accurately, as most of it was captured. The *Confiance* rated for years in our lists as a frigate of the class of the *Constellation, Congress,* and *Macedonian;* she was thus of over 1,200 tons. (Cooper says more, "nearly double the tonnage of the *Saratoga.*") She carried on her main-deck thirty long 24's, fifteen in each broadside. She did not have a complete spar-deck; on her poop, which came forward to the mizzen-mast, were two 32-pound (or possibly 42-pound) carronades and on her spacious top-gallant forecastle were four 32- (or 42-) pound carronades, and a long 24 on a pivot.[1] She had aboard her a furnace for heating shot; eight or ten of which heated shot were found with the furnace.[2] This was, of course, a perfectly legitimate advantage. The *Linnet,* Captain Daniel Pring, was a brig of the same size as the *Ticonderoga,* mounting 16 long 12's. The *Chubb* and *Finch,* Lieutenants James McGhie and William Hicks, were formerly the American sloops *Growler* and *Eagle,* of 112 and 110 tons respectively. The former mounted ten 18-pound carronades and one long 6; the latter, six 18-pound carronades, four long 6's, and one short 18. There were twelve gun-boats.[3] Five of these were large, of about 70 tons each; three mounted a long 24 and a 32-pound carronade each; one mounted a long 18 and a 32-pound carronade; one a long 18 and a short 18. Seven were smaller, of about 40 tons each; three of these carried each a long 18, and four carried each a 32-pound carronade. There is greater difficulty in finding out the number of men in the British fleet. American historians are unanimous in stating it at from 1,000 to 1,100; British historians never do any thing but copy James blindly. Midshipman Lea of the *Confiance,* in a letter (already quoted) published in the "London Naval Chronicle," vol. xxxii, p. 292, gives her crew as 300; but more than this amount of dead and prisoners were taken out of her. The number given her by Commander Ward in his "Naval Tactics," is probably nearest right—325.[4] The *Linnet* had about 125 men, and the *Chubb* and *Finch* about 50 men each. According to Admiral Paulding (given by Lossing, in his "Field-Book of the War of 1812," p. 868) their gun-boats averaged 50 men each. This is probably true, as they were manned largely by soldiers, any number of whom could be spared from Sir George Prevost's great army; but it may be best to consider the large ones as having 41, and the small 26 men, which were the complements of the American gun-boats of the same sizes.

---

[1] This is her armament as given by Cooper, on the authority of Lieutenant E. A. F. Lavallette, who was in charge of her for three months, and went aboard her ten minutes after the *Linnet* struck.

[2] James stigmatizes the statement of Commodore Macdonough about the furnace as "as gross a falsehood as ever was uttered"; but he gives no authority for the denial, and it appears to have been merely an ebullition of spleen on his part. Every American officer who went aboard the *Confiance* saw the furnace and the hot shot.

[3] Letter of General George Prevost, Sept. 11, 1814. All the American accounts say 13; the British official account had best be taken. James says only ten, but gives no authority; he appears to have been entirely ignorant of all things connected with this action.

[4] James gives her but 270 men,—without stating his authority.

The following, then, is the force of

DOWNIE'S SQUADRON

| NAME. | TONNAGE. | CREW. | BROADSIDE. | FROM WHAT GUNS, LONG OR SHORT. |
|---|---|---|---|---|
| *Confiance,* | 1,200 | 325 | 480 lbs. | long, 384<br>short, 96 |
| *Linnet,* | 350 | 125 | 96 " | long, 96 |
| *Chubb,* | 112 | 50 | 96 " | long, 6<br>short, 90 |
| *Finch,* | 110 | 50 | 84 " | long, 12<br>short, 72 |
| Five gun-boats, | 350 | 205 | 254 " | long, 12<br>short, 72 |
| Seven gun-boats, | 280 | 182 | 182 " | long, 54<br>short,128 |

In all, 16 vessels, of about 2,402 tons, with 937 men,[1] and a total of 92 guns, throwing at a broadside 1,192 lbs., 660 from long and 532 from short pieces.

These are widely different from the figures that appear in the pages of most British historians, from Sir Archibald Alison down and up. Thus, in the "History of the British Navy," by C. D. Yonge (already quoted), it is said that on Lake Champlain "our (the British) force was manifestly and vastly inferior, * * * their (the American) broadside outweighing ours in more than the proportion of three to two, while the difference in their tonnage and in the number of their crews was still more in their favor." None of these historians, or quasi-historians, have made the faintest effort to find out the facts for themselves, following James' figures with blind reliance, and accordingly it is only necessary to discuss the latter. This reputable gentleman ends his account ("Naval Occurrences," p. 424) by remarking that Macdonough wrote as he did because "he knew that nothing would stamp a falsehood with currency equal to a pious expression, * * * his falsehoods equalling in number the lines of his letter." These remarks are interesting as showing the unbiassed and truthful character of the author, rather than for any particular weight they will have in influencing any one's judgment on Commodore Macdonough. James gives the engaged force of the British as "8 vessels, of 1,426 tons, with 537 men, and throwing 765 lbs. of shot." To reduce the force down to this, he first excludes the *Finch,* because she "grounded opposite an American battery *before the engagement commenced,*" which reads especially well in connection with Capt. Pring's official letter: "Lieut. Hicks, of the *Finch,* had the mortification to strike on a reef of rocks to the eastward of Crab Island *about the middle of the engagement.*"[2] What James means

---

[1] About; there were probably more rather than less.
[2] The italics are mine. The letter is given in full in the "Naval Chronicle."

cannot be imagined; no stretch of language will convert "about the middle of" into "before." The *Finch* struck on the reef in consequence of having been disabled and rendered helpless by the fire from the *Ticonderoga*. Adding her force to James' statement (counting her crew only as he gives it), we get 9 vessels, 1,536 tons, 577 men, 849 lbs. of shot. James also excludes five gun-boats, because they ran away almost as soon as the action commenced (vol. vi, p. 501). This assertion is by no means equivalent to the statement in Captain Pring's letter "that the flotilla of gun-boats had abandoned the object assigned to them," and, if it was, it would not warrant his excluding the five gun-boats. Their flight may have been disgraceful, but they formed part of the attacking force nevertheless; almost any general could say that he had won against superior numbers if he refused to count in any of his own men whom he suspected of behaving badly. James gives his 10 gun-boats 294 men and 13 guns (two long 24's, five long 18's, six 32-pound carronades), and makes them average 45 tons; adding on the five he leaves out, we get 14 vessels, of 1,761 tons, with 714 men, throwing at a broadside 1,025 lbs. of shot (591 from long guns, 434 from carronades). But Sir George Prevost, in the letter already quoted, says there were 12 gun-boats, and the American accounts say more. Supposing the two gun-boats James did not include at all to be equal respectively to one of the largest and one of the smallest of the gun-boats as he gives them ("Naval Occurrences," p. 417); that is, one to have had 35 men, a long 24, and a 32-pound carronade, the other, 25 men and a 32-pound carronade, we get for Downie's force 16 vessels, of 1,851 tons, with 774 men, throwing at a broadside 1,113 lbs. of shot (615 from long guns, 498 from carronades). It must be remembered that so far I have merely corrected James by means of the authorities from which he draws his account—the official letters of the British commanders. I have not brought up a single American authority against him, but have only made such alterations as a writer could with nothing whatever but the accounts of Sir George Prevost and Captain Pring before him to compare with James. Thus it is seen that according to James himself Downie really had 774 men to Macdonough's 882, and threw at a broadside 1,113 lbs. of shot to Macdonough's 1,194 lbs. James says ("Naval Occurrences," pp. 410, 413): "Let it be recollected, no musketry was employed on either side," and "The marines were of no use, as the action was fought out of the range of musketry"; the 106 additional men on the part of the Americans were thus not of much consequence, the action being fought at anchor, and there being men enough to manage the guns and perform every other duty. So we need only attend to the broadside force. Here, then, Downie could present at a broadside 615 lbs. of shot from long guns to Macdonough's 480, and 498 lbs. from carronades to Macdonough's 714; or, he threw 135 lbs. of shot more from his long guns, and 216 less from his carronades. This is equivalent to Downie's having seven long 18's and one long 9, and Macdonough's having one 24-pound and six 32-pound carronades. A 32-pound carronade is not equal to a long 18; so that *even by James' own showing Downie's force was slightly the superior.*

Thus far, I may repeat, I have corrected James solely by the evidence of his own side; now I shall bring in some American authorities. These do not contradict the British official letters, for they virtually agree with them; but they do go against James' unsupported assertions, and, being made by naval officers of irreproachable reputation, will certainly outweigh them. In the first place, James asserts that on the main-deck of the *Confiance* but 13 guns were presented in broadside, two 32-pound carronades being thrust through the bridle- and two others through the stern-ports; so he excludes two of her guns from the broadside. Such guns would have been of great use to her at certain stages of the combat, and ought to be included in the force. But besides this the American officers positively say that she had a *broadside* of 15 guns. Adding these two guns, and making a trifling change in the arrangement of the guns in the row-galleys, we get a broadside of 1,192 lbs., exactly as I have given it above. There is no difficulty in accounting for the difference of tonnage as given by James and by the Americans, for we have considered the same subject in reference to the battle of Lake Erie. James calculates the American tonnage as if for sea-vessels of deep holds, while, as regards the British vessels, he allows for the shallow holds that all the lake craft had; that is, he gives in one the nominal, in the other the real, tonnage. This fully accounts for the discrepancy. It only remains to account for the difference in the number of men. From James we can get 772. In the first place, we can reason by analogy. I have already shown that, as regards the battle of Lake Erie, he is convicted (by English, not by American, evidence) of having underestimated Barclay's force by about 25 per cent. If he did the same thing here, the British force was over 1,000 strong, and I have no doubt that it was. But we have other proofs. On p. 417 of the "Naval Occurrences" he says the complement of the four captured British vessels amounted to 420 men, of whom 54 were killed in action, leaving 366 prisoners, including the wounded. But the report of prisoners, as given by the American authorities, gives 369 officers and seamen unhurt or but slightly wounded, 57 wounded men paroled, and other wounded whose number was unspecified. Supposing this number to have been 82, and adding 54 dead, we would get in all 550 men for the four ships, the number I have adopted in my list. This would make the British wounded 129 instead of 116, as James says: but neither the Americans nor the British seem to have enumerated all their wounded in this fight. Taking into account all these considerations, it will be seen that the figures I have given are probably approximately correct, and, at any rate, indicate pretty closely the *relative* strength of the two squadrons. The slight differences in tonnage and crews (158 tons and 55 men, in favor of the British) are so trivial that they need not be taken into account, and we will merely consider the broadside force. In absolute weight of metal the two combatants were evenly matched—almost exactly;—but whereas from Downie's broadside of 1,192 lbs. 660 were from long and 532 from short guns, of Macdonough's broadside of 1,194 lbs., but 480 were from long and 714 from short pieces. The forces were thus equal, except that Downie opposed 180 lbs. from long guns to 182 from carronades; as if

10 long 18's were opposed to ten 18-pound carronades. This would make the odds on their face about 10 to 9 against the Americans; in reality they were greater, for the possession of the *Confiance* was a very great advantage. The action is, as regards metal, the exact reverse of those between Chauncy and Yeo. Take, for example, the fight off Burlington on Sept. 28, 1813. Yeo's broadside was 1,374 lbs. to Chauncy's 1,288; but whereas only 180 of Yeo's was from long guns, of Chauncy's but 536 was from carronades. Chauncy's fleet was thus much the superior. At least we must say this: if Macdonough beat merely an equal force, then Yeo made a most disgraceful and cowardly flight before an inferior foe; but if we contend that Macdonough's force was inferior to that of his antagonist, then we must admit that Yeo's was in like manner inferior to Chauncy's. These rules work both ways. The *Confiance* was a heavier vessel than the *Pike,* presenting in broadside one long 24- and three 32-pound carronades more than the latter. James (vol. vi, p. 355) says: "The *Pike* alone was nearly a match for Sir James Yeo's squadron," and Brenton says (vol. ii, 503): "The *General Pike* was more than a match for the whole British squadron." Neither of these writers means quite as much as he says, for the logical result would be that the *Confiance* alone was a match for all of Macdonough's force. Still it is safe to say that the *Pike* gave Chauncy a great advantage, and that the *Confiance* made Downie's fleet much superior to Macdonough's.

Macdonough saw that the British would be forced to make the attack in order to get the control of the waters. On this long, narrow lake the winds usually blow pretty nearly north or south, and the set of the current is of course northward; all the vessels, being flat and shallow, could not beat to windward well, so there was little chance of the British making the attack when there was a southerly wind blowing. So late in the season there was danger of sudden and furious gales, which would make it risky for Downie to wait outside the bay till the wind suited him; and inside the bay the wind was pretty sure to be light and baffling. Young Macdonough (then but 28 years of age) calculated all these chances very coolly and decided to await the attack at anchor in Plattsburg Bay, with the head of his line so far to the north that it could hardly be turned; and then proceeded to make all the other preparations with the same foresight. Not only were his vessels provided with springs, but also with anchors to be used astern in any emergency. The *Saratoga* was further prepared for a change of wind, or for the necessity of winding ship, by having a kedge planted broad off on each of her bows, with a hawser and preventer hawser (hanging in bights under water) leading from each quarter to the kedge on that side. There had not been time to train the men thoroughly at the guns; and to make these produce their full effect the constant supervision of the officers had to be exerted. The British were laboring under this same disadvantage, but neither side felt the want very much, as the smooth water, stationary position of the ships, and fair range, made the fire of both sides very destructive.

Plattsburg Bay is deep and opens to the southward; so that a wind which would enable the British to sail up the lake would force them to beat when entering the bay. The east side of the mouth of the bay is formed by Cumberland Head; the entrance is about a mile and a half across, and the other boundary, southwest from the Head, is an extensive shoal, and a small, low island. This is called Crab Island, and on it was a hospital and one six-pounder gun, which was to be manned in case of necessity by the strongest patients. Macdonough had anchored in a north-and-south line a little to the south of the outlet of the Saranac, and out of range of the shore batteries, being two miles from the western shore. The head of his line was so near Cumberland Head that an attempt to turn it would place the opponent under a very heavy fire, while to the south the shoal prevented a flank attack. The *Eagle* lay to the north, flanked on each side by a couple of gun-boats; then came the *Saratoga,* with three gun-boats between her and the *Ticonderoga,* the next in line; then came three gun-boats and the *Preble.* The four large vessels were at anchor; the galleys being under their sweeps and forming a second line about 40 yards back, some of them keeping their places and some not doing so. By this arrangement his line could not be doubled upon, there was not room to anchor on his broadside out of reach of his carronades, and the enemy was forced to attack him by standing in bows on.

The morning of September 11th opened with a light breeze from the northeast. Downie's fleet weighed anchor at daylight, and came down the lake with the wind nearly aft, the booms of the two sloops swinging out to starboard. At half-past seven,[1] the people in the ships could see their adversaries' upper sails across the narrow strip of land ending in Cumberland Head, before the British doubled the latter. Captain Downie hove to with his four large vessels when he had fairly opened the Bay, and waited for his galleys to overtake him. Then his four vessels filled on the starboard tack and headed for the American line, going abreast, the *Chubb* to the north, heading well to windward of the *Eagle,* for whose bows the *Linnet* was headed, while the *Confiance* was to be laid athwart the hawse of the *Saratoga;* the *Finch* was to leeward with the twelve gun-boats, and was to engage the rear of the American line.

As the English squadron stood bravely in, young Macdonough, who feared his foes not at all, but his God a great deal, knelt for a moment, with his officers, on the quarter-deck; and then ensued a few minutes of perfect quiet, the men waiting with grim expectancy for the opening of the fight. The *Eagle* spoke first with her long 18's, but to no effect, for the shot fell short. Then, as the *Linnet* passed the *Saratoga,* she fired her broadside of long 12's, but her shot also fell short, except one that struck a hen-coop which happened to be aboard the *Saratoga.* There was a game cock inside, and, instead of being frightened at his sudden release, he jumped up on a gun-slide, clapped his wings, and crowed lustily. The men laughed and cheered; and immediately afterward Macdonough himself fired the first shot from one of the long guns. The 24-pound

---

[1] The letters of the two commanders conflict a little as to time, both absolutely and relatively. Pring says the action lasted two hours and three quarters; the American accounts, two hours and twenty minutes. Pring says it began at 8.00; Macdonough says a few minutes before nine, etc. I take the mean time.

ball struck the *Confiance* near the hawse-hole and ranged the length of her deck, killing and wounding several men. All the American long guns now opened and were replied to by the British galleys.

The *Confiance* stood steadily on without replying. But she was baffled by shifting winds, and was soon so cut up, having both her port bow-anchors shot away, and suffering much loss, that she was obliged to port her helm and come to while still nearly a quarter of a mile distant from the *Saratoga.* Captain Downie came to anchor in grand style,—securing every thing carefully before he fired a gun, and then opening with a terribly destructive broadside. The *Chubb* and *Linnet* stood farther in, and anchored forward the *Eagle's* beam. Meanwhile the *Finch* got abreast of the *Ticonderoga,* under her sweeps, supported by the gun-boats. The main fighting was thus to take place between the vans, where the *Eagle, Saratoga,* and six or seven gun-boats were engaged with the *Chubb, Linnet, Confiance,* and two or three gun-boats; while in the rear, the *Ticonderoga,* the *Preble,* and the other American galleys engaged the *Finch* and the remaining nine or ten English galleys. The battle at the foot of the line was fought on the part of the Americans to prevent their flank being turned, and on the part of the British to effect that object. At first the fighting was at long range, but gradually the British galleys closed up, firing very well. The American galleys at this end of the line were chiefly the small ones, armed with one 12-pounder apiece, and they by degrees drew back before the heavy fire of their opponents. About an hour after the discharge of the first gun had been fired the *Finch* closed up toward the *Ticonderoga,* and was completely crippled by a couple of broadsides from the latter. She drifted helplessly down the line and grounded near Crab Island; some of the convalescent patients manned the six-pounder and fired a shot or two at her, when she struck, nearly half of her crew being killed or wounded. About the same time the British gun-boats forced the *Preble* out of line, whereupon she cut her cable and drifted inshore out of the fight. Two or three of the British gun-boats had already been sufficiently damaged by some of the shot from the *Ticonderoga's* long guns to make them wary; and the contest at this part of the line narrowed down to one between the American schooner and the remaining British gun-boats, who combined to make a most determined attack upon her. So hastily had the squadron been fitted out that many of the matches for her guns were at the last moment found to be defective. The captain of one of the divisions was a midshipman, but sixteen years old, Hiram Paulding. When he found the matches to be bad he fired the guns of his section by having pistols flashed at them, and continued this through the whole fight. The *Ticonderoga's* commander, Lieut. Cassin, fought his schooner most nobly. He kept walking the taffrail amidst showers of musketry and grape, coolly watching the movements of the galleys and directing the guns to be loaded with canister and bags of bullets, when the enemy tried to board. The British galleys were handled with determined gallantry, under the command of Lieutenant Bell. Had they driven off the *Ticonderoga* they would have won the day for their side, and they pushed up till they were not a boat-hook's length distant, to try to carry her by boarding; but every attempt was repulsed and they were forced to draw off, some of them so crippled by the slaughter they had suffered that they could hardly man the oars.

Meanwhile the fighting at the head of the line had been even fiercer. The first broadside of the *Confiance*, fired from 16 long 24's, double shotted, coolly sighted, in smooth water, at point-blank range, produced the most terrible effect on the *Saratoga*. Her hull shivered all over with the shock, and when the crash subsided nearly half of her people were seen stretched on deck, for many had been knocked down who were not seriously hurt. Among the slain was her first lieutenant, Peter Gamble; he was kneeling down to sight the bow-gun, when a shot entered the port, split the quoin, and drove a portion of it against his side, killing him without breaking the skin. The survivors carried on the fight with undiminished energy. Macdonough himself worked like a common sailor, in pointing and handling a favorite gun. While bending over to sight it a round shot cut in two the spanker boom, which fell on his head and struck him senseless for two or three minutes; he then leaped to his feet and continued as before, when a shot took off the head of the captain of the gun and drove it in his face with such a force as to knock him to the other side of the deck. But after the first broadside not so much injury was done; the guns of the *Confiance* had been levelled to point-blank range, and as the quoins were loosened by the successive discharges they were not properly replaced, so that her broadsides kept going higher and higher and doing less and less damage. Very shortly after the beginning of the action her gallant captain was slain. He was standing behind one of the long guns when a shot from the *Saratoga* struck it and threw it completely off the carriage against his right groin, killing him almost instantly. His skin was not broken; a black mark, about the size of a small plate, was the only visible injury. His watch was found flattened, with its hands pointing to the very second at which he received the fatal blow. As the contest went on the fire gradually decreased in weight, the guns being disabled. The inexperience of both crews partly caused this. The American sailors overloaded their carronades so as to very much destroy the effect of their fire; when the officers became disabled, the men would cram the guns with shot till the last projected from the muzzle. Of course, this lessened the execution, and also gradually crippled the guns. On board the *Confiance* the confusion was even worse: after the battle the charges of the guns were drawn, and on the side she had fought one was found with a canvas bag containing two round of shot rammed home and wadded without any powder; another with two cartridges and no shot; and a third with a wad below the cartridge.

At the extreme head of the line the advantage had been with the British. The *Chubb* and *Linnet* had begun a brisk engagement with the *Eagle* and American gun-boats. In a short time the *Chubb* had her cable, bowsprit, and main-boom shot away, drifted within the American lines, and was taken possession of by one of the *Saratoga*'s midshipmen. The *Linnet* paid no attention to the American gun-boats, directing her whole fire against the *Eagle*, and the latter was, in addition, exposed to part of the fire of the *Confiance*. After keeping up a heavy fire for a long time her springs were shot away, and she came up into the wind, hanging so that she could not return a shot to the well-directed broadsides of the *Linnet*. Henly accordingly cut his cable, started home his top-sails, ran down, and anchored by the stern between and inshore of the *Confiance* and *Ticonderoga,* from which position he opened on the *Confiance*. The *Linnet* now directed her attention to the American gun-boats, which at this end of the line were very well fought, but she soon drove them off, and then sprung her broadside so as to rake the *Saratoga* on her bows.

Macdonough by this time had his hands full, and his fire was slackening; he was bearing the whole brunt of the action, with the frigate on his beam and the brig raking him. Twice his ship had been set on fire by the hot shot of the *Confiance;* one by one his long guns were disabled by shot, and his carronades were either treated the same way or else rendered useless by excessive overcharging. Finally but a single carronade was left in the starboard batteries, and on firing it the naval-bolt broke, the gun flew off the carriage and fell down the main hatch, leaving the Commodore without a single gun to oppose to the few the *Confiance* still presented. The battle would have been lost had not Macdonough's foresight provided the means of retrieving it. The anchor suspended astern of the *Saratoga* was let go, and the men hauled in on the hawser that led to the starboard quarter, bringing the ship's stern up over the kedge. The ship now rode by the kedge and by a line that had been bent to a bight in the stream cable, and she was raked badly by the accurate fire of the *Linnet*. By rousing on the line the ship was at length got so far round that the aftermost gun of the port broadside bore on the *Confiance*. The men had been sent forward to keep as much out of harm's way as possible, and now some were at once called back to man the piece, which then opened with effect. The next gun was treated in the same manner; but the ship now hung and would go no farther round. The hawser leading from the port quarter was then got forward under the bows and passed aft to the starboard quarter, and a minute afterward the ship's whole port battery opened with fatal effect. The *Confiance* meanwhile had also attempted to round. Her springs, like those of the *Linnet,* were on the starboard side, and so of course could not be shot away as the *Eagle*'s were; but, as she had nothing but springs to rely on, her efforts did little beyond forcing her forward, and she hung with her head to the wind. She had lost over half of her crew,[1] most of her guns on the engaged side were dismounted, and her stout masts had been splintered till they looked like bundles of matches; her sails had been torn to rags, and she was forced to strike, about two hours after she had fired the first broadside. Without pausing a minute the *Saratoga* again hauled on her starboard hawser till her broadside was sprung to bear on the *Linnet,* and the ship and brig began a brisk fight, which the *Eagle* from her position could take no part in, while the *Ticonderoga* was just finishing up the British galleys. The shattered and disabled state of the *Linnet*'s masts,

---

[1] Midshipman Lee, in his letter already quoted, says "not five men were left unhurt"; this would of course include bruises, etc., as hurts.

sails, and yards precluded the most distant hope of Capt. Pring's effecting his escape by cutting his cable; but he kept up a most gallant fight with his greatly superior foe, in hopes that some of the gun-boats would come and tow him off, and despatched a lieutenant to the *Confiance* to ascertain her state. The lieutenant returned with news of Capt. Downie's death, while the British gun-boats had been driven half a mile off; and, after having maintained the fight single-handed for fifteen minutes, until, from the number of shot between wind and water, the water had risen a foot above her lower deck, the plucky little brig hauled down her colors, and the fight ended, a little over two hours and a half after the first gun had been fired. Not one of the larger vessels had a mast that would bear canvas, and the prizes were in a sinking condition. The British galleys drifted to leeward, none with their colors up; but as the *Saratoga's* boarding-officer passed along the deck of the *Confiance* he accidentally ran against a lock-string of one of her starboard guns,[1] and it went off. This was apparently understood as a signal by the galleys, and they moved slowly off, pulling but a very few sweeps, and not one of them hoisting an ensign.

On both sides the ships had been cut up in the most extraordinary manner; the *Saratoga* had 55 shot-holes in her hull, and the *Confiance* 105 in hers, and the *Eagle* and *Linnet* had suffered in proportion. The number of killed and wounded can not be exactly stated; it was probably about 200 on the American side, and over 300 on the British.[2]

---

[1] A sufficient commentary, by the way, on James' assertion that the guns of the *Confiance* had to be fired by matches, as the gun-locks did not fit!

[2] Macdonough returned his loss as follows:

|  | KILLED. | WOUNDED. |
|---|---|---|
| *Saratoga*, | 28 | 29 |
| *Eagle*, | 13 | 20 |
| *Ticonderoga*, | 6 | 6 |
| *Preble*, | 2 | |
| *Boxer*, | 3 | 1 |
| *Centipede*, | | 1 |
| *Wilmer*, | | 1 |

A total of 52 killed and 58 wounded; but the latter head apparently only included those who had to go to the hospital. Probably about 90 additional were more or less slightly wounded. Captain Pring, in his letter of Sept. 12th, says the *Confiance* had 41 killed and 40 wounded; the *Linnet*, 10 killed and 14 wounded; the *Chubb*, 6 killed and 16 wounded; the *Finch*, 2 wounded: in all, 57 killed and 72 wounded. But he adds "that no opportunity has offered to muster * * * this is the whole as yet ascertained to be killed or wounded." The Americans took out 180 dead and wounded from the *Confiance*, 50 from the *Linnet*, and 40 from the *Chubb* and *Finch*; in all, 270. James ("Naval Occurrences," p. 412) says the *Confiance* had 83 wounded. As Captain Pring wrote his letter in Plattsburg Bay the day after the action, he of course could not give the loss aboard the British gun-boats; so James at once assumed that they suffered none. As well as could be found out they had between 50 and 100 killed and wounded. The total British loss was between 300 and 400, as nearly as can be ascertained. For this action, as already shown, James is of no use whatever. Compare his statements, for example, with those of Midshipman Lee, in the "Naval Chronicle." The comparative loss, as a means of testing the competitive prowess of the combatants, is not of much consequence in this case, as the weaker party in point of force conquered.

Captain Macdonough at once returned the British officers their swords. Captain Pring writes: "I have much satisfaction in making you acquainted with the humane treatment the wounded have received from Commodore Macdonough; they were immediately removed to his own hospital on Crab Island, and furnished with every requisite. His generous and polite attention to myself, the officers, and men, will ever hereafter be gratefully remembered." The effects of the victory were immediate and of the highest importance. Sir George Prevost and his army at once fled in great haste and confusion back to Canada, leaving our northern frontier clear for the remainder of the war; while the victory had a very great effect on the negotiations for peace.

In this battle the crews on both sides behaved with equal bravery, and left nothing to be desired in this respect; but from their rawness they of course showed far less skill than the crews of most of the American and some of the British ocean cruisers, such as the *Constitution, United States,* or *Shannon,* the *Hornet, Wasp,* or *Reindeer.* Lieut. Cassin handled the *Ticonderoga,* and Captain Pring the *Linnet,* with the utmost gallantry and skill, and, after Macdonough, they divide the honors of the day. But Macdonough in this battle won a higher fame than any other commander of the war, British or American. He had a decidedly superior force to contend against, the officers and men of the two sides being about on a par in every respect; and it was solely owing to his foresight and resource that we won the victory. He forced the British to engage at a disadvantage by his excellent choice of position; and he prepared beforehand for every possible contingency. His personal prowess had already been shown at the cost of the rovers of Tripoli, and in this action he helped fight the guns as ably as the best sailor. His skill, seamanship, quick eye, readiness of resource, and indomitable pluck, are beyond all praise. Down to the time of the Civil War he is the greatest figure in our naval history. A thoroughly religious man, he was as generous and humane as he was skilful and brave; one of the greatest of our sea-captains, he has left a stainless name behind him.

BRITISH LOSS

| NAME. | TONS. | GUNS. | REMARKS. |
|---|---|---|---|
| Brig, | 100 | 10 | Burnt by Lieut. Gregory, |
| *Magnet,* | 187 | 12 | " by her crew. |
| *Black Snake,* | 30 | 1 | Captured. |
| Gun-boat, | 50 | 2 | " |
| " | 50 | 3 | " |
| *Confiance,* | 1,200 | 37 | " |
| *Linnet,* | 350 | 16 | " |
| *Chubb,* | 112 | 11 | " |
| *Finch,* | 110 | 11 | " |
| 9 vessels, | 2,189 | 103 | |

## AMERICAN LOSS

| NAME. | TONS. | GUNS. | REMARKS. |
|---|---|---|---|
| *Growler,* | 81 | 7 | Captured. |
| Boat, | 50 | 2 | " |
| *Tigress,* | 96 | 1 | " |
| *Scorpion,* | 86 | 2 | " |
| *Ohio,* | 94 | 1 | " |
| *Somers,* | 98 | 2 | " |
| 6 vessels, | 505 | 15 | |

# IX

# 1815

# CONCLUDING OPERATIONS

*President* captured by Captain Hayes' squadron · Successful cutting-out expeditions of the Americans · Privateer brig *Chasseur* captures *St. Lawrence* schooner · *Constitution* captures *Cyane* and *Levant* · Escapes from a British squadron · The *Hornet* captures the *Penguin*, and escapes from a 74 · The *Peacock* and the *Nautilus* · Summary · Remarks on the war · Tables of comparative loss, etc. · Compared with results of Anglo-French struggle

The treaty of peace between the United States and Great Britain was signed at Ghent, Dec. 24, 1814, and ratified at Washington, Feb. 18, 1815. But during these first two months of 1815, and until the news reached the cruisers on the ocean, the warfare went on with much the same characteristics as before. The blockading squadrons continued standing on and off before the ports containing war-ships with the same unwearying vigilance; but the ice and cold prevented any attempts at harrying the coast except from the few frigates scattered along the shores of the Carolinas and Georgia. There was no longer any formidable British fleet in the Chesapeake or Delaware, while at New Orleans the only available naval force of the Americans consisted of a few small row-boats, with which they harassed the rear of the retreating British. The *Constitution,* Capt. Stewart, was already at sea, having put out from Boston on the 17th of December, while the blockading squadron (composed of the same three frigates she subsequently encountered) was temporarily absent.

The *Hornet,* Capt. Biddle, had left the port of New London, running in heavy weather through the blockading squadron, and had gone into New York, where the *President,* Commodore Decatur, and *Peacock,* Capt. Warrington, with the *Tom Bowline* brig were already assembled, intending to start on a cruise for the East Indies. The blockading squadron off the port consisted of the 56-gun razee *Majestic,* Capt. Hayes, 24-pounder frigate *Endymion,* Capt. Hope, 18-pounder frigate *Pomone,* Capt. Lumly, and 18-pounder frigate *Tene-*

*dos,* Capt. Parker.[1] On the 14th of January a severe snow-storm came on and blew the squadron off the coast. Next day it moderated, and the ships stood off to the northwest to get into the track which they supposed the Americans would take if they attempted to put out in the storm. Singularly enough, at the instant of arriving at the intended point, an hour before daylight on the 15th, Sandy Hook bearing W.N.W. 15 leagues, a ship was made out, on the *Majestic*'s weather-bow, standing S.E.[2] This ship was the unlucky *President.* On the evening of the 14th she had left her consorts at anchor, and put out to sea in the gale. But by a mistake of the pilots who were to place boats to beacon the passage the frigate struck on the bar, where she beat heavily for an hour and a half,[3] springing her masts and becoming very much hogged and twisted.[4] Owing to the severity of her injuries the *President* would have put back to port, but was prevented by the westerly gale.[5] Accordingly Decatur steered at first along Long Island, then shaped his course to the S.E., and in the dark ran into the British squadron, which, but for his unfortunate accident, he would thus have escaped. At daylight, the *President,* which had hauled up and passed to the northward of her opponents,[6] found herself with the *Majestic* and *Endymion* astern, the *Pomone* on the port and the *Tenedos* on the starboard quarter.[7] The chase now became very interesting.[8] During the early part of the day, while the wind was still strong, the *Majestic* led the *Endymion* and fired occasionally at the *President,* but without effect.[9] The *Pomone* gained faster than the others, but by Capt. Hayes' orders was signalled to go in chase of the *Tenedos,* whose character the captain could not make out[10]; and this delayed her several hours in the chase.[11] In the afternoon, the wind coming out light and baffling, the *Endymion* left the *Majestic* behind,[12] and, owing to the *President*'s disabled state and the amount of water she made in consequence of the injuries received while on the bar, gained rapidly on her,[13] although she lightened ship and did every thing else that was possible to improve her sailing.[14] But a shift of wind helped the *Endymion,*[15] and the latter was able at about 2.30, to begin skirmishing with her bow-chasers, answered by the stern-chasers of the *President.*[16] At 5.30 the *Endymion* began close

[1] Letter of Rear-Admiral Hotham, Jan. 23, 1815.

[2] Letter of Capt. Hayes, Jan. 17, 1815.

[3] Letter of Commodore Decatur, Jan. 18, 1815.

[4] Report of Court-martial, Alex. Murray presiding, April 20, 1815.

[5] Decatur's letter, Jan. 18th.

[6] Decatur's letter, Jan, 18th.

[7] James, vi, 529.

[8] Letter of Capt. Hayes.

[9] Letter of Commodore Decatur.

[10] James, vi, 529.

[11] Log of the *Pomone,* published at Bermuda, Jan. 29, and quoted in full in the "Naval Chronicle," xxxiii, 370.

[12] Letter of Captain Hayes.

[13] Letter of Decatur.

[14] Letter of Decatur.

[15] Cooper, ii, 466.

[16] Log of the *Pomone.*

action,[1] within half point-blank-shot on the *President*'s starboard quarter,[2] where not a gun of the latter could bear.[3] The *President* continued in the same course, steering east by north, the wind being northwest, expecting the *Endymion* soon to come up abeam; but the latter warily kept her position by yawing, so as not to close.[4] So things continued for half an hour during which the *President* suffered more than during all the remainder of the combat.[5] At 6.00 the *President* kept off, heading to the south, and the two adversaries ran abreast, the Americans using the starboard and the British the port batteries.[6] Decatur tried to close with his antagonist, but whenever he hauled nearer to the latter she hauled off[7] and being the swiftest ship could of course evade him; so he was reduced to the necessity of trying to throw her out of the combat[8] by dismantling her. He was completely successful in this, and after two hours' fighting the *Endymion*'s sails were all cut from her yards[9] and she dropped astern, the last shot being fired from the *President*.[10] The *Endymion* was now completely silent,[11] and Commodore Decatur did not board her merely because her consorts were too close astern[12]; accordingly the *President* hauled up again to try her chances at running, having even her royal studding-sails set,[13] and exposed her stern to the broadside of the *Endymion*,[14] but the latter did not fire a single gun.[15] Three hours afterward, at 11,[16] the *Pomone* caught up with the *President*, and luffing to port gave her the starboard broadside[17]; the *Tenedos* being two cables' length's distance astern, taking up a raking position.[18] The *Pomone* poured in another broadside, within musket shot,[19] when the *President* surrendered and was taken possession of by Capt. Parker of the *Tenedos*.[20] A considerable number of the *President*'s people were killed by these two last broadsides.[21] The *Endymion* was at this time out of sight astern.[22] She did

---

[1] Letter of Capt. Hayes.

[2] James, vi, 530.

[3] Letter of Decatur.

[4] Letter of Decatur.

[5] Cooper, 470.

[6] Log of the *Pomone*.

[7] Report of Court-martial.

[8] Letter of Commodore Decatur.

[9] Letter of Capt. Hayes.

[10] Log of the *Pomone*.

[11] Log of the *Pomone*.

[12] Report of Court-martial.

[13] James, vi, 538.

[14] Letter of Commodore Decatur.

[15] Log of the *Pomone*.

[16] Letter of Capt. Hayes.

[17] Log of the *Pomone*.

[18] Decatur's letter.

[19] Log of the *Pomone*.

[20] James, vi, 531.

[21] Letter of Commodore Decatur, March 6, 1815; deposition of Chaplain Henry Robinson before Admiralty Court at St. Georges, Bermuda, Jan. 1815.

[22] Letter of Decatur, Jan. 18th.

not come up, according to one account, for an hour and three quarters,[1] and according to another, for three hours[2]; and as she was a faster ship than the *President*, this means that she was at least two hours motionless repairing damages. Commodore Decatur delivered his sword to Capt. Hayes of the *Majestic*, who returned it, stating in his letter that both sides had fought with great gallantry.[3] The *President* having been taken by an entire squadron,[4] the prize-money was divided equally among the ships.[5] The *President's* crew all told consisted of 450 men,[6] none of whom were British.[7] She had thus a hundred more men than her antagonist and threw about 100 pounds more shot at a broadside; but these advantages were more than counterbalanced by the injuries received on the bar, and by the fact that her powder was so bad that while some of the British shot went through both her sides, such a thing did not once happen to the *Endymion*,[8] when fairly hulled. The *President* lost 24 killed and 55 wounded[9]; the *Endymion*, 11 killed and 14 wounded.[10] Two days afterward, on their way to the Bermudas, a violent easterly gale came on, during which both ships were dismasted, and the *Endymion* in addition had to throw over all her spar-deck guns.[11]

As can be seen, almost every sentence of this account is taken (very nearly word for word) from the various official reports, relying especially on the log of the British frigate *Pomone*. I have been thus careful to have every point of the narrative established by unimpeachable reference: first, because there have been quite a number of British historians who have treated the conflict as if it were a victory and not a defeat for the *Endymion;* and in the second place, because I regret to say that I do not think that the facts bear out the assertions, on the part of most American authors, that Commodore Decatur "covered himself with glory" and showed the "utmost heroism." As regards the first point, Captain Hope himself, in his singularly short official letter, does little beyond detail his own loss, and makes no claim to having vanquished his opponent. Almost all the talk about its being a "victory" comes from James; and in recounting this, as well as all the other battles, nearly every subsequent British historian simply gives James' statements over again, occasionally amplifying, but more often altering or omitting, the vituperation. The point at issue is simply this: could a frigate which, according to James himself, went out of action with every sail set, take another frigate which for two hours, according to the log of the *Pomone*, lay motionless and unmanageable on the waters, without a sail? To prove that it

---

[1] Log of the *Pomone*.
[2] Letter of Decatur, Mar. 6th.
[3] Letter of Capt. Hayes.
[4] Admiral Hotham's letter, Jan. 23d.
[5] Bermuda "Royal Gazette," March 8, 1815.
[6] Depositions of Lieut. Gallagher and the other officers.
[7] Deposition of Commodore Decatur.
[8] Bermuda "Royal Gazette," Jan. 6, 1818.
[9] Decatur's letter.
[10] Letter of Capt. Hope, Jan. 15, 1815.
[11] James, vi, 534.

could not, of course needs some not over-scrupulous manipulation of the facts. The intention with which James sets about his work can be gathered from the triumphant conclusion he comes to, that Decatur's name has been "sunk quite as low as that of Bainbridge or Porter," which, comparing small things to great, is somewhat like saying that Napoleon's defeat by Wellington and Blucher "sunk" him to the level of Hannibal. For the account of the American crew and loss, James relies on the statements made in the Bermuda papers, of whose subsequent forced retraction he takes no notice, and of course largely over-estimates both. On the same authority he states that the *President*'s fire was "silenced," Commodore Decatur stating the exact reverse. The point is fortunately settled by the log of the *Pomone*, which distinctly says that the last shot was fired by the *President*. His last resort is to state that the loss of the *President* was fourfold (in reality three-fold) that of the *Endymion*. Now we have seen that the *President* lost "a considerable number" of men from the fire of the *Pomone*. Estimating these at only nineteen, we have a loss of sixty caused by the *Endymion*, and as most of this was caused during the first half hour, when the *President* was not firing, it follows that while the two vessels were *both* fighting, broadside and broadside, the loss inflicted was about equal; or, the *President*, aiming at her adversary's rigging, succeeded in completely disabling her, and incidentally killed 25 men, while the *Endymion* did not hurt the *President*'s rigging at all, and, aiming at her hull, where, of course, the slaughter *ought* to have been far greater than when the fire was directed aloft, only killed about the same number of men. Had there been no other vessels in chase, Commodore Decatur, his adversary having been thus rendered perfectly helpless, could have simply taken any position he chose and compelled the latter to strike, without suffering any material additional loss himself. As in such a case he would neither have endured the unanswered fire of the *Endymion* on his quarter for the first half hour, nor the subsequent broadsides of the *Pomone*, the *President*'s loss would probably have been no greater than that of the *Constitution* in taking the *Java*. It is difficult to see how any outsider with an ounce of common-sense and fairmindedness can help awarding the palm to Decatur, as regards the action with the *Endymion*. But I regret to say that I must agree with James that he acted rather tamely, certainly not heroically, in striking to the *Pomone*. There was, of course, not much chance of success in doing battle with two fresh frigates; but then they only mounted eighteen-pounders, and, judging from the slight results of the cannonading from the *Endymion* and the two first (usually the most fatal) broadsides of the *Pomone*, it would have been rather a long time before they would have caused much damage. Meanwhile the *President* was pretty nearly as well off as ever as far as fighting and sailing went. A lucky shot might have disabled one of her opponents, and then the other would, in all probability, have undergone the same fate as the *Endymion*. At least it was well worth trying, and though Decatur could not be said to be disgraced, yet it is excusable to wish that Porter or Perry had been in his place. It is not very pleasant to criticise the actions of an American whose name is better known than that of almost any other single-ship captain of his time; but if a man is as much to be praised for doing fairly, or even badly, as for doing excellently, then there is no use in bestowing praise at all.

This is perhaps as good a place as any other to notice one or two of James' most common misstatements; they really would not need refutation were it not that they have been reëchoed, as usual, by almost every British historian of the war for the last 60 years. In the first place, James puts the number of the *President*'s men at 475; she had 450. An exactly parallel reduction must often be made when he speaks of the force of an American ship. Then he says there were many British among them, which is denied under oath by the American officers; this holds good also for the other American frigates. He says there were but 4 boys; there were nearly 30; and on p. 120 he says the youngest was 14, whereas we incidentally learn from the "Life of Decatur" that several were under 12. A favorite accusation is that the American midshipmen were chiefly masters and mates of merchant-men; but this was hardly ever the case. Many of the midshipmen of the war afterward became celebrated commanders, and most of these (a notable instance being Farragut, the greatest admiral since Nelson) were entirely too young in 1812 to have had vessels under them, and, moreover, came largely from the so-called "best families."

Again, in the first two frigate actions of 1812, the proportion of killed to wounded happened to be unusually large on board the American frigates; accordingly James states (p. 146) that the returns of the wounded had been garbled, under-estimated, and made "subservient to the views of the commanders and their government." To support his position that Capt. Hull, who reported 7 killed and 7 wounded, had not given the list of the latter in full, he says that "an equal number of killed and wounded, as given in the American account, hardly ever occurs, except in cases of explosion"; and yet, on p. 519, he gives the loss of the British *Hermes* as 25 killed and 24 wounded, disregarding the incongruity involved. On p. 169, in noticing the loss of the *United States*, 5 killed and 7 wounded, he says that "the slightly wounded, as in all other American cases, are omitted." This is untrue, and the proportion on the *United States*, 5 to 7, is just about the same as that given by James himself on the *Endymion*, 11 to 14, and *Nautilus*, 6 to 8. In supporting his theory, James brings up all the instances where the American wounded bore a larger proportion to their dead than on board the British ships, but passes over the actions with the *Reindeer, Epervier, Penguin, Endymion,* and *Boxer,* where the reverse was the case. One of James' most common methods of attempting to throw discredit on the much vilified "Yankees" is by quoting newspaper accounts of their wounded. Thus he says (p. 562, of the *Hornet,* that several of her men told some of the *Penguin*'s sailors that she lost 10 men killed, 16 wounded, etc. Utterly false rumors of this kind were as often indulged in by the Americans as the British. After the capture of the *President* articles occasionally appeared in the papers to the effect that some American sailor had counted "23 dead" on board the *Endymion,* that "more than 50" of her men were wounded, etc. Such statements were as commonly made and with as little foundation by one side as by the other, and it is absurd for a historian to take any notice of them. James does no worse than many of our own writers of the same date; but while their writings have passed into oblivion, his work is still often accepted as a standard. This must be my apology for devoting so much time to it. The severest criticism to which it can possibly be subjected is to compare it with the truth. Whenever dealing with purely American affairs, James' history is as utterly untrustworthy as its contemporary, "Niles' Register," is in matters purely British, while both are invaluable in dealing with things relating strictly to their own nation; they supplement each other.

—

On Jan. 8th General Packenham was defeated and killed by General Jackson at New Orleans, the *Louisiana* and the seamen of the *Carolina* having their full share in the glory of the day, and Captain Henly being among the very few American wounded. On the same day Sailing-master Johnson, with 28 men in two boats, cut out the British armed-transport brig *Cyprus,* containing provisions and munitions of war, and manned by ten men.[1] On the 18th the British abandoned the enterprise and retreated to their ships; and Mr. Thomas Shields, a purser, formerly a sea-officer, set off to harass them while embarking. At sunset on the 20th he left with five boats and a gig, manned in all with 53 men, and having under him Sailing-master Daily and Master's Mate Boyd.[2] At ten o'clock P.M. a large barge, containing 14 seamen and 40 officers and men of the 14th Light Dragoons, was surprised and carried by boarding after a slight struggle. The prisoners outnumbering their captors, the latter returned to shore, left them in a place of safety, and again started at 2 A.M. on the morning of the 22d. Numerous transports and barges of the enemy could be seen, observing very little order and apparently taking no precautions against attack, which they probably did not apprehend. One of the American boats captured a transport and five men; another, containing Mr. Shields himself and eight men, carried by boarding, after a short resistance, a schooner carrying ten men. The flotilla then re-united and captured in succession, with no resistance, five barges containing 70 men. By this time the alarm had spread and they were attacked by six boats, but these were repelled with some loss. Seven of the prisoners (who were now half as many again as their captors) succeed in escaping in the smallest prize. Mr. Shields returned with the others, 78 in number. During the entire expedition he had lost but three men, wounded; he had taken 132 prisoners, and destroyed eight craft whose aggregate tonnage about equalled that of the five gun-vessels taken on Lake Borgne.

On Jan. 30, 1815, information was received by Captain Dent, commanding at North Edisto, Ga., that a party of British officers and men, in four boats belonging to H.M.S. *Hebrus,* Capt. Palmer, were watering at one of the adjacent is-

---

[1] Letter of Sailing-master Johnson, Jan. 9, 1815.
[2] Letter of Thomas Shields to Com. Patterson, Jan. 25, 1815.

lands.[1] Lieut. Lawrence Kearney, with three barges containing about 75 men, at once proceeded outside to cut them off, when the militia drove them away. The frigate was at anchor out of gunshot, but as soon as she perceived the barges began firing guns as signals. The British on shore left in such a hurry that they deserted their launch, which, containing a 12-pound boat carronade and six swivels, was taken by the Americans. The other boats—two cutters, and a large tender mounting one long nine and carrying 30 men—made for the frigate; but Lieut. Kearney laid the tender aboard and captured her after a sharp brush. The cutters were only saved by the fire of the *Hebrus,* which was very well directed—one of her shot taking off the head of a man close by Lieut. Kearney. The frigate got under way and intercepted Kearney's return, but the Lieutenant then made for South Edisto, whither he carried his prize in triumph. This was one of the most daring exploits of the war, and was achieved at very small cost. On Feb. 14th a similar feat was performed. Lieutenant Kearney had manned the captured launch with 25 men and the 12-pound carronade. News was received of another harrying expedition undertaken by the British, and Captain Dent, with seven boats, put out to attack them, but was unable to cross the reef. Meanwhile Kearney's barge had gotten outside, and attacked the schooner *Brant,* a tender to H.M.S. *Severn,* mounting an 18-pounder, and with a crew of two midshipmen, and twenty-one marines and seamen. A running fight began, the *Brant* evidently fearing that the other boats might get across the reef and join in the attack; suddenly she ran aground on a sand-bank, which accident totally demoralized her crew. Eight of them escaped in her boat, to the frigate; the remaining fifteen, after firing a few shot, surrendered and were taken possession of.[2]

———

I have had occasion from time to time to speak of cutting-out expeditions, successful and otherwise, undertaken by British boats against American privateers; and twice a small British national cutter was captured by an overwhelmingly superior American opponent of this class. We now, for the only time, come across an engagement between a privateer and a regular cruiser of approximately equal force. These privateers came from many different ports and varied greatly in size. Baltimore produced the largest number; but New York, Philadelphia, Boston, and Salem, were not far behind; and Charleston, Bristol, and Plymouth, supplied some that were very famous. Many were merely small pilot-boats with a crew of 20 to 40 men, intended only to harry the West Indian trade. Others were large, powerful craft, unequalled for speed by any vessels of their size, which penetrated to the remotest corners of the ocean, from

---

[1] Letter of Lawrence Kearney of Jan. 30, 1815 (see in the Archives at Washington, "Captains' Letters," vol. 42, No. 100).

[2] Letter of Captain Dent, Feb. 16th (in "Captains' Letters," vol. 42, No. 130). Most American authors, headed by Cooper, give this exploit a more vivid coloring by increasing the crew of the *Brant* to forty men, omitting to mention that she was hard and fast aground, and making no allusion to the presence of the five other American boats which undoubtedly caused the *Brant's* flight in the first place.

Man to the Spice Islands. When a privateer started she was overloaded with men, to enable her to man her prizes; a successful cruise would reduce her crew to a fifth of its original size. The favorite rig was that of a schooner, but there were many brigs and brigantines. Each was generally armed with a long 24 or 32 on a pivot, and a number of light guns in broadside, either long 9's or short 18's or 12's. Some had no pivot gun, others had nothing else. The largest of them carried 17 guns (a pivotal 32 and 16 long 12's in broadside) with a crew of 150. Such a vessel ought to have been a match, at her own distance, for a British brig-sloop, but we never hear of any such engagements, and there were several instances where privateers gave up, without firing a shot, to a force superior, it is true, but not enough so to justify the absolute tameness of the surrender.[1] One explanation of this was that they were cruising as private ventures, and their object was purely to capture merchant-men with as little risk as possible to themselves. Another reason was that they formed a kind of sea-militia, and, like their compeers on land, some *could* fight as well as any regulars, while most would *not* fight at all, especially if there was need of concerted action between two or three. The American papers of the day are full of "glorious victories" gained by privateers over packets and Indiamen; the British papers are almost as full of instances where the packets and Indiamen "heroically repulsed" the privateers. As neither side ever chronicles a defeat, and as the narration is apt to be decidedly figurative in character, there is very little hope of getting at the truth of such meetings; so I have confined myself to the mention of those cases where privateers, of either side, came into armed collision with regular cruisers. We are then sure to find some authentic account.

The privateer brig *Chasseur*, of Baltimore, Captain Thomas Boyle, carried 16 long 12's, and had, when she left port, 115 men aboard. She made 18 prizes on her last voyage, and her crew was thus reduced to less than 80 men; she was then chased by the *Barossa* frigate, and threw overboard 10 of her long 12's. Afterward eight 9-pound carronades were taken from a prize, to partially supply the places of the lost guns; but as she had no shot of the calibre of these carronades each of the latter was loaded with one 4-pound and one 6-pound ball, giving her a broadside of 76 lbs. On the 26th of February, two leagues from Havana, the *Chasseur* fell in with the British schooner *St. Lawrence*, Lieut. H. C. Gordon, mounting twelve 12-pound carronades, and one long 9; her broadside was thus 81 lbs., and she had between 60 and 80 men aboard.[2] The *Chasseur*

---

[1] As when the *Epervier*, some little time before her own capture, took without resistance the *Alfred*, of Salem, mounting 16 long nines and having 108 men aboard.

[2] Letter of Captain Thomas Boyle, of March 2, 1815 (see Niles and Coggeshall); he says the schooner had two more carronades; I have taken the number given by James (p. 539). Captain Boyle says the *St. Lawrence* had on board 89 men and several more, including a number of soldiers and marines and gentlemen of the navy, as passengers; James says her crew amounted to 51 "exclusive of some passengers," which I suppose must mean at least nine men. So the forces were pretty equal; the *Chasseur* may have had 20 men more or 10 men less than her antagonist, and she threw from 5 to 21 lbs. less weight of shot.

mistook the *St. Lawrence* for a merchant-man and closed with her. The mistake was discovered too late to escape, even had such been Captain Boyle's intention, and a brief but bloody action ensued. At 1.26 P.M., the *St. Lawrence* fired the first broadside, within pistol shot, to which the *Chasseur* replied with her great guns and musketry. The brig then tried to close, so as to board; but having too much way on, shot ahead under the lee of the schooner, which put her helm up to wear under the *Chasseur*'s stern. Boyle, however, followed his antagonist's manœuvre, and the two vessels ran along side by side, the *St. Lawrence* drawing ahead, while the firing was very heavy. Then Captain Boyle put his helm a starboard and ran his foe aboard, when in the act of boarding, her colors were struck at 1.41 P.M., 15 minutes after the first shot. Of the *Chasseur*'s crew 5 were killed and 8 wounded, including Captain Boyle slightly. Of the *St. Lawrence*'s crew 6 were killed and 17 (according to James 18) wounded. This was a very creditable action. The *St. Lawrence* had herself been an American privateer, called the *Atlas*, and was of 241 tons, or just 36 less than the *Chasseur*. The latter could thus fairly claim that her victory was gained over a regular cruiser of about her own force. Captain Southcombe of the *Lottery*, Captain Reid of the *General Armstrong*, Captain Ordronaux of the *Neufchatel*, and Captain Boyle of the *Chasseur*, deserve as much credit as any regularly commissioned sea-officers. But it is a mistake to consider these cases as representing the *average*; an ordinary privateer was, naturally enough, no match for a British regular cruiser of equal force. The privateers were of incalculable benefit to us, and inflicted enormous damage on the foe; but in fighting they suffered under the same disadvantages as other irregular forces; they were utterly unreliable. A really brilliant victory would be followed by a most extraordinary defeat.

———

After the *Constitution* had escaped from Boston, as I have described, she ran to the Bermudas, cruised in their vicinity a short while, thence to Madeira, to the Bay of Biscay, and finally off Portugal, cruising for some time in sight of the Rock of Lisbon. Captain Stewart then ran off southwest, and on Feb. 20th, Madeira bearing W.S.W. 60 leagues,[1] the day being cloudy, with a light easterly breeze,[2] at 1 P.M. a sail was made two points on the port bow; and at 2 P.M., Captain Stewart, hauling up in chase, discovered another sail. The first of these was the frigate-built ship corvette *Cyane*, Captain Gordon Thomas Falcon, and the second was the ship sloop *Levant*, Captain the Honorable George Douglass.[3] Both were standing close hauled on the starboard tack, the sloop about 10 miles to leeward of the corvette. At 4 P.M. the latter began making signals to her consort that the strange sail was an enemy, and then made all sail before the wind to join the sloop. The *Constitution* bore up in chase, setting her topmast, top-gallant, and royal studding-sails. In half an hour she carried away her main royal mast, but immediately got another prepared, and at 5 o'clock

[1] Letter of Captain Stewart to the Secretary of the Navy, May 20, 1815.
[2] Log of *Constitution*, Feb. 20, 1815.
[3] "Naval Chronicle," xxxiii, 466.

began firing at the corvette with the two port-bow guns; as the shot fell short the firing soon ceased. At 5.30 the *Cyane* got within hail of the *Levant*, and the latter's gallant commander expressed to Captain Gordon his intention of engaging the American frigate. The two ships accordingly hauled up their courses and stood on the starboard tack; but immediately afterward their respective captains concluded to try to delay the action till dark, so as to get the advantage of manœuvring.[1] Accordingly they again set all sail and hauled close to the wind to endeavor to weather their opponent; but finding the latter coming down too fast for them to succeed they again stripped to fighting canvas and formed on the starboard tack in head and stern line, the *Levant* about a cable's length in front of her consort. The American now had them completely under her guns and showed her ensign, to which challenge the British ships replied by setting their colors. At 6.10 the *Constitution* ranged up to windward of the *Cyane* and *Levant*, the former on her port quarter, the latter on her port bow, both being distant about 250 yards from her[2]—so close that the American marines were constantly engaged almost from the beginning of the action. The fight began at once, and continued with great spirit for a quarter of an hour, the vessels all firing broadsides. It was now moonlight, and an immense column of smoke formed under the lee of the *Constitution*, shrouding from sight her foes; and, as the fire of the latter had almost ceased, Captain Stewart also ordered his men to stop, so as to find out the positions of the ships. In about three minutes the smoke cleared, disclosing to the Americans the *Levant* dead to leeward on the port beam, and the *Cyane* luffing up for their port quarter. Giving a broadside to the sloop, Stewart braced aback his main and mizzen top-sails, with top-gallant sails set, shook all forward, and backed rapidly astern, under cover of the smoke, abreast the corvette, forcing the latter to fill again to avoid being raked. The firing was spirited for a few minutes, when the *Cyane*'s almost died away. The *Levant* bore up to wear round and assist her consort, but the *Constitution* filled her top-sails, and, shooting ahead, gave her two stern rakes, when she at once made all sail to get out of the combat. The *Cyane* was now discovered wearing, when the *Constitution* herself at once wore and gave her in turn a stern rake, the former luffing to and firing her port broadside into the starboard bow of the frigate. Then, as the latter ranged up on her port quarter, she struck, at 6.50, just forty minutes after the beginning of the action. She was at once taken possession of, and Lieut. Hoffman, second of the *Constitution*, was put in command. Having manned the prize, Captain Stewart, at 8 o'clock, filled away after her consort. The latter, however, had only gone out of the combat to refit. Captain Douglass had no idea of re-

[1] "Naval Chronicle," xxxiii, 466.

[2] Testimony sworn to by Lieutenant W. B. Shubrick and Lieutenant of Marines Archibald Henderson before Thomas Welsh, Jr., Justice of the Peace, Suffolk St., Boston, July 20, 1815. The depositions were taken in consequence of a report started by some of the British journals that the action began at a distance of ¼ of a mile. All the American depositions were that all three ships began firing at once, when equidistant from each other about 250 yards, the marines being engaged almost the whole time.

treat, and no sooner had he rove new braces than he hauled up to the wind, and came very gallantly back to find out his friend's condition. At 8.50 he met the *Constitution,* and, failing to weather her, the frigate and sloop passed each other on opposite tacks, exchanging broadsides. Finding her antagonist too heavy, the *Levant* then crowded all sail to escape, but was soon overtaken by the *Constitution,* and at about 9.30 the latter opened with her starboard bow-chasers, and soon afterward the British captain hauled down his colors. Mr. Ballard, first of the *Constitution,* was afterward put in command of the prize. By one o'clock the ships were all in order again.

The *Constitution* had been hulled eleven times, more often than in either of her previous actions, but her loss was mainly due to the grape and musketry of the foe in the beginning of the fight.[1] The British certainly fired better than usual, especially considering the fact that there was much manœuvring, and that it was a night action. The Americans lost 3 men killed, 3 mortally, and 9 severely and slightly, wounded. The corvette, out of her crew of 180, had 12 men killed and 26 wounded, several mortally; the sloop, out of 140, had 7 killed and 16 wounded. The *Constitution* had started on her cruise very full-handed, with over 470 men, but several being absent on a prize, she went into battle with about 450.[2] The prizes had suffered a good deal in their hulls and rigging, and had received some severe wounds in their masts and principal spars. The *Cyane* carried on her main-deck twenty-two 32-pound carronades, and on her spar-deck two long 12's, and ten 18-pounder carronades. The *Levant* carried, all on one deck, eighteen 32-pound carronades and two long 9's, together with a shifting 12-pounder. Thus, their broadside weight of metal was 763 pounds, with a total of 320 men, of whom 61 fell, against the *Constitution*'s 704 pounds and 450 men, of whom 15 were lost; or, nominally, the relative force was 100 to 91, and the relative loss 100 to 24. But the British guns were almost exclusively carronades which, as already pointed out in the case of the *Essex* and in the battle off Plattsburg, are no match for long guns. Moreover, the scantling of the smaller ships was, of course, by no means as stout as that of the frigate, so that the disparity of force was much greater than the figures would indicate, although not enough to account for the difference in loss. Both the British ships were ably handled, their fire was well directed, and the *Levant* in especial was very gallantly fought.

As regards the *Constitution,* "her manœuvring was as brilliant as any recorded in naval annals," and it would have been simply impossible to surpass the consummate skill with which she was handled in the smoke, always keeping her antagonists to leeward, and, while raking both of them, not being once raked herself. The firing was excellent, considering the short time the ships were ac-

---

[1] Deposition of her officers as before cited.

[2] 410 officers and seamen, and 41 marines, by her muster-roll of Feb. 19th. (The muster-rolls are preserved in the Treasury Department at Washington.)

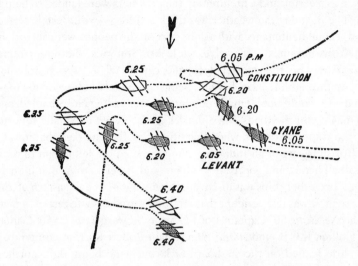

tually engaged, and the fact that it was at night. Altogether the fight reflected the greatest credit on her, and also on her adversaries.[1]

The merits of this action can perhaps be better appreciated by comparing it with a similar one that took place a few years before between a British sloop and corvette on the one side, and a French frigate on the other, and which is given in full by both James and Troude. Although these authors differ somewhat in the account of it, both agree that the Frenchman, the *Nereide*, of 44 guns, on Feb. 14, 1810, fought a long and indecisive battle with the *Rainbow* of 26 and *Avon* of 18 guns, the British sloops being fought separately, in succession. The relative force was almost exactly as in the *Constitution*'s fight. Each side claimed that the other fled. But this much is sure: the *Constitution* engaging the *Cyane* and *Levant* together, captured both; while the *Nereide*, engaging the *Rainbow* and *Avon* separately, captured neither.

The three ships now proceeded to the Cape de Verde, and on March 10th anchored in the harbor of Porto Praya, Island of San Jago. Here a merchant-brig

---

[1] There is no British official account of the action. James states that the entire British force was only 302 men of whom 12 were killed and 29 wounded. This is probably not based on any authority. Captain Stewart received on board 301 prisoners, of whom 42 were wounded, several mortally. Curiously enough James also underestimates the American loss, making it only 12. He also says that many attempts were made by the Americans to induce the captured British to desert, while the *Constitution*'s officers deny this under oath, before Justice Welsh, as already quoted, and state that, on the contrary, many of the prisoners offered to enlist on the frigate, but were all refused permission—as "the loss of the *Chesapeake* had taught us the danger of having renegades aboard." This denial, by the way, holds good for all the similar statements made by James as regards the *Guerrière, Macedonian*, etc. He also states that a British court-martial found various counts against the Americans for harsh treatment, but all of these were specifically denied by the American officers, under oath, as already quoted.

I have relied chiefly on Captain Stewart's narrative; but partly (as to time, etc.) on the British account in the "Naval Chronicle."

was taken as a cartel, and a hundred of the prisoners were landed to help fit her for sea. The next day the weather was thick and foggy, with fresh breezes.[1] The first and second lieutenants, with a good part of the people, were aboard the two prizes. At five minutes past twelve, while Mr. Shubrick, the senior remaining lieutenant, was on the quarter-deck, the canvas of a large vessel suddenly loomed up through the haze, her hull being completely hidden by the fog-bank. Her character could not be made out; but she was sailing close-hauled, and evidently making for the roads. Mr. Shubrick at once went down and reported the stranger to Captain Stewart, when that officer coolly remarked that it was probably a British frigate or an Indianman, and directed the lieutenant to return on deck, call all hands, and get ready to go out and attack her.[2] At that moment the canvas of two other ships was discovered rising out of the fog astern of the vessel first seen. It was now evident that all three were heavy frigates.[3] In fact, they were the *Newcastle*, 50, Captain Lord George Stewart; *Leander*, 50, Captain Sir Ralph Collier, K.C.B., and *Acasta*, 40, Captain Robert Kerr, standing into Porto Praya, close-hauled on the starboard tack, the wind being light northeast by north.[4] Captain Stewart at once saw that his opponents were far too heavy for a fair fight, and, knowing that the neutrality of the port would not be the slightest protection to him, he at once signalled to the prizes to follow, cut his cable, and, in less than ten minutes from the time the first frigate was seen, was standing out of the roads, followed by Hoffman and Ballard. Certainly a more satisfactory proof of the excellent training of both officers and men could hardly be given than the rapidity, skill, and perfect order with which every thing was done. Any indecision on the part of the officers or bungling on the part of the men would have lost every thing. The prisoners on shore had manned a battery and delivered a furious but ill-directed fire at their retreating conquerors. The frigate, sloop, and corvette, stood out of the harbor in the order indicated, on the port tack, passing close under the east point, and a gunshot to windward of the British squadron, according to the American, or about a league, according to the British, accounts. The Americans made out the force of the strangers correctly, and their own force was equally clearly discerned by the *Acasta*; but both the *Newcastle* and *Leander* mistook the *Cyane* and *Levant* for frigates, a mistake similar to that once made by Commodore Rodgers. The *Constitution* now crossed her top-gallant yards and set the foresail, main-sail, spanker, flying jib, and top-gallant sails; and the British ships, tacking, made all sail in pursuit. The *Newcastle* was on the *Constitution*'s lee quarter and directly ahead of the *Leander*, while the *Acasta* was on the weather-quarter of the *Newcastle*. All six ships were on the port tack. The *Constitution* cut adrift the boats towing astern, and her log notes that at 12.50 she found she was sailing about as fast as the ships on her lee quar-

---

[1] Log of *Constitution*, March 11, 1815.
[2] Cooper, ii, 459.
[3] Letter of Lieutenant Hoffman, April 10, 1815.
[4] Marshall's "Naval Biography," ii, 535.

ter, but that the *Acasta* was luffing into her wake and dropping astern. The log of the *Acasta* says, "We had gained on the sloops, but the frigate had gained on us." At 1.10 the *Cyane* had fallen so far astern and to leeward that Captain Stewart signalled to Lieutenant Hoffman to tack, lest he should be cut off if he did not. Accordingly the lieutenant put about and ran off toward the northwest, no notice being taken of him by the enemy beyond an ineffectual broadside from the sternmost frigate. At 2.35 he was out of sight of all the ships and shaped his course for America, which he reached on April 10th.[1] At 1.45 the *Newcastle* opened on the *Constitution* firing by divisions, but the shot all fell short, according to the American statements, about 200 yards, while the British accounts (as given in Marshall's "Naval Biography") make the distance much greater; at any rate the vessels were so near that from the *Constitution* the officers of the *Newcastle* could be seen standing on the hammock nettings. But, very strangely, both the 50-gun ships apparently still mistook the *Levant*, though a low, flush-decked sloop like the *Hornet*, for the "*President, Congress*, or *Macedonian*," Captain Collier believing that the *Constitution* had sailed with two other frigates in company.[2] By three o'clock the *Levant* had lagged so as to be in the same position from which the *Cyane* had just been rescued; accordingly Captain Stewart signalled to her to tack, which she did, and immediately afterward all three British ships tacked in pursuit. Before they did so, it must be remembered the *Acasta* had weathered on the *Constitution*, though left considerably astern, while the *Newcastle* and *Leander* had about kept their positions on her lee or starboard quarter; so that if any ship had been detached after the *Levant* it should have been the *Leander*, which had least chance of overtaking the American frigate. The latter was by no means as heavily armed as either of the two 50's, and but little heavier than the *Acasta*; moreover, she was shorthanded, having manned her two prizes. The *Acasta*, at any rate, had made out the force of the *Levant*, and, even had she been a frigate, it was certainly carrying prudence to an extreme to make more than one ship tack after her. Had the *Newcastle* and *Acasta* kept on after the *Constitution* there was a fair chance of overtaking her, for the *Acasta* had weathered on her, and the chase could not bear up for fear of being cut off by the *Newcastle*. At any rate the pursuit should not have been given up so early. Marshall says there was a mistake in the signalling. The British captains certainly bungled the affair; even James says (p. 558): "It is the most blundering piece of business recorded in these six volumes." As for Stewart and his men, they deserve the highest credit for the cool judgment and prompt, skilful seamanship they had displayed. The *Constitution*, having shaken off her pursuers, sailed to Maranham, where she landed her prisoners. At Porto Rico she learned of the peace, and forthwith made sail for New York, reaching it about the middle of May.

As soon as he saw Captain Stewart's signal, Lieutenant Ballard had tacked, and at once made for the anchorage at Porto Prayo, which he reached, though

---

[1] Letter of Lieutenant Hoffman, April 10, 1815.
[2] Marshall, ii, 533.

pursued by all his foes, and anchored within 150 yards of a heavy battery.[1] The wisdom of Captain Stewart's course in not trusting to the neutrality of the port, now became evident. The *Acasta* opened upon the sloop as soon as the latter had anchored, at 4.30[2] The *Newcastle*, as soon as she arrived, also opened, and so did the *Leander*, while the British prisoners on shore fired the guns of the battery. Having borne this combined cannonade for 15 minutes,[3] the colors of the *Levant* were hauled down. The unskilful firing of the British ships certainly did not redeem the blunders previously made by Sir George Collier, for the three heavy frigates during 15 minutes' broadside practice in smooth water against a stationary and unresisting foe, did her but little damage, and did not kill a man. The chief effect of the fire was to damage the houses of the Portuguese town.[4]

---

After the capture of the *President*, the *Peacock*, Captain Warrington, the *Hornet*, Captain Biddle, and *Tom Bowline*, brig, still remained in New York harbor. On the 22d of January a strong northwesterly gale began to blow, and the American vessels, according to their custom, at once prepared to take advantage of the heavy weather and run by the blockaders. They passed the bar by daylight, under storm canvas, the British frigates lying to in the southeast being plainly visible. They were ignorant of the fate of the *President*, and proceeded toward Tristan d'Acunha, which was the appointed rendezvous. A few days out the *Hornet* parted company from the two others; these last reached Tristan d'Acunha about March 18th, but were driven off again by a gale. The *Hornet* reached the island on the 23d, and at half-past ten in the morning, the wind being fresh S.S.W., when about to anchor off the north point, a sail was made in the southeast, steering west.[5] This was the British brig-sloop *Penguin*, Captain James Dickenson. She was a new vessel, having left port for the first time in September, 1814. While at the Cape of Good Hope she had received from Vice-Admiral Tyler 12 marines from the *Medway*, 74, increasing her complement to 132; and was then despatched on special service against a heavy American privateer, the *Young Wasp*, which had been causing great havoc among the homeward-bound Indiamen.

When the strange sail was first seen Captain Biddle was just letting go his topsail sheets; he at once sheeted them home, and, the stranger being almost instantly shut out by the land, made all sail to the west, and again caught sight of her. Captain Dickenson now, for the first time, saw the American sloop, and at once bore up for her. The position of the two vessels was exactly the reverse of the *Wasp* and *Frolic*, the Englishman being to windward. The *Hornet* hove to, to let her antagonist close; then she filled her maintop-sail and continued to yaw, wear-

---

[1] Letter of Lieutenant Ballard, May 2, 1815.
[2] *Newcastle's* log, as given by Marshall and James.
[3] Ballard's letter.
[4] James, vi, 551.
[5] Letter from Captain Biddle to Commodore Decatur, Mar. 25, 1815.

ing occasionally to prevent herself from being raked. At forty minutes past one the *Penguin,* being within musket-shot, hauled to the wind on the starboard tack, hoisted a St. George's ensign and fired a gun. The *Hornet* luffed up on the same tack, hoisting American colors, and the action began with heavy broadsides. The vessels ran along thus for 15 minutes, gradually coming closer together, and Captain Dickenson put his helm aweather, to run his adversary aboard. At this moment the brave young officer received a mortal wound, and the command devolved on the first lieutenant, Mr. McDonald, who endeavored very gallantly to carry out his commander's intention, and at 1.56 the *Penguin's* bowsprit came in between the *Hornet's* main- and mizzen-rigging on the starboard side. The American seamen had been called away, and were at their posts to repel boarders, but as the British made no attempt to come on, the cutlass men began to clamber into the rigging to go aboard the brig. Captain Biddle very coolly stopped them, "it being evident from the beginning that our fire was greatly superior both in quickness and effect." There was a heavy sea running, and as the *Hornet* forged ahead, the *Penguin's* bowsprit carried away her mizzen shrouds, stern davits, and spanker boom; and the brig then hung on her starboard quarter, where only small arms could be used on either side. An English officer now called out something which Biddle understood, whether correctly or not is disputed, to be the word of surrender; accordingly he directed his marines to cease firing, and jumped on the taffrail. At that minute two of the marines on the *Penguin's* forecastle, not 30 feet distant, fired at him, one of the balls inflicting a rather severe wound in his neck. A discharge of musketry from the *Hornet* at once killed both the marines, and at that moment the ship drew ahead. As the vessels separated the *Penguin's* foremast went overboard, the bowsprit breaking short off. The *Hornet* at once wore, to present a fresh broadside, while the *Penguin's* disabled condition prevented her following suit, and having lost a third of her men killed and wounded (14 of the former and 28 of the latter), her hull being riddled through and through, her foremast gone, main-mast tottering, and most of the guns on the engaged side dismounted, she struck her colors at two minutes past two, twenty-two minutes after the first gun was fired. Of the *Hornet's* 150 men, 8 were absent in a prize. By actual measurement she was two feet longer and slightly narrower than her antagonist. Her loss was chiefly caused by musketry, amounting to 1 marine killed, 1 seaman mortally, Lieutenant Conner very severely, and Captain Biddle and

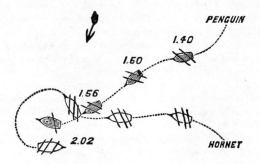

seven seamen slightly, wounded. Not a round shot struck the hull, nor was a mast or spar materially injured, but the rigging and sails were a good deal cut, especially about the fore and main top-gallant masts. The *Hornet*'s crew had been suffering much from sickness, and 9 of the men were unable to be at quarters, thus reducing the vessels to an exact equality. Counting in these men, and excluding the 8 absent in a prize, we get as

COMPARATIVE FORCE

| | TONNAGE. | NO. GUNS. | WEIGHT METAL. | CREW. | LOSS. |
| --- | --- | --- | --- | --- | --- |
| *Hornet* | 480 | 10 | 279 | 142[1] | 11 |
| *Penguin* | 477 | 10 | 274 | 132 | 42 |

Or, the force being practically equal, the *Hornet* inflicted fourfold the loss and tenfold the damage she suffered. Hardly any action of the war reflected greater credit on the United States marine than this; for the cool, skilful seamanship and excellent gunnery that enabled the Americans to destroy an antagonist of equal force in such an exceedingly short time. The British displayed equal bravery, but were certainly very much behind their antagonists in the other qualities which go to make up a first-rate man-of-warsman. Even James says he "cannot offer the trifling disparity of force in this action as an excuse for the *Penguin*'s capture. The chief cause is * * * the immense disparity between the two vessels in * * * the effectiveness of their crews."[2]

The *Penguin* was so cut up by shot that she had to be destroyed. After the stores, etc., had been taken out of her, she was thoroughly examined (Captain Biddle, from curiosity, taking her measurements in comparison with those of the *Hornet*). Her destruction was hastened on account of a strange sail heaving in sight; but the latter proved to be the *Peacock*, with the *Tom Bowline* in com-

---

[1] This number of men is probably too great; I have not personally examined the *Hornet*'s muster-roll for that period. Lieutenant Emmons in his "History," gives her 132 men; but perhaps he did not include the nine sick, which would make his statement about the same as mine. In response to my inquiries, I received a very kind letter from the Treasury Department (Fourth Auditor's office), which stated that the muster-roll of the *Hornet* on this voyage showed "101 officers and crew (marines excepted)." Adding the 20 marines would make but 121 in all. I think there must be some mistake in this, and so have considered the *Hornet*'s crew as consisting originally of 150 men, the same as on her cruises in 1812.

The *Penguin* was in reality slightly larger than the *Hornet*, judging from the comparisons made in Biddle's letter (for the original of which see in the Naval Archives, "Captains' Letters," vol 42, No. 112). He says that the *Penguin*, though two feet shorter on deck than the *Hornet*, had a greater length of keel, a slightly greater breadth of beam, stouter sides, and higher bulwarks, with swivels on the capstan and tops, and that she fought both her "long 12's" on the same side. I have followed James, however, as regards this; he says her long guns were 6-pounders, and that but one was fought on a side.

[2] After the action but one official account, that of Captain Biddle, was published; none of the letters of the defeated British commanders were published after 1813. As regards this action, every British writer has followed James, who begins his account thus: "Had the vessel in sight to windward been rigged with three masts instead of two, and had she proved to be a British cruiser, Captain Biddle would have marked her down in his log as a 'frigate,' and have made off with all the canvas he could possibly spread. Had the ship overtaken the *Hornet* and been in reality a trifle superior in force, Captain Biddle, we have

pany. The latter was now turned to account by being sent in to Rio de Janeiro as a cartel with the prisoners. The *Peacock* and *Hornet* remained about the island till April 13th, and then, giving up all hopes of seeing the *President*, and rightly supposing she had been captured, started out for the East Indies. On the 27th of the month, in lat. 38°30′ S. and long. 33° E.,[1] the *Peacock* signalled a stranger in the S.E., and both sloops crowded sail in chase. The next morning they came down with the wind aft from the northwest, the studding-sails set on both sides. The new 22-gun sloops were not only better war-vessels, but faster ones too, than any other ships of their rate; and the *Peacock* by afternoon was two leagues ahead of the *Hornet*. At 2 P.M. the former was observed to manifest some hesitation about approaching the stranger, which instead of avoiding had rather hauled up toward them. All on board the *Hornet* thought her an Indiaman, and "the men began to wonder what they would do with the silks," when, a few minutes before four, the *Peacock* signalled that it was a line-of-battle ship, which reversed the parts with a vengeance. Warrington's swift ship was soon out of danger, while Biddle hauled close to the wind on the port tack, with the *Cornwallis*, 74, bearing the flag of Admiral Sir George Burleton, K.C.B.,[2] in hot pursuit, two leagues on his lee quarter. The 74 gained rapidly on the *Hornet*, although she stopped to pick up a marine who had fallen overboard. Finding he had to deal with a most weatherly craft, as well as a swift sailer, Captain Biddle, at 9 P.M., began to lighten the *Hornet* of the mass of stores taken from the *Penguin*. The *Cornwallis* gained still, however, and at 2 A.M. on the 29th was ahead of the *Hornet*'s lee or starboard beam, when the sloop put about and ran off toward the west. Daylight showed the 74 still astern and to leeward, but having gained so much as to be within gunshot, and shortly afterward she opened fire, her shot passing over the *Hornet*. The latter had recourse anew to the lightening process. She had already hove overboard the sheet-anchor, several heavy spare spars, and a large quantity of shot and ballast; the remaining anchors and cables, more shot, six guns, and the launch now followed suit, and, thus relieved, the *Hornet* passed temporarily out of danger; but the breeze shifted gradually round to the east, and the liner came looming up till at noon she was within a mile, a shorter range than that at which the *United States* crippled and cut up the *Macedonian*; and had the *Corn-*

no doubt, would have exhausted his eloquence in lauding the blessings of peace before he tried a struggle for the honors of war." After this preface (which should be read in connection with the *Hornet*'s unaccepted challenge to the *Bonne Citoyenne*, a ship "a trifle superior in force") it can be considered certain that James will both extenuate and also set down a good deal in malice. One instance of this has already been given in speaking of the *President*'s capture. Again, he says, "the *Hornet* received several round shot in her hull," which she did—a month after this action, from the *Cornwallis*, 74; James knew perfectly well that not one of the *Penguin*'s shot hit the *Hornet*'s hull. The quotations I have given are quite enough to prove that nothing he says about the action is worth attending to. The funniest part of his account is where he makes Captain Biddle get drunk, lose his "native cunning," and corroborate his (James') statements. He does not even hint at the authority for this.

[1] Letter of Captain Biddle, June 10th, and extracts from her log.
[2] James, vi, 564.

*wallis'* fire been half as well aimed as that of the *States,* it would have been the last of the *Hornet.* But the 74's guns were very unskilfully served, and the shot passed for the most part away over the chase, but three getting home. Captain Biddle and his crew had no hope of ultimate escape, but no one thought of giving up. All the remaining spare spars and boats, all the guns but one, the shot, and in fact every thing that could be got at, below or on deck, was thrown overboard. This increased the way of the *Hornet,* while the *Cornwallis* lost ground by hauling off to give broadsides, which were as ineffectual as the fire from the chase-guns had been. The *Hornet* now had gained a little, and managed to hold her own, and shortly afterward the pluck and skill of her crew[1] were rewarded. The shift in the wind had been very much against them, but now it veered back again so as to bring them to windward; and every minute, as it blew fresher and fresher, their chances increased. By dark the *Cornwallis* was well astern, and during the night the wind kept freshening, blowing in squalls, which just suited the *Hornet,* and when day broke the liner was hull down astern. Then, on the morning of the 30th, after nearly 48 hours' chase, she abandoned the pursuit. The *Hornet* was now of course no use as a cruiser, and made sail for New York, which she reached on June 9th. This chase requires almost the same comments as the last chase of the *Constitution.* In both cases the American captains and their crews deserve the very highest praise for plucky, skilful seamanship; but exactly as Stewart's coolness and promptitude might not have saved the *Constitution* had it not been for the blunders made by his antagonists, so the *Hornet* would have assuredly been taken, in spite of Biddle's stubbornness and resource, if the *Cornwallis* had not shown such unskilful gunnery, which was all the more discreditable since she carried an admiral's flag.

The *Peacock* was thus the only one left of the squadron originally prepared for the East Indies; however, she kept on, went round the Cape of Good Hope, and cruised across the Indian Ocean, capturing 4 great Indiamen, very valuable prizes, manned by 291 men. Then she entered the Straits of Sunda, and on the 30th of June, off the fort of Anjier fell in with the East India Company's cruiser *Nautilus,* Lieut. Boyce, a brig of 180 (American measurement over 200) tons, with a crew of 80 men, and 14 guns, 4 long 9's and ten 18-pound carronades.[2] Captain Warrington did not know of the peace; one of the boats of the *Nautilus,* however, with her purser, Mr. Bartlett, boarded him. Captain Warrington declares the latter made no mention of the peace, while Mr. Bartlett swears that he did before he was sent below. As the *Peacock* approached, Lieut. Boyce hailed to ask if she knew peace had been declared.

---

[1] It is perhaps worth noting that the accounts incidentally mention the fact that almost the entire crew consisted of native Americans, of whom *quite a number had served as impressed seamen on board British war-ships.* James multiplies these threefold and sets them down as British.

[2] "History of the Indian Navy," by Charles Rathbone Low (late lieutenant of the Indian Navy), London, 1877, p. 285.

Captain Warrington, according to his letter, regarded this as a ruse to enable the brig to escape under the guns of the fort, and commanded the lieutenant to haul down his colors, which the latter refused to do, and very gallantly prepared for a struggle with a foe of more than twice his strength. According to Captain Warrington, one, or, by the deposition of Mr. Bartlett,[1] two broadsides were then interchanged, and the brig surrendered, having lost 7 men, including her first lieutenant, killed and mortally wounded, and 8 severely or slightly wounded. Two of her guns and the sheet-anchor were disabled, the bends on the starboard side completely shivered from aft to the forechains, the bulwarks from the chess-tree aft much torn, and the rigging cut to pieces.[2] The *Peacock* did not suffer the slightest loss or damage. Regarding the affair purely as a conflict between vessels of nations at war with each other, the criticism made by Lord Howard Douglass on the action between the *President* and *Little Belt* applies here perfectly. "If a vessel meet an enemy of even greatly superior force, it is due to the honor of her flag to try the effect of a few rounds; but unless in this gallant attempt she leave marks of her skill upon the larger body, while she, the smaller body, is hit at every discharge, she does but salute her enemy's triumph and discredit her own gunnery."[3] There could not have been a more satisfactory exhibition of skill than that given by Captain Warrington; but I regret to say that it is difficult to believe he acted with proper humanity. It seems impossible that Mr. Bartlett did not mention that peace had been signed; and when the opposing force was so much less than his own it would have been safe at least to defer the order "haul down your flag" for a short time, while he could have kept the brig within half pistol-shot, until he could have inquired into the truth of the report. Throughout this work I have wherever possible avoided all references to the various accusations and recriminations of some of the captains about "unfairness," "cruelty," etc., as in most cases it is impossible to get at the truth, the accounts flatly contradicting one another. In this case, however, there certainly seems some ground for the rather fervent denunciations of Captain Warrington indulged in by Lieut. Low. But it is well to remember that a very similar affair, with the parties reversed, had taken place but a few months before on the coast of America. This was on Feb. 22d, after the boats of the *Erebus*, 20, and *Primrose*, 18, under Captains Bartholomew and Phillot, had been beaten off with a loss of 30 men (including both captains wounded), in an expedition up St. Mary's River, Ga. The two captains and their vessels then joined Admiral Cockburn at Cumberland Island, and on the 25th of February were informed officially of the existence of peace. Three weeks afterward the American gunboat No. 168, Mr. Hurlburt, sailed from Tybee Bar, Ga., bearing des-

[1] As quoted by Low.
[2] Letter of Lieut. Boyce to Company's Marine Board, as quoted by Low.
[3] "Naval Gunnery," p. 3.

patches for the British admiral.[1] On the same day in the afternoon she fell in with the *Erebus,* Captain Bartholomew. Peace having been declared, and having been known to exist for over three weeks, no effort was made to avoid the British vessel; but when the gunboat neared the latter she was suddenly hailed and told to heave to. Mr. Hurlburt answered that he had dispatches for Admiral Cockburn, to which Captain Bartholomew responded, with many oaths, that he did not care, he would sink her if she did not send a boat aboard. When Mr. Hurlburt attempted to answer some muskets were discharged at him, and he was told to strike. He refused, and the *Erebus* immediately opened fire from her great guns; the gunboat had gotten so far round that her pivot-gun would not bear properly, but it was discharged across the bows of the *Erebus,* and then Mr. Hurlburt struck his colors. Although he had lain right under the foe's broadside, he had suffered no loss or damage except a few ropes cut, and some shot-holes in the sails. Afterward Captain Bartholomew apologized, and let the gunboat proceed.

This attack was quite as wanton and unprovoked as Warrington's, and Bartholomew's foe was relatively to himself even less powerful; moreover, while the *Peacock*'s crew showed great skill in handling their guns, the crew of the *Erebus* most emphatically did not. The intent in both cases was equally bad, only the British captain lacked the ability to carry his out.

## SUMMARY

The concluding operations of the war call for much the same comments as those of the preceding years. The balance of praise certainly inclines toward the Americans. Captain John Hayes' squadron showed great hardihood, perseverance and judgment, which were rewarded by the capture of the *President;* and Decatur's surrender seems decidedly tame. But as regards the action between the *President* and *Endymion* (taking into account the fact that the former fought almost under the guns of an overwhelming force, and was therefore obliged to expose herself far more than she otherwise would have), it showed nearly as great superiority on the side of the Americans as the frigate actions of 1812 did—in fact, probably quite as much as in the case of the *Java.* Similarly, while the *Cyane* and *Levant* did well, the *Constitution* did better; and Sir George Collier's ships certainly did not distinguish themselves when in chase of *Old Ironsides.* So with the *Hornet* in her two encounters; no one can question the pluck with which the *Penguin* was fought, but her gunnery was as bad as that of the *Cornwallis* subsequently proved. And though the skirmish between the *Peacock* and *Nautilus* is not one to which an American cares to look back, yet, regarding it purely from a fighting stand-point, there is no question which crew was the best trained and most skilful.

[1] Letter from Com. Campbell to Sec. of Navy, Mar. 29, 1815, including one from Sailing-master John H. Hurlburt of Mar. 18, 1815, preserved in the Naval Archives, in vol. 43, No. 125, of "Captains' Letters." See also "Niles' Register," viii, 104, 118, etc.

LIST OF SHIPS BUILT IN 1815

| NAME. | RATE. | WHERE BUILT. | COST. |
|---|---|---|---|
| *Washington* | 74 | Portsmouth | $235,861.00 |
| *Independence* | 74 | Boston | 421,810.41 |
| *Franklin* | 74 | Philadelphia | 438,149.40 |
| *Guerrière* | 44 | " | 306,158.56 |
| *Java* | 44 | Baltimore | 232,767.38 |
| *Fulton* | 30 | New York | 320,000.00 |
| *Torpedo* | | " | |

These ships first put to sea in this year. For the first time in her history the United States possessed line-of-battle ships; and for the first time in all history, the steam frigate appeared on the navy list of a nation. The *Fulton*, with her clumsy central wheel, concealed from shot by the double hull, with such thick scantling that none but heavy guns could harm her, and relying for offensive weapons not on a broadside of thirty guns of small calibre, but on two pivotal 100-pounder columbiads, or, perhaps, if necessary, on blows from her hog snout,—the *Fulton* was the true prototype of the modern steam ironclad, with its few heavy guns and ram. Almost as significant is the presence of the *Torpedo.* I have not chronicled the several efforts made by the Americans to destroy British vessels with torpedoes; some very nearly succeeded, and although they failed it must not be supposed that they did no good. On the contrary, they made the British in many cases very cautious about venturing into good anchorage (especially in Long Island Sound and the Chesapeake), and by the mere terror of their name prevented more than one harrying expedition. The *Fulton* was not got into condition to be fought until just as the war ended; had it continued a few months, it is more than probable that the deeds of the *Merrimac* and the havoc wrought by the Confederate torpedoes would have been forestalled by nearly half a century. As it was, neither of these engines of war attracted much attention. For ten or fifteen years the *Fulton* was the only war-vessel of her kind in existence, and then her name disappears from our lists. The torpedoes had been tried in the Revolutionary War, but their failure prevented much notice from being taken of them, and, besides, at that time there was a strong feeling that it was dishonorable to blow a ship up with a powder-can concealed *under* the water, though highly laudable to burn her by means of a fire-raft floating *on* the water—a nice distinction in naval ethics that has since disappeared.[1]

AMERICAN VESSELS DESTROYED, ETC.

BY OCEAN CRUISERS.

| NAME. | GUNS. | TONNAGE. | REMARKS. |
|---|---|---|---|
| *President* | 52 | 1,576 | captured by squadron. |
| | 52 guns. | 1,576 tons. | |

[1] James fairly foams at the mouth at the mere mention of torpedoes.

### BRITISH VESSELS DESTROYED, ETC.

#### A.—BY PRIVATEERS.[1]

| NAME. | GUNS. | TONNAGE. | REMARKS. |
|---|---|---|---|
| *Chasseur* | 12 | 240 | by privateer *St. Lawrence.* |

#### B.—BY OCEAN CRUISERS.

| NAME. | GUNS. | TONNAGE. | REMARKS. |
|---|---|---|---|
| *Cyane* | 34 | 659 | by *Constitution.* |
| *Levant* | 20 | 500 | retaken. |
| *Penguin* | 19 | 477 | by *Hornet.* |
| | 85 guns, | 1,876 tons. | |
| | 20 | 500 | (subtracting *Levant*). |
| | 65 guns, | 1,376 tons. | |

In summing up the results of the struggle on the ocean it is to be noticed that very little was attempted, and nothing done, by the American Navy that could *materially* affect the result of the war. Commodore Rodgers' expedition after the Jamaica plate fleet failed; both the efforts to get a small squadron into the East Indian waters also miscarried; and otherwise the whole history of the struggle on the ocean is, as regards the Americans, only the record of individual cruises and fights. The material results were not very great, at least in their effect on Great Britain, whose enormous navy did not feel in the slightest degree the loss of a few frigates and sloops. But morally the result was of inestimable benefit to the United States. The victories kept up the spirits of the people, cast down by the defeats on land; practically decided in favor of the Americans the chief question in dispute—Great Britain's right of search and impressment—and gave the navy, and thereby the country, a world-wide reputation. I doubt if ever before a nation gained so much honor by a few single-ship duels. For there can be no question which side came out of the war with the greatest credit. The damage inflicted by each on the other was not very unequal in amount, but the balance was certainly in favor of the United States, as can be seen by the following tables, for the details of which reference can be made to the various years:

| | AMERICAN LOSS | | BRITISH LOSS | |
|---|---|---|---|---|
| CAUSED:— | TONNAGE. | GUNS. | TONNAGE.[1] | GUNS. |
| By Ocean Cruisers | 5,984 | 278 | 8,451 | 351 |
| On the Lakes | 727 | 37 | 4,159 | 212 |
| By the Army | 3,007 | 116 | 500 | 22 |
| By Privateers | — | — | 402 | 20 |
| Total, | 9,718 | 431 | 13,512 | 605 |

[1] The tonnage can only be given approximately, as that of the vessels on Lake Champlain is not exactly known, although we know about what the two fleets tonned relatively to one another.

In addition we lost 4 revenue-cutters, mounting 24 guns, and, in the aggregate, of 387 tons, and also 25 gun-boats, with 71 guns, and, in the aggregate, of nearly 2,000 tons. This would swell our loss to 12,105 tons, and 526 guns[1]; but the loss of the revenue-cutters and gun-boats can fairly be considered to be counterbalanced by the capture or destruction of the various British Royal Packets (all armed with from 2 to 10 guns), tenders, barges, etc., which would be in the aggregate of at least as great tonnage and gun force, and with more numerous crews.

But the comparative material loss gives no idea of the comparative honor gained. The British navy, numbering at the outset a thousand cruisers, had accomplished less than the American, which numbered but a dozen. Moreover, most of the loss suffered by the former was in single fight, while this had been but twice the case with the Americans, who had generally been overwhelmed by numbers. The *President* and *Essex* were both captured by more than double their force simply because they were disabled before the fight began, otherwise they would certainly have escaped. With the exceptions of the *Chesapeake* and *Argus* (both of which were taken fairly, because their antagonists, though of

---

[1] This differs greatly from the figures given by James in his "Naval Occurrences" (App. ccxv). He makes the American loss 14,844 tons, and 660 guns. His list includes, for example, the "*Growler* and *Hamilton,* upset in carrying sail to avoid Sir James' fleet"; it would be quite as reasonable to put down the loss of the *Royal George* to the credit of the French. Then he mentions the *Julia* and *Growler,* which were recaptured; the *Asp,* which was also recaptured; the "*New York,* 46, destroyed at Washington," which was *not* destroyed or harmed in any way, and which, moreover, was a condemned hulk; the "*Boston,* 42 (in reality 32), destroyed at Washington," which had been a condemned hulk for ten years, and had no guns or anything else in her, and was as much a loss to our navy as the fishing up and burning of an old wreck would have been; and 8 gun-boats whose destruction was either mythical, or else which were not national vessels. By deducting all these we reduce James' total by 120 guns, and 2,600 tons; and a few more alterations (such as excluding the swivels in the *President*'s tops, which he counts, etc.), brings his number down to that given above—and also affords a good idea of the value to be attached to his figures and tables. The British loss he gives at but 530 guns and 10,273 tons. He omits the 24-gun ship burnt by Chauncy at York, although including the frigate and corvette burnt by Ross at Washington; if the former is excluded the two latter should be, which would make the balance still more in favor of the Americans. He omits the guns of the *Gloucester,* because they had been taken out of her and placed in battery on the shore, but he includes those of the *Adams,* which had been served in precisely the same way. He omits all reference to the British 14-gun schooner burnt on Ontario, and to all 3- and 4-gun sloops and schooners captured there, although including the corresponding American vessels. The reason that he so much underestimates the tonnage, especially on the lakes, I have elsewhere discussed. His tables of the relative loss in men are even more erroneous, exaggerating that of the Americans, and greatly underestimating that of the British; but I have not tabulated this on account of the impossibility of getting fair estimates of the killed and wounded in the cutting-out expeditions, and the difficulty of enumerating the prisoners taken in descents, etc. Roughly, about 2,700 Americans and 3,800 British were captured; the comparative loss in killed and wounded stood much more in our favor.

I have excluded from the British loss the brigs *Detroit* and *Caledonia,* and schooner *Nancy* (aggregating 10 guns and about 500 tons), destroyed on the upper lakes, because I hardly know whether they could be considered national vessels; the schooner *Highflyer,* of 8 guns, 40 men, and 209 tons, taken by Rodgers, because she seems to have been merely a tender; and the *Dominica,* 15, of 77 men, and 270 tons, because her captor, the privateer *Decatur,* though nominally an American, was really a French vessel. Of course both tables are only approximately exact; but at any rate the balance of damage and loss was over 4 to 3 in our favor.

only equal force, were better fighters), the remaining loss of the Americans was due to the small cruisers stumbling from time to time across the path of some one of the innumerable British heavy vessels. Had Congressional forethought been sufficiently great to have allowed a few line-of-battle ships to have been in readiness some time previous to the war, results of weight might have been accomplished. But the only activity ever exhibited by Congress in materially increasing the navy previous to the war, had been in partially carrying out President Jefferson's ideas of having an enormous force of very worthless gun-boats—a scheme whose wisdom was about on a par with some of that states-man's political and military theories.

Of the twelve[1] single-ship actions, two (those of the *Argus* and *Chesapeake*) undoubtedly redounded most to the credit of the British, in two (that of the *Wasp* with the *Reindeer,* and that of the *Enterprise* with the *Boxer*), the honors were nearly even, and in the other eight the superiority of the Americans was very manifest. In three actions (those with the *Penguin, Frolic,* and *Shannon*) the com-batants were about equal in strength, the Americans having slightly the advan-tage; in all the others but two, the victors combined superiority of force with superiority of skill. In but two cases, those of the *Argus* and *Epervier,* could any lack of courage be imputed to the vanquished. The second year alone showed to the advantage of the British; the various encounters otherwise were as cred-itable to the Americans at the end as at the beginning of the war. This is worth attending to, because many authors speak as if the successes of the Americans were confined to the first year. It is true that no frigate was taken after the first year, but this was partly because the strictness of the blockade kept the Ameri-can frigates more in port, while the sloops put out to sea at pleasure, and partly because after that year the British 18-pounder frigates either cruised in couples, or, when single, invariably refused, by order of the Board of Admiralty, an en-counter with a 24-pounder; and though much of the American success was un-questionably to be attributed to more men and heavier guns, yet much of it was not. The war itself gives us two instances in which defeat was owing solely, it may be said, to inferiority of force, courage and skill being equal. The *Wasp* was far heavier than the *Reindeer,* and, there being nothing to choose between them in any thing else, the damage done was about proportionate to this difference. It follows, as a matter of course, that the very much greater disproportion in loss in the cases of the *Avon, Epervier,* etc., where the disproportion in force was much less (they mounting 32's instead of 24's, and the victors being all of the same class), is only to be explained by the inferiority in skill on the part of the van-quished. These remarks apply just as much to the *Argus.* The *Reindeer,* with her 24's, would have been almost exactly on a par with her, and yet would have taken

[1] Not counting the last action of the *Constitution,* the *President'*s action, or the capture of the *Essex,* on account of the difficulty of fairly estimating the amount of credit due to each side. In both the first actions, however, the American ships seem to have been rather more ably fought than their antagonists, and, taking into account the overwhelming disadvantages under which the *Essex* labored, her defence displayed more desperate bravery than did that of any other ship during the war.

her with even greater ease than the *Peacock* did with her 32's. In other words, the only effect of our superiority in metal, men, and tonnage was to increase somewhat the disparity in loss. Had the *Congress* and *Constellation,* instead of the *United States* and *Constitution,* encountered the *Macedonian* and *Java,* the difference in execution would have been less than it was, but the result would have been unchanged, and would have been precisely such as ensued when the *Wasp* met the *Frolic,* or the *Hornet* the *Penguin.* On the other hand, had the *Shannon* met the *Constitution* there would have been a repetition of the fight between the *Wasp* and *Reindeer;* for it is but fair to remember that great as is the honor that Broke deserves, it is no more than that due to Manners.

The Republic of the United States owed a great deal to the excellent make and armament of its ships, but it owed still more to the men who were in them. The massive timbers and heavy guns of *Old Ironsides* would have availed but little had it not been for her able commanders and crews. Of all the excellent single-ship captains, British or American, produced by the war, the palm should be awarded to Hull.[1] The deed of no other man (excepting Macdonough) equalled his escape from Broke's five ships, or surpassed his half-hour's conflict with the *Guerrière.* After him, almost all the American captains deserve high praise— Decatur, Jones, Blakely, Biddle, Bainbridge, Lawrence, Burrows, Allen, Warrington, Stewart, Porter. It is no small glory to a country to have had such men upholding the honor of its flag. On a par with the best of them are Broke, Manners, and also Byron and Blythe. It must be but a poor-spirited American whose veins do not tingle with pride when he reads of the cruises and fights of the sea-captains, and their grim prowess, which kept the old Yankee flag floating over the waters of the Atlantic for three years, in the teeth of the mightiest naval power the world has ever seen; but it is equally impossible not to admire Broke's chivalric challenge and successful fight, or the heroic death of the captain of the *Reindeer.*

Nor can the war ever be fairly understood by any one who does not bear in mind that the combatants were men of the same stock, who far more nearly resembled each other than either resembled any other nation. I honestly believe that the American sailor offered rather better material for a man-of-warsman than the British, because the freer institutions of his country (as compared with the Britain of the drunken Prince Regent and his dotard father—a very different land from the present free England) and the peculiar exigencies of his life tended to make him more intelligent and self-reliant; but the difference, when there was any, was very small, and disappeared entirely when his opponents had been drilled for any length of time by men like Broke or Manners. The advantage consisted in the fact that our *average* commander was equal to the best, and higher than the average, of the opposing captains; and this held good throughout the various grades of the officers. The American officers knew they had redoubtable foes to contend with, and made every preparation accordingly. Owing

---

[1] See "Naval Tactics," by Commander J. H. Ward, and "Life of Commodore Tatnall," by Charles C. Jones, Jr.

their rank to their own exertions, trained by practical experience and with large liberty of action, they made every effort to have their crews in the most perfect state of skill and discipline. In Commodore Tatnall's biography (p. 15) it is mentioned that the blockaded *Constellation* had her men well trained at the guns and at target practice, though still lying in the river, so as to be at once able to meet a foe when she put out to sea. The British captain, often owing his command to his social standing or to favoritism, hampered by red tape,[1] and accustomed by 20 years' almost uninterrupted success to regard the British arms as invincible, was apt to laugh at all manœuvring,[2] and scorned to prepare too carefully for a fight, trusting to the old British "pluck and luck" to carry him through. So, gradually he forgot how to manœuvre or to prepare. The *Java* had been at sea six weeks before she was captured, yet during that time the entire exercise of her crew at the guns had been confined to the discharge of six broadsides of blank cartridges ( James, vi, 184); the *Constitution,* like the *Java,* had shipped an entirely new and raw crew previous to her first cruise, and was at sea but five weeks before she met the *Guerrière,* and yet her men had been trained to perfection. This is a sufficient comment on the comparative merits of Captain Hull and Captain Lambert. The American prepared himself in every possible way; the Briton tried to cope with courage alone against courage united to skill. His bad gunnery had not been felt in contending with European foes[3] as unskilful as himself. Says Lord Howard Douglass (p. 3): "We entered with too much confidence into a war with a marine much more expert than any of our European enemies * * * there was inferiority of gunnery as well as of force," etc. Admiral Codrington, commenting on the *Epervier's* loss, says, as before quoted, that, owing to his being chosen purely for merit, the American captain was an overmatch for the British, unless "he encountered our best officers on equal terms."

The best criticism on the war is that given by Capitaine Jurien de la Gravière.[4] After speaking of the heavier metal and greater number of men of the American ships, he continues: "And yet only an enormous superiority in the precision and rapidity of their fire can explain the difference in the losses sustained by the combatants. * * * Nor was the skill of their gunners the only cause to which the Americans owed their success. Their ships were faster; the crews, composed of chosen men, manœuvred with uniformity and precision; their captains had that practical knowledge which is only to be acquired by long experience of the sea; and it is not to be wondered at that the *Constitution,* when chased during three days by a squadron of five English frigates, succeeded in escaping, by surpassing them in manœuvring, and by availing herself of every ingenious resource and skilful

---

[1] For instance, James mentions that they were forbidden to use more than so many shot in practice, and that Capt. Broke utterly disregarded this command.

[2] Lord Howard Douglass, "Naval Gunnery," states this in various places.—"Accustomed to condemn all manœuvring."

[3] Lord Howard Douglass; he seems to think that in 1812 the British had fallen off absolutely, though not relatively to their European foes.

[4] "Guerres Maritimes," ii, pp. 269, 272, 274 (Paris, 1847).

expedient that maritime science could suggest. * * * To a marine exalted by success, but rendered negligent by the very habit of victory, the Congress only opposed the best of vessels and most formidable of armaments. * * * "[1]

It is interesting to compare the results of this inter-Anglian warfare, waged between the Insular and the Continental English, with the results of the contest that the former were at the same time carrying on with their Gallo-Roman neighbors across the channel. For this purpose I shall rely on Troude's "Batailles Navales," which would certainly not give the English more than their due. His account of the comparative force in each case can be supplemented by the corresponding one given in James. Under drawn battles I include all such as were indecisive, in so far that neither combatant was captured; in almost every case each captain claimed that the other ran away.

During the years 1812 to 1815 inclusive, there were eight actions between French and English ships of approximately equal force. In three of these the English were victorious.

In 1812 the *Victorious,* 74, captured the *Rivoli,* 74.

COMPARATIVE FORCE

BROADSIDES, METAL, LBS.

|  | TROUDE. | JAMES. |
|---|---|---|
| *Victorious* | 1,014 | 1,060 |
| *Rivoli* | 1,010 | 1,085 |

In 1814 the *Tagus* captured the *Ceres* and the *Hebrus* captured the *Étoile.*

BROADSIDES, METAL, LBS.

|  | TROUDE. | JAMES. |
|---|---|---|
| *Tagus* | 444 | 467 |
| *Ceres* | 428 | 463 |
| *Hebrus* | 467 | 467 |
| *Étoile* | 428 | 463 |

The *Ceres,* when she surrendered, had but one man wounded, although she had suffered a good deal aloft. The fight between the 74's was murderous to an almost unexampled degree, 125 English and 400 French falling. The *Hebrus* lost 40 and the *Étoile* 120 men.

Five actions were "drawn."

In 1812 the *Swallow* fought the *Renard* and *Garland.* The former threw 262, the latter 290 lbs. of shot at a broadside.

---

[1] The praise should be given to the individual captains and *not* to Congress, however; and none of the American ships had picked crews. During the war the *Shannon* had the only crew which could with any fairness be termed "picked," for her men had been together seven years, and all of her "boys" must have been well-grown young men, much older than the boys on her antagonist.

In 1815 the *Pilot,* throwing 262 lbs., fought a draw with the *Egerie* throwing 260.

In 1814 two frigates of the force of the *Tagus* fought a draw with two frigates of the force of the *Ceres;* and the *Eurotas,* with 24-pounders failed to capture the *Chlorinde,* which had only 18-pounders.

In 1815 the *Amelia* fought a draw with the *Aréthuse,* the ships throwing respectively 549 and 463 lbs., according to the English, or 572 and 410 lbs., according to the French accounts. In spite of being superior in force the English ship lost 141 men, and the French but 105. This was a bloodier fight than even that of the *Chesapeake* with the *Shannon;* but the gunnery was, nevertheless, much worse than that shown by the two combatants in the famous duel off Boston harbor, one battle lasting four hours and the other 15 minutes.

There were a number of other engagements where the British were successful but where it is difficult to compare the forces. Twice a 74 captured or destroyed two frigates, and a razee performed a similar feat. An 18-gun brig, the *Weasel,* fought two 16-gun brigs till one of them blew up.

The loss of the two navies at each other's hands during the four years was:—

| ENGLISH SHIPS. | FRENCH SHIPS. |
|---|---|
| 1 16-gun brig | 3 line-of-battle ships |
| 1 12-gun brig | 11 frigates |
| 1 10-gun cutter | 2 26-gun flûtes |
| | 2 16-gun brigs |
| | 1 10-gun brig |
| | many gun-boats, etc. |

Or one navy lost three vessels, mounting 38 guns, and the other 19 vessels, mounting 830 guns.

During the same time the English lost to the Danes one 14-gun brig, and destroyed in return a frigate of 46 guns, a 6-gun schooner, a 4-gun cutter, two galliots and several gun-brigs.

In the above lists it is to be noticed how many of the engagements were indecisive, owing chiefly to the poor gunnery of the combatants. The fact that both the *Eurotas* and the *Amelia,* though more powerfully armed and manned than the *Hebrus,* yet failed to capture the sister ships of the frigate taken by the latter, shows that heavy metal and a numerous crew are not the only elements necessary for success; indeed the *Eurotas* and *Amelia* were as superior in force to their antagonists as the *Constitution* was to the *Java.*

But the chief point to be noticed is the overwhelming difference in the damage the two navies caused each other. This difference was, roughly, as five to one against the Danes, and as fifty to one against the French; while it was as four to three in favor of the American. These figures give some idea of the effectiveness of the various navies. At any rate they show that we had found out what the European nations had for many years in vain striven to discover—a way to do more damage than we received in a naval contest with England.

# X

# 1815

# THE BATTLE

# OF NEW ORLEANS

The war on land generally disastrous · British send great expedition against New Orleans · Jackson prepares for the defence of the city · Night attack on the British advance guard · Artillery duels · Great battle of January 8, 1815 · Slaughtering repulse of the main attack · Rout of the Americans on the right bank of the river · Final retreat of the British · Observations on the character of the troops and commanders engaged

While our navy had been successful, the war on land had been for us full of humiliation. The United States then formed but a loosely knit confederacy, the sparse population scattered over a great expanse of land. Ever since the Federalist party had gone out of power in 1800, the nation's ability to maintain order at home and enforce respect abroad had steadily dwindled; and the twelve years' nerveless reign of the Doctrinaire Democracy had left us impotent for attack and almost as feeble for defence. Jefferson, though a man whose views and theories had a profound influence upon our national life, was perhaps the most incapable Executive that ever filled the presidential chair; being almost purely a visionary, he was utterly unable to grapple with the slightest actual danger, and, not even excepting his successor, Madison, it would be difficult to imagine a man less fit to guide the state with honor and safety through the stormy times that marked the opening of the present century. Without the prudence to avoid war or the forethought to prepare for it, the Administration drifted helplessly into a conflict in which only the navy prepared by the Federalists twelve years before, and weakened rather than strengthened during the intervening time, saved us from complete and shameful defeat. True to its theories, the House of Virginia made no preparations, and thought the war could be fought by "the nation in arms"; the exponents of this particular idea, the militiamen, a partially armed mob, ran like sheep whenever brought into the field. The regulars were not much better. After two years of warfare, Scott records in his autobiography that there were but two books of tactics (one written in French) in the entire army on the Niagara frontier; and officers and men were on such a dead level of ignorance that he had to spend a month drilling all of the former, divided into squads, in the school of the soldier and school of the company.[1] It is small wonder that such troops were utterly unable to meet the English. Until near the end, the generals were as bad as the armies they commanded, and the administration of the War Department continued to be a triumph of imbecility to the very last.[2] With the exception of the brilliant and successful charge of the Kentucky mounted infantry at the battle of the Thames, the only bright spot in the war in the North was the campaign on the Niagara frontier during the summer of 1814; and even here, the chief battle, that of Lundy's Lane, though reflecting as much honor on the Americans as on the British, was for the former a defeat, and not a victory, as most of our writers seem to suppose.

But the war had a dual aspect. It was partly a contest between the two branches of the English race, and partly a last attempt on the part of the Indian tribes to check the advance of the most rapidly growing one of these same two branches; and this last portion of the struggle, though attracting comparatively little attention, was really much the most far-reaching in its effect upon history. The triumph of the British would have distinctly meant the giving a new lease of life to the Indian nationalities, the hemming in, for a time, of the United States, and the stoppage, perhaps for many years, of the march of English civilization across the continent. The English of Britain were doing all they could to put off the day when their race would reach to a world-wide supremacy.

There was much fighting along our Western frontier with various Indian tribes; and it was especially fierce in the campaign that a backwoods general of Tennessee, named Andrew Jackson, carried on against the powerful confederacy of the Creeks, a nation that was thrust in like a wedge between the United States proper and their dependency, the newly acquired French province of Louisiana. After several slaughtering fights, the most noted being the battle of the Horse-shoe Bend, the power of the Creeks was broken for ever; and afterward, as there was much question over the proper boundaries of what was then the Latin land of Florida, Jackson marched south, attacked the Spaniards and drove them from Pensacola. Meanwhile the British, having made a successful and ravaging summer campaign through Virginia and Maryland, situated in the heart of the country, organized the most formidable expedition of the war for a winter campaign against the outlying land of Louisiana, whose defender Jackson of necessity became. Thus, in the course of events, it came about that Louisiana was the theatre on which the final and most dramatic act of the war was played.

---

[1] "Memoirs of Lieutenant-General Scott," written by himself (2 vols., New York, 1864), i, p. 115.

[2] Monroe's biographer (see "James Monroe," by Daniel C. Gilman, Boston, 1883, p. 123) thinks he made a good Secretary of War; I think he was as much a failure as his predecessors, and a harsher criticism could not be passed on him. Like the other statesmen of his school, he was mighty in word and weak in action; bold to plan but weak to perform. As an instance, contrast his fiery letters to Jackson with the fact that he never gave him a particle of practical help.

—

Amid the gloomy, semi-tropical swamps that cover the quaking delta thrust out into the blue waters of the Mexican Gulf by the strong torrent of the mighty Mississippi, stood the fair, French city of New Orleans. Its lot had been strange and varied. Won and lost, once and again, in conflict with the subjects of the Catholic king, there was a strong Spanish tinge in the French blood that coursed so freely through the veins of its citizens; joined by purchase to the great Federal Republic, it yet shared no feeling with the latter, save that of hatred to the common foe. And now an hour of sore need had come upon the city; for against it came the red English, lords of fight by sea and land. A great fleet of war vessels—ships of the line, frigates and sloops—under Admiral Cochrane, was on the way to New Orleans, convoying a still larger fleet of troop ships, with aboard them some ten thousand fighting men, chiefly the fierce and hardy veterans of the Peninsular War,[1] who had been trained for seven years in the stern school of the Iron Duke, and who were now led by one of the bravest and ablest of all Wellington's brave and able lieutenants, Sir Edward Packenham.

On the 8th of December 1814, the foremost vessels, with among their number the great two-decker *Tonnant,* carrying the admiral's flag, anchored off the Chandeleur Islands[2]; and as the current of the Mississippi was too strong to be easily breasted, the English leaders determined to bring their men by boats through the bayous, and disembark them on the bank of the river ten miles below the wealthy city at whose capture they were aiming. There was but one thing to prevent the success of this plan, and that was the presence in the bayous of five American gun-boats, manned by a hundred and eighty men, and commanded by Lieutenant Comdg. Catesby Jones, a very shrewd fighter. So against him was sent Captain Nicholas Lockyer with forty-five barges, and nearly a thousand sailors and marines, men who had grown gray during a quarter of a century of unbroken ocean warfare. The gun-boats were moored in a head-and-stern line, near the Rigolets, with their boarding-nettings triced up, and every thing ready to do desperate battle; but the British rowed up with strong, swift strokes, through a murderous fire of great guns and musketry; the vessels were grappled amid fierce resistance; the boarding-nettings were slashed through and cut away; with furious fighting the decks were gained; and one by one, at push of pike and cutlass stroke, the gun-boats were carried in spite of their stubborn defenders; but not till more than one barge had been sunk, while the assailants had lost a hundred men, and the assailed about half as many.

There was now nothing to hinder the landing of the troops; and as the scattered transports arrived, the soldiers were disembarked, and ferried through the sluggish water of the bayous on small flat-bottomed craft; and finally, Dec. 23d, the advance guard, two thousand strong, under General Keane, emerged at

---

[1] "The British infantry embarked at Bordeaux, some for America, some for England." ("History of the War in the Peninsula," by Major-General Sir W. F. P. Napier, K.C.B. New edition. New York, 1882, vol. v, p. 200.) For discussion of numbers, see farther on.

[2] See, *ante,* p. 343.

the mouth of the canal Villeré, and camped on the bank of the river,[1] but nine miles below New Orleans, which now seemed a certain prize, almost within their grasp.

Yet, although a mighty and cruel foe was at their very gates, nothing save fierce defiance reigned in the fiery creole hearts of the Crescent City. For a master-spirit was in their midst. Andrew Jackson, having utterly broken and destroyed the most powerful Indian confederacy that had ever menaced the Southwest, and having driven the haughty Spaniards from Pensacola, was now bending all the energies of his rugged intellect and indomitable will to the one object of defending New Orleans. No man could have been better fitted for the task. He had hereditary wrongs to avenge on the British, and he hated them with an implacable fury that was absolutely devoid of fear. Born and brought up among the lawless characters of the frontier, and knowing well how to deal with them, he was able to establish and preserve the strictest martial law in the city without in the least quelling the spirit of the citizens. To a restless and untiring energy he united sleepless vigilance and genuine military genius. Prompt to attack whenever the chance offered itself, seizing with ready grasp the slightest vantage-ground, and never giving up a foot of earth that he could keep, he yet had the patience to play a defensive game when it so suited him, and with consummate skill he always followed out the scheme of warfare that was best adapted to his wild soldiery. In after-years he did to his country some good and more evil; but no true American can think of his deeds at New Orleans without profound and unmixed thankfulness.

He had not reached the city till December 2d, and had therefore but three weeks in which to prepare the defence. The Federal Government, throughout the campaign, did absolutely nothing for the defence of Louisiana; neither provisions nor munitions of war of any sort were sent to it, nor were any measures taken for its aid.[2] The inhabitants had been in a state of extreme despondency up to the time that Jackson arrived, for they had no one to direct them, and they were weakened by factional divisions[3]; but after his coming there was nothing but the utmost enthusiasm displayed, so great was the confidence he inspired, and so firm his hand in keeping down all opposition. Under his direction earthworks were thrown up to defend all the important positions, the whole population working night and day at them; all the available artillery was mounted, and every ounce of war material that the city contained was seized; martial law was proclaimed; and all general business was suspended, every thing being rendered subordinate to the one grand object of defence.

Jackson's forces were small. There were two war vessels in the river. One was the little schooner *Carolina*, manned by regular seamen, largely New Englan-

---

[1] Letter of Major-General John Keane, Dec. 26, 1814.

[2] "Historical Memoir of the War in West Florida and Louisiana" (by Major A. Lacarriex Latour, translated from the French by H. P. Nugent, Philadelphia, 1816), p. 66.

[3] Latour, 53.

ders. The other was the newly built ship *Louisiana,* a powerful corvette; she had of course no regular crew, and her officers were straining every nerve to get one from the varied ranks of the maritime population of New Orleans; long-limbed and hard-visaged Yankees, Portuguese and Norwegian seamen from foreign merchantmen, dark-skinned Spaniards from the West Indies, swarthy Frenchmen who had served under the bold privateersman Lafitte,—all alike were taken, and all alike by unflagging exertions were got into shape for battle.[1] There were two regiments of regulars, numbering together about eight hundred men, raw and not very well disciplined, but who were now drilled with great care and regularity. In addition to this Jackson raised somewhat over a thousand militiamen among the citizens. There were some Americans among them, but they were mostly French creoles,[2] and one band had in its formation something that was curiously pathetic. It was composed of free men of color,[3] who had gathered to defend the land which kept the men of their race in slavery; who were to shed their blood for the Flag that symbolized to their kind not freedom but bondage; who were to die bravely as freemen, only that their brethren might live on ignobly as slaves. Surely there was never a stranger instance than this of the irony of fate.

But if Jackson had been forced to rely only on these troops New Orleans could not have been saved. His chief hope lay in the volunteers of Tennessee, who, under their Generals, Coffee and Carroll, were pushing their toilsome and weary way toward the city. Every effort was made to hurry their march through the almost impassable roads, and at last, in the very nick of time, on the 23d of December, the day on which the British troops reached the river-bank, the vanguard of the Tennesseeans marched into New Orleans. Gaunt of form and grim of face; with their powder-horns slung over their buckskin shirts; carrying their long rifles on their shoulders and their heavy hunting-knives stuck in their belts; with their coon-skin caps and fringed leggings; thus came the grizzly warriors of the backwoods, the heroes of the Horse-Shoe Bend, the victors over Spaniard and Indian, eager to pit themselves against the trained regulars of Britain, and to throw down the gage of battle to the world-renowned infantry of the island English. Accustomed to the most lawless freedom, and to giving free rein to the full violence of their passions, defiant of discipline and impatient of the slightest restraint, caring little for God and nothing for man, they were soldiers who, under an ordinary commander, would have been fully as dangerous to themselves and their leaders as to their foes. But Andrew Jackson was of all men the one best fitted to manage such troops. Even their fierce natures quailed before the ungovernable fury of a spirit greater than their own; and their sullen, stubborn wills were bent at last before his unyielding temper and iron hand. Moreover, he was one of themselves; he

---

[1] Letter of Commodore Daniel G. Patterson, Dec. 20, 1814.
[2] Latour, 110.
[3] Latour, 111.

typified their passions and prejudices, their faults and their virtues; he shared their hardships as if he had been a common private, and, in turn, he always made them partakers of his triumphs. They admired his personal prowess with pistol and rifle, his unswerving loyalty to his friends, and the relentless and unceasing war that he waged alike on the foes of himself and his country. As a result they loved and feared him as few generals have ever been loved or feared; they obeyed him unhesitatingly; they followed his lead without flinching or murmuring, and they ever made good on the field of battle the promise their courage held out to his judgment.

It was noon of December 23d when General Keane, with nineteen hundred men, halted and pitched his camp on the east bank of the Mississippi; and in the evening enough additional troops arrived to swell his force to over twenty-three hundred soldiers.[1] Keane's encampment was in a long plain, rather thinly covered with fields and farmhouses, about a mile in breadth, and bounded on one side by the river, on the other by gloomy and impenetrable cypress swamps; and there was no obstacle interposed between the British camp and the city it menaced.

At two in the afternoon word was brought to Jackson that the foe had reached the river bank, and without a moment's delay the old backwoods fighter prepared to strike a rough first blow. At once, and as if by magic, the city started from her state of rest into one of fierce excitement and eager preparation. The alarm-guns were fired; in every quarter the war-drums were beaten; while, amid the din and clamor, all the regulars and marines, the best of the creole militia, and the vanguard of the Tennesseeans, under Coffee,—forming a total of a little more than two thousand men,[2]—were assembled in great haste; and the gray of the winter twilight saw them, with Old Hickory at their head, marching steadily along the river bank toward the camp of their foes. Patterson, meanwhile, in the schooner *Carolina*, dropped down with the current to try the effect of a flank attack.

Meanwhile the British had spent the afternoon in leisurely arranging their camp, in posting the pickets, and in foraging among the farm-houses. There was no fear of attack, and as the day ended huge campfires were lit, at which the hungry soldiers cooked their suppers undisturbed. One division of the troops

[1] James ("Military Occurrences of the Late War," by Wm. James, London, 1818), vol. ii, p. 362, says 2,050 rank and file; the English returns, as already explained, unlike the French and American, never included officers, sergeants, drummers, artillerymen, or engineers, but only "sabres and bayonets" (Napier, iv, 252). At the end of Napier's fourth volume is given the "morning state" of Wellington's forces on April 10, 1814. This shows 56,030 rank and file and 7,431 officers, sergeants, and trumpeters or drummers; or, in other words, to get at the real British force in an action, even supposing there are no artillerymen or engineers present, 13 per cent. must be added to the given number, which includes only rank and file. Making this addition, Keane had 2,310 men. The Americans greatly overestimated his force, Latour making it 4,980.

[2] General Jackson, in his official letter, says only 1,500; but Latour, in a detailed statement, makes it 2,024; exclusive of 107 Mississippi dragoons who marched with the column, but being on horseback had to stay behind, and took no part in the action. Keane thought he had been attacked by 5,000 men.

had bivouacked on the high levee that kept the waters from flooding the land near by; and about half past seven in the evening their attention was drawn to a large schooner which had dropped noiselessly down, in the gathering dusk, and had come to anchor a short distance off shore, the force of the stream swinging her broadside to the camp.[1] The soldiers crowded down to the water's edge, and, as the schooner returned no answer to their hails, a couple of musket-shots were fired at her. As if in answer to this challenge, the men on shore heard plainly the harsh voice of her commander, as he sung out, "Now then, give it to them for the honor of America"; and at once a storm of grape hurtled into their ranks. Wild confusion followed. The only field-pieces with Keane were two light 3-pounders, not able to cope with the *Carolina*'s artillery; the rocket guns were brought up, but were speedily silenced; musketry proved quite as in-effectual; and in a very few minutes the troops were driven helter-skelter off the levee, and were forced to shelter themselves behind it, not without having suffered severe loss.[2] The night was now as black as pitch; the embers of the de-serted camp-fires, beaten about and scattered by the schooner's shot, burned with a dull red glow; and at short intervals the darkness was momentarily lit up by the flashes of the *Carolina*'s guns. Crouched behind the levee, the British sol-diers lay motionless, listening in painful silence to the pattering of the grape among the huts, and to the moans and shrieks of the wounded who lay beside them. Things continued thus till toward nine o'clock, when a straggling fire from the pickets gave warning of the approach of a more formidable foe. The American land-forces had reached the outer lines of the British camp, and the increasing din of the musketry, with ringing through it the whip-like crack of the Tennesseean rifles, called out the whole British army to the shock of a des-perate and uncertain strife. The young moon had by this time struggled through the clouds, and cast on the battle-field a dim, unearthly light that but partly relieved the intense darkness. All order was speedily lost. Each officer, American or British, as fast as he could gather a few soldiers round him, at-tacked the nearest group of foes; the smoke and gloom would soon end the struggle, when, if unhurt, he would rally what men he could and plunge once more into the fight. The battle soon assumed the character of a multitude of individual combats, dying out almost as soon as they began, because of the dif-ficulty of telling friend from foe, and beginning with ever-increasing fury as soon as they had ended. The clatter of the firearms, the clashing of steel, the rallying cries and loud commands of the officers, the defiant shouts of the men, joined to the yells and groans of those who fell, all combined to produce so terrible a noise and tumult that it maddened the coolest brains. From one

---

[1] I have taken my account of the night action chiefly from the work of an English soldier who took part in it; Ensign (afterward Chaplain-General) H. R. Gleig's "Narrative of the Campaigns of the British Army at Washington, Baltimore, and New Orleans." (New edition, Philadelphia, 1821, pp. 286–300.)

[2] General Keane, in his letter, writes that the British suffered but a single casualty; Gleig, who was present, says (p. 288): "The deadly shower of grape swept down numbers in the camp."

side or the other bands of men would penetrate into the heart of the enemy's lines, and would there be captured, or would cut their way out with the prisoners they had taken. There was never a fairer field for the fiercest personal prowess, for in the darkness the firearms were of little service, and the fighting was hand to hand. Many a sword, till then but a glittering toy, was that night crusted with blood. The British soldiers and the American regulars made fierce play with their bayonets, and the Tennesseeans, with their long hunting-knives. Man to man, in grimmest hate, they fought and died, some by bullet and some by bayonet-thrust or stroke of sword. More than one in his death agony slew the foe at whose hand he himself had received the mortal wound; and their bodies stiffened as they lay, locked in the death grip. Again the clouds came over the moon; a thick fog crept up from the river, wrapping from sight the ghastly havoc of the battle-field; and long before midnight the fighting stopped perforce, for the fog and the smoke and the gloom were such that no one could see a yard away. By degrees each side drew off.[1] In sullen silence Jackson marched his men up the river, while the wearied British returned to their camp. The former had lost over two hundred,[2] the latter nearly three hundred[3] men; for the darkness and confusion that added to the horror, lessened the slaughter of the battle.

Jackson drew back about three miles, where he halted and threw up a long line of breastworks, reaching from the river to the morass; he left a body of mounted riflemen to watch the British. All the English troops reached the field on the day after the fight; but the rough handling that the foremost had received made them cautious about advancing. Moreover, the left division was kept behind the levee all day by the *Carolina,* which opened upon them whenever they tried to get away; nor was it till dark that they made their escape out of range of her cannon. Christmas-day opened drearily enough for the invaders. Although they were well inland, the schooner, by greatly elevating her guns, could sometimes reach them, and she annoyed them all through the day[4]; and as the Americans had cut the levee in their front, it at one time seemed likely that they would be drowned out. However, matters now took a turn for the better. The river was so low that the cutting of the levee instead of flooding the plain[5] merely filled the shrunken bayous, and rendered it easy

---

[1] Keane writes: "The enemy thought it prudent to retire, and did not again dare to advance. It was now 12 o'clock, and the firing ceased on both sides"; and Jackson: "We should have succeeded ... in capturing the enemy, had not a thick fog, which arose about (?) o'clock, occasioned some confusion.... I contented myself with lying on the field that night." Jackson certainly failed to capture the British; but equally certainly damaged them so as to arrest their march till he was in condition to meet and check them.

[2] 24 killed, 115 wounded, 74 missing.

[3] 46 killed, 167 wounded, 64 missing. I take the official return for each side, as authority for the respective force and loss.

[4] "While sitting at table, a loud shriek was heard.... A shot had taken effect on the body of an unfortunate soldier ... who was fairly cut in two at the lower portion of the belly!" (Gleig, p. 306.)

[5] Latour, 113.

for the British to bring up their heavy guns; and on the same day their trusted leader, Sir Edward Packenham, arrived to take command in person, and his presence gave new life to the whole army. A battery was thrown up during the two succeeding nights on the brink of the river opposite to where the *Carolina* lay; and at dawn a heavy cannonade of red-hot shot and shell was opened upon her from eleven guns and a mortar.[1] She responded briskly, but very soon caught fire and blew up, to the vengeful joy of the troops whose bane she had been for the past few days. Her destruction removed the last obstacle to the immediate advance of the army; but that night her place was partly taken by the mounted riflemen, who rode down to the British lines, shot the sentries, engaged the out-posts, and kept the whole camp in a constant state of alarm.[2]

In the morning Sir Edward Packenham put his army in motion, and marched on New Orleans. When he had gone nearly three miles he suddenly, and to his great surprise, stumbled on the American army. Jackson's men had worked like beavers, and his breastworks were already defended by over three thousand fighting men,[3] and by half a dozen guns, and moreover were flanked by the corvette *Louisiana*, anchored in the stream. No sooner had the heads of the British columns appeared than they were driven back by the fire of the American batteries; the field-pieces, mortars, and rocket guns were then brought up, and a sharp artillery duel took place. The motley crew of the *Louisiana* handled their long ship guns with particular effect; the British rockets proved of but little service[4]; and after a stiff fight, in which they had two field-pieces and a light mortar dismounted,[5] the British artillerymen fell back on the infantry. Then Packenham drew off his whole army out of cannon shot, and pitched his camp facing the intrenched lines of the Americans. For the next three days the British battalions lay quietly in front of their foe, like wolves who have brought to bay a gray boar, and crouch just out of reach of his tusks, waiting a chance to close in.

Packenham, having once tried the strength of Jackson's position, made up his mind to breach his works and silence his guns with a regular battering train. Heavy cannon were brought up from the ships, and a battery was established on the bank to keep in check the *Louisiana*. Then, on the night of the last day of the year, strong parties of workmen were sent forward, who, shielded by the darkness, speedily threw up stout earthworks, and mounted therein fourteen

[1] Gleig, 307. The Americans thought the battery consisted of 5 18- and 12-pounders; Gleig says 9 field-pieces (9- and 6-pounders), 2 howitzers, and a mortar.

[2] Gleig, 310.

[3] 3,282 men in all, according to the Adjutant-General's return for Dec. 28, 1814.

[4] Latour, 121.

[5] Gleig, 314. The official returns show a loss of 18 Americans and 58 British, the latter suffering much less than Jackson supposed. Lossing, in his "Field-Book of the War of 1812," not only greatly overestimates the British loss, but speaks as if this was a serious attack, which it was not. Packenham's army, while marching, unexpectedly came upon the American intrenchment, and recoiled at once, after seeing that his field-pieces were unable to contend with the American artillery.

heavy guns,[1] to face the thirteen[2] mounted in Jackson's lines, which were but three hundred yards distant.

New Year's day dawned very misty. As soon as the haze cleared off the British artillerymen opened with a perfect hail of balls, accompanied by a cloud of rockets and mortar shells. The Americans were taken by surprise, but promptly returned the fire, with equal fury and greater skill. Their guns were admirably handled; some by the cool New England seaman lately forming the crew of the *Carolina,* others by the fierce creole privateersmen of Lafitte, and still others by the trained artillerymen of the regular army. They were all old hands, who in their time had done their fair share of fighting, and were not to be flurried by any attack, however unexpected. The British cannoneers plied their guns like fiends, and fast and thick fell their shot; more slowly but with surer aim, their opponents answered them.[3] The cotton bales used in the American embrasures caught fire, and blew up two powder caissons; while the sugar hogsheads of which the British batteries were partly composed were speedily shattered and splintered in all directions. Though the British champions fought with unflagging courage and untiring energy, and though they had long been versed in war, yet they seemed to lack the judgment to see and correct their faults, and most of their shot went too high.[4] On the other hand, the old sea-dogs and trained regulars who held the field against them, not only fought their guns well and skilfully from the beginning, but all through the action kept coolly correcting their faults and making more sure their aim. Still, the fight was stiff and well contested. Two

---

[1] 10 long 18's and 4 24-pound carronades ( James, ii, 368). Gleig says (p. 318), "6 batteries mounting 30 pieces of heavy cannon." This must include the "brigade of field-pieces" of which James speaks. 9 of these, 9- and 6-pounders, and 2 howitzers, had been used in the attack on the *Carolina;* and there were also 2 field-mortars and 2 3-pounders present; and there must have been 1 other field-piece with the army, to make up the 30 of which Gleig speaks.

[2] viz.: 1 long 32, 3 long 24's, 1 long 18, 3 long 12's, 3 long 6's, a 6-inch howitzer, and a small carronade (Latour, 147); and on the same day Patterson had in his water-battery 1 long 24 and 2 long 12's (see his letter of Jan. 2d), making a total of 16 American guns.

[3] The British historian, Alison, says ("History of Europe," by Sir Archibald Alison, 9th edition, Edinburgh and London, 1852, vol. xii, p. 141): "It was soon found that the enemy's guns were so superior in weight and number, that nothing was to be expected from that species of attack." As shown above, at this time Jackson had on both sides of the river 16 guns; the British, according to both James and Gleig, between 20 and 30. Jackson's long guns were 1 32, 4 24's, 1 18, 5 12's, and 3 6's, throwing in all 224 pounds; Packenham had 10 long 18's, 2 long 3's, and from 6 to 10 long 9's and 6's, thus throwing between 228 and 258 pounds of shot; while Jackson had but 1 howitzer and 1 carronade to oppose 4 carronades, 2 howitzers, 2 mortars, and a dozen rocket guns; so in both number and weight of guns the British were greatly superior.

[4] In strong contrast to Alison, Admiral Codrington, an eyewitness, states the true reason of the British failure: ("Memoir of Admiral Sir Edward Codrington," by Lady Bourchier, London, 1873, vol. i, p. 334.) "On the 1st we had our batteries ready, by severe labor, in situation, from which the artillery people were, as a matter of course, to destroy and silence the opposing batteries, and give opportunity for a well-arranged storm. But, instead, not a gun of the enemy appeared to suffer, and our own firing too high was not discovered till" too late. "Such a failure in this boasted arm was not to be expected, and I think it a blot on the artillery escutcheon."

of the American guns were disabled and 34 of their men were killed or wounded. But one by one the British cannon were silenced or dismounted, and by noon their gunners had all been driven away, with the loss of 78 of their number.

The *Louisiana* herself took no part in this action. Patterson had previously landed some of her guns on the opposite bank of the river, placing them in a small redoubt. To match these the British also threw up some works and placed in them heavy guns, and all through New Year's day a brisk cannonade was kept up across the river between the two water-batteries, but with very little damage to either side.

For a week after this failure the army of the invaders lay motionless facing the Americans. In the morning and evening the defiant, rolling challenge of the English drums came throbbing up through the gloomy cypress swamps to where the grim riflemen of Tennessee were lying behind their log breastworks, and both day and night the stillness was at short intervals broken by the sullen boom of the great guns which, under Jackson's orders, kept up a never-ending fire on the leaguering camp of his foes.[1] Nor could the wearied British even sleep undisturbed; all through the hours of darkness the outposts were engaged in a most harassing bush warfare by the backwoodsmen, who shot the sentries, drove in the pickets, and allowed none of those who were on guard a moment's safety or freedom from alarm.[2]

But Packenham was all the while steadily preparing for his last and greatest stroke. He had determined to make an assault in force as soon as the expected reinforcements came up; nor, in the light of his past experience in conflict with foes of far greater military repute than those now before him, was this a rash resolve. He had seen the greatest of Napoleon's marshals, each in turn, defeated once and again, and driven in headlong flight over the Pyrenees by the Duke of Wellington; now he had under him the flower of the troops who had won those victories; was it to be supposed for a moment that such soldiers[3] who, in a dozen battles, had conquered the armies and captured the forts of the mighty French emperor, would shrink at last from a mud wall guarded by rough backwoodsmen? That there would be loss of life in such an assault was certain; but was loss of life to daunt men who had seen the horrible slaughter through which the stormers moved on to victory at Ciudad Rodrigo, Badajos, and San Sebastian? At the battle of Toulouse an English army, of which Packenham's troops then formed part, had driven Soult from a stronger position than was

---

[1] Gleig, 322.

[2] Gleig, 323.

[3] Speaking of Soult's overthrow a few months previous to this battle, Napier says (v, 209): "He was opposed to one of the greatest generals of the world, at the head of unconquerable troops. For what Alexander's Macedonians were at Arbela, Hannibal's Africans at Cannæ, Cæsar's Romans at Pharsalia, Napoleon's Guards at Austerlitz—such were Wellington's British soldiers at this period.... Six years of uninterrupted success had engrafted on their natural strength and fierceness a confidence that made them invincible."

now to be assailed, though he held it with a veteran infantry. Of a surety, the dashing general who had delivered the decisive blow on the stricken field of Salamanca,[1] who had taken part in the rout of the ablest generals and steadiest soldiers of Continental Europe, was not the man to flinch from a motley array of volunteers, militia, and raw regulars, led by a grizzled old bush-fighter, whose name had never been heard of outside of his own swamps, and there only as the savage destroyer of some scarcely more savage Indian tribes.

Moreover, Packenham was planning a flank attack. Under his orders a canal was being dug from the head of the bayou up which the British had come, across the plain to the Mississippi. This was to permit the passage of a number of ships' boats, on which one division was to be ferried to the opposite bank of the river, where it was to move up, and, by capturing the breastworks and water-battery on the west side, flank Jackson's main position on the east side.[2] When this canal was nearly finished the expected reinforcements, two thousand strong, under General Lambert, arrived, and by the evening of the 7th all was ready for the attack, which was to be made at daybreak on the following morning. Packenham had under him nearly 10,000[3] fighting men; 1,500 of these, under Colonel Thornton were to cross the river and make the attack on the west bank. Packenham himself was to superintend the main assault, on the east bank, which was to be made by the British right under General Gibbs, while the left moved forward under General Keane, and General Lambert commanded the reserve.[4] Jack-

---

[1] It was about 5 o'clock when Packenham fell upon Thomiéres. . . . From the chief to the lowest soldier, all [of the French] felt that they were lost, and in an instant Packenham, the most frank and gallant of men, commenced the battle. The British columns formed lines as they marched, and the French gunners, standing up manfully for the honor of their country, sent showers of grape into the advancing masses, while a crowd of light troops poured in a fire of musketry, under cover of which the main body endeavored to display a front. But, bearing onwards through the skirmishers with the might of a giant, Packenham broke the half-formed lines into fragments, and sent the whole in confusion upon the advancing supports. . . . Packenham, bearing onwards with conquering violence, . . . formed one formidable line two miles in advance of where Packenham had first attacked; and that impetuous officer, with unmitigated strength, still pressed forward, spreading terror and disorder on the enemy's left." (Napier, iv, 57, 58, 59.)

[2] "A particular feature in the assault was our cutting a canal into the Mississippi. . . . to convey a force to the right bank, which . . . might surprise the enemy's batteries on that side. I do not know how far this measure was relied on by the general, but, as he ordered and made his assault at daylight, I imagine he did not place much dependence upon it." (Codrington, i, 335.)

[3] James (ii, 373) says the British "rank and file" amounted to 8,153 men, including 1,200 seamen and marines. The only other place where he speaks of the latter is in recounting the attack on the right bank, when he says "about 200" were with Thornton, while both the admirals, Cochrane and Codrington, make the number 300; so he probably underestimates their number throughout, and at least 300 can be added, making 1,500 sailors and marines, and a total of 8,453. This number is corroborated by Major McDougal, the officer who received Sir Edward's body in his arms when he was killed; he says (as quoted in the "Memoirs of British Generals Distinguished During the Peninsular War," by John William Cole, London, 1856, vol. ii, p. 364) that after the battle and the loss of 2,036 men, "we had still an effective force of 6,400," making a total before the attack of 8,436 rank and file. Calling it 8,450, and adding (see *ante*, note 10) 13.3 per cent. for the officers, sergeants, and trumpeters, we get about 9,600 men.

[4] Letter of Major-General John Lambert to Earl Bathurst, Jan. 10, 1815.

son's[1] position was held by a total of 5,500 men.[2] Having kept a constant watch on the British, Jackson had rightly concluded that they would make the main attack on the east bank, and had, accordingly, kept the bulk of his force on that side. His works consisted simply of a mud breastwork, with a ditch in front of it, which stretched in a straight line from the river on his right across the plain, and some distance into the morass that sheltered his left. There was a small, unfinished redoubt in front of the breastworks on the river bank. Thirteen pieces of artillery were mounted on the works.[3] On the right was posted the Seventh regular infantry, 430 strong; then came 740 Louisiana militia (both French creoles and men of color, and comprising 30 New Orleans riflemen, who were Americans), and 240 regulars of the Forty-fourth regiment; while the rest of the line was formed by nearly 500 Kentuckians and over 1,600 Tennesseeans, under Carroll and Coffee, with 250 creole militia in the morass on the extreme left, to

---

[1] 4,698 on the east bank, according to the official report of Adjutant-General Robert Butler, for the morning of January 8th. The details are as follow:

| | |
|---|---|
| At batteries . . . . . . . . . . . . . . . . . . . . . . . . . . . . . . . . . . . . . | 154 |
| Command of Col. Ross (671 regulars and 742 Louisiana militia) . . . . . . . . . . . | 1,413 |
| Command of General Carroll (Tennesseeans, and somewhat under 500 Kentuckians) . . . . | 1,562 |
| General Coffee's command (Tennesseeans, and about 250 Louisiana militia) . . . . . . . | 813 |
| Major Hind's dragoons . . . . . . . . . . . . . . . . . . . . . . . . . . . . . | 230 |
| Col. Slaughter's command . . . . . . . . . . . . . . . . . . . . . . . . . . . . | 526 |
| Total, | 4,698 |

These figures tally almost exactly with those given by Major Latour, except that he omits all reference to Col. Slaughter's command, thus reducing the number to about 4,100. Nor can I anywhere find any allusion to Slaughter's command as taking part in the battle; and it is possible that these troops were the 500 Kentuckians ordered across the river by Jackson; in which case his whole force but slightly exceeded 5,000 men.

On the west bank there were 546 Louisiana militia—260 of the First regiment, 176 of the Second, and 110 of the Sixth. Jackson had ordered 500 Kentucky troops to be sent to reinforce them; only 400 started, of whom but 180 had arms. Seventy more received arms from the Naval Arsenal; and thus a total of 250 armed men were added to the 546 already on the west bank.

[2] Two thousand Kentucky militia had arrived, but in wretched plight; only 500 had arms, though pieces were found for about 250 more; and thus Jackson's army received an addition of 750 very badly disciplined soldiers.

"Hardly one third of the Kentucky troops, so long expected, are armed, and the arms they have are not fit for use." (Letter of Gen. Jackson to the Secretary of War, Jan. 3d.)

[3] Almost all British writers underestimate their own force and enormously magnify that of the Americans. Alison, for example, quadruples Jackson's *relative* strength, writing: "About 6,000 combatants were on the British side; a slender force to attack double their number, intrenched to the teeth in works bristling with bayonets and loaded with heavy artillery." Instead of double, he should have said half; the bayonets only "bristled" metaphorically, as less than a quarter of the Americans were armed with them; and the British breaching batteries had a heavier "load" of artillery than did the American lines. Gleig says that "to come nearer the truth" he "will choose a middle course, and suppose their whole force to be about 25,000 men" (p. 325). Gleig, by the way, in speaking of the battle itself, mentions one most startling evolution of the Americans, namely, that "without so much as lifting their faces above the ramparts, they swung their firelocks by one arm over the wall and discharged them" at the British. If any one will try to perform this feat, with a long, heavy rifle held in one hand, and with his head hid behind a wall, so as not to see the object aimed at, he will get a good idea of the likelihood of any man in his senses attempting it.

guard the head of a bayou. In the rear were 230 dragoons, chiefly from Mississippi, and some other troops in reserve; making in all 4,700 men on the east bank. The works on the west bank were farther down stream, and were very much weaker. Commodore Patterson had thrown up a water-battery of nine guns, three long 24's and six long 12's, pointing across the river, and intended to take in flank any foe attacking Jackson. This battery was protected by some strong earthworks, mounting three field-pieces, which were thrown up just below it, and stretched from the river about 200 yards into the plain. The line of defence was extended by a ditch for about a quarter of a mile farther, when it ended, and from there to the morass, half a mile distant, there were no defensive works at all. General Morgan, a very poor militia officer,[1] was in command, with a force of 550 Louisiana militia, some of them poorly armed; and on the night before the engagement he was reinforced by 250 Kentuckians, poorly armed, undisciplined, and worn out with fatigue.[2]

All through the night of the 7th a strange, murmurous clangor arose from the British camp, and was borne on the moist air to the lines of their slumbering foes. The blows of pickaxe and spade as the ground was thrown up into batteries by gangs of workmen, the rumble of the artillery as it was placed in position, the measured tread of the battalions as they shifted their places or marched off under Thornton,—all these and the thousand other sounds of warlike preparation were softened and blended by the distance into one continuous humming murmur, which struck on the ears of the American sentries with ominous foreboding for the morrow. By midnight Jackson had risen and was getting every thing in readiness to hurl back the blow that he rightly judged was soon to fall on his front. Before the dawn broke his soldiery was all on the alert. The bronzed and brawny seamen were grouped in clusters around the great guns. The creole soldiers came of a race whose habit it has ever been to take all phases of life joyously; but that morning their gayety was tempered by a dark undercurrent of fierce anxiety. They had more at stake than any other men on the field. They were fighting for their homes; they were fighting for their wives and their daughters. They well knew that the men they were to face were very brave in battle and very cruel

---

[1] He committed every possible fault, except showing lack of courage. He placed his works at a very broad instead of at a narrow part of the plain, against the advice of Latour, who had Jackson's approval (Latour, 167). He continued his earthworks but a very short distance inland, making them exceedingly strong in front, and absolutely defenceless on account of their flanks being unprotected. He did not mount the lighter guns of the water-battery on his lines, as he ought to have done. Having a force of 800 men, too weak anyhow, he promptly divided it; and, finally, in the fight itself, he stationed a small number of absolutely raw troops in a thin line on the open, with their flank in air; while a much larger number of older troops were kept to defend a much shorter line, behind a strong breastwork, with their flanks covered.

[2] Latour, 170.

in victory[1]; they well knew the fell destruction and nameless woe that awaited their city should the English take it at the sword's point. They feared not for themselves; but in the hearts of the bravest and most careless there lurked a dull terror of what that day might bring upon those they loved.[2] The Tennesseeans were troubled by no such misgivings. In saturnine, confident silence they lolled behind their mud walls, or, leaning on their long rifles, peered out into the gray fog with savage, reckless eyes. So, hour after hour, the two armies stood facing each other in the darkness, waiting for the light of day.

---

[1] To prove this, it is only needful to quote from the words of the Duke of Wellington himself; referring, it must be remembered, to their conduct in a friendly, not a hostile, country. "It is impossible to describe to you the irregularities and outrages committed by the troops. They are never out of sight of their officers, I might almost say, out of sight of the commanding officers of the regiments that outrages are not committed.... There is not an outrage of any description which has not been committed on a people who have uniformly received them as friends." "I really believe that more plunder and outrages have been committed by this army than by any other that ever was in the field." "A detachment seldom marches...that a murder, or a highway robbery, or some act of outrage is not committed by the British soldiers composing it. They have killed eight people since the army returned to Portugal." "They really forget every thing when plunder or wine is within reach."

[2] That these fears were just can be seen by the following quotations, from the works of a British officer, General Napier, who was an eye-witness of what he describes. It must be remembered that Ciudad Rodrigo, Badajos, and San Sebastian were friendly towns, only the garrisons being hostile. "Now commenced that wild and desperate wickedness which tarnished the lustre of the soldiers' heroism. All, indeed, were not alike, for hundreds risked and many lost their lives in striving to stop the violence; but the madness generally prevailed, and as the worst men were leaders here, all the dreadful passions of human nature were displayed. Shameless rapacity, brutal intemperance, savage lust, cruelty and murder, shrieks and piteous lamentations, groans, shouts, imprecations, the hissing of fires bursting from the houses, the crashing of doors and windows, the reports of muskets used in violence, resounded for two days and nights in the streets of Badajos. On the third, when the city was sacked, when the soldiers were exhausted by their own excesses, the tumult rather subsided than was quelled." (Vol. iii, 377.) And again: "This storm seemed to be a signal from hell for the perpetration of villainy which would have shamed the most ferocious barbarians of antiquity. At Rodrigo intoxication and plunder had been the principal object; at Badajos lust and murder were joined to rapine and drunkenness; but at San Sebastian the direst, the most revolting cruelty was added to the catalogue of crimes—one atrocity, of which a girl of seventeen was the victim, staggers the mind by its enormous, incredible, indescribable barbarity...a Portuguese adjutant, who endeavored to prevent some wickedness, was put to death in the market-place, not with sudden violence from a single ruffian, but deliberately, by a number of English soldiers.... and the disorder continued until the flames, following the steps of the plunderer, put an end to his ferocity by destroying the whole town." Packenham himself would have certainly done all in his power to prevent excesses, and has been foully slandered by many early American writers. Alluding to these, Napier remarks, somewhat caustically: "Pre-eminently distinguished for detestation of inhumanity and outrage, he has been, with astounding falsehood, represented as instigating his troops to the most infamous excesses; but from a people holding millions of their fellow-beings in the most horrible slavery, while they prate and vaunt of liberty until all men turn in loathing from the sickening folly, what can be expected?" (Vol. v, p. 31.) Napier possessed to a very eminent degree the virtue of being plain-spoken. Elsewhere (iii, 450), after giving a most admirably fair and just account of the origin of the Anglo-American war, he alludes, with a good deal of justice, to the Americans of 1812, as "a people who (notwithstanding the curse of black slavery which clings to them, adding the most horrible ferocity to the peculiar baseness of their mercantile spirit, and rendering their republican vanity ridiculous) do, in their general government, uphold civil institutions which have startled the crazy despotisms of Europe."

At last the sun rose, and as its beams struggled through the morning mist they glinted on the sharp steel bayonets of the English, where their scarlet ranks were drawn up in battle array, but four hundred yards from the American breastworks. There stood the matchless infantry of the island king, in the pride of their strength and the splendor of their martial glory; and as the haze cleared away they moved forward, in stern silence, broken only by the angry, snarling notes of the brazen bugles. At once the American artillery leaped into furious life; and, ready and quick, the more numerous cannon of the invaders responded from their hot, feverish lips. Unshaken amid the tumult of that iron storm the heavy red column moved steadily on toward the left of the American line, where the Tennesseeans were standing in motionless, grim expectancy. Three fourths of the open space was crossed, and the eager soldiers broke into a run. Then a fire of hell smote the British column. From the breastwork in front of them the white smoke curled thick into the air, as rank after rank the wild marksmen of the backwoods rose and fired, aiming low and sure. As stubble is withered by flame, so withered the British column under that deadly fire; and, aghast at the slaughter, the reeling files staggered and gave back. Packenham, fit captain for his valorous host, rode to the front, and the troops, rallying round him, sprang forward with ringing cheers. But once again the pealing rifle-blast beat in their faces; and the life of their dauntless leader went out before its scorching and fiery breath. With him fell the other general who was with the column, and all of the men who were leading it on; and, as a last resource, Keane brought up his stalwart Highlanders; but in vain the stubborn mountaineers rushed on, only to die as their comrades had died before them, with unconquerable courage, facing the foe, to the last. Keane himself was struck down; and the shattered wrecks of the British column, quailing before certain destruction, turned and sought refuge beyond reach of the leaden death that had overwhelmed their comrades. Nor did it fare better with the weaker force that was to assail the right of the American line. This was led by the dashing Colonel Rennie, who, when the confusion caused by the main attack was at its height, rushed forward with impetuous bravery along the river bank. With such headlong fury did he make the assault, that the rush of his troops took the outlying redoubt, whose defenders, regulars and artillerymen, fought to the last with their bayonets and clubbed muskets, and were butchered to a man. Without delay Rennie flung his men at the breastworks behind, and, gallantly leading them, sword in hand, he, and all around him, fell, riddled through and through by the balls of the riflemen. Brave though they were, the British soldiers could not stand against the singing, leaden hail, for if they stood it was but to die. So in rout and wild dismay they fled back along the river bank, to the main army. For some time afterward the British artillery kept up its fire, but was gradually silenced; the repulse was entire and complete along the whole line; nor did the cheering news of success brought from the west bank give any hope to the British commanders, stunned by their crushing over-throw.[1]

Meanwhile Colonel Thornton's attack on the opposite side had been suc-cessful, but had been delayed beyond the originally intended hour. The sides of the canal by which the boats were to be brought through to the Mississippi caved in, and choked the passage,[2] so that only enough got through to take over a half of Thornton's force. With these, seven hundred in number,[3] he crossed, but as he did not allow for the current, it carried him down about two miles below the proper landing-place. Meanwhile General Morgan, having under him eight hundred militia[4] whom it was of the utmost importance to have kept together, promptly divided them and sent three hundred of the rawest and most poorly armed down to meet the enemy in the open. The in-evitable result was their immediate rout and dispersion; about one hundred got back to Morgan's lines. He then had six hundred men, all militia, to op-pose to seven hundred regulars. So he stationed the four hundred best disci-plined men to defend the two hundred yards of strong breastworks, mounting three guns, which covered his left; while the two hundred worst disciplined were placed to guard six hundred yards of open ground on his right, with their flank resting in air, and entirely unprotected.[5] This truly phenomenal arrangement ensured beforehand the certain defeat of his troops, no matter how well they fought; but, as it turned out, they hardly fought at all. Thornton, pushing up the river, first attacked the breastwork in front, but was checked by a hot fire; deploying his men he then sent a strong force to march round and take Morgan on his exposed right flank.[6] There, the already demoralized Kentucky militia, extended in thin order across an open space, outnumbered, and taken in flank by regular troops, were stampeded at once, and after firing a single volley they took to their heels.[7] This exposed

---

[1] According to their official returns the British loss was 2,036; the American accounts, of course, make it much greater. Latour is the only trustworthy American contemporary historian of this war, and even he at times absurdly exaggerates the British force and loss. Most of the other American "histories" of that period were the most preposterously bombastic works that ever saw print. But as regards this bat-tle, none of them are as bad as even such British historians as Alison; the exact reverse being the case in many other battles, notably Lake Erie. The devices each author adopts to lessen the seeming force of his side are generally of much the same character. For instance, Latour says that 800 of Jackson's men were employed on works at the rear, on guard duty, etc., and deducts them; James, for precisely similar rea-sons, deducts 853 men: by such means one reduces Jackson's total force to 4,000, and the other gives Packenham but 7,300. Only 2,000 Americans were actually engaged on the east banks.

[2] Codrington, i, 386.

[3] James says 298 soldiers and about 200 sailors; but Admiral Cochrane in his letter (Jan. 18th) says 600 men, half sailors; and Admiral Codrington also (p. 335) gives this number, 300 being sailors: adding 13¼ per cent. for the officers, sergeants, and trumpeters, we get 680 men.

[4] 796. (Latour, 164–172.)

[5] Report of Court of Inquiry, Maj.-Gen. Wm. Carroll presiding.

[6] Letter of Col. W. Thornton, Jan. 8, 1815.

[7] Letter of Commodore Patterson, Jan. 13, 1815.

the flank of the better disciplined creoles, who were also put to flight; but they kept some order and were soon rallied.[1] In bitter rage Patterson spiked the guns of his water-battery and marched off with his sailors, unmolested. The American loss had been slight, and that of their opponents not heavy, though among their dangerously wounded was Colonel Thornton.

This success, though a brilliant one, and a disgrace to the American arms, had no effect on the battle. Jackson at once sent over reinforcements under the famous French general, Humbert, and preparations were forthwith made to retake the lost position. But it was already abandoned, and the force that had captured it had been recalled by Lambert, when he found that the place could not be held without additional troops.[2] The total British loss on both sides of the river amounted to over two thousand men, the vast majority of whom had fallen in the attack on the Tennesseeans, and most of the remainder in the attack made by Colonel Rennie. The Americans had lost but seventy men, of whom but thirteen fell in the main attack. On the east bank, neither the creole militia nor the Forty-fourth regiment had taken any part in the combat.

The English had thrown for high stakes and had lost every thing, and they knew it. There was nothing to hope for left. Nearly a fourth of their fighting men had fallen; and among the officers the proportion was far larger. Of their four generals, Packenham was dead, Gibbs dying, Keane disabled, and only Lambert left. Their leader, the ablest officers, and all the flower of their bravest men were lying, stark and dead, on the bloody plain before them; and their bodies were doomed to crumble into mouldering dust on the green fields where they had fought and had fallen. It was useless to make another trial. They had learned to their bitter cost, that no troops, however steady, could advance over open ground against such a fire as came from Jackson's lines. Their artillerymen had three times tried conclusions with the American gunners, and each time they had been forced to acknowledge themselves worsted. They would never have another chance to repeat their flank attack, for Jackson had greatly strengthened and enlarged the works on the west bank, and had seen that they were fully manned and ably commanded. Moreover, no sooner had the assault failed, than the Americans again began their old harassing warfare. The heaviest cannon, both from the breastwork and the water-battery, played on the British camp, both night and day, giving the army no rest, and the mounted riflemen kept up a trifling, but incessant and annoying, skirmishing with their pickets and outposts.

---

[1] Alison outdoes himself in recounting this feat. Having reduced the British force to 340 men, he says they captured the redoubt, "though defended by 22 guns and 1,700 men." Of course, it was physically impossible for the water-battery to take part in the defence; so there were but 3 guns, and by halving the force on one side and trebling it on the other, he makes the relative strength of the Americans just sixfold what it was,—and is faithfully followed by other British writers.

[2] The British Col. Dickson, who had been sent over to inspect, reported that 2,000 men would be needed to hold the battery; so Lambert ordered the British to retire. (Lambert's letter, Jan. 10th.)

The British could not advance, and it was worse than useless for them to stay where they were, for though they, from time to time, were reinforced, yet Jackson's forces augmented faster than theirs, and every day lessened the numerical inequality between the two armies. There was but one thing left to do, and that was to retreat. They had no fear of being attacked in turn. The British soldiers were made of too good stuff to be in the least cowed or cast down even by such a slaughtering defeat as that they had just suffered, and nothing would have given them keener pleasure than to have had a fair chance at their adversaries in the open; but this chance was just what Jackson had no idea of giving them. His own army, though in part as good as an army could be, consisted also in part of untrained militia, while not a quarter of his men had bayonets; and the wary old chief, for all his hardihood, had far too much wit to hazard such a force in fight with a superior number of seasoned veterans, thoroughly equipped, unless on his own ground and in his own manner. So he contented himself with keeping a sharp watch on Lambert; and on the night of January 18th the latter deserted his position, and made a very skilful and rapid retreat, leaving eighty wounded men and fourteen pieces of cannon behind him.[1] A few stragglers were captured on land, and, while the troops were embarking, a number of barges, with over a hundred prisoners, were cut out by some American seamen in row-boats; but the bulk of the army reached the transports unmolested. At the same time, a squadron of vessels, which had been unsuccessfully bombarding Fort Saint Philip for a week or two, and had been finally driven off when the fort got a mortar large enough to reach them with, also returned; and the whole fleet set sail for Mobile. The object was to capture Fort Boyer, which contained less than four hundred men, and, though formidable on its sea-front,[2] was incapable of defence when regularly attacked on its land side. The British landed, February 8th, some 1,500 men, broke ground, and made approaches; for four days the work went on amid a continual fire, which killed or wounded 11 Americans and 31 British; by that time the battering guns were in position and the fort capitulated, February 12th, the garrison marching out with the honors of war. Immediately afterward the news of peace arrived and all hostilities terminated.

In spite of the last trifling success, the campaign had been to the British both bloody and disastrous. It did not affect the results of the war; and the decisive

---

[1] Letter of General Jackson, Jan. 19th, and of General Lambert, Jan. 28th.

[2] "Towards the sea its fortifications are respectable enough; but on the land side it is little better than a block-house. The ramparts being composed of sand not more than three feet in thickness, and faced with plank, are barely cannon-proof; while a sand hill, rising within pistol-shot of the ditch, completely commands it. Within, again, it is as much wanting in accommodation as it is in strength. There are no bomb-proof barracks, nor any hole or arch under which men might find protection from shells; indeed, so deficient is it in common lodging-rooms, that great part of the garrison sleep in tents.... With the reduction of this trifling work all hostilities ended." (Gleig, 357.)

General Jackson impliedly censures the garrison for surrendering so quickly; but in such a fort it was absolutely impossible to act otherwise, and not the slightest stain rests upon the fort's defenders.

battle itself was a perfectly useless shedding of blood, for peace had been declared before it was fought. Nevertheless, it was not only glorious but profitable to the United States. Louisiana was saved from being severely ravaged, and New Orleans from possible destruction; and after our humiliating defeats in trying to repel the invasions of Virginia and Maryland, the signal victory of New Orleans was really almost a necessity for the preservation of the national honor. This campaign was the great event of the war, and in it was fought the most important battle as regards numbers that took place during the entire struggle; and the fact that we were victorious, not only saved our self-respect at home, but also gave us a prestige abroad which we should otherwise have totally lacked. It could not be said to entirely balance the numerous defeats that we had elsewhere suffered on land—defeats which had so far only been offset by Harrison's victory in 1813 and the campaign in Lower Canada in 1814—but it at any rate went a long way toward making the score even.

Jackson is certainly by all odds the most prominent figure that appeared during this war, and stands head and shoulders above any other commander, American or British, that it produced. It will be difficult, in all history, to show a parallel to the feat that he performed. In three weeks' fighting, with a force largely composed of militia, he utterly defeated and drove away an army twice the size of his own, composed of veteran troops, and led by one of the ablest of European generals. During the whole campaign he only erred once, and that was in putting General Morgan, a very incompetent officer, in command of the forces on the west bank. He suited his movements admirably to the various exigencies that arose. The promptness and skill with which he attacked, as soon as he knew of the near approach of the British, undoubtedly saved the city; for their vanguard was so roughly handled that, instead of being able to advance at once, they were forced to delay three days, during which time Jackson entrenched himself in a position from which he was never driven. But after this first attack the offensive would have been not only hazardous, but useless, and accordingly Jackson, adopting that mode of warfare which best suited the ground he was on and the troops he had under him, forced the enemy always to fight him where he was strongest, and confined himself strictly to the pure defensive—a system condemned by most European authorities,[1] but which has at times succeeded to admiration in America, as witness Fredericksburg, Gettysburg, Kenesaw Mountain, and Franklin. Moreover, it must be remembered that Jackson's success was in no wise owing either to chance or to the errors of his adversary.[2] As far as fortune favored ei-

[1] Thus Napier says (vol. v, p. 25): "Soult fared as most generals will who seek by extensive lines to supply the want of numbers or of hardiness in the troops. Against rude commanders and undisciplined soldiers, lines may avail; seldom against accomplished commanders, never when the assailants are the better soldiers." And again (p. 150), "Offensive operations must be the basis of a good defensive system."

[2] The reverse has been stated again and again with very great injustice, not only by British, but even by American writers (as *e.g.*, Prof. W. G. Sumner, in his "Andrew Jackson as a Public Man," Boston, 1882). The climax of absurdity is reached by Major McDougal, who says (as quoted by Cole in his "Memoirs

ther side, it was that of the British[1]; and Packenham left nothing undone to accomplish his aim, and made no movements that his experience in European war did not justify his making. There is not the slightest reason for supposing that any other British general would have accomplished more or have fared better than he did.[2] Of course Jackson owed much to the nature of the ground on which he fought; but the opportunities it afforded would have been useless in the hands of any general less ready, hardy, and skilful than Old Hickory.

A word as to the troops themselves. The British infantry was at that time the best in Europe, the French coming next. Packenham's soldiers had formed part of Wellington's magnificent peninsular army, and they lost nothing of their honor at New Orleans. Their conduct throughout was admirable. Their steadiness in the night battle, their patience through the various hardships they had to undergo, their stubborn courage in action, and the undaunted front they showed in time of disaster (for at the very end they were to the full as ready and eager to fight as at the beginning), all showed that their soldierly qualities were of the highest order. As much cannot be said of the British artillery, which, though very bravely fought was clearly by no means as skilfully handled as was the case with the American guns. The courage of the British officers of all arms is mournfully attested by the sadly large proportion they bore to the total on the lists of the killed and wounded.

An even greater meed of praise is due to the American soldiers, for it must not be forgotten that they were raw troops opposed to veterans; and indeed, nothing but Jackson's tireless care in drilling them could have brought them into shape at all. The regulars were just as good as the British, and no better. The Kentucky militia, who had only been 48 hours with the army and were badly armed and totally undisciplined, proved as useless as their brethren of New York and Virginia, at Queenstown Heights and Bladensburg, had previously shown themselves to be. They would not stand in the open at all, and even

---

of British Generals," ii, p. 364): "Sir Edward Packenham fell, not after an utter and disastrous defeat, but at the very moment when the arms of victory were extended towards him"; and by James, who says (ii, 388): "The premature fall of a British general saved an American city." These assertions are just on a par with those made by American writers, that only the fall of Lawrence prevented the *Chesapeake* from capturing the *Shannon*.

British writers have always attributed the defeat largely to the fact that the 44th regiment, which was to have led the attack with fascines and ladders, did not act well. I doubt if this had any effect on the result. Some few of the men with ladders did reach the ditch, but were shot down at once, and their fate would have been shared by any others who had been with them; the bulk of the column was never able to advance through the fire up to the breastwork, and all the ladders and fascines in Christendom would not have helped it. There will always be innumerable excuses offered for any defeat; but on this occasion the truth is simply that the British regulars found they could not advance in the open against a fire more deadly than they had ever before encountered.

[1] *E.g.:* The unexpected frost made the swamps firm for them to advance through; the river being so low when the levee was cut, the bayous were filled, instead of the British being drowned out; the *Carolina* was only blown up because the wind happened to fail her; bad weather delayed the advance of arms and reinforcements, etc., etc.

[2] "He was the next man to look to after Lord Wellington" (Codrington, i, 339).

behind a breastwork had to be mixed with better men. The Louisiana militia, fighting in defence of their homes, and well trained, behaved excellently, and behind breastworks were as formidable as the regulars. The Tennesseeans, good men to start with, and already well trained in actual warfare under Jackson, were in their own way unsurpassable as soldiers. In the open field the British regulars, owing to their greater skill in manœuvring, and to their having bayonets, with which the Tennesseeans were unprovided, could in all likelihood have beaten them; but in rough or broken ground the skill of the Tennesseeans, both as marksmen and woodsmen, would probably have given them the advantage; while the extreme deadliness of their fire made it far more dangerous to attempt to storm a breastwork guarded by these forest riflemen than it would have been to attack the same work guarded by an equal number of the best regular troops of Europe. The American soldiers deserve great credit for doing so well; but greater credit still belongs to Andrew Jackson, who, with his cool head and quick eye, his stout heart and strong hand, stands out in history as the ablest general the United States produced, from the outbreak of the Revolution down to the beginning of the Great Rebellion.

# APPENDIX A

According to Act of Congress (quoted in "Niles' Register," iv, 64), the way of measuring double-decked or war-vessels was as follows:

"Measure from fore-part of main stem to after-part of stern port, above the upper deck; take the breadth thereof at broadest part above the main wales, one half of which breadth shall be accounted the depth. Deduct from the length three fifths of such breadth, multiply the remainder by the breadth and the product by the depth; divide by 95; the quotient is tonnage."

$$(i.e., \text{ If length} = x, \text{ and breadth} = y;$$
$$\text{Tonnage} = \frac{(x - \tfrac{3}{5}y) \times y \times \tfrac{1}{2}y.)}{95}$$

Niles states that the British mode, as taken from Steele's "Shipmaster's Assistant," was this: Drop plumb-line over stem of ship and measure distance between such line and the after part of the stern port at the load water-mark; then measure from top of said plumb-line in parallel direction with the water to perpendicular point immediately over the load water-mark of the fore part of main stem; subtract from such admeasurement the above distance; the remainder is ship's extreme length, from which deduct 3 inches for every foot of the load-draught of water for the rake abaft, and also three fifths of the ship's breadth for the rake forward; remainder is length of keel for tonnage. Breadth shall be taken from outside to outside of the plank in broadest part of the ship either above or below the main wales, exclusive of all manner of sheathing or doubling. Depth is to be considered as one half the length. Tonnage will then be the length into the depth into breadth, divided by 94.

Tonnage was thus estimated in a purely arbitrary manner, with no regard to actual capacity or displacement and, moreover, what is of more importance, the British method differed from the American so much that a ship measured in the latter way would be nominally about 15 per cent. larger than if measured by British rules. This is the exact reverse of the statement made by the British naval historian, James. His mistake is pardonable, for great confusion existed on the subject at that time, even the officers not knowing the tonnage of their own ships. When the *President* was captured, her officers stated that she measured about 1,400 tons; in reality she tonned 1,576, American measure. Still more singular was the testimony of the officers of the *Argus,* who thought her to be of about 350 tons, while she was of 298, by American, or 244, by British measurement. These errors were the more excusable as they occurred also in higher quarters. The earliest notice we have about the three 44-gun frigates of the *Constitution's* class, is in the letter of Secretary of the Navy, Benjamin Stoddart, on Dec. 24, 1798,[1] where they are expressly said to be of 1,576 tons; and this tonnage is given them in every navy list that mentions it for 40 years afterward; yet Secretary Paul Hamilton in one of his letters incidentally alludes to them as of 1,444 tons. Later, I think about the year 1838, the method of measuring was changed, and their tonnage was put down as 1,607. James takes the American tonnage from Secretary Hamilton's letter as 1,444, and states (vol. vi, p. 5), that this is equivalent to 1,533 tons, English. But in reality, by American measurement, the tonnage was 1,576; so that even according to James' own figures the British way of measurement made the frigate 43 tons smaller than the American way did; actually the difference was nearer 290 tons. James' statements as to the size of our various ships would seem to have been largely mere guesswork, as he sometimes makes them smaller and sometimes larger than they were according to the official navy lists. Thus, the *Constitution, President,* and *United States,* each of 1,576, he puts down as of 1,533; the *Wasp,* of 450, as of 434; the *Hornet,* of 480, as of 460; and the *Chesapeake,* of 1,244, as of 1,135 tons. On the other hand the *Enterprise,* of 165 tons, he states to be of 245; the *Argus* of 298, he considers to be of 316, and the *Peacock, Frolic,* etc., of 509 each, as of 539. He thus certainly adopts different standards of measurement, not only for the American as distinguished from the British vessels, but even among the various American vessels themselves. And there are other difficulties to be encountered; not only were there different ways of casting tonnage from given measurements, but also there were different ways of getting what purported to be the same measurement. A ship, that, according to the British method of measurement was of a certain length, would, according to the American method, be about 5 per cent. longer; and so if two vessels were the same size, the American would have the greatest nominal tonnage. For example, James in his "Naval Occurrences" (p. 467) gives the length of the *Cyane's* main deck as 118 feet 2 inches. This same *Cyane* was carefully surveyed and measured, under orders from the United States navy department, by Lieut. B. F. Hoffman, and in his published report[2] he gives, among the other

---

[1] "American State Papers," xiv, 57.

[2] "American State Papers," xiv, p. 417.

dimensions: "Length of spar-deck, 124 feet 9 inches," and "length of gun-deck 123 feet 3 inches." With such a difference in the way of taking measurements, as well as of computing tonnage from the measurements when taken, it is not surprising that according to the American method the *Cyane* should have ranked as of about 659 tons, instead of 539. As James takes no account of any of these differences I hardly know how to treat his statements of comparative tonnage. Thus he makes the *Hornet* 460 tons, and the *Peacock* and *Penguin,* which she at different times captured, about 388 each. As it happens both Captain Lawrence and Captain Biddle, who commanded the *Hornet* in her two successful actions, had their prizes measured. The *Peacock* sank so rapidly that Lawrence could not get very accurate measurements of her; he states her to be four feet shorter and half a foot broader than the *Hornet.* The British naval historian Brenton (vol. v, p. 111), also states that they were of about the same tonnage. But we have more satisfactory evidence from Captain Biddle. He stayed by his prize nearly two days, and had her thoroughly examined in every way; and his testimony is, of course, final. He reports that the *Penguin* was by actual measurement two feet shorter, and somewhat broader than the *Hornet,* and with thicker scantling. She tonned 477, compared to the *Hornet*'s 480—a difference of about one half of one per cent. This testimony is corroborated by that of the naval inspectors who examined the *Epervier* after she was captured by the *Peacock.* Those two vessels were respectively of 477 and 509 tons, and as such they ranked on the navy lists. The American *Peacock* and her sister ships were very much longer than the brig sloops of the *Epervier*'s class, but were no broader, the latter being very tubby. All the English sloops were broader in proportion than the American ones were; thus the *Levant,* which was to have mounted the same number of guns as the *Peacock,* had much more beam, and was of greater tonnage, although of rather less length. The *Macedonian,* when captured, ranked on our lists as of 1,325 tons,[1] the *United States* as of 1,576; and they thus continued until, as I have said before, the method of measurement was changed, when the former ranked as of 1,341, and the latter as of 1,607 tons. James, however, makes them respectively 1,081, and 1,533. Now to get the comparative force he ought to have adopted the first set of measurements given, or else have made them 1,081 and 1,286. Out of the twelve single-ship actions of the war, four were fought with 38-gun frigates like the *Macedonian,* and seven with 18-gun brig sloops of the *Epervier*'s class; and as the *Macedonian* and *Epervier* were both regularly rated in our navy, we get a very exact idea of our antagonists in those eleven cases. The twelfth was the fight between the *Enterprise* and the *Boxer,* in which the latter was captured; the *Enterprise* was apparently a little smaller than her foe, but had two more guns, which she carried in her bridle ports.

As my purpose in giving the tonnage is to get it comparatively, and not absolutely, I have given it throughout for both sides as estimated by the American method of that day. The tonnage of the vessels on the lakes has been already noticed.

---

[1] See the work of Lieutenant Emmons, who had access to all the official records.

# APPENDIX B

Very few students of naval history will deny that in 1812 the average American ship was superior to the average British ship of the same strength; and that the latter was in turn superior to the average French ship. The explanation given by the victor is in each case the same; the American writer ascribes the success of his nation to "the aptitude of the American character for the sea," and the Briton similarly writes that "the English are inherently better suited for the sea than the French." Race characteristics may have had some little effect between the last pair of combatants (although only a little), and it is *possible* that they somewhat affected the outcome of the Anglo-American struggle, but they did not form the main cause. This can best be proved by examining the combats of two preceding periods, in which the English, French, and Americans were at war with one another.

During the years 1798–1800, the United States carried on a desultory conflict with France, then at war with England. Our navy was just built, and was rated in the most extraordinary manner; the *Chesapeake*, carrying 18-pounders, was called a 44; and the *Constellation*, which carried 24's, a 36; while the *Washington*, rating 24, was really much heavier than the *Boston*, rating 28. On Feb. 9, 1799, after an hour's conflict, the *Constellation* captured the French frigate *l'Insurgente*; the Americans lost 3, the French 70 men, killed and wounded. The *Constitution* carried but 38 guns; 28 long 24's, on the main-deck, and 10 long 12's on the quarter-deck, with a crew of 309 men. According to Troude (iii, 169), *l'Insurgente* carried 26 long 12's, 10 long 6's, and 4 36-pound carronades; the Americans report her number of men as nearly four hundred. Thus in actual[1] (not nominal) weight of shot the *Constellation* was superior by about 80 pounds, and was inferior in crew by from 50 to 100 men. This would make the vessels apparently nearly equal in force; but of course the long 24's of the *Constellation* made it impossible that *l'Insurgente*, armed only with long 12's, should contend with her. As already said, a superiority in number of men makes very little difference, provided each vessel has ample to handle the guns, repair damages, work the sails, etc. Troude goes more into details than any other French historian; but I think his details are generally wrong. In this case he gives the *Constellation* 12's, instead of the 24's she really carried; and also supplies her with 10 32-pound carronades—of which species of ordnance there was then not one piece in our navy. The first carronades we ever had were those carried by the same frigate on her next voyage. She had completely changed her armament, having 28 long 18's on the main-deck, ten 24-pound carronades on the quarter-deck; and, I believe, 6 long 12's on the forecastle, with a crew of 310 men. Thus armed, she encountered and fought a drawn battle with *la Vengeance*. Troude (vol. iii, pp. 201, and 216) describes the armament of the latter as 26 long 18's, 10 long 8's, and 4 36-pound carronades. On board of her was an American prisoner, James Howe, who swore she had 52 guns, and 400 men (see Cooper, i, 306). The French and American accounts thus radically disagree. The point is settled definitely by the report of the British captain Milne, who, in the *Seine* frigate, captured *la Vengeance* in the same year, and then reported her armament as being 28 long 18's, 16 long 12's, and 8 36-pound carronades, with 326 men. As the American and British accounts, written entirely independently of one another, tally almost exactly, it is evident that Troude was very greatly mistaken. He blunders very much over the *Constellation's* armament.

Thus in this action the American frigate fought a draw with an antagonist, nearly as much superior to herself as an American 44 was to a British 38. In November, 1800, the "28-gun frigate," *Boston*, of 530 tons, 200 men, carrying 24 long 9's on the main-deck, and on the spar-deck 8 long 6's (or possibly 12-pound carronades) captured, after two hours action, the French corvette *Berceau*, of 24 guns, long 8's; the *Boston* was about the same size as her foe, with the same number of men, and superior in metal about as ten to nine. She lost 15, and the *Berceau* 40 men. Troude (iii, p. 219) gives the *Berceau* 30 guns, 22 long 8's, and 8 12-pound carronades. If this is true she was in reality of equal force with the *Boston*. But I question if Troude really knew anything about the combatants; he gives the *Boston* (of the same size and build as the *Cyane*) 48 guns—a number impossible for her to

---

[1] French shot was really very much heavier than the nominally corresponding English shot, as the following table, taken from Captain T. L. Simmon's work on "Heavy Ordnance" (London, 1837, p. 62) will show:

| NOMINAL FRENCH WEIGHT OF SHOT. | ACTUAL WEIGHT OF SAME SHOT IN ENGLISH POUNDS. |
|---|---|
| 36 lbs. | 43 lbs. 4 oz. |
| 24 " | 28 " 8¾ " |
| 18 " | 21 " 4½ " |
| 12 " | 14 " 7 " |

carry. He continually makes the grossest errors; in this same (the third) volume, for example, he arms a British 50-gun-ship with 72 cannon, giving her a broadside fifty per cent. heavier than it should be (p. 141); and, still worse, states the ordinary complement of a British 32-gun frigate to be 384 men, instead of about 220 (p. 417). He is by no means as trustworthy as James, though less rancorous.

The United States schooner *Experiment*, of 12 guns, long 6's, and 70 men, captured the French man-of-war three-masted schooner *La Diane*, of 14 guns (either 4- or 6-pounders), with a crew of 60 men, and 30 passengers; and the *Enterprise*, the sister vessel of the *Experiment*, captured numerous strong privateers. One of them, a much heavier vessel than her captor, made a most obstinate fight. She was the *Flambeau* brig of fourteen 8-pounders and 100 men, of whom half were killed or wounded. The *Enterprise* had 3 killed and 7 wounded.

Comparing these different actions, it is evident that the Americans were superior to the French in fighting capacity during the years 1799 and 1800. During the same two years there had been numerous single contests between vessels of Britain and France, ending almost invariably in favor of the former, which I mention first in each couple. The 12-pounder frigate *Dædalus* captured the 12-pounder frigate *Prudente*, of equal force. The British 18-pounder frigate *Sybille* captured the frigate *Forte*, armed with 52 guns, 30 of them long 24's on the main-deck; she was formidably armed and as heavy as the *Constitution*. The *Sybille* lost 22 and the *Forte* 145 men killed and wounded. The 18-pounder frigate *Clyde*, with the loss of 5 men, captured the 12-pounder frigate *Vestale*, which lost 32. The cutter *Courser*, of twelve 4-pounders and 40 men, captured the privateer *Guerrière*, of fourteen 4-pounders and 44 men. The cutter *Viper*, of fourteen 4-pounders and 48 men, captured the privateer *Suret*, of fourteen 4-pounders and 57 men. The 16-gun ship-sloop *Peterel*, with 89 men, engaged the *Cerf*, 14, *Lejoille*, 6, and *Ligurienne*, 16, with in all 240 men, and captured the *Ligurienne*. The 30-gun corvette *Dart* captured by surprise the 38-gun frigate *Desirée*. The *Gypsey*, of ten 4-pounders and 82 men, captured the *Quidproquo*, of 8 guns, 4- and 8-pounders, and 98 men. The schooner *Milbrook* of sixteen 18-pounder carronades and 47 men, fought a draw with the privateer *Bellone*, of 24 long 8's and six 36-pound carronades. Finally, six months after the *Vengeance* had escaped from the *Constellation* (or beaten her off, as the French say) she was captured by the British frigate *Seine*, which threw a broadside about 30 pounds more than the American did in her action, and had some 29 men less aboard. So that her commander, Captain Milne, with the same force as Commodore Truxton, of the *Constellation*, accomplished what the latter failed to do.

Reviewing all these actions, it seems pretty clear that, while the Americans were then undoubtedly much superior to the French, they were still, at least slightly, inferior to the British.

From 1777 to 1782 the state of things was very different. The single combats were too numerous for me to mention them here; and besides it would be impossible to get at the truth without going to a great deal of trouble—the accounts given by Cooper, Sohomberg, and Troude differing so widely that they can often hardly be recognized as treating of the same events. But it is certain that the British were very much superior to the Americans. Some of the American ships behaved most disgracefully, deserting their consorts and fleeing from much smaller foes. Generally the American ship was captured when opposed by an equal force—although there were some brilliant exceptions to this. With the French things were more equal; their frigates were sunk or captured time and again, but nearly as often they sunk or captured their antagonists. Some of the most gallant fights on record are recounted of French frigates of this period; in 1781 the *Minerve*, 32, resisted the *Courageous*, 74, till she had lost 73 men and had actually inflicted a loss of 17 men on her gigantic antagonist, and the previous year the *Bellepoule*, 32, had performed a similar feat with the *Nonsuch*, 64, while the *Capricieuse*, 32, had fought for five hours before surrendering to the *Prudente* and *Licorne*, each of force equal to herself. She lost 100 men, inflicting a loss of 55 upon her two antagonists. Such instances make us feel rather ashamed when we compare them with the fight in which the British ship *Glasgow*, 20, beat off an American squadron of 5 ships, including two of equal force to herself, or with the time when the *Ariadne*, 20, and *Ceres*, 14, attacked and captured without resistance the *Alfred*, 20, the latter ship being deserted in the most outrageously cowardly manner by her consort the *Raleigh*, 32. At that period the average American ship was certainly by no means equal to the average French ship of the same force, and the latter in turn was a little, but only a little, inferior to the average British ship of equal strength.

Thus in 1782 the British stood first in nautical prowess, separated but by a very narrow interval from the French, while the Americans made a bad third. In 1789 the British still stood first, while the Americans had made a great stride forward, coming close on their heels, and the French had fallen far behind into the third place. In 1812 the relative positions of the British and French were unchanged, but the Americans had taken another very decided step in advance, and stood nearly as far ahead of the British as the latter were ahead of the French.

The explanation of these changes is not difficult. In 1782 the American war vessels were in reality privateers; the crews were unpracticed, the officers untrained, and they had none of the traditions and discipline of a regular service. At the same time the French marine was at its highest point; it was commanded by officers of ability and experience, promoted largely for merit, and with crews thoroughly trained, especially in gunnery, by a long course of service on the sea. In courage, and in skill in the management of guns, musketry, etc., they were the full equals of their English antagonists; their slight *average* inferiority in seamanship may, it is possible, be fairly put down to the difference in race. (It seems certain that, when serving in a neutral vessel, for example, the Englishmen aboard are apt to make better sailors than the Frenchmen.) In 1799 the revolution had deprived the French of all their best officers, had let the character of the marine run down, and the discipline of the service become utterly disorganized; this exposed them to frightful reverses, and these in turn prevented the character of the service from recovering its former tone. Meanwhile the Americans had established for the first time a regular navy, and, as there was excellent material to work with, it at once came up close to the English; constant and arduous service, fine discipline, promotion for merit, and the most unflagging attention to practical seamanship and gunnery had in 1812 raised it far above even the high English standard. During all these three periods the English marine, it must be remembered, did not fall off, but at least kept its position; the French, on the contrary, *did* fall off, while the American navy advanced by great strides to the first place.

# APPENDIX C

After my work was in press I for the first time came across Prof. J. Russell Soley's "Naval Campaign of 1812," in the "Proceedings of the United States Naval Institute," for October 20, 1881. It is apparently the precursor of a more extended history. Had I known that such a writer as Professor Soley was engaged on a work of this kind I certainly should not have attempted it myself.

In several points our accounts differ. In the action with the *Guerrière* his diagram differs from mine chiefly in his making the *Constitution* steer in a more direct line, while I have represented her as shifting her course several times in order to avoid being raked, bringing the wind first on her port and then on her starboard-quarter. My account of the number of the crew of the *Guerrière* is taken from the *Constitution's* muster-book (in the Treasury Department at Washington), which contains the names of all the British prisoners received aboard the *Constitution* after the fight. The various writers used "larboard" and "starboard" with such perfect indifference, in speaking of the closing and the loss of the *Guerrière's* mizzen-mast, that I hardly knew which account to adopt; it finally seemed to me that the only way to reconcile the conflicting statements was by making the mast act as a rudder, first to keep the ship off the wind until it was dead aft and then to bring her up into it. If this was the case, it deadened her speed, and prevented Dacres from keeping his ship yardarm and yardarm with the foe, though he tried to steady his course with the helm; but, in this view, it rather delayed Hull's raking than helped him. If Professor Soley's account is right, I hardly know what to make of the statement in one of the American accounts that the *Constitution* "luffed across the enemy's bow," and of Cooper's statement (in *Putnam's Magazine*) that the *Guerrière's* bowsprit pressed against the *Constitution's* "lee or port quarter."

In the action of the *Wasp* with the *Frolic*, I have adopted James' statement of the latter's force; Professor Soley follows Captain Jones' letter, which gives the brig three additional guns and 18 pounds more metal in broadside. My reason for following James was that his account of the *Frolic*'s force agrees with the regular armament of her class. Captain Jones gives her *two* carronades on the topgallant forecastle, which must certainly be a mistake; he makes her chase-guns long 12's, but all the other British brigs carried 6's; he also gives her another gun in broadside, which he calls a 12-pounder, and Lieutenant Biddle (in a letter to his father) a 32-pound carronade. His last gun should perhaps be counted in; I excluded it because the two American officials differed in their account of it, because I did not know through what port it could be fought, and because James asserted that it was dismounted and lashed to the forecastle. The *Wasp* left port with 138 men; subtracting the pilot and two men who were drowned, makes 135 the number on board during the action. As the battle was fought, I doubt if the loss of the brig's main-yard had much effect on the result; had it been her object to keep on the wind, or had the loss of her after-sails enabled her antagonist to cross her stern (as in the case of the *Argus* and *Pelican*), the accident could fairly be said to have had a decided effect upon the contest. But as a short time after the fight began the vessels were running nearly free, and as the *Wasp* herself was greatly injured aloft at the time, and made no effort to cross her foe's stern, it is difficult to see that it made much difference. The brig's head-sails were all right, and, as she was not close-hauled, the cause of her not being kept more under command was probably purely due to the slaughter on her decks.

Professor Soley represents the combat of the *States* and *Macedonian* as a plain yardarm and yardarm action after the first forty minutes. I have followed the English authorities and make it a running fight throughout. If Professor Soley is right, the enormous disparity in loss was due mainly to the infinitely greater accuracy of the American fire; according to my diagram the chief cause was the incompetency of the *Macedonian*'s commander. In one event the difference was mainly in the gunnery of the crews, in the other, it was mainly in the tactical skill of the captains. The question is merely as to how soon Carden, in his headlong, foolishly rash approach, was enabled to close with Decatur. I have represented the closing as taking place later than Professor Soley has done; very possibly I am wrong. Could my work now be rewritten I think I should adopt his diagram of the action of the *Macedonian*.

But in the action with the *Java* it seems to me that he is mistaken. He has here followed the British accounts; but they are contradicted by the American authorities, and besides have a very improbable look. When the *Constitution* came round for the second time, on the port tack, James declares the *Java* passed directly across her stern, almost touching, but that the British crew, overcome by astonishment or awe, did not fire a shot; and that shortly afterward the manœuvre was repeated. When this incident is said to have occurred the *Java*'s crew had been hard at work fighting the guns for half an hour, and they continued for an hour and a half afterward; it is impossible to believe that they would have foreborne to fire more than one gun when in such a superb position for inflicting damage. Even had the men been struck with temporary lunacy the officers alone would have fired some of the guns. Moreover, if the courses of the vessels were such as indicated on Professor Soley's diagram the *Java* would herself have been previously exposed to a terrible raking fire, which was not the case. So the alleged manœuvres have, *per se*, a decidedly apocryphal look; and besides they are flatly contradicted by the American accounts which state distinctly that the *Java* remained to windward in every portion of the fight. On this same tack Professor Soley represents the *Java* as forereaching on the *Constitution;* I have reversed this. At this time the *Java* had been much cut up in her rigging and aloft generally, while the *Constitution* had set much additional sail, and in consequence the latter forged ahead and wore in the smoke unperceived. When the ships came foul Professor Soley has drawn the *Constitution* in a position in which she would receive a most destructive stern rake from her antagonist's whole broadside. The positions could not have been as there represented. The *Java's* bowsprit came foul in the *Constitution's* mizzen rigging and as the latter forged ahead she pulled the former gradually round till when they separated the ships were in a head and stern line. Commodore Bainbridge, as he particularly says, at once "kept away to avoid being raked," while the loss of the headsails aboard the *Java* would cause the latter to come up in the wind, and the two ships would again be running parallel, with the American to leeward. I have already discussed fully the reasons for rejecting in this instance the British report of their own force and loss. This was the last defeat that the British officially reported; the admiralty were smarting with the sting of successive disasters and anxious at all costs to put the best possible face on affairs (as witness Mr. Croker's response to Lord Dundonald's speech in the House). There is every reason for believing that in this case the reports were garbled; exactly as at a later date the official correspondence preceding the terrible disasters at Cabul was tampered with before being put before the public (see McCarthy's "History of Our Own Times").

It is difficult to draw a diagram of the action between the *Hornet* and *Peacock,* although it was so short, the accounts contradicting one another as to which ship was to windward and which on the "larboard tack"; and I do not know if I have correctly represented the position of the combatants at the close of the engagement. Lieutenant Conner reported the number of men aboard the *Hornet* fit for duty as 135; Lawrence says she had 8 absent in a prize and 7 too sick to be at quarters. This would make an original complement of 150, and tallies exactly with the number of men left on the *Hornet* after the action was over, as mentioned by Lawrence in his account of the total number of souls aboard. The log-book of the *Hornet* just before starting on her cruise, states her entire complement as 158; but 4 of these were sick and left behind. There is still a discrepancy of 4 men, but during the course of the cruise nothing would be more likely than that four men should be gotten rid of, either by sickness, desertion, or dismissal. At any rate the discrepancy is very trivial. In her last cruise, as I have elsewhere said, I have probably overestimated the number of the *Hornet's* crew; this seems especially likely when it is remembered that toward the close of the war our vessels left port with fewer supernumeraries aboard than earlier in the contest. If such is the case, the *Hornet* and *Penguin* were of almost exactly equal force.

My own comments upon the causes of our success, upon the various historians of the war, etc., are so similar to those of Professor Soley, that I almost feel as if I had been guilty of plagiarism; yet I never saw his writings till half an hour ago. But in commenting on the actions of 1812, I think the Professor has laid too much stress on the difference in "dash" between the combatants. The *Wasp* bore down with perfect confidence to engage an equal foe; and the *Hornet* could not tell till the *Peacock* opened fire that the latter was inferior in force, and moreover fought in sight of another hostile vessel. In the action with the *Guerrière* it was Hull and not Dacres who acted boldly, the Englishman delaying the combat and trying to keep it at long range for some time. In this fight it must be remembered that neither foe knew the exact force of the other until the close work began; then, it is true, Dacres fought most bravely. So with the *Macedonian;* James particularly says that she did not know the force of her foe, and was confident of victory. The *Java*, however, must have known that she was to engage a superior force. In neither of the first two frigate actions did the Americans have a chance to display any courage in the actual fighting, the victory was won with such ease. But in each case they entered as bravely, although by no means as rashly or foolishly, into the fight as their antagonists did. It must always be remembered that until this time it was by no means proved that 24-pounders were better guns than 18's to put on frigates; exactly as at a little later date it was vigorously contended that 42-pounders were no more effective guns for two-deckers than 32-pounders were. Till 1812 there had been no experience to justify the theory that the 24-pounder was the better gun. So that in the first five actions it cannot be said that the British showed any especial courage in *beginning* the fight; it was more properly to be called ignorance. After the fight was once begun they certainly acted very bravely and, in particular, the desperate nature of the *Frolic*'s defence has never been surpassed.

But admitting this is a very different thing from admitting that the British fought more bravely than their foes; the combatants were about on a par in this respect. The Americans, it seems to me, were always to the full as ready to engage as their antagonists were; on each side there were few over-cautious men, such as Commodore Rodgers and Sir George Collier, the opposing captains on Lake Ontario, the commander of the *Bonne Citoyenne*, and perhaps Commodore Decatur, but as a rule either side jumped at the chance of a fight. The difference in tactics was one of skill and common sense, not one of timidity. The *United States* did not "avoid close action" from over-caution, but simply to take advantage of her opponent's rashness. Hull's approach was as bold as it was skilful; had the opponent to leeward been the *Endymion*, instead of the *Guerrière*, her 24-pounders would not have saved her from the fate that overtook the latter. Throughout the war I think that the Americans were as bold in beginning action, and as stubborn in continuing it, as were their foes—although no more so. Neither side can claim any superiority on the average, though each can in individual cases, as regards courage. Foolhardiness does not imply bravery. A prize-fighter who refused to use his guard would be looked upon as exceptionally brainless, not as exceptionally brave; yet such a case is almost exactly parallel to that of the captain of the *Macedonian*.

# APPENDIX D

In the "Historical Register of the United States" (edited by T. H. Palmer, Philadelphia, 1814), vol. 1, p. 105 (State Papers), is a letter from Lieut. L. H. Babbitt to Master-commandant Wm. U. Crane, both of the *Nautilus,* dated Sept. 13, 1812, in which he says that of the six men imprisoned by the British on suspicion of being of English birth, four were native-born Americans, and two naturalized citizens. He also gives a list of six men who deserted, and entered on the *Shannon,* of whom two were American born—the birthplaces of the four others not being given. Adding these last, we still have but six men as the number of British aboard the *Nautilus.* It is thus seen that the crack frigate *Shannon* had American deserters aboard her—although these probably formed a merely trifling faction of her crew, as did the British deserters aboard the crack frigate *Constitution.*

On p. 108, is a letter of Dec. 17, 1812, from Geo. S. Wise, purser of the *Wasp,* stating that twelve of that ship's crew had been detained "under the pretence of their being British subjects"; so that nine per cent. of her crew may have been British—or the proportion may have been very much smaller.

On p. 117, is a letter of Jan. 14, 1813, from Commodore J. Rodgers, in which he states that he encloses the muster-rolls of H.B.M. ships *Moselle* and *Sappho,* taken out of the captured packet *Swallow;* and that these muster-rolls show that in August, 1812, one eighth of the crews of the *Moselle* and *Sappho,* was composed of Americans.

These various letters thus support strongly the conclusions reached on a former page as to the proportion of British deserters on American vessels.

In "A Biographical Memoir of the Late Commodore Joshua Barney, from Autographical Notes and Journals" (edited by Mary Barney, Boston, 1832), on pages 263, and 315, are descriptions of the flotilla destroyed in the Patuxent. It consisted of one gun-boat, carrying a long 24; one cutter, carrying a long 18, a columbiad 18, and four 9-pound carronades; and thirteen row barges, each carrying a long 18 or 12 in the bow, with a 32-pound or 18-pound carronade in the stern. On p. 256, Barney's force in St. Leonard's Creek, is described as consisting of one sloop, two gun-boats, and thirteen barges, with in all somewhat over 500 men; and it is claimed that the flotilla drove away the blockading frigates, entirely unaided; the infantry force on shore rendering no assistance. The work is of some value, as showing that James had more than doubled the size, and almost doubled the strength, of Barney's various gun-boats.

It may be mentioned that on p. 108, Commodore Barney describes the Dutch-American frigate *South Carolina*, which carried a crew of 550 men, and was armed with 28 long 42's on the maindeck, and 12 long 12's on the spardeck. She was far heavier than any of our 44-gun frigates of 1812, and an overmatch for anything under the rank of a 74. This gives further emphasis to what I have already stated— that the distinguishing feature of the war of 1812, is *not* the introduction of the heavy frigate, for heavy frigates had been in use among various nations for thirty years previously, but the fact that for the first time the heavy frigate was used to the best possible advantage.

# APPENDIX E

In the last edition of James' "Naval History of Great Britain," published in London, in 1886, by Richard Bentley & Son, there is an appendix by Mr. H. T. Powell, devoted to the war of 1812, mainly to my account thereof.

Mr. Powell begins by stating with naïf solemnity that "most British readers will be surprised to learn that, notwithstanding the infinite pains taken by William James to render his history a monument of accuracy, and notwithstanding the exposure he brought upon contemporary misstatements, yet to this day the Americans still dispute his facts." It is difficult to discuss seriously any question with a man capable of writing down in good faith such a sentence as the above. James (unlike Brenton and Cooper) knew perfectly well how to be accurate; but if Mr. Powell will read the comments on his accounts which I have appended to the description of almost every battle, he will see that James stands convicted beyond possibility of doubt, not merely of occasional inaccuracies or errors, but of the systematic, malicious, and continuous practice of every known form of wilful misstatement, from the suppression of the truth and the suggestion of the false to the lie direct. To a man of his character the temptation was irresistible; for when he came to our naval war, he had to appear as the champion of the beaten side, and to explain away defeat instead of chronicling victory. The contemporary American writers were quite as boastful and untruthful. No honorable American should at this day endorse their statements; and similarly, no reputable Englishman should permit his name to be associated in any way with James' book without explicitly disclaiming all share in, or sympathy with, its scurrilous mendacity.

Mr. Powell's efforts to controvert my statements can be disposed of in short order. He first endeavors to prove that James was right about the tonnage of the ships; but all that he does is to show that his author gave for the English frigates and sloops the correct tonnage by English and French rules. This I never for a moment disputed. What I said was that the *comparative* tonnage of the various pairs of combatants as given by James was all wrong; and this Mr. Powell does not even discuss. James applied one system correctly to the English vessels; but he applied quite another to the American (especially on the lakes). Mr. Powell actually quotes Admiral Chads as a witness, because he says that his father considered James' account of the *Java*'s fight accurate; if he wishes such testimony, I can produce many relatives of the Perrys, Porters, and Rodgers of 1812, who insist that I have done much less than justice to the American side. He says I passed over silently James' schedule of dimensions of the frigates and sloops. This is a mistake; I showed by the testimony of Captains Biddle and Warrington and Lieutenant Hoffman that his *comparative* measurements (the absolute measurements being of no consequence) for the American and British sloops are all wrong; and the same holds true of the frigates.

Mr. Powell deals with the weight of shot exactly as he does with the tonnage—that is, he seeks to show what the *absolute* weight of the British shot was; but he does not touch upon the point at issue, the *comparative* weight of the British and American shot.

When he comes to the lake actions, Mr. Powell is driven to conclude that what I aver must be accurate, because he thinks the *Confiance* was the size of the *General Pike* (instead of half as large again; she mounted 30 guns in battery on her main deck, as against the *Pike*'s 26, and stood to the latter as the *Constellation* did to the *Essex*), and because an American writer (very properly) expresses dissatisfaction with Commodore Chauncy! What Mr. Powell thinks this last statement tends to prove would be difficult to say. In the body of my work I go into the minute details of the strength of the combatants in the lake action; I clearly show that James was guilty of gross and wilful falsification of the truth; and no material statement I make can be successfully controverted.

So much for Mr. Powell. But a much higher authority, Mr. Frank Chiswell, has recently published some articles which tend to show that my conclusions as to the tonnage of the sea vessels (not as to the lake vessels, which are taken from different sources) are open to question. In the appendix to my first edition I myself showed that it was quite impossible to reconcile all the different statements; that the most that could be done was to take one method and apply it all through, admitting that even in this way it would be impossible to make all the cases square with one another.

Mr. Chiswell states that "the American tonnage measurements, properly taken, never could give results for frigates varying largely from the English tonnage." But a statement like this is idle; for the answer to the "never could" is that they *did*. If Mr. Chiswell will turn to James' "Naval Occurrences," he will find the *Chesapeake* set down as 1,135 tons, and the *Macedonian* as of 1,081; but in the American Navy lists, which are those I followed, the *Chesapeake* is put down as of 1,244 tons. A simple application of the rule of three shows that even if I accepted James' figures, I would be obliged to consider the *Macedonian* as of about 1,185 tons, to make her correspond with the system I had adopted for the American ships.

But this is not all. James gives the length of the *Macedonian* as 154 ft. 6 in. In the Navy Department at Washington are two plans of the *Macedonian*. One is dated 1817, and gives her length as 157 ft. 3 in. This difference in measurement would make a difference of 20 odd tons; so that by the American mode she must certainly have been over 1,200 tons, instead of under 1,100, as by the British rules. The second plan in the Navy Department, much more elaborate than the first, is dated 1829, and gives the length as 164 ft.; it is probably this that Emmons and the United States Navy lists have followed—as I did myself in calling the tonnage of the *Macedonian* 1,325. Since finding the plan of 1817, however, I think it possible that the other refers to the second vessel of the name, which was built in 1832. If this is true, then the *Macedonian* (as well as the *Guerrière* and *Java*) should be put down as about 120 tons less than the measurements given by Emmons and adopted by me; but even if this is so, she must be considered as tonning over 1,200, using the method I have applied to the *Chesapeake*. Therefore, adopting the same system that I apply to the American 38-gun frigates, the British 38-gun frigates were of over 1,200, not under 1,100, tons.

As for the *Cyane,* James makes her but 118 ft. and 2 in. long, while the American *Peacock* he puts at 119 ft. 5 in. But Lieut. Hoffman's official report makes the former 123 ft. 3 in., and the plans in the State Department at Washington make the latter 117 ft. 11 in. in length. I care nothing for the different methods of measuring different vessels; what I wish to get at is the comparative measurement, and this stands as above. The comparative tonnage is thus the very reverse of that indicated by James' figures.

Finally, as to the brigs, James makes them some ten feet shorter than the American ship-sloops. In the Washington archives I can find no plan on record of the measurements of the captured *Epervier;* but in the Navy Department, volume 10, of the "Letters of Master Commandants, 1814," under date of May 12th, is the statement of the Surveyor of the Port of Charleston that she measured 467 tons (in another place it is given as 477). James makes her 388; but as he makes the American *Wasp* 434, whereas she stands on our list as of 450, the application of the same rule as with the frigates gives us, even taking his own figures, 400 as her tonnage, when measured as our ships were. But the measurements of the Surveyor of the Port who examined the *Epervier* are corroborated by the statements of Captain Biddle, who captured her sister brig, the *Penguin*. Biddle reported that the latter was two feet shorter and a little broader than his own ship, the *Hornet*, which was of 480 tons. This would correspond almost exactly with the Surveyor's estimate.

It still seems impossible to reconcile all these conflicting statements; but I am inclined to think that, on the whole, in the sea (not the lake) vessels I have put the British tonnage too high. On the scale I have adopted for the American 44-gun and 38-gun frigates and 18-gun sloops like the *Hornet* and *Wasp*, the British 38-gun frigates ought to be put down as of a little over 1,200, and the British 18-gun sloops as of between 400 and 450, tons. In other words, of the twelve single-ship actions of the war five, those of the *Chesapeake* and *Shannon, Enterprise* and *Boxer, Wasp* and *Frolic, Hornet* and *Peacock, Hornet* and *Penguin,* were between vessels of nearly equal size; in six the American was the superior about in the proportion of five to four (rather more in the case of the frigates, rather less in the case of the brigs); and in one, that of the *Argus* and *Pelican,* the British sloop was the bigger, in a somewhat similar ratio.

This correction would be in favor of the British. But in a more important particular I think I have done injustice to the Americans. I should have allowed for the short weight of American metal on the lakes, taking off seven per cent. from the nominal broadsides of Perry and Macdonough; for the American ordnance was of exactly the same quality as that on the ocean vessels, while the British was brought over from England, and must have shown the same superiority that obtained on the seagoing ships.

Moreover, I am now inclined to believe that both the *Guerrière* and the *Java*, which were originally French ships, still carried French 18's on their main-deck, and that, therefore, about 20 pounds should be added to the broadside weight of metal of each. The American accounts stated this to be the case in both instances; but I paid no heed to them until my attention was called to the fact that the English had captured enormous quantities of French cannon and shot and certainly used the captured ordnance on some of their ships.

In writing my history I have had to deal with a mass of confused and contradictory testimony, which it has sometimes been quite impossible to reconcile, the difficulty being greatly enhanced by the calculated mendacity of James and some others of the earlier writers, both American and British. Often I have had simply to balance probabilities, and choose between two sets of figures, aware that, whichever I chose, much could be said against the choice. It has, therefore, been quite impossible to avoid errors; but I am confident they have been as much in favor of the British as the Americans; and in all important points my statements are substantially accurate.

I do not believe that my final conclusions on the different fights can be disputed. James asserts that the American ships were officered by cunning cowards, and manned to the extent of half their force in point of effectiveness by renegade British. I show that the percentage of non-American seamen aboard the American ships was probably but little greater than the percentage of non-British seamen aboard the British ships; and as for the charges of cowardice, there were but two instances in which it could be fairly urged against a beaten crew—that of the British *Epervier* and that of the American *Argus* (for the cases of Sir George Collier, Commodore Rodgers, Chauncy, Yeo, the commander of the *Bonne Citoyenne*, etc., etc., cannot be considered as coming under this head). James states that there was usually a great superiority of force on the side of the Americans; this is true; but I show that it was not nearly as great as he makes it, and that in dealing with the lake flotillas his figures are absolutely false, to the extent of even reversing the relative strength of the combatants on Lake Champlain, where the Americans won, although with an inferior force. In the one noteworthy British victory, that of the *Shannon,* all British authors fail to make any allowance for the vital fact that the *Shannon's* crew had been drilled for seven years, whereas the *Chesapeake* had an absolutely new crew, and had been out of port just eight hours; yet such a difference in length of drill is more important than disparity in weight of metal.

As a whole, it must be said that both sides showed equal courage and resolution; that the Americans usually possessed the advantage in material force; and that they also showed a decided superiority in fighting skill, notably in marksmanship.

# INDEX

# Index to Chapter X

### A Note on the Type

The principal text of this Modern Library edition
was set in a digitized version of Janson,
a typeface that dates from about 1690 and was cut by Nicholas Kis,
a Hungarian working in Amsterdam. The original matrices have
survived and are held by the Stempel foundry in Germany.
Hermann Zapf redesigned some of the weights and sizes for Stempel,
basing his revisions on the original design.